Interorganizational Relations

Edited by William M. Evan

Interorganizational Relations

Selected Readings

Edited by William M. Evan

University of Pennsylvania Press

1978

American edition 1978 by the University of Pennsylvania Press
under special arrangement with Penguin Books Ltd.

Library of Congress Cataloging in Publication Data

Main entry under title:

Interorganizational relations.

    Includes bibliographies and indexes.
    1.   Interorganizational relations—Addresses,
essays, lectures.   I.   Evan, William M.
HM133.I56   1978   301.18′32   77-25062
ISBN 0-8122-7745-7

Printed in the United States of America

To my GSB Students

Contents

8 Contents

Introduction

A turning point has been reached in the field of organization theory. For at least two decades, there has been an extensive amount of theoretical and empirical work on the internal structure and functioning of organizations. Researchers from several disciplines – psychology, sociology, economics, political science, business administration, management science and others – have joined in the exploration of the anatomy and physiology, so to speak, of organizations. As might be expected, the modes of theorizing and the methodologies have varied greatly. One basic assumption, however, has unified researchers from diverse disciplines and vantage points, viz., that a significant amount of the variance of organizational phenomena can be accounted for by concentrating on intraorganizational variables. Ironically, Weber's bureaucracy model has stimulated much research attention on internal organizational problems, notwithstanding his own sweeping historical concerns which far transcended the boundaries of a bureaucracy.

In recent years, one can detect a rising tide of discontent with the predominantly *intraorganizational* focus of organizational research. One expression of this discontent is as follows:

Too much sociological theory and research has been based mainly on the model of a single organization, and attention has been focused on its internal processes, by and large. Surely this dominant model is not sufficient to analyze newer and more complex organizational forms such as the interlocking networks of organization in the civil service, the multi-campus state university, regional consortia of educational institutions, multi-outlet distributive organizations in business, and multi-plant industrial concerns. Having become rooted in its social and technological environment and more complex ways, organizations find themselves both constraining and being constrained by these environments in new ways. Yet investigators of formal organizations have barely begun to attack these new relationships (Smelser and Davis, 1969, p. 65).

Surely, the environment of organizations, which includes a

multitude of organizations, must interact in a variety of ways with internal organizational variables. Some efforts have, therefore, been made to break out of the prevailing research paradigm. This, it turns out, is no mean feat. New models have to be developed to relate organizations to environing organizations; and new methodologies especially appropriate for studying *interorganizational* relations have to be developed. Moreover, a new style of research, namely, that of the collaborative team instead of the ubiquitous solo researcher, will perforce emerge to cope with the sheer complexities of studying interorganizational relations. Progress along these lines is barely discernible. Empirical studies using explicit or implicit models of interorganizational relations and employing methodologies varying in degree of utility have been conducted by researchers from diverse disciplines. And some researchers have even ventured to speculate about the normative implications of interorganizational research, namely, how to design and manage interorganizational systems.

All of these beginnings, theoretical, empirical, methodological and normative, are, to be sure, still faltering. Isn't it, therefore, premature to report the progress to date in book form? Yet because these efforts point in a new and significant direction, they merit close attention by students and researchers who may either be still committed to traditional research paradigms in organization theory or else may be moving toward the new frontier; they also deserve the attention of managers of various organizations who grapple with complex boundary problems. This, then, is the justification for a collection of readings on models (Part One), empirical studies (Parts Two and Three), methodologies (Part Four) and design implications (Part Five) of interorganizational relations.

A critical analysis of the selections in this book will, hopefully, stimulate the reader to a new perspective on organizations, thus accelerating the emergence of new paradigms for research on interorganizational relations and generating new approaches to the solution of interorganizational problems. Progress in research on interorganizational relations will very likely pave the way for analytically linking the study of organizations with the study of total societies, an unsolved problem in macrosociology as well as in comparative sociology (Evan, 1966, p. 188; 1976).

References

EVAN, W. M. (1966), 'The organization-set: toward a theory of interorganizational relations', in J. D. Thompson (ed.), *Approaches to Organizational Design*, Pittsburgh, University of Pittsburgh Press, pp. 175–91.

EVAN, W. M. (1976), *Organization Theory*, New York, Wiley.

SMELSER, N. J., and DAVIS, J. A. (eds.) (1969), *Sociology*, Englewood Cliffs, N.J., Prentice-Hall.

Part One
Models of Interorganizational Relations

Few explicit models of interorganizational relations have thus far
been developed. As the volume of research in this area increases
we can expect an increase in the formulation of models that are
both more explicit and more operational. In Part One, six models
have been selected because of their general heuristic value. The
first is by an economist, Phillips, who presents a behavioural
micro-economic model of the firm in an oligopolistic market.
Phillips's concept of the 'interfirm organization' and his four
propositions (pp. 20–22) have stimulated a fellow-economist,
Williamson, to develop a differential equations model of interfirm
behaviour which interrelates three endogenous variables (adherence to interfirm goals, interfirm communication, and performance) with the condition of the environment as an exogenous
variable.

Underlying both models is a process of coalition formation
which Axelrod develops with the aid of the concept of conflict of
interest. Interactions among organizations involve a process of
exchange of economic as well as non-economic utilities. In Blau's
model, economic and social exchange are distinguished, which, in
turn, clarifies the emergence of processes of differentiation,
integration, conflict and legitimation among organizations.

In Parsons's model, three types of organizational members –
technical, managerial, and institutional – differentially located in
the hierarchy of the organization, affect the interaction of the
organization with its environment. Linking the role-set relations
of different categories of organizational members, particularly
those occupying boundary roles, with environing organizations,
Evan's model of input and output organization-sets of the focal
organization generates propositions on the relationships between

intraorganizational and interorganizational variables (pp. 81–7).

None of the six models presented in Part One is sufficiently general to provide organizational researchers with an analytical apparatus to encompass the gamut of interorganizational linkages and interactions. A general systems analysis model, building on these six models, is necessary to cope with interorganizational problems varying in levels of aggregation from a network consisting of but two organizations to one consisting of numerous interacting organizations.

1 A. Phillips

A Theory of Interfirm Organization

A. Phillips, 'A theory of interfirm organization', *Quarterly Journal of Economics*, vol. 74, November 1960, pp. 602–13.

It appears that a new and more realistic theory of oligopoly is emerging. It is based in part on a willingness to drop the assumption of profit-maximizing behaviour. More important, it is based too on a growing recognition that firms in oligopolistic markets are members of a group (or interfirm organization) which has an identity apart from the individuals of which it is comprised. Paradoxically, until recently the theory of industrial organization has been lacking in organizational content; market behaviour has been treated as an amalgamation of individual motives and actions. To understand oligopolistic behaviour and performance, the interfirm organization as well as the firms in the group must be studied. As with people, firms may behave differently in a group than they do in isolation.

The study of group behaviour has been an objective of the behavioural sciences – of sociologists and social psychologists. In this paper I shall attempt to show that recent developments in the theory of group behaviour and in organization theory, when applied to oligopolistic markets, can make significant contributions to the theory of value. Combining economics with the behavioural sciences suggests some generalizations concerning interrelations between market structure, market performance, and firm behaviour which may be pertinent to public policy.

Interfirm organizations

Simple oligopoly

It has long been recognized that firms in a simple oligopolistic market are likely to behave as though an agreement restricting the rivalry among them had been reached. Moreover, while no one has shown how such firms can achieve the degree of market stability necessary to keep them in business without this pattern of behaviour, it is generally agreed the restraint imposed on competition by their parallel behaviour may produce market performance which is less than 'workably' competitive.

The parallel action of oligopolists is evidence that they recognize themselves as members of a group. Their behaviour, not surprisingly, is similar to that observed in other small groups. Many of Thrasher's (1927) conclusions with respect to group behaviour, derived from a study of juvenile gangs, have equal validity for oligopoly. He finds, for example, the development of an unwritten code and that such fighting as occurs *within* the gang follows rules established by that code. An analogue in oligopoly is the frequent unwillingness to engage in price competition, on the one hand, and the vigour of nonprice competition, on the other. As in other groups, the behavioural code of the oligopolists may be the result of conscious decisions and express communication but, with so few members, it may easily arise as 'unconscious sensitivity to certain stimuli,' or a 'learned response' based on past experience. No verbal communication of any kind is necessary.

The behavioural sciences place emphasis on one point which has not been stressed in economics. The difference in the behavioural science approach is the recognition of the fact that the firms have established an interfirm organization, however informal it may be. This carried connotations which go beyond Fellner's (1949) 'quasi-agreements' and Henderson's (1954) 'mutual restraint' since both of these focus attention on the individual firms.

Clark and Ackoff (1959, p. 280) define an organization as follows:

1. An organization is a social group, a collection of individuals all of whose members can (potentially or actually) communicate with each other.

2. The group has at least one objective (or goal). Some of the individual members of the group may not be interested in this objective, but collectively (as opposed to distributively) they are.

3. The group has a functional division of labor relative to pursuit of the group goal.

This division of labor implies the existence of subgoals for the organizational components. The attempts to achieve these subgoals can result in conflict situations among the functionally defined subgroups, and necessitate compromise between these subgroups in order to attain the group goal.

The similarity between this definition of an organization, even though it was conceived to cope with intrafirm groups, and the identifying characteristics of mutually interdependent firms is striking. The firms do comprise a group and they are able to communicate, either expressly or through mutual understanding. The group, as opposed to its individual members, does have a general objective – to resolve the indeterminacy which accompanies oligopolistic markets. There is a division of labour, though it may not be functional in the sense in which Clark and Ackoff use the term. Looked at one way, the division is one of duplication, with each firm performing somewhat the same functions as the others. Looked at in another way, the division of labour among the firms arises because each has an individual identity and individual goals concerning profits, output, price, etc. These are the subgoals which may result in conflict (competition) among the firms. Compromise is necessary since there are probably differences in the cost and demand functions of the firms in the group which make it impossible to find price-output combinations which optimally satisfy the firms' subgoals simultaneously. If, for example, maximum profits are the subgoals, firms with higher costs or less elastic demand would prefer higher prices; those with lower costs or more elastic demand, lower prices. The interfirm organization – tacit and informal in this instance – resolves these conflicts to the mutual advantage of all, if not to the unique advantage of any.

Complex or linked oligopoly

Clair Wilcox (1950) has argued forcefully that oligopoly is not so ubiquitous as many economists believe. His argument, based on concentration ratios which show the presence of numerous firms in many lines of production, is not conclusive. It may be true that high concentration ratios are good indicia of the absence of pure competition, but the converse is not true. Low concentration ratios give little assurance that monopolistic competition or a more complex form of oligopoly does not prevail among the firms in question. Henderson (1954, p. 565) describes the more complex form of oligopoly as follows:

There may be thousands of grocers, yet each grocer will be intimately affected by a *very small number* of neighboring grocers – who may be close geographically, or similar in type of customer to whom they cater. Among dozens of makers of electrical machinery, each will have his own *small group* of particular rivals. An industry is like a forest: each tree is far from almost all the rest, but each has some close neighbors. What looks, at first sight, like an imperfectly competitive industry turns out to be a series of linked oligopolies.

Reflection suggests that even though simple oligopoly is not ubiquitous, linked oligopoly may be. In the latter, however, the group problem and its solution are less obvious than is the case in simple oligopoly. Interdependence, action and reaction, and conjectural variations still exist due to the few close rivals each firm has. But unlike simple oligopoly, the informal, tacit, interfirm organization is not an efficient means for achieving the group objective.

A combination of organization theory and the theory of small groups suggest four generalizations concerning various structures of complex oligopolistic markets and the efficiency of interfirm organizations. The first relates to the number of firms linked together. The complex oligopoly may involve but a dozen firms or it may contain thousands. *The interfirm organization must become more formal, better planned, and better coordinated if the efficiency of simple oligopoly is to be maintained with a larger number of firms in the group.* The probability of mutual understanding and implicit agreements bringing the same efficiency decreases as the number of firms increases. Two-way communication is difficult, especially if the individuals have conflicting interests, and this difficulty compounds as the dimensions of the required communication multiply. The group objective has to be understood by more individuals, more individuals have to recognize that their own objectives must be compromised for the sake of the group and, ultimately, for the sake of each, and to do this some well-formulated and directed programme becomes in-increasingly necessary as numbers increase. In addition, with a larger number of firms, it becomes more probable that one will stray from the group, moving prices downward, for example, and forcing the others to follow. Because of this, a need arises for executive or directive action by some leader of the organization and, very likely, the placing in his hands of power to discipline recalcitrants.

This point about numbers is hardly different from organizational problems within an office, firm, or government bureau. Hierarchical authority and red tape accompany increases in size. In relation to restraints on competition, it is important to recognize that it may be differences in numbers, not differences in goals of the group or its members, which create the tendency toward more formal and express agreements. The restraint imposed on individual action and open rivalry among the members may be no greater when a large number of firms, linked oligopolistically, enter into formal organizations than when a few firms tacitly collude. Identical efficiency in achieving the same objectives requires more elaborate organization among the many than among the few.

The second generalization pertains to leadership within the group and the equality with which market power is distributed among the firms. Populations of economic units, like populations of insects, animals, people, and even college professors, do not typically have power equally distributed among the members. Some lead in various capacities while others follow. In general, *the more asymmetrical the distribution of power, given the number of firms, the less formal need the interfirm organization be to achieve the efficiency of simple oligopoly.* The powerful unit, almost definitionally, has the ability to assure coordinated efforts toward the group's goal and the requisite sublimation of subgroup goals without elaborate plans and detailed lines of authority.

The power to make others follow can be traced to a number of sources. One firm (or a coalition of firms) may have a large volume of sales relative to each of the others and, because of this, have an advantage in cross-demand elasticities. In the event of open conflict, the larger firm is apt to have the bigger guns and the greater staying power. Fearing the strength of size, the smaller firms may be willing to follow even when, from their individual points of view, the market decisions made by the leader are not optimal. A number of other factors might be mentioned, going down to such vague influences as historical prominence and a reputation for wisdom and fairness. But whatever the cause, powerful leadership is an alternative to formal organization.

The third generalization concerns the similarity of the value systems among the firms in the group. If the firms are substantially similar with respect to costs, degrees of capacity being utilized, the extent to which various prices and profit levels are thought to attract new competitors, their feelings towards the way the market ought to be shared among them, etc., the interfirm organization is presented with few conflicts and, hence, need not be equipped to use either force or persuasion to resolve them. *In general, as the value systems of the members of the group become more unlike, it becomes increasingly necessary to formalize the organization if the efficiency of simple oligopoly is to be effected.* One function of the organization may be to establish homogeneity of value systems through such devices as product standardization, uniform costing methods, and the provision of information.

Interfirm organizations, like intrafirm groups, have to cope with problems which arise from without the group and over which they have no direct control. Suppliers exert an influence, as do customers. Usually these outside groups are organized themselves, and to some extent the function of each group is to offset the power of other groups with which it is in conflict. This is seen clearly in the relations of a union with a group of employers. It is seen less clearly, but it is not less important, when a group of selling firms organizes (either expressly or through tacit understanding) to combat the pressure placed on prices by an organization of buying firms. *Again generalizing, the better organized and more efficient are the groups from which purchases and to which sales are made, the more formal and the more centrally directed must an interfirm organization be to retain a given level of efficiency.*

Private groups are not the only outside influence with which an interfirm organization must cope. Of perhaps equal importance are the vague mores and customs of the society in which the organization functions and the host of laws and regulations imposed on the organization by the several governments under whose jurisdictions it operates. In a world of organizations, the pressure to be a 'good citizen' as well as the fear of the policeman may have significant effects on what a group will and will not do.

Market structure, market performance and the interfirm organization

The actual analysis of the restraining influences exerted by an interfirm organization is more complex than the preceding pages indicate. For the sake of clarity, each of the four generalizations was advanced with the assumption of given goals and the formality of the organization was, in each instance, varied to maintain the efficiency of simple oligopoly in achieving the goals. In reality, there is interaction among the four influences. Analysis of this interaction leads to observations concerning market performance, market structure, and the interfirm organization.

It was indicated above that simple oligopolies, even with no formal interfirm organization, may produce market performance which is less than workably competitive. That is, the interfirm organization, despite its informality, may be too efficient in achieving group goals. At the opposite end of the structural-organizational spectrum is the industry with many firms scattered geographically in linked oligopolistic relations, producing relatively homogeneous products, and without a formal organization. With these characteristics, the industry will tend to be excessively competitive. The individual firms, seeking to optimize the achievement of their own subgoals, will produce so competitive a performance that even the most efficient will have their survival threatened. In the face of such performance, either the organizational or the structural characteristics of the industry will tend to change.

The organizational problem in rationalizing excessive competition in a linked oligopolistic industry with a large number of firms is quite different from that in simple oligopoly. A formal interfirm organization with means of penalizing recalcitrants is required because of the large numbers and the temptation on the part of each to 'chisel' on any restraining agreement. It is not coincidental that the most formal interfirm organizations are sanctioned by law in many 'large-number' industries. The Fair Trade laws are an excellent but by no means exclusive example. Privately sponsored interfirm organizations also tend to be more formal in the large-number industries. Here are found basing point pricing systems, uniform list prices, standard costing, product standardization and numerous other techniques.

It can hardly be denied that the formal interfirm organizations may have too great a restraining influence on competition. Again, the Fair Trade laws are a prime example. Customers of the firms involved may be denied any real alternative among the suppliers and the organization may be so successful in perpetuating the given structure of the industry that technical inefficiency and overinvestment are the result. The creation of workably competitive conditions is not assured if the interfirm organization is abolished, however. The performance of the industry will tend to become more competitive as the formality of the organization is reduced. Up to a point, the increase in competition is beneficial since it encourages a more efficient structure through its tendency to lower prices and profits. But, if the formality of the organization is reduced beyond this point, the continued increase in the degree of competition will tend to produce structural change as an alternative to a more formal organization.

The most likely changes in structure will be those occasioned by failures and consolidations which reduce the number of firms, create power positions for leadership, and encourage the remaining firms to put less weight on their own value systems and more weight on group goals. Paradoxically, while the lacking or denial of an effective interfirm organization is the cause of this structural change, the final outcome of the process is not a market without a restraining interfirm organization. Instead, the change continues, approaching more and more the simple oligopolistic market in which a very informal, implicit organization becomes an effective means of solving the problem of mutual interdependence.

The interrelations among structure, performance, and the organization of firms suggest the need for a balance. Ideally, the interfirm organization would not be so formal that a structure which is technologically inefficient is maintained. Neither should it possess such power that the public is harmed because of too little competitive influence on price, whether or not the structure is technically efficient. If the organization does not produce these results, however, it is not obvious that reducing its formality will be for the public good. The result is apt to be a more monopolistic structure than is required for technological reasons, not improved performance.

Concluding observations on profit-maximization and traditional supply and demand analysis

Little attention has been given the subgoals of the individual firms in the interfirm organization. Actually, nothing in the theory is inconsistent with the assumption that the principal subgoal of each firm is to have profits as large as possible. The phrase, 'as large as possible,' is devoid of much content, though. The theory views each firm as a member of a group and, as a consequence, suggests that it is unreasonable to conceive of a firm blindly pursuing the maximization of its own profits without considering the impact of this behaviour on others in the group. This does not constitute an attack on *profit*-maximization, per se, for similar qualifications would apply to any other assumed subgoal so long as conflict situations with other firms result when one firm attempts to achieve its subgoal unilaterally. The theory of interfirm organization is based on the premise that it is inappropriate to assume that individual firms attempt unilaterally to maximize anything, whether it be profits, sales, or even a 'general-preference function' if all the dimensions of the function are variables *internal* to the firm. For that matter, the theory points with equal validity to the inadequacies of attempts to explain firm behaviour on the basis of 'satisficing' objectives (Simon, 1957), or organizational factors (Cyert and March, 1955; 1956) if only intrafirm influences are considered. In its simplest form the theory of interfirm organization posits the fact that firms are members of groups and that the explanation of group behaviour requires assumptions beyond those relating to the motivation of the individuals in the group. Assumptions with respect to individual motives are necessary but not sufficient to explain group behaviour.

Finally, the theory of interfirm organization should add to, not detract from, the usefulness of traditional supply and demand analysis. Nothing about the theory, for example, denies that increases in demand or decreases in supply tend to cause prices to rise. Instead, the theory points out that other circumstances of the market may override such tendencies and offers tools to investigate interfirm factors which influence the responsiveness of price to variations in supply and demand.

References

CLARK, D. F., and ACKOFF, R. L. (1959), 'A report on some organizational experiments', *Operations Research*, vol. 7, May–June, pp. 279–93.

CYERT, R. M., and MARCH, J. G. (1955), 'Organizational structure and pricing behavior in an oligopolistic market', *American Economic Review*, vol. 45, March, pp. 44–64.

CYERT, R. M., and MARCH, J. G. (1956), 'Organizational factors in the theory of oligopoly', *Quarterly Journal of Economics*, vol. 70, February, pp. 44–64.

FELLNER, W. (1949), *Competition Among the Few*, New York, Knopf.

HENDERSON, A. (1954), 'The theory of duopoly', *Quarterly Journal of Economics*, vol. 68, November, pp. 565–84.

SIMON, H. A. (1957), *Models of Man*, New York, Wiley.

THRASHER, F. M. (1927), *The Gang*, University of Chicago Press.

WILCOX, C. (1950), 'On the the alleged ubiquity of oligopoly', *American Economic Review, Papers and Proceedings*, vol. 40, May, pp. 63–73.

2 O. E. Williamson

A Dynamic Theory of Interfirm Behaviour

O. E. Williamson, 'A dynamic theory of interfirm behavior', *Quarterly Journal of Economics*, vol. 79, November 1965, pp. 579–607.

A survey of the failures of oligopoly theory has led Almarin Phillips (1960) to take the position that a theory of 'interfirm organization' is required if we are to obtain significant insights into certain types of oligopoly behaviour. He argues that a unified framework that combines organizational with economic variables is frequently needed, and he proposes a general set of relationships designed to achieve this end.

The present analysis is directed at a similar objective. However, it differs from Phillips's approach in two important ways. First, whereas he is concerned from the outset with devising a general approach to the subject, we direct our initial attention instead at discovering the factors that are responsible for generating a particular class of oligopoly behaviour. Once we have devised a model that reproduces the basic features of the behaviour in question (and is in other ways satisfactory), we then elaborate the model to examine issues that range beyond the initial description. Second, the proposed model is dynamic rather than static. Although this complicates the analysis in some respects, it permits us to extract implications that are not easily, if at all obtainable otherwise.

The phenomenon that occupies our attention is the widely reported tendency for certain classes of oligopolistic industries to alternate between competitive and collusive solutions. Boulding (1963) has characterized this behaviour in the following terms:

... it is of some interest to note that under conditions of perfect oligopoly there is some tendency for price wars to break out, and then we are apt to have rather curious fluctuations around some equilibrium, with prices falling in the price war and then rising again in what I suppose we ought to call a price peace, in which a happy state of collusion, gentlemanliness, or just plain political organization prevails.

Based on this recurrent cycle of cooperation and conflict, we take as our preliminary objective the following paradigm suggested by Simon (1962, p. 479): 'given the description of some natural phenomena, . . . find the differential equations for processes that will produce the phenomena'.

A gross description

The factor that appears to be mainly responsible for shifting the firms in an oligopoly between cooperative and conflict solutions is the condition of the environment. Thus, although oligopolists can be assumed to be continuously aware of their interdependency relationship and of the collective advantages of pursuing a qualified joint profit maximization strategy, adherence to a joint profit maximization agreement may be made difficult during times of adversity by current pressing demands that cause short-run own-goals of one or more of the members to override collective considerations. Assuming that when adversity is experienced by one it is experienced generally, deviation by one member of the coalition is likely to induce defensive responses by others and the entire relationship tends quickly to deteriorate into one of conflict and active competition. As the condition of the environment improves, however, the oligopolists are likely to perceive own-needs as less pressing and hence a return to a cooperative solution becomes feasible.

The above description appears to characterize the primary factors that influence the recurrent cycle of cooperation and conflict that we have taken as the dynamic phenomenon requiring explanation. Similar descriptions have been reported elsewhere. Thus Kaysen (1949, p. 112) observes that 'in a general environment of declining demand for the product of the group, . . . each (oligopolist) has a poor income prospect. . . . Since any gain by one oligipolist can be made only at the expense of his rivals, all changes in prices are likely to be viewed as aggressive, and lead to retaliation. . . . Tacit agreements are unlikely to last.' Hence, he concludes, oligopolists 'are more likely to maintain agreements, and thus act monopolistically, in periods of rising . . . demand.' Similarly Mitchell's (1941, pp. 134–5) observations of interfirm behaviour led him to conclude that 'pools, working agreements, and combinations of other kinds become far more difficult to sustain in the face of a buyers' market, and many of them go to pieces because their members suspect one another of secret undercutting of rates.'

In terms of more specific examples we have Bain's (1959, pp. 309–10) description of price behaviour in the steel industry in the 1920s and 1930s. Thus he observes:

... the steel industry had long been the scene ... of a fairly elaborate tacitly collusive system of price determination. ... The major evident imperfection is that of secret price shading. ... The incidence of this shading ... was apparently variable with the state of the market, or the relation of demand to available capacity. In the first half of the 1920's, and again in 1941 and 1942, for example, with relatively good demand, price concessions were very infrequent and on the average extremely small. But in 1939 and 1940, when there was considerable excess capacity ..., significant price shading affected as much as 70 to 80 per cent of all steel tonnage sold. ... For most of the decade of the 1930's, ... detailed findings are not available, but ... [with] much unutilized capacity, a high incidence of price shading was probably experienced.

A more recent (and more spectacular) example is afforded by the electrical equipment conspiracy in the 1950s. Indeed, at one stage or another of their histories, this alternating pattern of behaviour appears to be representative of a wide variety of oligopolies.

In addition to the influence of the condition of the environment on interfirm relations, are there any other salient features of this process that require attention? If we are to take seriously the argument that socialization influences are important, explicit concern for the communication process by which interfirm agreements are achieved and maintained may be essential. Obviously the effectiveness of the electrical equipment conspiracy rested on the coordinated exchange of information, and presumably this is true more generally. Thus Simon (1957, p. 7) inquires 'What corresponds, in the social sciences, to the postulate of "no action at a distance"? I think the direct analogue is "no influence without communication".' And Kaysen and Turner (1959, p. 145) observe that 'parallel price changes by a large number of firms will almost inevitably require ... (an extensive) machinery of intercommunication. . . . Even industry of small numbers will typically require agreement.' Hence, in addition to a mechanism that transmits changes in the condition of the environment through the system, a communication mechanism may also be warranted.

A dynamic model

The interfirm relationships

The most important question to raise in attempting to develop a model that possesses the indicated properties is: what are the critical endogenous variables? Once these have been specified, a connected framework with which to investigate them can be devised and this can then be augmented to include a variety of exogenous influences. The endogenous variables that I have chosen for this purpose are: (1) a performance variable; (2) an adherence to group goals variable; (3) an interfirm communication variable. The values that these variables take on are not independent but are mutually determined as part of a simultaneous system.

The performance variable is an index of the level of achievement of the firms in the industry. Ordinarily this will be a profits measure, and obviously it will depend, among other things, on the condition of competition that prevails in the industry. Such a variable is essential to transmit the influence of changes in the condition of the environment that occupied an essential role in the description of interfirm behaviour above. We shall also use it in our analysis of the effects of structural conditions and regulatory restraints.

Adherence to group goals is a measure of what Lange (1944, p. 41) has called the 'discipline' of the group, which he defines as the 'degree to which the individual firms are willing to act in unison as members of the group.' The group goal will be taken to be one of qualified joint profit maximization, and the willingness of firms to place such a long-run collective goal ahead of short-run own-goals is a measure of the strength of adherence.

The interfirm communication variable is a measure of the amount of valid information transfer between firms within the industry. Explicit treatment of the role of communication is frequently omitted from economists' descriptions of the interfirm coordination process. It is obvious, however, that communication is essential to coordinated response and it is our contention that the amount of communication both affects and is affected by the level of adherence.

To these three endogenous variables we need to add the condition of the environment as an exogenous variable. The direct effect of an increase in demand is to improve the level of performance and a deterioration leads to a decline.

In a gross sense, these are the basic variables and relationships that the proposed model rests on. Our objective now is to elaborate the description of the qualitative relations that exist between the variables by resorting to the organization theory and social psychology literature on small group interaction. With this completed, we will be in a position to develop a model that possesses the indicated attributes.

The proposed relationships between the endogenous variables are the following:

1. The level of collective performance varies directly with the degree of adherence to group goals and with the condition of the environment.

2. The degree of adherence varies directly with the amount of interfirm communication and with the level of performance.

3. The amount of communication varies directly with the degree of adherence, at least initially.

The proposition that the level of collective performance increases as the member firms adhere more closely to the group goal of qualified joint profit maximization follows from the definition of terms. It similarly follows that the direct effect of an improvement in the condition of the environment is to increase the level of performance. The second and third relations are perhaps less obvious (although neither are they counter-intuitive), and thus deserve additional elaboration.

The observation that communication tends to enhance adherence has been widely recorded. It can be found in the organizational studies of Barnard, March and Simon, Thompson, and Cartwright and Zander, among others. Although the precise statement of the relation varies slightly, the general proposition that intragroup communication promotes shared goals appears to be a well-established empirical finding. That the level of performance also has a positive influence on the degree of adherence has been less widely observed. However, March and Simon (1958, pp. 120, 126) argue that a deterioration in performance (due to an unfavourable change in the condition of the environment) causes the group to reinterpret the relationship between the membership as being more competitive than cooperative, and conflict is apt to result. Barnard (1938, pp. 60–61) also observes that cooperation is conditional on the capacity of the environment to produce satisfaction, and thus adversity poses a threat to an adherence relationship which had been quite stable under more favourable conditions.

The proposition that the influence of communication on adherence is reciprocated has been made by March and Simon (1958, p. 66) and constitutes one of the basic linkages in Homans's (1950, p. 101) observations of group activity. That is, not only does communication promote adherence, but adherence in turn induces communication.

In a very general sense, therefore, we emerge with the following basic relations:

1 $\qquad \pi = \pi(A; E) \qquad \pi_A > 0, \pi_E > 0$

2 $\qquad A = A(\pi, C) \qquad A_\pi > 0, A_C > 0$

3 $\qquad C = C(A) \qquad C_A > 0$

where π, A, and C are performance, adherence, and communication respectively and E refers to the condition of the environment. Our objective in the next part of this section will be to consider the effects of lagged responses on the dynamic behaviour of this system, to examine the equilibrium relations that obtain, and to develop the dynamic response of the system to changes in the condition of the environment.

A differential equations model

We hypothesize that the changes in the level of performance in response to changes in either adherence or the condition of the environment occur very rapidly but that the adjustments in the attitude of the group (adherence) and in the interaction between group members (communication) take time. That is, the social processes that characterize group behaviour are assumed to require time to come into adjustment, whereas the economic response of the system is assumed to occur relatively quickly. Considering the inertia that is generally associated with making social adjustments, as compared with the immediacy with which changes in demand or in the degree of interfirm competition affect prices and output, this view seems plausible. Thus we reformulate our system as follows (where (t) designates the time period to which the measures apply):

1 $\quad \pi(t) = \pi[A(t); E(t)] \qquad \pi_A > 0, \pi_E > 0$

2′ $\quad \dfrac{dA(t)}{dt} = g[\pi(t), C(t), A(t)] \qquad g_\pi > 0, g_C > 0, g_A < 0$

3′ $\quad \dfrac{dC(t)}{dt} = \psi[A(t), C(t)] \qquad \psi_A > 0$ for low A

$\qquad\qquad\qquad\qquad\qquad\qquad\qquad \psi_A < 0$ for high A
$\qquad\qquad\qquad\qquad\qquad\qquad\qquad \psi_C < 0$

The first two expressions are completely consistent with our discussion of the connections between the variables on pp. 30–32 and in the response relations indicated above. The last expression is likewise consistent with the preceding discussion with one exception. It indicates that the directional influence of adherence on communication may depend on the level of adherence, whereas previously it was assumed that this influence was always positive. Certainly at low levels of adherence an increase in adherence will tend to promote more complete transfer of information so that the amount of communication will increase in response. At very high levels of adherence, however, the consensus becomes so widely shared and highly articulated that the degree of understanding which prevails may reduce both the urge and the necessity to communicate. That this latter seems plausible is our reason for introducing it into the system. It is not, however, essential to the analysis.

By substituting equation 1 into equation 2′ we obtain:

$$\frac{dA(t)}{dt} = g\{\pi[A(t); E(t)], C(t), A(t)\}.$$

This can be re-expressed as:

2"
$$\frac{dA(t)}{dt} = \phi[C(t), A(t); E(t)]$$

which together with equation 3',

3'
$$\frac{dC(t)}{dt} = \psi[A(t), C(t)],$$

reduces our system to a pair of differential equations for the determination of $A(t)$ and $C(t)$.

The system represented by equations 2" and 3' can be represented graphically in the C–A plane. At any point in the plane, the direction of adjustment can be obtained from the equation of the trajectory, namely

$$\frac{dA}{dC} = \frac{dA/dt}{dC/dt} = \frac{\phi[C, A; E]}{\psi[A, C]}.$$

This gives the rate of change of A relative to C for each possible pair of (C, A) values. To each point there corresponds one and only one possible response and connecting consecutive points along the direction of indicated response yields an integral curve. The collection of such curves provides the direction field of the system. Several such curves are shown in Figure 1 by the curved arrow constructions.

The character of the direction field depends on the nature of our partial equilibrium relationships. That is, consider the set of points at which the level of adherence is in equilibrium, namely where

4
$$\frac{dA}{dt} = \phi(C, A; E) = 0.$$

At any point on this curve there is no tendency for the level of adherence to the group goal to adjust. Hence the trajectory,

$$\frac{dA}{dC},$$

must be horizontal everywhere along this curve, moving to the right or to the left according to whether ψ is positive or negative at the point in question. Similarly the set of points where

$$5 \qquad \frac{dC}{dt} = \psi(A, C) = 0$$

defines a curve in the C–A plane along which there is no tendency for the level of communication to change. The trajectory at every point along this curve will thus be vertical, moving up or down depending on whether ϕ is positive or negative.

At the points where 4 and 5 intersect, that is where both relations are satisfied simultaneously, the system will be in equilibrium. The stability of these points depends on the character of the direction field in the neighbourhood of the equilibrium. As shown in Figure 1, points K and M are stable equilibrium positions while L is an unstable equilibrium.

Although the basic assumptions that are embodied in Figure 1 have already been stated, some additional comments on the relationships shown are warranted.

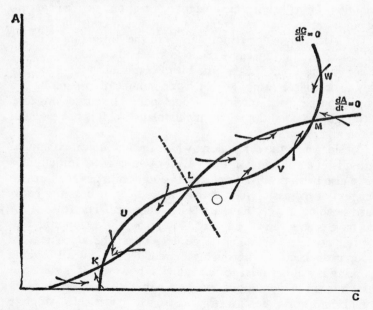

Figure 1

First, consider the curve along which the adherence to group goals variable is in equilibrium. It is drawn with a positive slope, to reflect the assumption that the equilibrium level of adherence increases in response to increases in communication, and the slope goes through an increasing then decreasing phase. Only the second phase is essential to the analysis and it is due to a saturation phenomenon. That is, given the condition of the environment, the effect of increasing the amount of communication is assumed eventually to encounter a diminishing response region where subsequent increases in communication produce successively smaller increases in the equilibrium level of adherence. This can result from the combination of two effects. First, the early communications may be concerned with more essential matters for obtaining coordination among the rivals than are later ones. In addition, the susceptibility to influence is almost certainly going to reach a saturation point as long as a difference between individual and group goals exists. This latter is related to Fellner's argument that, short of merger, rivals are apt to achieve only a qualified joint profit maximization position; agreements to advance group goals are subject to significant constraints.

The increasing slope region shown in the lower ranges of the adherence equilibrium curve is due to assumed economies of scale in communication. Thus a little bit of communication produces only a negligible response, but as communication cumulates a much sharper definition of group goals becomes possible. Although this condition seems highly plausible, it is not essential to the argument.

Consider next the curve along which the amount of communication is in equilibrium at every level of adherence. Initially this curve also has a positive slope but, in addition to passing through a region of increasing then decreasing returns, it becomes backward bending at very high levels of adherence. The reasons for this have been given already. It follows from the assumption that the felt need to communicate declines when the agreement on group goals becomes thoroughly shared. This backward bending property is not essential to the analysis, however. It is sufficient that saturation conditions set in so that the communication equilibrium curve need merely approach a vertical asymptote rather than turn back on itself at very high levels of adherence.

As drawn, the curve

$$\frac{dC}{dt} = 0$$

has its intercept along the C axis to the right of the intercept

$$\frac{dA}{dt} = 0.$$

That is, at zero adherence the equilibrium level of communication exceeds the level of communication required to maintain zero adherence. As a result, a system initially in a position of very low adherence will, due to a felt need to communicate even when every member is motivated to attend solely to his own interests, tend to move to an equilibrium level of adherence that exceeds zero (to a position such as K). In other words, a completely fractionated industry is an unnatural condition; the level of dealings necessary to transact business in an orderly way generally promotes an identity of interest that exceeds zero. Under extreme conditions this relationship between the two intercepts might be violated, in which case the system would then possess only a single equilibrium position. It would be at the intercept of the communication equilibrium curve with the C axis.

So much, then, for the shapes and positions of the curves. As indicated earlier, the intersections K and M are stable equilibria. Should the system start out at any point above the dashed line through L it would move towards the high level equilibrium at M, while if it should start out anywhere below it would move (asymptotically) to the low level equilibrium at K. The high level equilibrium being a position of substantial communication and adherence will, through the mechanism of equation 1, lead to a high level of performance while the low level equilibrium, being one where independent rather than joint actions are preferred, yields a lower level of individual and collective achievement.

More interesting than the equilibrium properties of the system, however, is the dynamic response of the system to changes in the condition of the environment (E). A change in the condition of the environment has a direct effect on performance via equation 1. But performance in turn influences the level of adherence through equation 2. Thus the environment has an effect on adherence and acts as a shift parameter on this relation (equation 2″). The communication relation, however, is not directly influenced by the environment. Hence the curve

$$\frac{dC}{dt} = 0$$

remains fixed as changes in E occur while the curve

$$\frac{dA}{dt} = 0$$

is shifted by changes in the condition of the environment.

More precisely, a decline in E tends to produce a condition of excess supply (evaluated at normal price) and the curve

$$\frac{dA}{dt} = 0$$

is shifted down. Thus at every level of adherence, a higher level of communication is necessary in order to maintain equilibrium with respect to the adherence relation when the environment deteriorates than when the environment is favourable. The unfavourable environment tends to amplify differences between own and group goals so that, in order to encourage collective rather than independent action, a higher level of information exchange is required. Thus, although from the point of view of the industry the economic incentive to act collectively and maximize joint profits is always operative, a tendency for disparity to develop in the attitudes of the individual members during periods of adversity makes a policy of collective action difficult to sustain. An improvement in the condition of the environment reverses these forces and the curve

$$\frac{dA}{dt} = 0$$

is shifted up.

Consider the system initially at a high level equilibrium position when a decline in the environment begins. If the point M is above the point W in Figure 1 (the maximum value of C on the curve

$$\frac{dC}{dt} = 0),$$

the first effects of the decline will be to increase communication but decrease adherence. If the deterioration continues, the curve

$$\frac{dA}{dt} = 0$$

will pass through W; beyond this point both A and C will decline. As the curve

$$\frac{dA}{dt} = 0$$

continues to shift down, the points L and M will begin to converge. When the point V is reached, tangency between the two partial equilibrium relations occurs, L and M will have become identical, and the equilibrium will be unstable from below but stable from above. Thus any further decline in E will send the system to a low level (stable) equilibrium at K.

As soon as an improvement in the environment begins, the adherence equilibrium curve will shift up. However, the system will tend to persist at its low level equilibrium position, K. Thus even after the system re-establishes tangency at V and moves back towards its original position (as shown in Figure 1), there will only occur a modest increase in adherence and communication. Not until the curve

$$\frac{dA}{dt} = 0$$

moves so far as to obtain tangency with the curve

$$\frac{dC}{dt} = 0$$

at U (at which position L and K converge) and the equilibrium becomes stable from below but unstable from above will the system be ready to move to a new high level position. If improvements in the condition of the environment shift the curve

$$\frac{dA}{dt} = 0$$

beyond tangency at U, a new high level equilibrium will be re-established. The cyclical sequence of adjustment is shown in Figure 2.

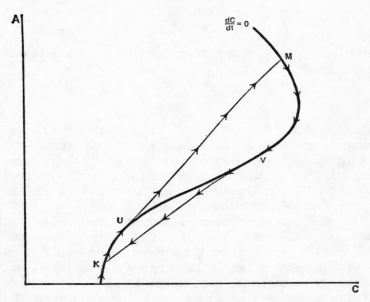

Figure 2

The movements between *V* and *K* and between *U* and *M* occur very rapidly, since they are movements from disequilibrium to equilibirum positions, whereas the movements between *M* and *V* and *K* and *U* occur only in response to continuing changes in the condition of the environment. Thus the system has the property that once a low level equilibrium is achieved there will tend to be persistence at a low level whereas once a shift to a high level occurs persistence at a high level will develop.

In other words, if the system is operating at a low level of adherence and communication (i.e., the competitive solution), a substantial improvement in the environment will be necessary before the system will shift to a high level of adherence and communication. *Indeed, the condition of the environment required to drive the system to the collusive solution is much higher than the level required to maintain it once it has achieved this position.*

Similarly a much more unfavourable condition of the environment is required to move the system from a high to a low level equilibrium than is required to maintain it there. These conditions are displayed graphically in Figure 3.

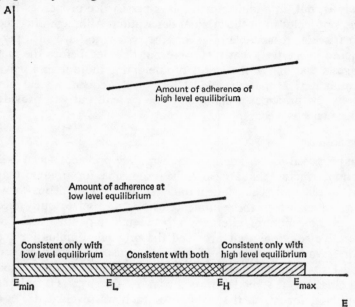

Figure 3

The cross-hatched area reveals that there is a wide range of environmental conditions over which the system can be in either high or low level equilibrium, depending on where it originates. Thus if the system is in a low level equilbrium position the condition of the environment must exceed E_H before the system will shift to a high level equilibrium position. But once it has shifted to a high level equilibrium, the condition of the environment must fall to E_L before a low level equilibrium will be restored.[1]

1. By replacing adherence by communication along the ordinate in Figure 3, the same relationships would apply to communication (except that at high levels of E the backward bending character of the locus

$$\frac{dC}{dt} = 0$$

would give rise to a slight decline in C).

This is not an intuitively obvious property for such a system to possess and is a refutable implication. Indeed, we find that not only is the dynamic model capable of reproducing the cyclical behaviour that was taken as the immediate objective of the analysis, but, in addition, it displays persistence properties that were not included in the original description. Although after the fact it seems reasonable to expect the system to have such persistence properties; that they were not detected before the fact suggests that one of the merits of attempting more than a naive formulation[2] is that the model itself will frequently yield not merely the principal properties of the system, but will provide refinements as well.

Conclusions

The proposed model attempts to merge the principal social and economic factors that appear to be responsible for an important class of oligopoly behaviour into a system of simultaneous equations within which these influences work themselves out. Since the phenomenon of alternation between competitive and co-operative solutions that provided the original stimulus for the analysis involves a process of dynamic adjustment, the proposed model was formulated as a system of differential equations. Upon examination, the model was shown to display: (1) multiple equilibria, for which the stability of each was evaluated; (2) a capacity to generate the alternation phenomenon in question in response to changes in the condition of the environment; (3) persistence behaviour that went undetected in the original description of the dynamic characteristics of the system. Thus the model not only reproduced the gross characteristics of the behaviour under examination, but it suggested refinements as well.

2. As an example of a naive formulation consider the model $A = f(E)$, $f_E > 0$. In some gross sense this captures the influence of changes in demand on the degree of adherence. It fails to reveal the type of persistence properties that we have indicated, however, and indeed if the relations shown in Figure 3 are substantially correct, a simple regression of A on E such as is suggested by this naive model lead to a quite unsatisfactory fit.

References

BAIN, J. S. (1959), *Industrial Organization*, New York, Wiley, pp. 309–10.

BARNARD, C. I. (1938), *The Functions of the Executive*, Cambridge, Mass., Harvard University Press.

BOULDING, K. E. (1963), 'The uses of price theory', *Models of Markets*, ed. A. R. Oxenfeldt, New York, Columbia University Press, pp. 146–62.

HOMANS, G. C. (1950), *The Human Group*, New York, Harcourt, Brace.

KAYSEN, C. (1949), 'A dynamic aspect of the monopoly problem', *Review of Economics and Statistics*, vol. 31, May, pp. 109–13.

KAYSEN, C., and TURNER, D. F. (1959), *Antitrust Policy*, Cambridge, Mass., Harvard University Press.

LANGE, O. (1944), *Price Flexibility and Employment*, Bloomington, Indiana, Principia Press.

MARCH, J. G., and SIMON, H. A. (1958), *Organizations*, New York, Wiley.

MITCHELL, W. C. (1941), *Business Cycles and Their Causes*, Berkeley and Los Angeles, University of California Press.

PHILLIPS, A. (1960), 'A theory of interfirm organization', *Quarterly Journal of Economics*, vol. 74, November, pp. 602–13.

SIMON, H. A. (1957), *Models of Man*, New York, Wiley.

SIMON, H. A. (1962), 'The architecture of complexity', *Proceedings of the American Philosophical Society*, vol. 106, December, pp. 467–82.

3 R. Axelrod

A Coalition Theory Based on Conflict of Interest

R. Axelrod, *Conflict of Interest*, Markham Publishing Co., 1970, pp. 165–75.

In a parliamentary democracy, political parties contend for legislative seats in a popular election. A cabinet is then formed which seeks to attain a vote of confidence from the legislature. If it is successful, the cabinet and its legislative supporters control the formation and execution of public policy. This situation lasts until the cabinet loses a vote of confidence or until the next general election.

In some parliamentary democracies, such as the United Kingdom, the legislature is usually controlled by a single party. This party can then form a cabinet and govern the nation without having to rely on the support of any other party. However, in other parliamentary democracies, such as Sweden, the Netherlands, France during the Fourth Republic, Italy, and Israel, the legislature usually cannot be controlled by any one party. In order for a cabinet to attain a vote of confidence from the legislature in these countries, the cabinet must be supported by a coalition that includes several different political parties. The question to be examined is which coalitions are likely to form and prove durable.

Contribution of conflict of interest

Predicting which coalition will form can be a difficult matter. For example, if there are seven political parties represented in the legislature (and not infrequently there are even more), then there are 128 possible coalitions. If a simple majority is needed in only one chamber to attain a vote of confidence, then half of these potential coalitions, or 64, are able to govern.[1] With eight parties

1. The proof is trivial. For n parties there are 2^n potential coalitions, including the coalition with no support and the coalitions with only one

there are 256 possible coalitions, including 128 coalitions which can govern.

The key point is that not all of the possible coalitions have the same likelihood of forming. The various parties have differing goals, but a given party has goals that are more similar to those of some of the parties than of others. In other words, some potential coalitions have less incompatibility of goals among their members than do others. This of course means that some potential coalitions have less conflict of interest than others.

If some potential coalitions have less conflict of interest among their members than others, perhaps this fact can be used to predict the behaviour of the parties in joining and staying in coalitions. The general hypothesis asserts that the more conflict of interest there is, the more likely is conflictful behaviour. Sociologists and psychologists have identified many types of conflictful behaviour in groups (e.g., Coser, 1956, and M. Deutsch, 1949), and conceivably the general hypothesis could be used to relate conflict of interest in coalitions to each of these types of behaviour.

For the present purposes the forms of behaviour that are important to predict are the ones with direct political significance. Among the most important political questions about the behaviour of parties in a parliamentary democracy are which coalitions they are most likely to form, and which coalitions are most likely to prove durable.

The general hypothesis can be reformulated to say that the less conflict of interest there is, the more likely is cooperative behaviour. Examples of cooperative behaviour are the formation of a coalition and the continued support of an existing coalition. The formation of a coalition is a form of cooperative behaviour among the member parties because by the very act of forming a coalition these parties work together to support a specific cabinet. The member parties also work together to some extent to cooperate on the passage of agreed-upon items of public policy. The continued existence of a coalition also requires cooperative behaviour because the cabinet falls as soon as it loses a vote of

---

member. Each one of these coalitions can be matched with its complement. Either the coalition or its complement has a majority (assuming there are enough seats to make tie votes unlikely). Thus exactly one-half of all coalitions contain a majority of the seats.

confidence. These interpretations of political acts provide two predictions which are applications of the general hypothesis:

1. The less conflict of interest there is in a coalition, the more likely the coalition will form.

2. The less conflict of interest there is in a coalition, the more likely the coalition will have long duration if formed.

These predictions are not based on a strong assumption of rationality on the part of the various parties. Even if people who make the decisions on behalf of the parties do not have a clear conception of the policy goals of the other parties, and even if they do not understand that some coalitions have less conflict of interest than others, the predictions need not fail. The reason is that negotiations for coalitions that have low conflict of interest will simply be easier to conclude successfully, and hence these coalitions can be expected to be more likely to form – even if the political leaders are not able to identify them beforehand. Likewise, a coalition with low conflict of interest can be expected to last longer once formed than an average coalition, just because disputes within such a coalition will be easier to resolve. In a sense, this is a theory of 'natural selection' and survival of viable political coalitions.

Ordinal policy space

The concept of a policy space has been used in the analysis of conflict of interest in societies. The same concept can also be applied to the study of political parties in legislatures. If the policy preferences of the public can be structured on a left-right dimension, for example, it would not be surprising that the political parties of the same country could also be regarded as occupying positions on a left-right policy dimension.

Fortunately, most of the restrictive assumptions used in the analysis of societal conflict of interest are not needed for a study of conflict of interest in the coalition process. In fact, the most parsimonious of all spatial models is sufficient to develop a testable theory of coalitions based on conflict of interest. All that needs to be assumed is the existence of an ordinal policy dimension, which means that the size of the intervals between positions has no significance. This means that the political parties need only be listed in order (say from left to right). Instead of assuming that utility loss is linear with distance, all that needs to be assumed is the property Black (1958, p. 7) calls 'single-peaked preferences.' This is the assumption used by Downs (1957, pp. 115f) in his spatial model. It simply means that of two policy positions on one side of a political party, the party prefers the closer one. Even the assumption of no anti-system behaviour can be dropped because it is not needed for the results that are to be derived from the ordinal model.

This gives the simplest of all policy spaces: a one-dimensional ordinal policy space with ordinal utilities. This spatial model is completely specified by listing the parties in order from one end of the policy dimension to the other.

Conflict of interest in coalitions

The hypotheses relating conflict of interest to behaviour are that the less conflict of interest there is in a coalition, the more likely it will form and the more likely it will be durable if it does form. The possible outcomes are each of the possible combinations of political parties into coalitions. The parties' utilities are incompletely, but sufficiently, specified by their positions in the ordinal policy space.

Now comes the question of how conflict of interest for a coalition can be defined. Since utilities have been specified in only an ordinal fashion for the parties, it is impossible to assign an exact numerical value to the amount of conflict of interest of each potential coalition. However, this is not necessary. It is sufficient to be able to identify the potential coalitions that have comparatively low conflict of interest. If this is done, the predictions that these coalitions are most likely to form and be durable can be tested.

The treatment of conflict of interest in spatial models of society provides clues to analysing conflict of interest in coalitions. Using certain strong assumptions, conflict of interest in a two-person bargaining game is proportional to the square of the policy distance between the two people. Next, using the same strong assumptions, it was shown that conflict of interest between large numbers of people can be regarded as equivalent to the variance of the distribution of their positions in the policy space. These results employed the assumptions that distance in the policy space can be measured numerically and that utility loss is proportional to policy distance.

What do these results suggest about an ordinal policy space where utility loss can only be said to increase as distance in one direction increases? The answer seems to be that the less dispersion there is in the policy positions of the members of a coalition, the less conflict of interest there is. Of course, the dispersion of a coalition cannot be precisely measured in a strictly ordinal space. Nevertheless, the list of the political parties in order from one end of the policy dimension to the other does provide some information about how dispersed a given coalition is.

For illustration, suppose that the parties are labelled A, B, C, D, E, F, and G in order of their positions from left to right on the policy dimension. In an ordinal policy dimension, the dispersion of the coalition consisting of parties A, B, and C cannot be compared to the disperson of the coalition consisting of B, C, and D. However, the coalition consisting of the adjacent parties A, B, and C is certain to be less dispersed than the coalition consisting of A, B, and D. For this reason, a coalition consisting of adjacent parties, or a *connected coalition* as it can be called, tends to have relatively low dispersion and thus low conflict of interest for its size.

Of course, the property of a coalition's being connected does not take into account its total spread or dispersion. The coalition ABC has less dispersion than the coalition ABCD. Therefore ABC has less conflict of interest than ABCD, even though both coalitions are connected. Thus the size as well as the connectedness of a coalition affects its conflict of interest.

A third property concerning the strategic capabilities of a coalition can be added to these two properties relating to conflict of interest. The constitution of each parliamentary democracy indicates what a coalition must do to provide a vote of confidence for a cabinet. Typically, it must obtain a simple majority vote in one or both chambers of the legislature. A coalition that meets the requirement for providing a vote of confidence can thus control the formation and execution of public policy through its control of the legislative and executive branches of the government. Such a coalition is called a *winning coalition*.

These three properties of coalitions can be put together to describe the kind of coalitions predicted by a theory based on conflict of interest. The coalition has to be a winning coalition in order to be able to support a cabinet, and it should be connected but not too large in order to have low conflict of interest. This suggests the following definition:

Definition. A minimal connected winning coalition (or an *MCW coalition*) is a coalition that is connected (consists of adjacent members); is a winning coalition (can give a cabinet a vote of confidence); and is minimal in the sense that it can lose no member party without ceasing to be connected and winning.

For example, if the seven parties A, B, C, D, E, F, and G are all of equal size and a simple majority is needed for control, then a coalition of any four or more parties is a winning coalition. There are 64 winning coalitions out of a total of 128 coalitions.[2] The connected coalitions consist of adjacent members. There are 28 connected coalitions.[3] The minimal connected winning coalitions in this example are those coalitions with exactly four adjacent parties. There are only four of these: ABCD, BCDE, CDEF, and DEFG. Regardless of the distribution of legislative seats among the parties there are no more than $(n + 1)/2$ minimal connected winning coalitions if there are n parties and if a simple majority of the seats is needed to win.[4]

Another formulation of the definition is that a coalition that is connected and winning is also minimal if the exclusion of either of

2. See preceding footnote for proof.

3. Seven connected coalitions have party A as their leftmost member, six have B as their leftmost member and so on. This gives $7 + 6 + 5 + 4 + 3 + 2 + 1 = 28$.

4. Here is the proof. Define the median party as the party that has a majority of seats on neither side of it. The median party must be in every MCW coalition. Suppose that the median party is the kth from the nearest end. For example, suppose the median party is the third from the left, i.e. party C. Then there are no more than 3 MCW coalitions because no more than one can begin with each of A, B, and C and none can begin with a party to the right of C. In general, if the median party is the kth from the nearest end, there can be no more than k MCW coalitions. The largest k can be is $(n + 1)/2$ which happens when the median party has an equal number of parties on each side of it.

its exterior members leaves a coalition that is no longer a winning coalition. Thus BCDEF is not a minimal connected winning coalition in the example because the exclusion of either B or F leaves a new coalition that is still winning (and of course it is still connected because only an exterior member was excluded).

Now that the definition of a minimal connected winning coalition has been given, the predictions of the coalition theory based on conflict of interest can be precisely stated.

Hypotheses. In a parliamentary democracy in which the parties can be placed in a one-dimensional ordinal policy space, minimal connected winning coalitions:

1. are likely to form more often than would be indicated by chance (even compared to just the other winning coalitions), and

2. once formed are likely to be of longer duration than other coalitions.

If these predictions are confirmed the theory succeeds, otherwise it fails. Thus, if there are other factors such as personal friendships between some of the party leaders which cannot be represented as positions of the parties in the policy space, then these factors will show up as failures of the predictions. Likewise if there are any short-term changes in the relationships between the parties which cannot be treated in terms of the ordinal model and minimal connected winning coalitions, these changes can also appear as failures of the predictions.

Relationship to other coalition theories

There is no need to provide here a comprehensive review of the large amount of theoretical and laboratory work that has been done on coalitions because two excellent critical reviews already exist. The first of these is by Luce and Raiffa (1957, pp. 155–274) and covers roughly the first decade of game theory which began with the work of Von Neumann and Morgenstern (second edition, 1947). A critical review of work on coalitions in the second decade is provided by Leiserson (1966, pp. 38–170).

Although it is not necessary to review here all the contributions of game theory to the study of coalitions, it will be useful to compare the predictions of present theory to those of earlier coalition theories. The four earlier theories all assume that the coalition process is a zero-sum game and do not take into account the ideological positions of the parties.

1. Von Neumann and Morgenstern (1947, pp. 420ff.) predict that a coalition will include no parties that are not needed to win. The idea is that in a zero-sum game the winners will not want to share the spoils with any more parties than are necessary.

2. Leiserson's bargaining theory (1968) selects from among those winning coalitions that include no unnecessary parties only those with the fewest number of parties. The idea is that the bargaining process over the formation of a winning coalition is easier if the coalition has only a few parties as members.

3. Riker's basic theory (1962, p. 32) predicts that of all the winning coalitions only the one of smallest size will form. His idea is that the winning coalition with the least number of seats will be able to give its members the best distribution of the spoils.

4. Riker's modified theory (1962, pp. 77ff.) predicts that since information is not perfect winning coalitions slightly larger than the smallest one may form. For present purposes I will operationalize the modified theory to allow a 5 per cent margin of error, so that any winning coalition with less than 55 per cent of the seats is predicted.

To compare these four theories consider a simple example. Suppose there is a legislature with 31 seats divided among four parties from left to right as follows:

A has 14 seats
B has 3 seats
C has 12 seats
D has 2 seats

If a simple majority is needed to win, the coalition predicted to form by each theory will obviously have at least 16 seats.

Von Neumann and Morgenstern predict that a coalition that forms will not be able to exclude one of its parties and still have a majority. Thus they predict that AB, AC, AD or BCD will form. Leiserson's bargaining theory predicts the coalition with the fewest parties, which in this case is two parties. Thus AB, AC, and AD are his predictions. Riker's basic theory predicts that the coalition will be as small as possible, which in this case means 16 seats, and therefore must be AD. Riker's modified theory allows for winning coalitions with up to 5 per cent of the seats, which in this case is 16 or 17 seats, so AB, AD, or BCD is predicted. None of these theories takes account of the order in which the parties are placed.

In contrast, the theory of coalitions based on conflict of interest predicts that the coalition must be connected. Furthermore, it singles out coalitions that are not able to exclude either of their exterior parties and still have a majority. The only coalitions that fulfil these conditions are AB and BCD.

The coalition theory based on conflict of interest does not assume that the participants are in a zero-sum game. On the contrary, the idea of conflict of interest has been developed precisely to be able to analyse the extent to which situations vary between being partnership games and zero-sum games.

In the ordinal model of policy space, for example, the parties may all have some common interests and some conflicting interests. The assumption used in the present theory of coalitions is that the preferences for public policy of the parties near each other on the policy dimension are similar. This leads to the idea of a minimal connected winning coalition as a coalition which can be expected to have relatively low conflict of interest. Thus, unlike the zero-sum theories, the present theory predicts that the policy preferences of a party greatly influence which other parties it is likely to join with in a coalition. To oversimplify, the present theory denies that coalition politics makes strange bedfellows.

Leiserson (1966) has proposed another coalition theory for non-zero-sum interactions. This theory assumes that parties search for other parties that are close to them ideologically. With iterated search procedures used by the parties, coalitions are built up which have minimal ideological diversity. Ideological diversity is defined in terms of an ideological space similar to the ordinal policy space used in this chapter. The prediction that coalitions will have minimal ideological diversity is virtually identical to the first hypothesis of the theory of coalitions based on conflict of interest (namely that MCW coalitions are more likely to form than other coalitions).

The theory of coalitions based on conflict of interest is so close to Leiserson's ideological theory that the present theory can be regarded as a derivative of that theory from more fundamental considerations. In other words, the specific form that ideological diversity takes in a spatial model is just another application of the definition of conflict of interest. The prediction of which coalitions will form is just another application of the general hypothesis for bargaining games.

Leiserson developed his ideological theory of political coalitions after conducting and studying four-person laboratory games. In the present study, a theoretical analysis of conflict of interest in various contexts (first the bargaining game, later society, and now multiparty coalitions) has provided an alternate route to a virtually identical theory of coalitions.

Needless to say, knowing the nature of Leiserson's theory of ideological diversity aided the development of the present coalition theory based on conflict of interest. Unfortunately, Leiserson's insightful work contains ambiguities in parts of the theory. For this reason an exact comparison of his ideological theory and the theory of coalitions based on conflict of interest is not possible at this time.

The conflict of interest approach does have several advantages over the more empirical approach based on laboratory gaming.

1. The conflict of interest approach helps place the coalition theory in a broader context as a special case of a much more general theory.

2. By eliminating some of the *ad hoc* quality of the theory, the conflict of interest approach leads to a more parsimonious model. In particular, the need to assume special search strategies by the participants is replaced by an application of the general hypothesis in the explanation of why certain coalitions are more likely to form than others.

3. The conflict of interest approach suggests an additional hypothesis which goes beyond the prediction of which coalitions will form. This additional hypothesis, of course, is that the MCW coalitions will last longer than other coalitions that form because they are expected to have less internal conflict of interest and

hence less internal conflictful behaviour. Coalition *formation* has been the main subject of the study of coalition in the game theoretic context (including Leiserson's theory). The conflict of interest approach suggests how the important political question of coalition *maintenance* can also be treated.

References

BLACK, D. (1958), *The Theory of Committees and Elections*, Cambridge, Cambridge University Press.

COSER, L. (1956), *The Functions of Social Conflict*, New York, Free Press of Glencoe.

DEUTSCH, M. (1949), 'A theory of co-operation and competition', *Human Relations*, vol. 2, pp. 129–52.

DOWNS, A. (1957), *An Economic Theory of Democracy*, New York, Harper & Row.

LEISERSON, M. (1966), *Coalition in Politics*, Ph.D. Dissertation, New Haven, Conn., Yale University (mimeo).

LEISERSON, M. (1968), 'Factions and coalitions in one-party Japan: an interpretation based on the theory of games', *American Political Science Review*, vol. 62, pp. 770–87.

LUCE, R. D., and RAIFFA, H. (1957), *Games and Decisions*, New York, Wiley.

RIKER, W. H. (1962), *The Theory of Political Coalitions*, New Haven, Conn., Yale University Press.

VON NEUMANN, J., and MORGENSTERN, O. (1947), *Theory of Games and Economic Behavior*, 2nd ed., Princeton, N.J., Princeton University Press.

4 P. M. Blau

Social Exchange Among Collectivities

P. M. Blau, *Exchange and Power in Social Life*, John Wiley & Sons, Inc., 1964, pp. 312–15, 327–38.

Two fundamental questions can be asked in the analysis of inter-personal relations, what attracts individuals to the association and whether their transactions are symmetrical or not. The first distinction is that between associations that participants experience as intrinsically rewarding, as in love relations, and social interactions in which individuals engage to obtain some extrinsic benefits, as in instrumental cooperation. Extrinsic benefits are, in principle, detachable from their social source – that is, the persons who supply them – and thus furnish external criteria for choosing between associates, for example, for deciding which colleague to ask for advice. No such objective criteria of comparison exist when an association is an end-in-itself, since the fused rewards that make it intrinsically attractive cannot be separated from the association itself. The second distinction is that between reciprocal and unilateral social transactions. Cross classification of these two dimensions yields four types of associations between persons:

	Intrinsic	*Extrinsic*
Reciprocal	Mutual attraction	Exchange
Unilateral	One-sided attachment	Power

The structures of social associations in groups and societies can also be analysed in terms of two underlying dimensions. In this case, the first question is whether particularistic or universalistic standards govern the pattern of social relations and orientations in a collectivity. That is, whether the structure of social relations reveals preferences among persons with similar status attributes or universal preferences throughout the collectivity for persons with given attributes. Particularistic standards refer to status attributes that are valued only by the ingroup, such as religious or political beliefs, whereas universalistic standards refer to attributes that are generally valued, by those who do not have them as well as by those who do, such as wealth or competence. The second question is whether the patterns of social interaction under consideration are the emergent aggregate result of the diverse endeavours of the members of the collectivity, or whether they are organized and explicitly focused on some common, immediate or ultimate, objectives. Cross classification of these two dimensions yields four facets of social structure:

	Particularism	Universalism
Emergent	Integration	Differentiation
Goal-focused	Opposition	Legitimation

A serious limitation of such typologies derived from underlying dimensions, however, is that they imply a static conception of social life and social structure. Although the explicit inclusion of opposition, a major generator of social change, as one of the types is an attempt to overcome this limitation, the schemas still fail to indicate the manifold conflicts between social forces and the dynamic processes of social change. The prime significance of the contrast between reciprocity and imbalance, for example, is not as a dimension for classifying social associations but as a dynamic force that transforms simple into increasingly complex social processes and that serves as a catalyst of ubiquitous change in social structures. There is a strain toward reciprocity in social associations, but reciprocity on one level creates imbalances on others, giving rise to recurrent pressures for re-equilibration and social change. In complex social structures with many interdependent, and often interpenetrating, substructures, particularly, every movement toward equilibrium precipitates disturbances and disequilibria and thus new dynamic processes. The perennial adjustments and counteradjustments find expression in a dialectical pattern of social change.

• • •

Social exchange is the basic concept in terms of which the associations between persons have been analysed. The prototype is the *reciprocal* exchange of *extrinsic* benefits. People often do favours for their associates, and by doing so they obligate them to return favours. The anticipation that an association will be a rewarding experience is what initially attracts individuals to it, and the exchange of various rewarding services cements the social bonds between associates. Either dimension of 'pure' exchange can become modified, however, yielding the two special cases of intrinsic attraction and power based on unilateral services. When an association is intrinsically rewarding, as in love, the exchange of extrinsic benefits is merely a means to attain and sustain the ultimate reward of reciprocated attraction. The supply of recurrent unilateral services is a source of power, since it obliges those who cannot reciprocate in kind to discharge their obligations to the supplier by complying with his wishes.

There are a number of similarities between social exchange and economic exchange. Individuals who do favours for others expect a return, at the very least in the form of expressions of gratitude and appreciation, just as merchants expect repayment for economic services. Individuals must be compensated for social rewards lest they cease to supply them, because they incur costs by doing so, notably the cost of the alternatives foregone by devoting time to the association. The principle of the eventually diminishing marginal utility applies to social as well as economic commodities. Thus the social approval of the first few colleagues is usually more important to a newcomer in a work group than that of the last few after the rest have already accepted him. In addition to these similarities, however, there are also fundamental differences between social and strictly economic exchange.

In contrast to economic transactions, in which an explicit or implicit formal contract stipulates in advance the precise obligations incurred by both parties, social exchange entails unspecified obligations. There is no contract, and there is no exact price. A person to whom others are indebted for favours performed has the general expectation that they will discharge their obligations by doing things for him, but he must leave the exact nature of the return up to them. He cannot bargain with them over how much his favours are worth, and he has no recourse if they fail to reciprocate altogether, except, of course, that he can, and probably will, discontinue to do favours for them. Since there is no contract that can be enforced, social exchange requires trust. But little trust is required for the minor transactions with which exchange relations typically start, and the gradual expansion of the exchange permits the partners to prove their trustworthiness to each other. Processes of social exchange, consequently, generate trust in social relations. The mutual trust between committed exchange partners encourages them to engage in a variety of transactions – to exchange advice, help, social support, and compansionship – and these diffuse transactions give the partnership some intrinsic significance. Only impersonal economic exchange remains exclusively focused on specific extrinsic benefits, whereas in social exchange the association itself invariably assumes a minimum of intrinsic significance.

Four facets of social structures have been distinguished – integration, differentiation, legitimation, and opposition. The first two emerge in the course of social transactions without any explicit design, whereas the last two are the result of organized efforts focused on some collective objectives or ideals. Integration and opposition rest on particularistic values that unite ingroups and divide them from outgroups. Differentiation and legitimation are governed by universalistic standards that specify the achievements and qualities that are generally valued within the compass of the collectivity under consideration and that bestow superior status on those who exhibit them. Two of these four facets of social structure can be directly derived from an analysis of exchange, and the other two, more indirectly.

Social exchange has been defined by two criteria, associations oriented largely to extrinsic rather than purely intrinsic rewards and reciprocal rather than unilateral transactions. In the course of recurrent reciprocal exchange of extrinsic benefits, partnerships of mutual trust develop that assume some intrinsic significance for the partners, introjecting an intrinsic element into social interaction. At the same time, some individuals can supply important services to others for which the latter cannot appropriately reciprocate, and the unilateral transactions that consequently take place give rise to differentiation of status. Exchange processes, therefore, lead to the emergence of bonds of intrinsic attraction and social integration, on the one hand, and of unilateral services and social differentiation, on the other.

The development of social integration and differentiation in a collectivity creates a fertile soil for the establishment of an organization designed to coordinate endeavours in the pursuit of common objectives. Integrative bonds provide opportunities for communication about common problems, some of which can only be solved through concerted action, and in these social communications agreement on collective goals tends to arise. In the process of social differentiation, some individuals have demonstrated their ability to make outstanding contributions to the welfare of the rest, and these become apparent candidates for directing collective endeavours, that is, for leadership. Agreement on social objectives is a prerequisite for organization and leadership in a collectivity, because common objectives are the incentives for organizing and coordinating the activities of various members, and because they provide the conditions that permit leaders to arise. For a leader to be able to guide the activities in a collectivity, all or most members must be obliged to comply with his directives. A common purpose makes it possible for a man, by making crucial contributions to its achievement, to obligate all members simultaneously and thus command the compliance of all of them. In groups without a common purpose, a man commands the compliance of others by contributing to their individual ends, and this makes it impossible, except in very small groups, for leadership to evolve, since no man has the time to furnish services to a large number of men singly.[1]

Formal organizations are explicitly instituted to achieve given objectives. Their full establishment requires that the objectives they are intended to serve and the authority of their leadership become legitimated by social values. The contributions effective leadership makes to the welfare of the rest create joint obligations and social approval, which give rise to social norms among

1. Reference here is to direct services rendered by a person to others. The situation is different if a man has the resources to pay wages to many others. Such financial resources are a major source of extensive power over large numbers of men, since money as a general medium of exchange makes indirect transactions on a large scale possible.

followers that demand compliance with the orders of leaders and effectuate their authority. The enforcement of compliance with the directives of superiors *by the collectivity of subordinates* is the distinctive characteristic of legitimate authority. Some organizations, such as voluntary associations and unions, consist mostly of members, whose ends the organization is designed to serve, and who are expected to receive a share of the profits. Other organizations, such as business concerns, consist mostly of employees, who are compensated for services that further the ends of others, and who are not entitled to a share of the profits. In strong voluntary organizations with powerful leaders, however, this distinction becomes obscured, since leaders need to distribute only sufficient rewards to members to act as incentives for compliance and contributions and can keep the rest at their own disposal, which means that they treat members, in effect, as management treats employees.

Within the organization, indirect exchange processes become substituted for direct ones, although direct ones persist in interstitial areas, such as informal cooperation among colleagues. The development of authority illustrates the transformation of direct into indirect exchange transactions. As long as subordinates obey the orders of a superior primarily because they are obligated to him for services he has rendered and favours he has done for them individually, he does not actually exercise authority over the subordinates, and there is a direct exchange between him and them, of the type involving unilateral services. The establishment of authority means that normative constraints that originate among the subordinates themselves effect their compliance with the orders of the superior – partly through public pressure and partly through enforcement actions by the dominant groups among subordinates – and indirect exchanges now take the place of the former direct ones. The individual subordinate offers compliance to the superior in exchange for approval from his colleagues; the collectivity of subordinates enforces compliance with the superior's directives to repay its joint obligations to the superior; and the superior makes contributions to the collectivity in exchange for the self-enforced voluntary compliance of its members on which his authority rests.

The performance of many duties in formal organizations

entails indirect exchange. Supervisors and staff personnel have the official duty to provide assistance to operating employees, in return for which they are compensated, not by these employees, but by the organization, which ultimately benefits from their contributions to the work of others. Officials in bureaucratic organizations are expected to treat clients impersonally in accordance with the rules, which requires that they refrain from engaging in exchange transactions with them. They must, of course, not accept bribes or gratuities, and neither must they reward clients with more favourable treatment for expressions of gratitude and appreciation lest impartial service to all clients in conformity with official procedures suffer. In return for offering services to clients without accepting rewards from them, officials receive material rewards from the organization and colleague approval for conforming with accepted standards. The clients make contributions to the community, which furnishes the resources to the organization that enable it to reward its members. Professional service involves a similar chain of indirect exchange, the central link of which is colleague approval for service to clients in accordance with professional standards and hence in disregard of considerations of social exchange. The obligations created in exchange transactions would make undeviating adherence to impersonal bureaucratic or professional standards impossible. The absence of exchange transactions with clients is a prerequisite of bureaucratic or professional detachment toward them. To maintain such detachment, therefore, requires that colleague approval or other rewards compensate practitioners for the advantages foregone by refraining from entering into exchanges with clients.

Indirect transactions are characteristic of the complex structures in large collectivities generally. Since direct contact between most members in a large collectivity is not possible, the interrelations between them uniting them in a social structure are primarily indirect, and social values serve as the media of these indirect links and transactions. Particularistic values create a common solidarity and integrative ties that unify the members of the collectivity and divide them from other collectivities, functioning both as substitutes for the personal bonds of attraction that solidify face-to-face groups and as a basis for such bonds in the collectivity and its subgroups. Universalistic standards define achievements and qualifications that are generally acknowledged as valuable, making indirect exchange transactions possible, notably in the form of enabling individuals and groups to accumulate social status and power in one setting and gain advantages from them in another. Legitimating values expand the scope of social control beyond the limits of personal influence by establishing authority that commands willing compliance enforced by the subordinates themselves, and these values become the foundation for organizing collective effort on a large scale. Opposition ideals serve as rallying points of opposition movements and as catalysts of social change and reorganization. These four types of value standards constitute media of social associations and transactions; they are the social context that moulds social relations, and they act as mediating links for indirect connections in the social structure.

One characteristic that distinguishes macrostructures from microstructures is that social processes in the macrostructures are mediated by prevailing values. Another differentiating criterion is that macrostructures are composed of interrelated social structures, whereas the constituent elements of microstructures are interrelated individuals in direct social contact. Furthermore, parts of the complex social structures in societies assume enduring form as institutions. Institutionalization involves two complementary social mechanisms through which social patterns are perpetuated from generation to generation. On the one hand, external social arrangements are historically transmitted, partly through written documents that circumscribe and preserve them, as exemplified by the form of government in a society resting on its constitution and laws. On the other hand, internalized cultural values are transmitted in processes of socialization and give the traditional external manifestations of institutions continuing meaning and significance. These institutional mechanisms are implemented by the power structure, since the powerful groups in a society tend to be most identified with its institutions, and since they tend to use their power to preserve the traditional institutions.

Once organized collectivities have developed, social transactions occur between them. A basic distinction can be made between two major types of processes that characterize the transactions of organized collectivities – as well as those of individuals, for that matter – competitive processes reflecting endeavours to maximize scarce resources and exchange processes reflecting some form of interdependence. Competition occurs only among like social units that have the same objective and not among unlike units with different objectives – among political parties and among business concerns but not between a party and a firm – whereas exchange occurs only between unlike units – between a political party and various interest groups but not among the different parties (except when two form a coalition and thus cease to be two independent political units). Competition promotes hierarchical differentiation between the more and the less successful organizations, and exchange promotes horizontal differentiation between specialized organizations of diverse sorts. Extensive hierarchical differentiation, however, makes formerly alike units unlike in important respects and unlike ones alike in their power and opportunity to attain a dominant position. Hence, exchange relations may develop between units that once were alike as the result of differential success in competition, and competition for dominance may develop among unlike units made alike by their success. The first of these developments is illustrated by the exchange relation between a giant manufacturing concern and an unsuccessful competitor who becomes the other's supplier of parts, and the second, by the competition among major business concerns, strong unions, and other organized interest groups for a position of dominant influence in the community.

Competition among collectivities that belong in some respect to the same general type is manifest in patterns of mobility of individuals from one to another, which continually modify their boundaries and internal structure. Organized collectivities typically compete for members and contributors – for experienced executives, skilled employees, customers, voters, religious converts, and so forth. Successful competition provides more resources for rewarding members and thus spells further success, since the greater rewards discourage members of the collectivity from defecting from it to others and encourage members of other collectivities to leave them for it. The internal differentiation of status and consequent differential distribution of rewards in a collectivity, however, create differences in incentives for mobility among its members. If different value standards prevail in the various social groupings, as is the case for religious denominations or political parties, the marginal members of low standing in one collectivity have most incentive to move to another. But if social groupings are hierarchically ranked in terms of the same universalistic standards that prevail throughout all of them, as is the case for social classes, individuals with high social standing within a social stratum have most incentive to leave it, since they have the best chance of moving up to a higher one. The typical patterns of mobility under these conditions are from a superior position in a lower stratum to an inferior position in a higher one and vice versa. The opportunity for such movements confronts individuals with the choice between being a big fish in a little pond and a little fish in a big pond, which entails the alternatives of either deriving social rewards from occupying a superordinate position in daily social intercourse or obtaining the advantages and privileges that accrue from membership in a higher social class at the cost of having to assume a subordinate role in recurrent social interaction.

The interdependent organizations in a society engage in exchange and various related transactions (Thompson and McEwen, 1958). Formal organizations often exchange services. For example, welfare and health organizations refer clients to each other (Levine and White, 1961), parties adopt programmes that serve the interests of various groups in exchange for political support, and, of course, firms exchange a large variety of products and services for a price. Many organizational exchanges are mediated through the community. Thus, the police provides protection to the members of the community, schools furnish training for the young, universities supply research knowledge, hospitals render health services, and they all receive support from the community in exchange for their services. Organizations sometimes form coalitions committing them to joint decisions and actions. Small parties unite forces in a political campaign, for instance, several unions agree to carry out a strike together, and churches join in an ecumenical council. Coalitions among organizations may become mergers that destroy the former boundaries between them. But even without complete mergers, transactions between organized collectivities often lead to their interpenetration and obscure their boundaries. A political party that is primarily supported by two occupational groupings, for example, cannot be said to constitute a social entity distinct from these groups that engages in exchange relations with them. Rather, representative segments of these occupational groups are constituent elements of the party, and competition and bargaining occur between them within the party as each seeks to influence its political programme and course of action.

Transactions among organized collectivities, then, may give rise to social ties that unite them, just as social exchange among individuals tends to produce integrative bonds. These transactions also differentiate competing organizations and may result in the elimination or absorption of competitors and the dominance of one or a few organizations – a few giant corporations, two major parties, a universal church – just as unilateral transactions and competition among individuals generate hierarchical differentiation and may result in the dominance of one or a few leaders in a group. The existence of a differentiated structure of relations among organized collectivities creates the conditions for its formalization and the explicit establishment of an overall political organization in order to maintain order and protect the power of the organizations and ruling groups, which rests on the distribution of needed benefits, against being overthrown by violence, which is the major threat to it. For a political organization to become instituted in a society, however, requires that social values legitimate its objectives and invest it with authority. This process is again analogous to the development of a single organization when the emergent social integration and differentiation in a collectivity are complemented by social values that legitimate common endeavours and the authority to pursue them. No claim is made that the conception outlined represents the actual historical evolution of social organization. It is merely a theoretical model, in which political organization is analytically derived from transactions among organized collectivities and these organizations, in turn, are traced back to simpler processes of social exchange. This model can be schematically presented in the following form:

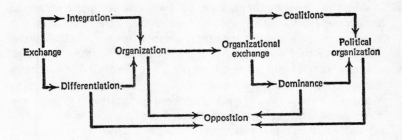

The dynamics of organized social life has its source in opposition forces. The dominant power of individuals, groups, or organizations over others makes it possible for them to establish legitimate authority by exercising their power fairly and with moderation and by making it profitable for others to remain under their protective influence. Dominant power, however, also makes it possible to exploit others and thereby gain advantages, and it consequently is often exercised oppressively. Serious deprivations caused by the unfair exercise of power tend to engender a desire for retaliation. If the exploitation is experienced in a group situation, particularly in a group comparatively isolated from the rest of the community, communication among the oppressed socially justifies and reinforces their feeling of hostility against existing powers by giving rise to an opposition ideology that transforms this hostility from a selfish expression of revenge into a noble cause pursued to further the welfare of one's fellow men. While oppression is not the sole reason for opposition, ideological identification with a cause is essential for the support of radical movements, inasmuch as existing powers have the sanctions to assure that such support harms a man's self-interest and thus is not warranted on purely rational grounds. Opposition ideals create a surplus of resources, since devotion to them frees social energies by making men willing to sacrifice material welfare for their sake, and the opposition movement they inspire constitutes a new social investment that brings about social change and reorganization.

Vested interests and powers create rigidities in social structures, and so does the institutionalization of social arrangements through which they are perpetuated beyond the life-span of individuals. Social institutions are crystallized forms of organized social life that have their base in historical traditions and that are supported by major cultural values internalized in childhood and passed on from generation to generation. Traditional institutions, endowed by profound values with symbolic significance, tend to defy innovation and reform even when changes in social conditions have made them obsolete. Powerful groups whose interests are served by existing institutional arrangements defend them against attack and fortify them. Institutions meet the need for social order and stability in a society at the cost of rigidities and inequities that often cause serious hardships. Vigorous social opposition is required to produce a change in institutions, and it constitutes a countervailing force against institutional rigidities.

Not all opposition takes the form of radical rebellions. Conditions in complex social structures with their interlaced substructures recurrently engender opposing forces. Particularistic values integrate the members of collectivities into solidary units and simultaneously produce divisive boundaries between them that frequently create problems of social solidarity in the encompassing social structure. Universalistic standards of achievement give rise to differentiated social strata in which vested powers and particularistic allegiances restrict upward mobility on the basis of universalistic criteria of achievement alone. Legitimate centralized authority and the autonomy of its component organizations often come into conflict. Even the reorganizations effected by successful opposition movements tend to have repercussions that cause fresh problems and new needs for reorganization. Moreover, the many intersecting organized collectivities with interlocking memberships typical of modern society stimulate a multitude of crisscrossing conflicts, since many issues arise among organized groups, and since individuals are drawn by their organizational affiliations into these controversies. Cross-cutting conflicts that periodically realign opposition forces prevent conflicts from becoming cumulative and dividing the community into two hostile camps, and they are manifest in dialectical patterns of change and reorganization.

References

LEVINE, S., and WHITE, P. E. (1961), 'Exchange as a conceptual framework for the study of interorganizational relationships', *Administrative Science Quarterly*, vol. 5, pp. 583–601.

THOMPSON, J. D., and McEWEN, W. J. (1958), 'Organization goals and environment', *American Sociological Review*, vol. 23, pp. 23–31.

5 T. Parsons

Three Levels in the Hierarchical Structure of Organization

T. Parsons, *Structure and Process in Modern Societies*, Free Press, 1960, pp. 59–69.

The theory of 'bureaucracy' has been so strongly influenced by the conception of 'line' authority that there has been a tendency to neglect the importance of what in some sense are qualitative breaks in the continuity of the line structure. There is much sound observation and comment on many relevant problems but little direct attempt to analyse them in a more formal way. I would like to suggest a way of breaking down the hierarchical aspect of a system of organization – of examining, for example, the line within a school system that runs all the way from the chairman of the school board to the teacher of most junior status, or even to the non-teaching employee in the humblest position. I make this breakdown according to three references of function or responsibility, which become most clearly marked in terms of the external references of the organization to its setting or to the next higher order in the hierarchy. These three may be called, respectively, the 'technical' system, the 'managerial' system, and the 'community' or 'institutional' system.

The three system-levels

In the first place, every formal organization has certain 'technical' functions. In an educational organization these are the actual processes of teaching; in a government bureau, the administrative process in direct relation to the public (e.g., tax collecting by the Bureau of Internal Revenue); in a business firm, the process of physical production of goods, etc. There is, then, always a type of suborganization whose 'problems' are mainly those of effectively performing this 'technical' function – the conduct of classes by the teacher, the processing of income tax returns and the handling of recalcitrants by the bureau, the processing of material and supervision of these operations in the case of physical production. The primary exigencies to which this suborganization is oriented are those imposed by the nature of the technical task, such as the 'materials' – physical, cultural, or human – which must be processed, the kinds of cooperation of different people required to get the job done effectively.

I assume, however, that on the level of social differentiation with which we are here concerned, there is another set of 'problems' which becomes the focus of a different order of organizational setup. In the area where parents teach their own children, for example, to speak their language, there is no problem of the selection and appointment of teachers, or even of their qualifications; the status of parent *ipso facto* makes him the appropriate teacher. But in a school system teachers have to be especially appointed and allocated to teach particular classes. Moreover, classrooms have to be provided; the teacher does not automatically control adequate facilities for performing the function. Furthermore, while it is taken for granted that a child should learn to speak the language of his parents, what should be taught in what schools to what children is by no means automatically given.

In a complex division of labour, both the resources necessary for performing technical functions and the relations to the population elements on whose behalf the functions are performed have become problematical. Resources are made available by special arrangements; they are not simply 'given' in the nature of the context of the function. And who shall be the beneficiary of what 'product' or 'service' on what terms is problematical; this becomes the focus of organizational arrangements of many different kinds.

When the division of labour has progressed beyond a certain point, decisions that pertain to this division must take precedence over those on the 'technical' level. Thus it does not make sense to set up classrooms without having decided what children should be taught what things by what kinds of teachers, or without knowing whether specific teachers and specific physical facilities can be made available. Similarly, the Bureau of Internal Revenue does not just 'collect taxes' in general; it collects specific taxes assessed by a higher authority, from specific categories of persons. And the plant does not just produce goods without anyone's worrying about how the materials will be procured, who will do the actual work on what terms, and who wants the goods anyway – again on what terms. In the case of a subsistence farm family there is no problem: its members have to eat; they have access to soil, seeds, and some simple equipment; and they work to produce their own food. But this is not the typical case for a modern society.

We may say then that the more complex technical functions are performed by suborganizations controlled and serviced – in various ways and at a variety of levels – by higher-order organizations. The higher-order organization is sometimes called an 'administration'. In the business case it is usually called the 'firm', whereas the technical organization is called the 'plant'. In the field of government, 'bureaus' are mainly technical organizations, while the 'political' parts of government are, literally, the 'policy-making' parts (in our system, principally legislative[1] and higher executive). Perhaps a good name for this level of organization is, as suggested above, a 'managerial' system.

The relations between such a managerial system and the technical system can be divided into two categories: mediation between the organization and the external situation, and 'administration' of the organization's internal affairs. Both involve the 'decision-making' processes which have been the centre of so much recent attention.

At the level I have in mind, there are two main foci of the external reference and responsibility. The primary one is to mediate between the technical organization and those who use its 'products' – the 'customers', pupils, or whoever. The second is to procure the resources necessary for carrying out the technical functions (i.e., financial resources, personal, and physical facilities).

In one set of connections, decisions made in the management system control the operations of the technical system. This is certainly true for such matters as the broad technical task which is to be performed in the technical system – the scale of operations, employment and purchasing policy, etc. But, as in other cases of functional differentiation, this is by no means simply a one-way relation, for managerial personnel usually are only

1. The legislative function may, however, be placed mainly at the still higher level, which I call 'institutional' and which will be discussed below.

partially competent to plan and supervise the execution of the technical operations. The managers present specifications to the technical subsystem, but vice versa, the technical people present 'needs' which constitute specifications to the management; on various bases the technical people are closest to the operating problems and know what is needed. Perhaps the most important of these bases is the technical *professional* competence of higher personnel in technical systems, a professional competence not often shared by the administrative personnel who – in the line sense – are the organizational superiors of the technicians.

In its external relations, the managerial system is oriented to the 'markets' for the disposal of the 'product' and for 'procurement' of the resources required by the organization to perform its functions. But those 'lateral' external relations do not exhaust the 'external' problem foci of a managerial system. The organization which consists of both technical and managerial suborganizations never operates subject only to the exigencies of disposal to and procurement from other agencies (which stand on an approximately equal level) as 'customers' or as sources of supply. There is always some 'organized superior' agency with which the organization articulates.

A formal organization in the present sense is a mechanism by which goals somehow important to the society, or to various subsystems of it, are implemented and to some degree defined. But not only does such an organization have to operate in a social environment which imposes the conditions governing the processes of disposal and procurement, it is also part of a wider social system which is the source of the 'meaning', legitimation, or higher-level support which makes the implementation of the organization's goals possible. Essentially, this means that just as a technical organization (at a sufficiently high level of the division of labour) is controlled and 'serviced' by a managerial organization, so, in turn, is the managerial organization controlled by the 'institutional' structure and agencies of the community.

The ways in which the managerial system fits into the higher-order institutional system vary widely according to the character of the managerial system's functions and the organization's position on both the 'lateral' and the 'vertical' axes of the larger social system. But it is a cardinal thesis of this analysis that no organization is ever wholly 'independent'. In terms of 'formal' controls it may be relatively so, but in terms of the 'meaning' of the functions performed by the organization and hence of its 'rights' to command resources and to subject its 'customers' to disciplines, it never is wholly independent.

As noted, this third level of organization, which articulates with the managerial, may take many forms. In the educational field, for instance, I would put school boards with their representative functions in the local community in this category; similarly with trustees of the various types of private, non-profit organizations and, indeed, under the fully-developed corporate form, with the boards of directors of business corporations.[2] These, and possibly other agencies, are the mediating structures between the particular managerial organization – and hence the technical organization it controls – and the higher-order community interests which, on some level, it is supposed to 'serve'.

Without attempting to be more circumstantial and formal at this stage, I may merely suggest that the foci of these higher-level controls which stand 'over' the managerial organization are of three main types, which often appear in combination. One control is universal: the operation of the organization is subjected to generalized norms, valid throughout a wider community. These range from the rules formally codified in the law to standards of 'good practice' informally accepted. So far as control is of this type, the distinctive thing is that no organized agency continually supervises the managerial organization; intervention is likely only when deviant practice is suspected – such control is exerted, for example, through litigation or by law-enforcement agencies, trade and professional associations, and relevant 'public opinion'.

The second type of control mechanism is some formal organization which is interstitial between the managerial structure and a more diffuse basis of 'public interest'. The fiduciary board which supervises the typical private non-profit organization is the type case, though in many respects the directors of business corporations also belong in this category.

2. For the business case one may thus designate the three organizational levels as plant, firm, and corporation. The 'central office' may be thought of as the 'plant' of the administrative organization of the firm.

Finally, the third type is that which brings the managerial organization directly into a structure of 'public authority' at some level. In our society this is usually 'political' authority, i.e., some organ of government; but in the past, religious authorities have also performed this function, and even now, for example, the Catholic school system should be treated as belonging to this type. The relation to superior authority may in turn be 'administrative' or 'regulative'.

The points of articulation between the three system-levels

I have emphasized these *three* different levels of the organization hierarchy because at each of the two points of articulation between them we find a qualitative break in the simple continuity of 'line' authority. School boards, boards of directors, or trustees and political superiors do not, in the nature of the case, simply tell the people at the next level down 'what to do'. This is essentially because the people 'lower down' typically must exercise types of competence and shoulder responsibilities which cannot be regarded as simply 'delegated' by their 'superiors'. This again is because the *functions* at each level are qualitatively different; those at the second level are not simply 'lower-order' spellings-out of the 'top' level functions.

In the case of the technical organization, I illustrate this by the case of the higher level technical functions. When the personnel of the technical organization reach a full professional level of competence, a crucial problem of organization appears. For no matter how far removed these professionals may be from certain levels of concrete 'operations', they must necessarily have the last word in planning and evaluating these operations (i.e., setting the *criteria* of effective operation in technical terms), simply because their managerial superiors are seldom, if at all, equally competent in the technical field. Organizational arrangements are extremely varied; sometimes such people have important positions in the 'firm' or other managerial organization, and they should be regarded, like the foreman, as interstitial. In any case, their position cannot be a simple 'line' position. Nor, indeed, is it adequate to assign them to the 'staff' and say that their function is to 'advise' the 'lay' executive. This implies that it is the executive who *really* makes the decisions. But this is not correct. The technical expert must, in the nature of the case, *participate* in the technically crucial decisions. He does not simply lay the alternatives with their consequences before his 'boss' and say, 'Take *your* choice.' The technical expert takes responsibility for *his* judgement, and when the decision has fallen a given way, he must assume his share of responsibility for the consequences. Hence, if he feels that he cannot take this responsibility, his recourse is to resign, exactly as in the case of an executive. A decision is arrived at not by the executive's deciding in the light of the expert's advice but by a process of weighing the considerations for which each is responsible and then reaching some kind of a balance of agreement. Because of the functions of the managerial organization, the executive has some kind of 'last word'. But this is a veto power, not a capacity to implement, because the executive is powerless to implement or plan implementation without the competence of the expert. The most the executive can do is to fire one expert and hire another in his place.

This leads to another crucial point. The technical expert at the professional level may be a member of the managerial organization, and of the technical system under it, but his allegiance is never exhausted by these two. Though degrees of formal organization vary greatly, the expert is typically a member of one or more collectivities of specialists sharing a type of competence which cuts across the structure of managerial and specific technical organizations. Thus no one industrial firm employs all the engineers, nor one hospital all the doctors, nor one school system all the teachers. The 'reference group' to which the expert looks in connection with his competence and the definition of its standards is not his 'managerial' boss but his professional peers and colleagues.

Similar considerations apply at the point of articulation between the managerial and the institutional system. But the qualitative break in line authority at this point is obscured because we have tended to describe organizational situations according to one of two extreme types. One is exemplified by the business firm where the 'top man' is thought of as beholden to no one; he is 'on his own'. He is thought of as responsible only to his own conscience, and everyone else in the organization is under his orders. The other type of organization is that in which the managerial unit is incorporated in a 'political' structure, so that the nominal head of the unit is thought of merely as a subordinate of his political superiors.

The essential focus of the qualitative break in line authority I have in mind here is the managerial *responsibility* assumed by the executive and the managerial organization which he, in many cases, heads. This also is not a mere 'delegation' where the executive is commissioned to carry out the 'details' while his superiors decide all the 'policies'. This is because it is not possible to perform the functions of focusing legitimation and community support for the organization and at the same time act as the active management of it – that is, when the differentiation of function in the structure has gone far enough. The 'board', or whatever structural form it takes, is a mediating structure between the affairs of the organization at the managerial level and its 'public'. It can become absorbed in the managerial structure only at the expense of its primary function.

Of course the degree to which legitimation and support are essential functions varies from case to case. In some cases, most nearly approached but by no means reached in the business world, the 'automatic' institutional controls constitute the main regulatory mechanism. Perhaps near the extreme in the other direction is the case of the school board in a community where a great many issues touching the operation of the school system are politically 'hot'. Then the superintendent may be sorely in need of a buffer between himself and various 'pressure groups' in the community, but by the same token the board itself may be 'bent' by the pressures of these groups. Its failure to protect the 'professional'[3] element in the school system is not, however, an adequate measure of its dispensability.

Not least of the reasons why the board does not merely delegate functions to the managerial executive is the type of relation the latter must maintain with the technical personnel. The same holds, however, for the executive's external responsibilities. The essential point is that the executive must perform his functions by coming to terms with categories of other people – experts,

3. Note the ambiguity of the term 'professional'. Ordinarily I use the term in a sense denoting *technical* competence. When used otherwise, I shall put it in quotation marks.

customers, and resource people – who are in a position (within limits) to exact their own terms independently. Therefore, to be effective, the executive must have considerable freedom to use his own judgement as to what terms are good for the organization. He can be reasonably bound by broad policies and rules laid down from above, but these cannot be too restrictive. Certainly he cannot be regarded as the mere implementing agent of other people's decisions. Furthermore, he must be in a position to present *his* problems to his board and to negotiate with them from a position of relative strength, not just to go to them for 'instructions'.

I may generalize about the nature of the two main breaks in line authority which I have outlined by saying that at each of the two points of articulation between subsystems there is a *two-way* interchange of inputs and outputs. What has to be 'contributed' from each side is qualitatively different. Either side is in a position, by withholding its important contribution, to interfere seriously with the functioning of the other and of the larger organization. Hence the *institutionalization* of these relations must typically take a form where the relative independence of each is protected. Since, however, there is an actual hierarchy, since in some sense the 'higher' authority must be able to have some kind of 'last word', the problem of protection focuses on the status of the lower-order element. Accordingly, we find that such institutions as tenure serve, in part at least, to protect professional personnel from pressures exerted by management – pressures that are often passed on down from board levels.

6 W. M. Evan

An Organization-Set Model of Interorganizational Relations

W. M. Evan, 'An organization-set model of interorganizational relations', in M. F. Tuite, M. Radnor and R. K. Chisholm (eds.), *Interorganizational Decision Making*, Aldine-Atherton Publishing Co., 1972, pp. 181–200.

The pattern of research in the field of organizational behaviour over the past two decades has been the reverse of that in behaviouristic psychology. Instead of looking at the stimulus and response, social scientists, with the exception of some economists,[1] have studied what behaviourists refer to as the 'black box', that is, the internal structures and processes of an organization. This strategy is justified in view of the complexity and variability of formal organizations, but it is a highly restricted approach to the analysis of organizational phenomena which consist of many external as well as internal interactions. It has nevertheless provided an indispensable prologue to the analysis of the problems of interorganizational relations that some social scientists and practitioners are now attempting to study.

A systems model

For several decades social scientists engaged in research on organizations have conceived of formal organizations as social systems. However, they have rarely pursued the implication of this conceptualization, which is to acknowledge that a systems analysis is required to guide the conduct of research. A systems approach to organizational phenomena begins with the postulate that organizations are 'open' systems which, of necessity, engage in various modes of exchange with their environment.

In further postulating the interrelationships of components of a given system, a systems approach identifies input elements, process elements, output elements, and feedback effects. Moreover, it focuses attention on the interrelation of at least three

1. See for example Phillips (1960) and Williamson (1965).

levels of analysis: the subsystems of an organization, the organizational system in its entirety, and the suprasystem. Analysing the subsystems of an organization entails a study of the interaction patterns of various subunits. Analysing the organizational system includes an examination of (a) the cultural components, viz., its values and goals, (b) the structural components, which consist of the various relationships among the subunits, and (c) the technological components. The suprasystem level of analysis of an organization necessitates, at the very least, an inquiry into the network of interactions or linkages of a given organization with various organizations in its environment.

The particular systems model of interorganizational relations explored here is one elsewhere referred to as an 'organization-set' model (Evan, 1966a). The points of departure of this model are several concepts in role theory developed by Merton (1957) and Gross *et al.* (1958). Instead of selecting a status as the unit of analysis and charting the complex of role relationships in which the status occupant is involved, as Merton does in his analysis of role-sets, let us take as the unit of analysis an organization or a class of organizations and trace its interactions with the various organizations in its environment, viz., its 'organization-set'. Following Gross, Mason and McEachern's use of the term 'focal position' in their analysis of roles, the organization or class of organizations that is the point of reference is referred to as the 'focal organization' (Evan, 1966a, p. 178). As in the case of role-set analysis, the focal organization interacts with a complement of organizations in its environment, i.e., its 'organization-set'. A systems analysis perspective, however, suggests that we partition the organization-set into an 'input-organization-set' and an 'output-organization-set'. By an input-organization-set is meant a complement of organizations that provides resources to the focal organization. Similarly, by an output-organization-set is meant all organizations which receive the goods and/or services, including organizational decisions, generated by the focal organization. Furthermore, a systems analysis requires that we trace feedback effects from the output-organization-set to the focal organization and thence to the input-organization-set, or directly from the output- to the input-organization-set. These feedback effects can, of course, be positive or negative, as well as anticipated or unanticipated, but it is easier to postulate these effects than to operationalize them to facilitate empirical inquiry.

The four components of the model – focal organization, input-organization-set, output-organization-set, and feedback effects – may jointly be conceived as comprising an 'interorganizational system'. Figure 1 summarizes the structural elements of the model of interorganizational relations.

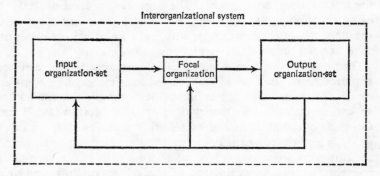

Figure 1 Some elements of an organization-set model of interorganizational relations

For purposes of illustration, if we take as a focal organization the Ford Motor Company, the input-organization-set may include a variety of suppliers of raw materials, trade unions, government agencies, courts, universities, research and development organizations, etc. The input resources are very heterogeneous, including human, material, financial, legal, etc. These inputs are transformed by the focal organization's social structure and technology into products and services that are exported to the members of the output-organization-set, which include principally automobile dealers. The output-organization-set may also include advertising agencies concerned with increasing the sale of its products, trade associations to which information is provided and which may undertake to influence the course of future legislation, community chest organizations to which financial contributions are made, etc. The success with which the focal organization, in this case the Ford Motor Company, manages its multifaceted relations with the members of its output-organization-set, in turn, has feedback effects on itself as well as on the input-organization-set which again triggers the cycle of interorganizational systemic relations.

If instead of the Ford Motor Company we take as a focal organization all four automobile manufacturers for the purpose of studying how they 'negotiate their environment' (Cyert and March, 1963, pp. 119–20), the analysis would focus on the 'interfirm organization' (Phillips, 1960) in an oligopolistic market and the members of the output-organization-set. Such questions as the following might be asked: How does the focal organization decide on output, prices, policies with respect to automobile dealers, strategy with respect to trade associations, legislatures, etc.? In other words, given the problem formulation, it may not be especially relevant to inquire about the interactions of the focal organization with members of its input-organization-set. If the analysis of this particular focal organization were extended to the members of the input-organization-set, two potential members would be the Department of Justice and the Federal Trade Commission, one or both of which might inquire into possible violations of antitrust law.

Dimensions of organization-sets

It should be clear from the context of this analysis that the phrase 'member of an organization-set' refers to an organizational entity with which a focal organization interacts, not an individual member of one of the environing organizations. Apart from distinguishing between input- and output-organization-sets, various other dimensions of organization-sets need to be explored if we are to generate some propositions about inter-organizational interactions. For present purposes three dimensions may be singled out that, prima facie, have significant consequences for the focal organization, viz., the size and diversity of the input- and output-organization-sets and the network configuration.[2] Size of set, of course, refers to the sheer number of input and output organizations with which the focal organization interacts; by diversity of the input- and output-organization-set is meant the number of organizations in the input- and output-sets differing in gross, manifest functions such as industrial organizations, courts,

2. For other dimensions of organization-sets, see Evan (1966a), pp. 178–180.

legislatures, community organizations, prisons, professional associations, hospitals, etc. The network configuration refers to the formal properties of interaction among the members of the input- and output-organization-sets. At least four types of inter-action configurations, shown in Figure 2, that have loomed large

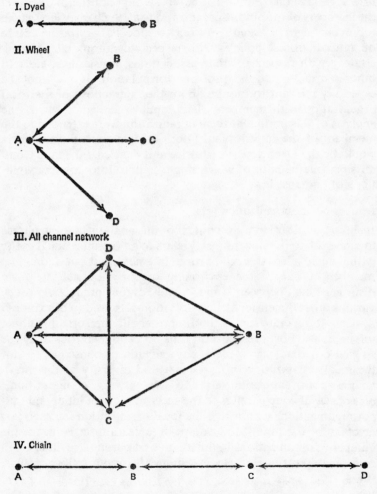

Figure 2 Four network configurations of organization-sets

in the experimental literature on group communication network experiments will be mentioned: (a) *a dyad*, in which focal organization A interacts with B, an individual organization or a class of organizations, in either the input- or output-set; (b) *a wheel network*, in which the focal organization interacts with more than one organization of a particular type but where there are no mutual interactions among the members of the set; (c) *an all-channel network*, in which all members of the set interact with each other and each interacts with the focal organization; and (d) *a chain network*, in which the members of a set are linked in series with the focal organization which has only direct interaction with the first link, so to speak, in the chain.

Examples of network configurations from the real world might make these four types appear more plausible. An illustration of a dyadic relationship is the interaction of a trade union with a business organization. A wheel-type configuration would describe the interaction of automobile manufacturers with 30,000–40,000 individual automobile dealers prior to the formation of the National Automobile Dealers Association (Macaulay, 1965; Assael, 1969). With the establishment of this association, the interaction configuration was transformed to a modified channel network, thus increasing the relative bargaining power of the automobile dealers. The chain configuration commonly occurs in manufacturing and in distribution processes, e.g., the sequential pattern of interaction of automobile suppliers, automobile manufacturers, and automobile dealers. Obviously these four network configurations are meant to be only illustrative of the formal properties of input- and output-organization-sets. Other types may be postulated, such as a limited-channel network with only one link to the focal organization. An exploration of the empirically observable formal properties of sets is but one of the many unsolved analytical problems of interorganizational relations.

An analysis of the formal properties of organization-sets points to an intriguing question concerning the relationship between these formal properties and modes of interaction between the focal organization and members of the input- and output-sets. Thus, for example, under what conditions in a dyadic linkage between the focal organization and a member of its input-set will we observe evidence of cooptation, bargaining, and amalgamation? In a wheel-type configuration, do we find the focal organization dominating the members of the set? If so, under what conditions will pressures emerge to transform the dominance-submission relationship into a bargaining relationship? In an all-channel network or a limited-channel network, would we find a tendency for a coalition to emerge, *vis-à-vis* the focal organization? And, finally, under what conditions would we find in a chain network both cooperation and conflict because of the pressures arising from the constrained pattern of interdependence? Inasmuch as the focal organization will often be involved in diverse network configurations with members of its input- and output-sets, the question arises as to the relative frequency of different modes of interaction, given the frequency of different network configurations.

Apart from having consequences for modes of interaction between the focal organization and members of its input- and output-sets, each of the formal properties probably has some reverberations in the internal structure and internal processes of the focal organization, such as in the formation of new subunits, the formation of new organizational norms, and the articulation of new goals. One hypothetical example will suffice: A state university whose principal source of financial support is derived from the state legislature is an illustration of a dyadic linkage between the focal organization and a member of the input-organization-set. In this familiar situation it is difficult to justify substantial budget increases over time for various departments and schools of a university unless new functional units are established. As a consequence, financial constraints encourage subunit differentiation in the focal organization; for example, sociology and anthropology are divided into separate departments; similarly, operations research and statistics, finance and economics, etc. By establishing new organizational subunits, which may increase student enrollment, it becomes easier to justify substantial increases in the budget of the total university as well as of its components.

Role-sets of boundary personnel

An analysis of modes of interaction between the focal organization and members of its organization-sets, with the aid of the three dimensions discussed above, has one serious limitation. On this level of aggregation there is not only a danger of hypostatizing organizations, i.e., treating them as disembodied entities, but also of losing sight of the intervening mechanisms that contribute to the various modes of interaction. It is, therefore, essential to descend to a lower level of aggregation of social structure and examine the system linkages observable in the role-set relations of boundary personnel. It is through the behaviour of incumbents of various statuses at the boundary of the focal organization, such as top executives, lawyers, purchasing agents, marketing specialists, personnel officers, etc., that various environmental interactions are mediated. Corresponding to the distinction between an input- and output-organization-set, let us distinguish between input and output boundary roles. As a result of the network of role-set relations of boundary personnel of the focal organization, with their role partners in organizations comprising the input- and output-organization-sets, various transactions occur involving the flows of people, information, capital, influence, goods and services, etc.

Apart from distinguishing between input and output boundary roles, other dimensions need to be identified if we are to generate new propositions about interorganizational relations. The most obvious way of distinguishing between the input and output boundary personnel of one organization compared with another is in sheer number, absolute or relative. One could devise various ratios of boundary to nonboundary personnel of the focal organization's input- and output-sets. A second dimension is the quality of formal education or the degree of expertise of boundary personnel. It makes a substantial difference whether the house counsel, for example, is a graduate of an Ivy League law school or a night law school.

A third dimension is position in the organizational hierarchy. Whether the boundary person is a shipping clerk, a director of research and development, or a top executive will obviously influence his relationship to his role partners in other organizations. Is the boundary person authorized to engage in organizational decision making, in pre-decision making activities, such as information gathering, or in non-decision making activities, viz., in the internal technical activities of the organization? Parsons's conceptualization of the three levels in the hierarchical structure of organizations is especially suggestive when applied to boundary roles (Parsons, 1960, pp. 60–9). At the 'technical' level in an organization there may be a relatively large number of boundary roles as well as boundary personnel engaged in the primary operations of the organization, such as foremen, supervisors, purchasing agents, salesmen, clerks, etc. Individually they may have little impact on interorganizational relations, but collectively their effect may be of considerable significance. At the 'managerial' level in an organization, the number of boundary roles is smaller but the salience of the manager's behaviour, individually and collectively, for interorganizational relations is probably greater than the behaviour of boundary personnel at the 'technical' level. Managers also differ from the personnel at the 'technical' level in that they are preoccupied with the tactics of organizational goal formation and decision making. At the 'institutional' level in an organization's hierarchy, where the focus is on strategies of goal formation and decision making, there are substantially fewer boundary roles and boundary personnel than at the managerial level; however, the decision making power of such personnel – top executives, members of boards of directors, or boards of trustees – in their role-set relations at the interface of the focal organization, is appreciably greater.

A fourth dimension of boundary roles is the normative-reference-group orientation of boundary personnel. Do they orient themselves to the norms and values of their own organization, i.e., of the focal organization, or to those of some other organization? Boundary personnel whose normative reference group is their own organization, i.e., the focal organization, will exhibit greater loyalty in their external role-set relations than those whose normative reference group is an outside organization. Organizations employing large numbers of professionals, such as universities, hospitals, research and development organizations, bear the brunt of a 'cosmopolitan' normative-reference-group orientation which may result in behaviour impeding organizational goal attainment, including the costs entailed in a high turnover rate (Gouldner, 1957, 1958).

An analysis of the personnel occupying the boundary roles of a focal organization would be guided by the dimensions identified above as well as by the dimensions of its input- and output-organization-set. By way of illustrating the heuristic value of our model, we suggest the following hypotheses:

1. As the size of the input-organization-set increases, the number of input boundary personnel of the focal organization increases.

2. As the diversity or heterogeneity of the input-organization-set increases, the input boundary roles within the focal organization become increasingly differentiated.

3. A similar positive relationship is anticipated between the size and diversity of the output-organization-set and the number and role differentiation of output boundary personnel of the focal organization.

4. As the input- and output-organization-sets become more 'turbulent' (Emery and Trist, 1965) and uncertain, the input and output boundary roles of the focal organization become more functionally differentiated.

5. If the boundary personnel of the focal organization are not commensurate in number, quality of education or expertise, position in the organizational hierarchy, and normative-reference-group orientation with the boundary personnel of organizations comprising the input- and output-organization-sets, the effectiveness of the focal organization will be impaired.

Implications of the model for a theory of organizational change

The organization-set model outlined above is incomplete in two respects: it needs to be further developed theoretically and also operationalized before it can be put to an empirical test. In its present state it is principally a systems approach to organizational structure and ecology. At first blush, the model may suggest a static approach to organizational phenomena. Upon closer examination, however, it should be evident that it has implications for a 'positive' as well as a 'normative' theory of organizational change. Insofar as it generates explanations for organizational stability as well as predictions concerning organizational change, it qualifies as a positive or a descriptive theory; and insofar as it suggests guidelines for effecting organizational change, it meets the test of a normative theory. In either case, the level of analysis of this model and its implications for a theory of organizational change are principally sociological in nature.

In attending to the internal structure of the focal organization, we are focusing on the structure of roles at the three levels in the hierarchy (technical, managerial, and institutional) and inquiring into (a) the characteristics of the boundary roles and boundary personnel in terms of the four dimensions identified above and (b) the functions performed by boundary personnel in relation to their role partners located in organizations comprising the input- and output-organization-sets. In examining the input- and output-set of the focal organization, such structural dimensions as size, diversity, and network configuration are considered in order to ascertain the sources of support for, opposition to, and constraints on, the focal organization.

From the concepts and assumptions of our model it follows that the effectiveness of the focal organization, regardless of its objectives, is a function of (a) internal structure, particularly its role structure, and (b) the characteristics of its input- and output-sets. We may also infer the following proposition, of a positive nature, with respect to organizational change: as the input- or output-organization-set undergoes change as regards size, diversity, network configuration, etc., the internal structure and level of effectiveness of the focal organization will also change. The direction of causality is in principle reversible; i.e., if the focal organization's internal structure (role structure and/ or technology) undergoes change, the input- and output-organization-sets will likewise change. Neither of these propositions, of course, precludes the occurrence of time lags before adaptive responses are triggered (Evan, 1966b). Organizational change, in the sense of growth, occurs when the feedback effects are positive but of a controlled nature. It goes without saying that uncontrolled positive feedback effects can destroy the focal organization; that excessive time lags before adaptive responses occur, especially on the part of boundary personnel at all three hierarchical levels of the focal organization, can undermine organizational effectiveness; and that if no 'appreciable' structural change occurs, within a given time interval, in the focal organization as well as in its input- and output-sets, the focal organization can be characterized as 'stable'.

Our model also has implications for a normative theory of organizational change in that it in effect directs change agents – whether internal or external – to intervene at several crucial junctures in organizational functioning. First and foremost, in recruiting personnel for boundary roles at the three hierarchical levels, special attention is warranted in assessing their potential efficacy in interactions with role partners in organizations comprising the input- and output-sets. Second, to the extent that the socialization of new and old members involves formal and planned activities, particular attention should be devoted to the handling of role-set problems of boundary personnel. In all likelihood, the incidence of role conflicts and role ambiguities is higher among the occupants of boundary roles than non-boundary roles. Hence, if boundary personnel were helped, via specially designed training programmes, to increase their level of competence in managing role-set conflicts and ambiguities, it could noticeably improve their role performance. Third, special efforts are necessary at each of the three levels in the hierarchy of the focal organization for redesigning the interaction network in the input- and output-organization-sets, with a view to increasing organizational effectiveness. Innovative ideas designed to alter the organizational ecology of the focal organization may include proposals for cooperation, cooptation, bargaining, coalition formation, consortia formation, amalgamation, etc., with members of the input- and output-organization-sets.

Clearly, normative guidelines, such as these, that are derived from our model differ from, but are not incompatible with, the psychological and social-psychological propositions of theories of change emerging under the rubric of organization development (Beckhard, 1969; Bennis, 1969; Blake and Mouton, 1969). Since few organizational field experiments have thus far been performed (Evan, 1971), we are not yet in a position to assess the relative merits of different normative theories of organizational change. Much systematic field experimentation will be needed to test the validity of propositions derivable from our model as compared with those derivable from 'organization development' models.

References

ASSAEL, H. (1969), 'Constructive role of interorganizational conflict', *Administrative Science Quarterly*, vol. 14, December, pp. 573–82.

BECKHARD, R. (1969), *Organization Development: Strategies and Models*, Reading, Mass., Addison-Wesley Publishing Co.

BENNIS, W. G. (1969), *Organization Development: Its Nature, Origins, and Prospects*, Reading, Mass., Addison-Wesley Publishing Co.

BLAKE, R. R., and MOUTON, J. S. (1969), *Building a Dynamic Corporation through Grid Organization Development*, Reading, Mass., Addison-Wesley Publishing Co.

CYERT, R. M., and MARCH, J. G. (1963), *A Behavioral Theory of the Firm*, Englewood Cliffs, New Jersey, Prentice-Hall, Inc.

EMERY, F. E., and TRIST, E. L. (1965), 'The causal texture of organizational environments', *Human Relations*, vol. 18, pp. 21–31.

EVAN, W. M. (1966a), 'The organization-set: toward a theory of interorganizational relations', *Approaches to Organizational Design*, James D. Thompson (ed.), Pittsburgh, University of Pittsburgh Press, pp. 175–91.

EVAN, W. M. (1966b), 'Organizational lag', *Human Organization*, vol. 25, pp. 51–3.

EVAN, W. M. (1971), *Organizational Experiments*, New York, Harper & Row.

GOULDNER, A. W. (1957), 'Cosmopolitans and locals: toward an analysis of latent social roles I', *Administrative Science Quarterly*, vol. 2, December, pp. 281–306.

GOULDNER, A. W. (1958), 'Cosmopolitans and locals: toward an analysis of latent social roles II', *Administrative Science Quarterly*, vol. 2, March, pp. 444–80.

GROSS, N., MASON, W. J., and MCEACHERN, A. W. (1958), *Explorations in Role Analysis: Studies of the School Superintendency Role*, New York, John Wiley & Sons, Inc.

MACAULAY, S. (1965), 'Changing a continuing relationship between a large corporation and those who deal with it: automobile manufacturers, their dealers and the legal systems', *Wisconsin Law Review*, Summer, pp. 483–575; Fall, pp. 740–858.

MERTON, R. K. (1957), *Social Theory and Social Structure*, rev. ed., Glencoe, Ill., The Free Press.

PARSONS, T. (1960), *Structure and Process in Modern Societies*, Glencoe, Ill., The Free Press.

PHILLIPS, A. (1960), 'A theory of interfirm organization', *Quarterly Journal of Economics*, vol. 74, November, pp. 602–13.

WILLIAMSON, O. E. (1965), 'A dynamic theory of interfirm behavior', *Quarterly Journal of Economics*, vol. 79, November, pp. 579–607.

Part Two
Research on Interorganizational Relations: Types of Linkage Mechanisms

That theory and research are not well coordinated is especially evident in newly developing research areas such as interorganizational relations. The research reports included in Part Two all deal with important problems, processes or mechanisms of interorganizational relations. Yet not all the reports are theoretically based, let alone on one of the six models presented in Part One.

Conceptualized in terms of social exchange, Baty, Evan and Rothermel analyse the flow of personnel among schools of business. Dooley and Pfeffer each investigate a common interorganizational linkage involving the 'institutional' personnel of an organization. Dooley discovers the persistence of a similar frequency of interlocking directorates from 1935 to 1964 and the influence of five significant contributory factors: (1) the size of the corporation, (2) the extent of management control, (3) the financial linkages of the corporation, (4) the relationship with competitors, and (5) the existence of local economic interests. Pfeffer finds that the size and composition of the board of directors are a function of the conditions of the external environment of an organization. Hirsch is also concerned with how organizations manage the uncertainty in their environments and applies the organization-set concept in a study of organizations in three 'cultural' industries: book publishing, phonograph records and motion pictures. He identifies three adaptive strategies to the uncertainties at the input and output boundaries: the development of 'contact' men, overproduction and differential promotion of new products, and cooptation of mass media gatekeepers.

Aiken and Hage investigate the relationship between interorganizational cooperation and intraorganizational structure. They find that health and welfare organizations that enter into joint programmes tend to be more complex, more innovative, have more active internal communication channels and more decentralized decision-making structures.

Schwarz is also concerned with interorganizational cooperation but of a type involving the formation and maintenance of coalitions in the European Economic Community and in the party system of Western Germany and Austria. In each case, Schwarz observes the operation of an enduring coalition and the use of a number of similar mechanisms to maintain the coalition: the partial exclusion of certain issues from impinging on the coalition's decision-making system, the establishment of a decision-making system in which either some or all of the members have a veto over important coalition decisions, and the promotion of a central 'broker' role within the coalitions.

Assael deals with conflicts among organizations that are members of a channel of distribution. In the post-World War Two years, distributive trade associations have been more successful in resolving manufacturer-distributor conflicts by means of self-regulation than by political action, viz., recourse to third parties such as the legislature.

The process of merger or amalgamation among organizations involves negotiating the terms of the merger as well as the implementation of the merger agreement. Dewey analyses the recent trend in union mergers in the US and the factors contributing to it.

The research reports presented in Part Two exemplify only some of the linkage mechanisms – various types of exchanges, conflicts, coalitions and mergers – that arise in the course of interorganizational relations. Future research will undoubtedly clarify the relationship among the diverse linkage mechanisms and, in turn, the relevance of different models for describing and explaining their occurrence.

7 P. C. Dooley

The Interlocking Directorate

P. C. Dooley, 'The interlocking directorate', *American Economic Review*, vol. 59, June 1969, pp. 314–23.

Early in this century interlocking directorates were publicly attacked from many quarters. Louis Brandeis, one of the most outspoken critics and one of President Wilson's chief advisers on the trust problem, described interlocking directorates with the following words:

The practice of interlocking directorates is the root of many evils. It offends laws human and divine. Applied to rival corporations, it tends to the suppression of competition and to violation of the Sherman law. Applied to corporations which deal with each other, it tends to disloyalty and to violation of the fundamental law that no man can serve two masters. In either event it leads to inefficiency; for it removes incentive and destroys soundness of judgement. It is undemocratic, for it rejects the platform: 'A fair field and no favors' – substituting the pull of privilege for the push of manhood (Brandeis, 1914, p. 51).

The Clayton Act of 1914 prohibited interlocking directorates among competing corporations, but it did not condemn the practice in general.

In the 1930s the National Resources Committee found that 225 of the 250 largest US corporations had at least one director who sat on the board of at least one other of the largest corporations. It further discovered that 106 of these corporations belonged to '. . . eight more or less clearly defined interest groups' (US National Resources Committee, 1939, p. 161). These findings have provoked repeated studies and comment by the government (US Federal Trade Commission, 1951; US House of Representatives, 1965, 1968), by economists (Gordon, 1945; Perlo, 1957), by sociologists (Mills, 1959; Warner *et al.*, 1967) and others (Domhoff, 1967; Villarejo, 1961). Paul Sweezy, who helped prepare the National Resources Committee study, has recently stated that the network of interlocking directorates has changed since the 1930s and that the concept of the interest group is now obsolete (Baran and Sweezy, 1966, pp. 17–20).

This paper investigates the nature of interlocking directorates and interest groups for 1965, compares the 1935 findings of the National Resources Committee with the current situation, and examines several reasons for the existence of interlocking directorates.

Interlocks: 1935 and 1965

The National Resources Committee studied the 200 largest non-financial corporations and the 50 largest financial corporations ranked by assets. This paper uses a similar group of corporations thirty years later. The list of corporations was taken from the Fortune Directory. Of course, membership in the top 250 corporations changed substantially over this period. Only 140 of the largest corporations in 1965 can readily be identified on the 1935 list, though the actual overlapping is greater than this due to mergers and reorganizations. The 200 largest non-financial corporations are here further subdivided into 115 industrial, 10 merchandising, 25 transportation, and 50 public utility corporations. The financial group includes 32 banks and 18 life insurance companies. The list of directors for these companies was obtained from Standard and Poor's *Register* for 1965.

The frequency of interlocks in 1935 and 1965 is remarkably similar. In 1965 a total of 4,007 directorships were held by 3,165 men. While most of these directors sat on a single board, 562 sat on two or more boards. Five men held six directorships each. In all, 1,404 directorships were held by multiple directors. In 1935 there were somewhat fewer directors and directorships, though the distribution of multiple directorships was slightly more concentrated than in 1965 (Table 1).[1]

More of the top 250 corporations were interlocked in 1965 than in 1935. In the earlier period 25 corporations did not interlock at all, while only 17 were not interlocked in the later period (Table 2). In 1965 these noninterlocked companies consisted of eleven

---

1. The Gini index of concentration is 20 for 1935 and 18 for 1965, where 00 indicates perfect equality.

industrials, four utilities, one merchandiser, and one life insurance company.

Table 1. Distribution of directorships

Number of directorships held by one man	1935[a]		1965	
	Number of men	Number of directorships	Number of men	Number of directorships
1	2,234	2,234	2,603	2,603
2	303	606	372	744
3	102	306	123	369
4	48	192	49	196
5	19	95	13	65
6	6	36	5	30
7	6	42		
8	3	24		
9	1	9		
Total	2,722	3,544	3,165	4,007

[a] US National Resources Committee, *The Structure of the American Economy*, Washington, 1939, p. 158.

Table 2. Interlocking directorates among the 250 largest US corporations in 1935 and 1965

	1935[a]		1965	
	Number of companies	Number of companies interlocked	Number of companies	Number of companies interlocked
Industrial and merchandising	107	91	125	113
Transportation	39	38	25	25
Utilities	54	46	50	46
All nonfinancial	200	175	200	184
All financial	50	50	50	49
Total	250	225	250	233

[a] US National Resources Committee, *The Structure of the American Economy*, Washington, 1939, p. 159.

Table 3. Distribution of interlocks by kind of business, 1965

Number of interlocks per corporation	Industrial	Merchandising	Transportation	Utility	Non-financial	Banks	Life insurance	Financial	Total
0	11	1	0	4	16	0	1	1	17
1–5	27	2	8	25	62	8	5	13	75
6–10	30	3	6	14	53	4	4	8	61
11–15	29	3	5	3	40	7	2	9	49
16–20	13	0	4	2	19	5	2	7	26
over 20	5	1	2	2	10	8	4	12	22
Total companies	115	10	25	50	200	32	18	50	250
Average number of interlocks	9·1	9·7	10·6	6·2	8·6	16·1	13·6	15·2	9·9

The number of interlocks per corporation was unevenly distributed. Three companies in 1965 had directors who held 40 or more outside directorships, while 19 additional companies interlocked 20 or more times with other corporations among the top 250. Financial companies interlocked more frequently than did nonfinancial companies. In 1965 banks interlocked an average of 16·1 times compared to 9·9 times for all 250 corporations (Table 3).

Why do interlocks occur?

The institution of the interlocking directorate has continued to exist since the early days of corporate capitalism. This is of some interest in itself, because it is doubtful that it would have survived without serving some material purpose. The critical question is what purpose (or purposes) does it serve.

Like many social phenomena, the interlocking directorate is shaped by a multitude of tangible and intangible forces. Yet interlocks occur with sufficient order to permit an empirical analysis of some of the more obvious forces. In this study five different factors were found to be significant: (1) the size of the corporation, (2) the extent of management control, (3) the financial connections of the corporation, (4) the relationship with competitors, and (5) the existence of local economic interests.

Size: The largest corporations tend to have the most interlocks (Table 4). This may occur because the directors of the largest corporations are the most knowledgeable, the most capable, and the most accomplished men available. Other corporations would naturally seek their advice and would rather have them on their board than men of less ability. This may also occur, however, because of factors unrelated to managerial ability. The director of a giant corporation undoubtedly has more personal influence with other companies, with potential investors, and with the government than the common man. Having the director from a large corporation on your board may also lead to profitable business with that corporation.

Management control: Management controlled companies, where management control is measured by the proportion of officers on the board of directors, tend to avoid interlocks with other corporations. The frequency of interlocks with other corporations declines as the proportion of active company officers (president, vice president, treasurer, etc.) on the board of directors increases (Table 5).

Table 4. Average number of interlocks by size of corporation, 1965

	Assets in billions of dollars							
	less than 0·5	0·5 to 0·9	1·0 to 1·4	1·5 to 1·9	2·0 to 2·9	3·0 to 3·9	4·0 to 4·9	5·0 and above
Nonfinancial	6·0	7·5	7·6	9·2	13·6	14·6	16·0	17·3
Financial	—	—	4·3	9·5	10·3	18·0	21·0	26·8
Total	6·0	7·5	6·8	9·2	12·4	16·4	19·1	23·7

Note: The simple correlation coefficients for number of interlocks in relation to size are 0·316, 0·489, and 0·467 for nonfinancial, financial, and all 250 corporations, respectively. However, since the relationship does not appear to be linear, these coefficients tend to understate the degree of correlation.

Table 5. Average number of interlocks in relation to management control, 1965

	Percentage of directors who are officers[a]									
	less than 10	10 to 19	20 to 29	30 to 39	40 to 49	50 to 59	60 to 69	70 to 79	80 to 89	90 to 100
Nonfinancial	7·1	7·7	10·1	9·7	7·1	6·6	1·7	3·5	2·0	[b]
Financial	19·0	11·0	11·5	[c]						
Total	13·6	8·6	10·2	9·7	7·1	6·6	1·7	3·5	2·0	

[a] Officers are defined to exclude the chairman of the board.

[b] No nonfinancial corporations had 90 per cent or more of their board of directors made up of officers.

[c] No financial corporations had 30 per cent or more of their board of directors made up of officers.

Note: The simple correlation coefficients for number of interlocks in relation to management control are −0·195, −0·291, and −0·292 for nonfinancial, financial and all 250 corporations, respectively. For the 115 manufacturing corporations alone the coefficient is −0·422. However, the relationship does not appear to be linear.

Management increases its autonomy by increasing its control over the board of directors. When outside directors do not sit on the board, management is free to pursue its own policies for good or bad and does not have to answer embarrassing questions.

Financial interlocks: For nonfinancial corporations roughly one-third of all interlocks are with financial institutions. For financial corporations the proportion is somewhat less (Table 6). These financial interlocks occur for several reasons.

Table 6. Interlocking directorates among the 250 largest US corporations, 1965

	Number of interlocks	Interlocks with financial institutions	Interlocks with competitors[a]	Interlocks within the same commercial centre
Industrial	1,049	378	133	500
Merchandising	97	32	0	51
Transportation	265	90	25	63
Utilities	309	116	2	148
Total nonfinancial	1,720	616	160	762
Banks	514	82	82	283
Life insurance	246	55	55	117
Total financial	760	137	137	400
All 250 corporations	2,480	753	297	1162

[a] For financial institutions interlocks with other financial institutions and with competitors are identical.

First, companies that are in financial difficulty, particularly those occasionally threatened with insolvency, tend to form a close association with one or more financial houses. By electing a banker to the board of directors, a company may expect to have more ready access to bank funds, while the banker can watch over the operation of the company and reduce the risk of lending to a distressed borrower.

Second, banks apparently find it advantageous to become associated with large companies by electing company officers to the bank's board of directors. This may attract large deposits as well as secure a reliable customer for bank loans.

A multiple regression analysis of the relationship between the financial position of the 200 nonfinancial corporations and the number of interlocks with financial corporations indicates that the incidence of interlocks between the two increases as the nonfinancial corporation becomes less solvent and as the assets of the nonfinancial corporation become larger. Thus, many corporations are partially dependent on financial houses for credit and in turn, financial institutions depend on the larger corporations for a substantial portion of their business.

While the modern corporation typically finances a large proportion of its new investment out of internally generated funds, the volume of outside financing is still large. For all 200 nonfinancial corporations, total liabilities were 62 per cent of equity. This percentage ranged from 102 for the 50 utilities to 50·8 for the 115 industrials. The importance of outside funds is further illustrated by the fact that on 31 December 1965 the total liabilities of the nonfinancial business sector in the Flow of Funds Accounts was $461·9 billion. Of this $276·1 billion was in the form of corporate bonds, mortgages, bank loans, and other loans, most of which was held by banks and life insurance companies. In turn, the business sector held $20·3 billion on deposit in commercial banks (Board of Governors, 1966, pp. 734–5).

Third, these financial interlocks also arise from the trust operations of banks (US House of Representatives, 1968). The trust departments of the major banks are often the principal stockholders of the largest corporations, because they gather together the wealth of many individuals. Consequently, they gain representation on the board of directors of other corporations.

Competition: Nearly one in every eight interlocks involves companies which are competitors (Table 6). The proportion is highest among life insurance companies, banks, and manufacturers; and lowest among merchandisers and utilities. While illegal under the Clayton Act, the law has not been effectively enforced;[2] so that the institution of interlocking directorates con-

2. In 1965 the Antitrust Subcommittee of the House Judiciary Committee concluded after a lengthy study of interlocks among competitors that: 'In operation, the body of Federal legislation has not effectively prevented interlocks in corporate managements in the fields it covers. Enforcement of the Clayton Act's prohibitions against interlocking directorates was neither prompt nor vigorous . . .

From its enactment on October 15, 1914, to January 1965, the FTC had

tinues to provide a vehicle for restricting competition. Perhaps it is not often used. Perhaps it can easily be abandoned when antitrust spokesmen raise their voice. Nonetheless the framework exists today as it existed earlier in the century.

Local interest groups: The most prevalent type of interlock involves companies which have their head offices in the same commercial centre (Table 6). Indeed, almost half of the largest 250 corporations belong to one of 15 clearly identifiable local interest groups each of which is held together by a network of interlocking directorates. In other words, the interest groups reported by the National Resources Committee in 1935 still exist today, but in a modified form. Of the eight major groups identified by the Committee, five were associated with names of well-known financial and industrial families (Morgan-First National, Rockefeller, Kuhn-Loeb, Mellon, and Du Pont). The remaining three groups could only be identified by their location (Chicago, Cleveland, and Boston) (US National Resources Committee, 1939, pp. 160–63). Today all have a local identity. Only one, the Mellon-Pittsburgh group, is clearly dominated by a single family, though the Rockefeller family occupies a position of primary importance in the New York group.

The 15 interest groups were identified by the number of times their members were interlocked together. They include corporations with head offices outside of the group city. Seven groups were classed as *tight-knit* because the corporations in those groups interlocked four or more times, while eight groups were classed as *loose-knit* because they interlocked only two or three times. New York is actually in a class by itself. So many corporations interlocked with the New York group that it was necessary to raise the

---

filed a total of 13 complaints under section 8 of the Clayton Act. Only one of these complaints resulted in a cease-and-desist order, and this was by consent; the remainder were dismissed when the directors involved discontinued the prohibited relationship.

The Department of Justice did not undertake a systematic program with respect to interlocking directorates until after World War Two, and the first cases to be litigated to a decision by a court were not filed until February 27, 1952, 38 years after the enactment of the Clayton Act. As of January 1965, the Department of Justice had instituted a total of 10 cases to enforce section 8, and 5 cases to enforce section 10' (US House of Representatives, 1965, pp. 226–7).

cut-off point for membership in the group to six or more interlocks (Table 7).

Table 7. **Interest groupings**

Tight-knit groups:[a]	Number of corporations
New York	38
Chicago	14
San Francisco	13
Pittsburgh	8
Los Angeles	6
Cleveland	5
Detroit	4
Loose-knit groups:[b]	
Hartford	6
Philadelphia	4
Milwaukee	7
Portland, Ore.	4
Minneapolis-St Paul	3
Boston	3
Dallas	2
Houston	2
Unallocated[c]	3
Total	122

[a] Interlocked four or more times, except for New
York where all corporations were interlocked six or
more times.

[b] Interlocked two or three times.

[c] Interlocked four or more times with two groups
and not allocated to either group. The three are Pan
American World Airways, the Pennsylvania Railroad,
and Union Oil.

Nearly all the groups share certain common characteristics.
Banks or life insurance companies form the central core of the
group and have the greatest number of interlocks with other
members of the group. Local public utilities form a second ring
about the central core and have the second greatest number of
interlocks. Finally, an outer ring is made up of manufacturing,
merchandising, and transportation companies that do a substantial portion of their business in the region of the group city.

The New York group is, in part, an exception to this general pattern. It contains the major New York banks, life insurance companies, and utilities, but it also contains a large number of companies whose business is clearly nationwide.

In 1935, the National Resources Committee designated two major New York City groups, the Morgan-First National and the Rockefeller. Today it is not possible to separate these groups. For that matter, it has not been easy to distinguish between them since the turn of the century, as John Moody observed in 1904:

It should not be supposed, however, that these two great groups of capitalists and financiers are in any real sense rivals or competitors for power, or that such a thing as a 'war' exists between them. For, as a matter of fact, they are not only friendly, but they are allied to each other by many close ties, and it would probably require only a little stretch of the imagination to describe them as a single great Morgan-Rockefeller group (Moody, 1904, pp. 492–3).

The Chicago group and the Pittsburgh group contain many of the companies they did in 1935. The Chicago group is made up of 14 corporations that have been prominent in the economic history of the city, while the Pittsburgh group includes the principal corporations that have long been associated with the Mellon name. San Francisco did not appear as a group in the 1935 study; however, today it is third in size. Like Chicago, the San Francisco group is dominated by local banks and utilities and by other important regional corporations. The remaining groups follow the same general pattern.

The arbitrary rules used to establish these groups involves three serious problems. First, 15 corporations qualified for membership in two groups, none qualified for membership in three. Such inter-group corporations were not allocated to any group unless there was a clear connection to a particular group in terms of location, ownership, or number of interlocks.[3] Second, some corporations were included in groups with which they have little in common (location, products, ownership) and from which they may be independent in every respect except the coincidence of their common directors. General Motors, for example, is included in the Pittsburgh group simply because two directors sit

3. Thirteen of the 15 inter-group corporations were interlocked four or more times with the New York group.

on its board who are multiple directors in the Pittsburgh group. Third, many significant interlocks and interlocking groups were omitted by restricting the study to just the 250 largest corporations. W. L. Warner, D. B. Unwalla, and J. H. Trimm have found in a sociological study of interlocks that 5,776 directors of their 500 large representative corporations interlocked a total of 8,872 corporations, ranging in size from less than a million dollars in net worth to over a billion dollars in assets (1967, pp. 130–34).

While these three definitional problems affect the number, size and membership of groups, it is doubtful that they affect the nature of interlocking groups in general. The *tight-knit* groups in particular are intertwined too many times to be significantly rearranged by minor changes in definition.

Conclusion

The institution of the interlocking directorate is extensive and enduring. Most of the larger corporations have been interlocked with other large corporations for many decades. This suggests that the structure of the American economy is markedly different from what is commonly supposed. The widely accepted views of A. A. Berle and G. C. Means (1932), R. A. Gordon (1945), R. J. Larner (1966), and J. K. Galbraith (1967) that the modern corporation is an independent and self-sufficient organ ruled by its own self-perpetuating management needs to be modified on several points.

The extreme view holds that: 'Major corporations in most instances do not seek capital. They form it themselves' (Berle, p. 40). This view contains an important element of truth, but it overlooks the fact that the total liabilities of nonfinancial business approach one-half trillion dollars, that about one-third of the assets of the 200 largest nonfinancial corporations are financed on credit, and that these 200 corporations interlock 616 times with the 50 largest banks and life insurance companies alone. Stock and bond issues, mergers and acquisitions, and other questions of high finance require expert counsel. Such questions are not the daily business of the salaried executives of nonfinancial corporations, the men who Gordon claims make '. . . the essential business decisions . . .' (1945, p. viii), nor do the anonymous men of Galbraith's 'technostructure' have the opportunity to develop competence in handling such occasional and specialized questions. This does not mean that a small clique of bankers controls every detail of corporate activity. However, the presence of knowledgeable men of finance on the board of directors cannot help but influence policies within the sphere of their competence and responsibility.

The presence of outside local business leaders on the board of directors must also force management to consider the interests of the local community, both in terms of its economic growth and in terms of its social and political development. In addition, the presence of competitors in the board room must direct the attention of the management to certain matters of common interest.

Thus, while it is accepted that the modern corporation is the central unit of production and capital accumulation today, its autonomy is a matter of degree. Its autonomy increases as management control over the board of directors increases, for then management can isolate itself from other points of view. For the typical corporation this control is far from absolute. Within its own walls it faces the constraining influence of the financier, the local interest, and the competitor.

References

BARAN, P. A., and SWEEZY, P. M. (1966), *Monopoly Capital*, New York, Monthly Review Press.

BERLE, A. A., and MEANS, G. C. (1932), *The Modern Corporation and Private Property*, New York, Macmillan.

BERLE, A. A. (1954), *The 20th Century Capitalist Revolution*, New York, Harcourt Brace.

BRANDEIS, L. D. (1914), *Other People's Money*, New York, Harper's Weekly.

DOMHOFF, G. W. (1967), *Who Rules America?*, Englewood Cliffs, Prentice-Hall.

GALBRAITH, J. K. (1967), *The New Industrial State*, Boston, Houghton Mifflin.

GORDON, R. A. (1945), *Business Leadership in the Large Corporation*, Washington, D.C., Brookings Institution.

LARNER, R. J. (1966), 'Ownership and control of the 200 largest nonfinancial corporations, 1929 and 1963', *American Economic Review*, vol. 56, September, pp. 777–87.

MILLS, C. W. (1959), *The Power Elite*, New York, Oxford University Press.

MOODY, J. (1904), *The Truth about the Trusts*, New York, Greenwood Press.

PERLO, V. (1957), *The Empire of High Finance*, New York, International Publishers.

VILLAREJO, D. (1961), 'Stock ownership and control of corporations', *New University Thought*, Autumn, pp. 33–77.

WARNER, W. L., UNWALLA, D. B. and TRIMM, J. H. (1967), *The Emergent American Society*, New Haven, Yale University Press.

BOARD OF GOVERNORS OF THE FEDERAL RESERVE SYSTEM (1966), *Federal Reserve Bulletin*, May, pp. 724–35.

STANDARD AND POOR'S (1965), *Poor's Register of Corporation Officers and Directors, United States and Canada*, 1965, New York, Standard and Poor's Corporation.

US FEDERAL TRADE COMMISSION (1951), *Report on Interlocking Directorates*, Washington, US Government Printing Office.

US HOUSE OF REPRESENTATIVES, COMMITTEE ON THE JUDICIARY, ANTITRUST SUBCOMMITTEE (1965), *Interlocks in Corporate Management*, Washington, US Government Printing Office.

US HOUSE OF REPRESENTATIVES, COMMITTEE ON BANKING AND CURRENCY, SUBCOMMITTEE ON DOMESTIC FINANCE (1968), *Commercial Banks and Their Trust Activities: Emerging Influence on the American Economy*, Washington, US Government Printing Office.

US NATIONAL RESOURCES COMMITTEE (1939), *The Structure of the American Economy: Part I. Basic Characteristics*, Washington, US Government Printing Office.

8 J. Pfeffer

Size and Composition of Corporate Boards of Directors: The Organization and its Environment

J. Pfeffer, 'Size and composition of corporate boards of directors', *Administrative Science Quarterly*, vol. 17, June 1972, pp. 218–28.

There has been an increasing emphasis on the importance of analysing the relationship between the organization and its environment (Katz and Kahn, 1966; Buckley, 1967; and Thompson, 1967). This research has had two separate themes running through it. Many authors have attempted to trace the impact of generalized environmental characteristics on internal organizational structure and functioning. Others have been concerned with the problem of interorganizational interaction, or the specific patterns of interaction between organizations. When conditions of the environment have substantial impact on the organization, it is logical to expect that organizations will attempt to take actions to ensure continued success and viability, or to make their environments more munificent. Thompson (1967) proposed that organizations seek to manage their dependence on the environment, and Starbuck's discussion of organizational growth (1965) also pursued the theme of the organization attempting to manage the environment and to make it more favourable.

There have not been many empirical studies delineating the mechanisms and the conditions under which the organization manages its relationships with the environment. Elling and Halebsky (1961), in a study of hospitals in New York, found that the organization's choice of goals and clientele had effects on its ability to attract community support. Starbuck noted that organizational growth provided some advantages to the organization in dealing with the environment. In particular, large organizations would be better able to survive mistakes; large organizations could potentially exercise more control over their environments because of their size; and through growth, organizations could diversify, reducing their dependence upon one particular sector of the environment.

Selznick (1949), in his study of the Tennessee Valley Authority, noted how an organization, faced with strong opposition, could partially neutralize it by bringing representatives of hostile groups onto the organization's governing boards. This case of cooptation illustrates another mechanism by which organizations can attempt to manage their environments. Price (1963) found that one of the central functions of commissioners on state wildlife governing boards was to mediate the interaction between the organization and the public interested in its operations. Zald (1967) noted the relationship between the composition of YMCA boards and characteristics of the environment in which the organization was located and later (1969) developed a theoretical argument concerning whether the board of an organization would serve a cooptative or managing function.

This article considers the organization's use of the board of directors as a vehicle for dealing with problems of external interdependence and uncertainty, resulting from its exchange of resources with important external organizations. It is seen that the size and composition of boards of directors are consistent, in important respects, with hypotheses derived from a model of rational organization response to interdependence. More important, organizations that deviate more from an optimal or preferred structure in their board of directors tend to be significantly less profitable, controlling for industry effects, than those which do not deviate as much. In other words, it can be shown that corporate boards are used as if they were instruments with which to deal with the environment. When organizations fail to use this instrument accordingly, they pay a real penalty in the form of reduced profits.

The board in management literature

Judging by the lack of literature pertaining to corporate boards of directors, the common notion that boards are unimportant could be easily reinforced. Most research has been nonquantitative (Baker, 1945) and prescriptive. There are books on what the duties of directors are and how they should function,[1] and other

1. A partial list includes McDougall (1969), Brown and Smith (1957), Koontz (1967) and Juran and Louden (1966).

treatises on the legal liabilities of directors.[2] There are also frequent pleas for management of corporations to make more effective use of boards, and it is frequently argued that the board is another valuable management tool in running a business.

Fiedler, Godfrey, and Hall (1957) have studied boards of farm cooperatives as decision groups to validate a model of contingent leadership effectiveness. They found that psychological distance among the directors was correlated with the success of the cooperative.

The descriptive work that has been done has been, for the most part, a gathering and presentation of information, rather than an attempt to determine either what forces control the size and composition of corporate boards, or whether the board of directors matters in the success of an organization. Thompson and Walsh (1965) found that present directors and senior executives usually suggested the candidates for board vacancies. The National Industrial Conference Board (Kinley, 1962) conducted periodic studies to determine such questions as the size, composition, and compensation of boards of directors in large economic organizations.

There have been two studies of boards of directors that have attempted to treat the composition of the board of directors as an independent variable. Vance (1964), in a study of 103 large companies, concluded that, on the average, inside boards of directors were superior in performance to outside boards.[3] He also could find no evidence that outside directors or directorates are more numerous or more important than they had previously been, and that they were not increasing in number; both findings run counter to the prevailing business folk wisdom.

Lanser (1969) studied new companies in California and treated board composition and size as independent measures, relating them to his measure of success, which was whether or not the organization was still in existence five years after the initial

2. For example, Knepper (1969).
3. Inside directors are directors who are currently involved in the management of the organization and, in some definitions, former executives as well. Inside boards, then, are composed of a majority of inside directors. Outside directors do not have a direct management relationship with the organization.

incorporation. He found that accommodation directors, or directors put on to serve outside interests, were inversely associated with the survival of the firm. He also concluded that larger boards tended to be more successful. The issue of inside versus outside boards could not be tested, since so many of the companies had boards of the minimum legal size, three members. The Lanser measure of success was a dichotomous one, and his sample would certainly not be representative of the types of companies covered in the Vance study.

In all of the writing cited, the board is viewed as a managing body. Thus, many of the arguments for inside or outside boards rest on such issues as who knows the problems of the company best, and the breadth and depth of business management experience the various board members bring to the company. This approach is inaccurate on two counts. First, the selection procedure by which board members are chosen guarantees that, in most cases, board members are hand-picked by management. In many practical respects, management is, therefore, in control of the board. Second, management may not wish to use the board to obtain additional management advice, but may, in fact, be using the board as an instrument with which to deal with the organization's external environment. To the extent that this is the case, the notion of whether or not management is making full use of its board cannot be evaluated by board participation in management, but rather by how well important external organizations and groups are being handled.

In a departure from this general approach, it is proposed here that the composition of the board is a dependent variable, reflecting the organization's perceived need to deal differentially with various important sectors or organizations in the environment. The effect of the board on company success will, then, depend on how well the board meets environmental requirements, or there will be a contingency model of board size and composition, with the dimensions of the contingencies being the organization's relationships to its external context.

Before delineating the empirical work that supports these latter conclusions, it is useful to review some elements of theories of interorganizational behaviour, so that the findings can be placed in this context.

Board size and composition

It is this article's thesis that business organizations (and other organizations) use their boards of directors as vehicles through which they coopt, or partially absorb, important external organizations with which they are interdependent. The strategy of cooptation involves exchanging some degree of control and privacy of information for some commitment for continued support from the external organization.

Cooptation, as a tactic, is likely to be utilized when total absorption is (1) legally proscribed, (2) impossible due to resource constraints, or (3) when partial inclusion is sufficient to solve the organization's problems of dealing with the external organization. With business boards of directors, one would expect cooptation to be used on (1) very large organizations, which would be costly to absorb completely, (2) financial institutions, where total absorption is frequently forbidden by law, and (3) political bodies important to the organization, where total absorption is infeasible.

Further, if cooptation is used as a rational response to environmental exigencies, some propositions can be developed to predict its expected use. One important set of external organizations includes those that provide funds for the organization. Cooptation of these organizations is hypothesized to be related to the need for these external funds, or the need for ready access to the capital markets. It can then be hypothesized that (1) organizations that have larger capital requirements will be more likely to have a greater percentage of their board of directors composed of representatives from financial institutions.

In addition to financial institutions, regulatory bodies cannot be directly absorbed, nor can they be directly coopted by the organization. Nevertheless, it is important to obtain a favourable regulatory climate, and the organization's success in doing so will affect its operation. Favourable regulation can be obtained by having outside representatives allied to the organization, with these outside representatives, in turn, possessing some political, economic, or social power that is of concern to the regulatory body membership. Tapping these bases of power and influence requires coopting a relatively large number of external representatives. Operating success may be determined more by the success of these political tactics than by considerations of internal efficiency. Consequently, it can be hypothesized that (2) organizations operating in regulated industries will tend to have a greater percentage of their board of directors composed of persons outside the management of the company.

The availability of outside capital is enhanced not only by the number of representatives of financial institutions directly on the board, but also by the percentage of outsiders in general. An outside director may sit on the board of a bank, or have close working relationships with others members of the financial community. The outside organization may also be an important purchaser of short-term debt instruments. The need for outside financing dictates a greater orientation to the external business community. For these reasons, firms with greater needs for access to the capital markets would be expected to have a smaller percentage of inside directors, or conversely, a greater percentage of outside representatives on their boards. It is, therefore, suggested that (3) the greater the organization's requirements for external financing and access to the capital markets, the smaller will be the percentage of inside directors on its board.

In addition to representatives of financial institutions, attorneys are often found on boards of directors of companies. In developing an outside board of directors, or one that has a relatively large percentage of outsiders on it, the inclusion of an attorney becomes more and more likely, simply because there are more and more positions to be filled. Thus, (4) the percentage of attorneys on boards of directors will be inversely related to the percentage of insiders on the board.

The use of outside financing, either debt or equity, customarily involves some legal documents and legal questions. Other things being equal, the need for legal services and legal advice is increased as the need for access to the external capital markets increases. Therefore, it can be hypothesized that: (5) the percentage of attorneys on a corporate board of directors will be directly related to the extent to which the corporation has a need for access to external capital markets.

The locally regulated organization must tap essentially local political power bases. This may involve selecting small businessmen, farmers, and representatives of important local business organizations. It will also probably involve obtaining a comprehensive geographic representation from the area being regulated. National regulation, on the other hand, emanates from Washington, and while outside representation is just as necessary for the board, there are fewer constraints on covering all the geographic bases, and the political power bases being tapped are fundamentally different. Regulation on a national basis, covering a much broader clientele, will tend to be more legalistic and formal, and much more visible. One would, therefore, expect that the percentage of attorneys on a board of directors would be related to whether or not the organization is nationally regulated, but perhaps not to whether the organization is locally regulated. It can then be predicted that (6) the percentage of attorneys on an organization's board will be directly related to whether or not the organization is regulated on a national basis.

It can also be noted that the size of the board of directors is affected by the relationships with the environment. If the organization has requirements for coopting important external elements of its environment, the greater this need for cooptation, the more members the organization will probably have to place on its board. Recalling the arguments based on the need for access to external capital, it can then be hypothesized that (7) the number of directors an organization has will be related to its need for access to external capital markets.

Similarly, cooptation has been thought to be related to whether or not the organization was regulated. It is then proposed that (8) the number of directors an organization has will be related to whether or not it is regulated.

Finally, the requirement for a large board undoubtedly increases as the size of the organization itself increases. This occurs, first, because large organizations are typically more diversified, and hence have a need to deal with relatively more sectors of the environment. Second, it occurs because large organizations have a greater impact on society and the economy because of their size, and thus there is again a greater need to have more members who can relate and legitimate the organization to its external environment. It is therefore hypothesized that (9) the number of directors an organization has will be directly related to the size of the organization.

Supporting evidence

The hypotheses previously developed and presented were tested using a random sample of eighty corporations drawn from the Dun and Bradstreet *Reference Book of Corporate Managements, 1969.* The sample specifically excluded holding companies, financial institutions, and companies in which ownership was highly concentrated in the hands of the officers and directors. The companies in the sample include utilities, transportation companies, manufacturing concerns, and retailing and distribution establishments. Because of the universe from which the sample was drawn, the companies tend to be large in size. The average size, as measured by total sales, is $531 million dollars, though there are many in the sample with sales of under $100 million.

Most of the variables in the hypotheses are operationalized in a straightforward manner. The need for access to capital markets is represented by the debt to equity ratio for the organization. (It was felt that firms with relatively large debt in their capital structure would face greater financing problems, and would have more frequent need to refinance or adjust their capital structure.) Inside directors are defined as directors that are either current managers in the organization or retired or former managers for the same organization. (Subsidiary organizations are assumed to be within the organization under consideration.) The size of the organization is measured by its total sales volume. (In terms of impact on the external environment, this seemed like a more meaningful figure than the related value of total assets.) Data are for the years 1969.

All simple correlations are computed based on the Spearman correlation coefficient formula, under the assumption that the data are defined only on an ordinal scale. It was felt that the data did not fulfil the parametric assumptions required for the computation of a Pearson correlation coefficient, and that, moreover, because of accounting controversies, and because of possible changes in some of the values as periods of time were adjusted, only ordinal measurements could be strongly claimed for the variables.

The results are strikingly supportive of the hypotheses. As predicted in (8) and (9), the number of directors on the organization's board is found to be significantly related to the organization's size, as measured by total sales volume, and to its need for access to the external capital markets, as measured by its debt–equity ratio. The expected relationship between the number of directors and either national or local regulation is not observed, though these correlations are in the expected direction. The results for the number of directors hypotheses are presented in Table 1.

Table 1. Correlations and levels of significance for hypotheses dealing with number of directors

Spearman correlation of number of directors with		
Variable	*Correlation*	*Level of significance*
Sales	0·47	0·001
Debt-equity	0·18	0·05
Local regulation	0·09	not significant
National regulation	0·05	not significant

Also, as expected, the percentage of inside directors is significantly inversely related to both the need for external capital, and to the existence of local or national regulation over the organization. These results are all statistically significant at less than the 0·002 level, which provides strong support to the hypotheses concerning the inside-outside composition of corporate boards. The results for the hypotheses about the percentage of inside directors are shown in Table 2.

Table 2. Correlations and levels of significance for hypotheses concerning the percentage of inside directors

Spearman correlation of percentage of inside directors with		
Variable	*Correlation*	*Level of significance*
Debt-equity	−0·34	0·001
Local regulation	−0·365	0·001
National regulation	−0·32	0·001

Confirming the first hypothesis, the percentage of board members representing financial institutions is significantly related to the need for access to external capital, as measured by the debt–equity ratio.[4] The Spearman rank order correlation between these two variables is 0·21, which is statistically significant at the 0·004 level.

Finally, the appearance of attorneys on the boards of directors is also as anticipated. The percentage of attorneys is positively related to the debt to equity ratio, to the occurrence of national (but not local) regulation, and is negatively related to the percentage of inside directors. These results are presented in Table 3.

Table 3. Spearman correlations and levels of significance for hypotheses concerning the percentage of attorneys on the board

Correlation of percentage of attorneys with

Variable	Correlation	Level of significance
Debt-equity	0·20	0·04
National regulation	0·18	0·05
Percentage of inside directors	−0·32	0·001

To summarize the findings, eight out of the nine hypotheses are confirmed at least at the 0·05 level of significance, and nine out of the eleven correlations that are relevant to these hypotheses are statistically significant. All eleven correlations are in the expected direction. The consistency of these results indicates that board size and composition are not random variables, but are, in fact, systematically related to the organization's apparent need to deal with important external sectors in the environment in such a way as to ensure successful operations and an adequate supply of resources for the future.

In addition to examining the pattern of individual relationships among variables, a multiple regression analysis was performed for two dimensions of size and composition for which there was more than one hypothesis.

The regression equation for the number of directors includes the variables for the size of the firm (S) in millions of dollars, the

4. Financial institutions include banks, investment banks, stock brokerages, and investment companies.

debt to equity ratio (D), and a dummy variable indicating whether or not the firm is locally regulated (LR). The resulting estimated equation is:

(1)   ND = 10·26 + 0·0026 S + 1·512 D + 0·59 LR
              (0·00057)   (0·917)   (1.44)   r = 0·48

where ND represents the number of directors, and the numbers in parentheses are the standard errors of the respective regression coefficients. The coefficient on the regulatory dummy variable is not significant, which coincides with the nonparametric simple correlational analysis. Both of the other variable coefficients are statistically significant at the 0·05 level, and the regression equation is able to account for about one-quarter of the variation in the number of directors.

Considering the percentage of inside directors (PI), a dummy variable representing whether or not the organization was regulated nationally (NR) was included, in addition to the previously used explanatory factors. The estimated equation is:

(2) PI = 59·93 − 0·00373 S − 5·560 D − 27·12 NR − 22·84 LR
         (0·00301)   (4·899)   (7·39)   (7·665)
                                              r = 0·54

In (2), S and D are not quite significant at the 0·05 level, though both are in the expected direction. This equation can account for some 30 per cent of the variation in the percentage of inside directors that are found on corporate boards. Both the coefficients of the dummy variables representing regulation are statistically significant at the 0·01 level.

A contingency model

While the results presented thus far support the notion of the use of the board of directors as a vehicle for dealing with the external environment, and most of the specific hypotheses were confirmed, how important are these results in the context of the large amount of residual unexplained variance? The percentage of inside or outside directors may be an important indicator of the extent to which the organization is externally or internally oriented. While this orientation has been found to be related to some hypothesized factors, only about one-third of the variation can be explained.

One possible explanation for this is that some people may believe that directors are unimportant in the organization. If, however, either directors matter, or more to the point, the extent of the organization's inside-outside orientation matters, then some consequences should be evident for those organizations that do or do not match well with environmental requirements. Specifically, it is hypothesized that (10) organizations that deviate relatively more from a preferred inside-outside director orientation should be relatively less successful when compared to industry standards than those that deviate less from a preferred board composition. To the extent it can be indicated that departures from a preferred inside-outside orientation are accompanied by real and important consequences to organizational performance, the previous results will be considerably strengthened.

Bowman (1963), in an industrial scheduling context, has noted that while individual manager estimates may be far from optimal, these estimates pooled over time, or over managers, frequently give optimal, or nearly optimal, results. For an optimal inside-outside director relationship, the values computed by (2) for each company were selected. The equation represents the pooled experience of some eighty randomly sampled companies. It was believed that the resulting relationship would more closely approximate a preferred relationship than any single datum point.

Hypothesis 10 was tested as follows. The absolute value of the difference between the actual percentage of insiders and the predicted percentage was computed for each company. This variable is denoted as DIF. Two measures of company performance commonly used in evaluating organizations were then computed. The first is the ratio of net income to sales (I/S), and the second is the ratio of net income to stockholders' equity (I/E). The first measure tells how well the company is performing relative to its sales volume, and the second how well it is utilizing the stockholders' investment. A Spearman rank order correlation analysis between DIF and the two measures of company performance, unadjusted, was not significant, but in the expected direction. This is not surprising, considering that, thus far, it has been possible to ignore the issue of differences among industries. A refined test of hypothesis 10, which coincides with how it is stated, involves comparing the two performance measures to measures for the organization's industry as a whole. In the process of doing this, eight companies were eliminated, as it was impossible to define a comparable industry, because they were so diversified. For the remaining seventy-two organizations, it can be asked whether deviations from the predicted percentage of insiders on the board are accompanied by decrements in performance, when compared to industry standards.[5] The results of this analysis are presented in Table 4. Deviations from the predicted relationship are very significantly correlated with substandard industry performance,

Table 4. **Profitability performance related to deviations from optimal board structure**

Spearman correlation of DIF with differences in		
Variable	*Correlation*	*Level of significance*
Income–sales	−0·30	0·005
Income–equity	−0·295	0·006

on either measure of financial effectiveness. Firms that deviated from the inside-outside orientation they were predicted to have from (2) performed poorly, and the greater the deviation, in general, the more poorly they performed, relative to standards for their industry.

Conclusions

Lawrence and Lorsch (1967) have noted that successful organizations tend to have internal structural characteristics that are congruent with environmental demands. The present study shows that deviations from predicted patterns of inside-outside orientations as reflected in board of director composition are also reflected in the dimensions of organizational performance. Whether the board itself makes the difference, by enabling the organization more successfully to handle its external relationships, or whether board composition merely reflects a general

5. Industry standards were derived from Dun and Bradstreet's *Key Business Ratios in 125 Lines* wherever possible, and from the Internal Revenue Service (1970) in other cases.

inside-outside orientation, remains to be seen in further research. It can be concluded, however, that board size and composition are not random or independent factors, but are, rather, rational organizational responses to the conditions of the external environment.

To what extent do organizations employ varying degrees of inclusion and what factors determine which strategies they use in dealing with the environment and conditions of interdependence are both important issues that recur throughout this discussion. Further attention is warranted for refinement of the analysis presented here, as well as consideration of other dimensions of organizational orientation to external environmental factors. The analysis has assumed a cooptative intent; it would be worthwhile to develop evidence on the efficacy of this strategy. By focusing this additional attention on the organization's context, better descriptive models of organizational responses to environmental demands can be developed and some normative guidance for those in quasipolitical roles charged with legitimating the organization and relating it to its environment can perhaps be provided.

References

BAKER, J. C. (1945), *Directors and Their Functions*, Boston, Harvard University Graduate School of Business Administration, Division of Research.

BOWMAN, E. H. (1963), 'Consistency and optimality in managerial decision-making', *Management Science*, vol. 9, pp. 310–21.

BROWN, C. C., and SMITH, E. E. (1957), *The Director Looks at His Job*, New York, Columbia University Press.

BUCKLEY, W. (1967), *Sociology and Modern Systems Theory*, Englewood Cliffs, Prentice-Hall.

DUN AND BRADSTREET (1968), *Key Business Ratios in 125 Lines*, New York, Dun & Bradstreet.

DUN AND BRADSTREET (1969), *Reference Book of Corporate Managements*, New York, Dun & Bradstreet.

ELLING, R. H., and HALEBSKY, S. (1961) 'Organizational differentiation and support: a conceptual framework', *Administrative Science Quarterly*, vol. 6, pp. 185–209.

FIEDLER, F. E., GODFREY, E. P. and HALL, D. M. (1957), *Boards, Management and Company Success*, Danville, Interstate Printers and Publishers.

INTERNAL REVENUE SERVICE (1970), *Statistics of Income, Corporation Income Tax Returns, 1966*, Washington, US Government Printing Office.

JURAN, J. M., and LOUDEN, J. K. (1966), *The Corporate Director*, New York, American Management Association.

KATZ, D., and KAHN, R. L. (1966), *The Social Psychology of Organizations*, New York, John Wiley.

KINLEY, J. R. (1962), *Corporate Directorship Practices*, New York, National Industrial Conference Board, Studies in Business Policy, no. 103.

KNEPPER, W. E. (1969), *Liability of Corporate Officers and Directors*, Indianapolis, Allen Smith Co.

KOONTZ, H. (1967), *The Board of Directors and Effective Management*, New York, McGraw-Hill.

LANSER, R. E. (1969), *Visible Traits of Boards of Directors*, Ph.D. Dissertation, Stanford University.

LAWRENCE, P., and LORSCH, J. (1967), *Organization and Environment*, Boston, Harvard University Press.

MCDOUGAL, W. J. (ed.) (1969), *The Effective Director*, London, Canada, University of Western Ontario, School of Business Administration.

PRICE, J. L. (1963), 'The impact of governing boards on organizational effectiveness and morale', *Administrative Science Quarterly*, vol. 8, pp. 361–78.

SELZNICK, P. (1949), *TVA and the Grass Roots*, Berkeley, University of California Press.

STARBUCK, W. H. (1965), 'Organizational growth and development', in J. G. March (ed.), *Handbook of Organizations*, Chicago, Rand-McNally, pp. 451–533.

THOMPSON, G. C., and WALSH, F. J., JR (1965), 'Selection of corporate directors', *Conference Board Record*, vol. 2, pp. 8–16.

THOMPSON, J. D. (1967), *Organizations in Action*, New York, McGraw-Hill.

VANCE, S. C. (1964), *Boards of Directors: Structure and Performance*, Eugene, University of Oregon Press.

ZALD, M. N. (1967), 'Urban differentiation, characteristics of boards of directors and organizational effectiveness', *American Journal of Sociology*, vol. 73, pp. 261–72.

ZALD, M. N. (1969), 'The power and function of boards of directors: a theoretical synthesis', *American Journal of Sociology*, vol. 75, pp. 97–111.

9 G. B. Baty, W. M. Evan and T. W. Rothermel

Personnel Flows as Interorganizational Relations

G. B. Baty, W. M. Evan and T. W. Rothermel, 'Personnel flows as interorganizational relations', *Administrative Science Quarterly*, vol. 16, December 1971, pp. 430–43.

Organizations are open social systems which necessarily engage in various exchanges with other organizations in their environment (Bertalanffy, 1962; Katz and Kahn, 1966). Although economic theories of the firm have developed concepts about the exchanges of products or services, organization theory has developed few concepts that can explain the processes involved in the exchange of people, information, and influence among organizations.

This exploratory study develops concepts and propositions that help explain the flow of personnel among organizations, specifically the movement of faculty among schools of business (Evan, 1966; 1968; 1972).

Flow of personnel among organizations

As open social systems pursuing specified goals, organizations must recruit various resources – human, financial, material, and so on – in order to survive and pursue their goals. The recruitment of human resources, a universal and recurrent organizational process, gives rise to the flow of personnel, and concurrently, to a flow of information among organizations; for just as members of a society are carriers of the culture which they transmit consciously and unconsciously to the next generation, so members of an organization are carriers of its subculture, which they transmit to new members. When new members are recruited, particularly in technical or professional occupations, new bodies of knowledge and skills are imported which are often the sources of innovative ideas in organizations (Evan and Black, 1967). Just as organizations operate in particular product or service markets, so they operate in particular labour markets in which personnel are exchanged. In this respect, the goals of an organization are constrained by the labour market; that is, the kinds of people that it can recruit.

In this exploratory study of personnel flows in schools of business, the focus is on the process of exchange (Homans, 1952; Blau, 1964). If two actors – in this case, organizations – enter into an exchange relationship, it should be possible to identify the nature of the units being exchanged. In the case of the flow of personnel, if a highly prestigious school sends one of its Ph.Ds to a school with relatively low prestige, what does the latter give the prestigious school in return? The less prestigious school is not likely to send its faculty or graduates to the prestigious school. It can, however, express deference and admiration in at least two forms: (1) by endorsing the curricular philosophy and by adapting elements of the curriculum of the prestigious school to its own curriculum, and (2) by sending graduate students to the prestigious school for further training.

In recent years, there has been a proliferation of schools of business because of the growing demand in industry and government for specialized managerial training (Gordon and Howell, 1959; Pierson, 1959; McGuire, 1963). Each school, in recruiting a new faculty member, probably considers how his training, experience, and status can contribute to its reputation, curriculum, and research programme. Among the variables that presumably affect faculty recruitment are the size of the student body, the ratio of students to teachers, the rate of growth of the school, the prestige of the school among schools of business, the geographic location of the school, and so on.

One consequence of the recruitment decision is the network of relationships, including friendships and scholarly connections, which develop; that is, each faculty member has a role-set (Gross *et al.*, 1959: 48–69; Merton, 1957: 368–80) which includes relationships with others in the academic community. This network of role relationships is not only a channel for the flow of knowledge but also a source of information about faculty members who might be recruited.

The school of business as a whole can be considered as having a set of relationships with other organizations; that is, an organization-set, of which it is the focal member (Evan, 1966).

This organization-set includes not only other schools of business with which it exchanges personnel and conducts joint activities, but also other professional schools, government agencies, industrial organizations, foundations, publishing companies, and so forth. Each business school also has various relations with the members of its organization-set other than those involving the recruiting and supplying of faculty personnel. It may take part in activities of an association of schools of business or collaborate with other schools in supplying information, for example, to the Educational Testing Service; nevertheless, the flow of personnel is undoubtedly one of the major forms of exchange among schools of business. Recruitment of new faculty therefore affords an opportunity for studying interorganizational relations.

In this study, special attention was devoted to the following five dimensions of the flow of personnel: (1) the number of schools of business with which faculty exchanges occurred, (2) the number of faculty members supplied to other schools of business, (3) the total number of faculty members exchanged, that is, the number exported to and imported from other schools of business, (4) the degree of inbreeding, that is, the number of faculty trained at their school of employment, and (5) the number of schools with reciprocal faculty interchanges.

Another question that received special attention was whether schools recruited faculty from other schools similar or dissimilar to themselves in curricular and other structural respects, that is, whether they were guided by a principle of structural similarity or structural complementarity.

The 11 independent variables, whose effects on the flow of personnel, the dependent variable, were explored in this study, might be characterized, following Lazarsfeld and Menzel (1961), as analytical and global properties of schools of business. Among the analytical variables were faculty size, growth rate of faculty size, student-faculty ratio, annual number of Ph.D. degrees awarded; among the global variables were age of school, prestige rating of school, type of curricular philosophy, degree to which high-ranking faculty predominated, shape of faculty rank structure, type of support of the university, that is, public or private, and geographic location.

Procedure

The basic source of the data for this study was the membership directory of the American Association of Collegiate Schools of Business (1960). Only faculty members of professorial rank were included in the study, and only the 79 schools offering graduate business programmes. Once the data were entered on punch cards, it was possible to generate a faculty interchange matrix of the origins of the faculty in 1960 of each of the schools included in the study (see Figure 4 for the list of schools).

The decision rule for associating a faculty member with a supplying institution was that of his last academic affiliation, whether as a student, a research associate, or a faculty member. Although this rule is arbitrary, it seemed a better choice than the other most obvious rule, the institution from which the last degree was obtained, since in many cases the professor had been out of school for years before entering the university with which he was affiliated in 1960. The rule also avoided our having to classify all the sources from which faculty had been recruited, for example, government, industry, and even retirement. Many schools received at least some of their faculty from business schools outside this population, and indeed, some received most of their faculty from outside this population and from academic departments other than business schools.

The sources of data from the 11 structural variables varied. Some, such as size of faculty, size of student body, age of business school, location, and so on, were readily obtained and did not require subjective judgement; whereas other variables, such as prestige and type of curriculum, did. To develop a rough measure of prestige of the various business schools on a five-point scale, 29 faculty members of business schools throughout the country were asked to rate as many of the 79 schools of which they had some definite knowledge. The value of this limited survey was reassured by the degree to which their ratings were consistent, at least for the more conspicuous schools. Nevertheless, it is appropriate to ask whether 29 other judges would produce ratings at all similar to those obtained.

Assessing the type of curriculum was perhaps the most difficult of all the variables for which data were gathered. Questionnaires were sent to all 79 schools, asking them to describe their educational philosophy, curricular goals, and so on, in a general way, and then to rate the importance of various elements of their curricula – for example, statistics, accounting, psychology, marketing. The questionnaire responses were supplemented by an examination of the catalogue of each school for both course offerings and general comments on the curriculum. Using the information available, each school was then assigned to one of the following curriculum categories:

1. social science
2. management science
3. general techniques
4. special techniques
5. case studies

Although these categories are not exhaustive or mutually exclusive, they made it possible to differentiate the principal curricular orientation of the schools.

Given the data on the interchange of faculty members and the 11 structural characteristics of the business schools, cluster analysis seemed a promising analytical approach. It does not, like clique analysis, identify a group of members who exchanged only among each other, but it does isolate, statistically, groups of members with a large number of attributes in common.

The computer program used to perform a cluster analysis was developed by Bonner (1964a; 1964b) and Pettit (1964) of IBM for use in syndrome identification from large amounts of clinical data in which no pattern could otherwise be discerned. The faculty interchange matrix was analysed for clusters of schools that either received their faculty from significantly similar sources or exported faculty to similar schools. The preliminary results were encouraging and led to the adoption of cluster analysis as the principal analytical tool.

Results

Identification of clusters

The cluster identification program was applied to the data and yielded several clusters, one of which was selected for detailed analysis, although other sets of results could have been selected based on different assumptions about threshold values and the other program parameters. The clusters chosen for analysis, although overlapping considerably, have the advantage that they included about two-thirds of the schools in the population. Had the clustering program parameters been changed to reduce overlapping, clusters with statistically higher similarity among members might have emerged but with fewer schools represented in them.

Figure 1 shows six receipt clusters, R; that is, groups of schools that recruited their faculties from significantly similar sources. Figure 2 shows six supply clusters, S; that is, schools that supplied faculty personnel to similar schools. The schools are coded from 1 to 79 in the cluster maps; that is, the same numbers used in the list of 79 graduate schools of business presented in Figure 4.

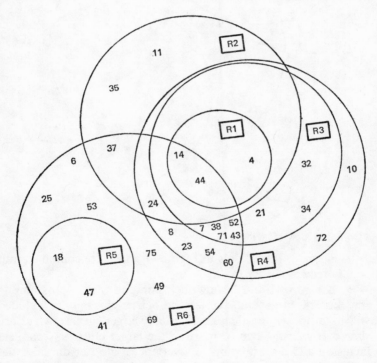

Figure 1 Receipt cluster map

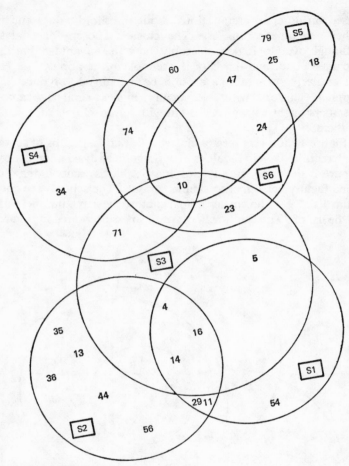

Figure 2 Supply cluster map

In Figure 3, the schools in Figures 1 and 2 are combined into supply-receipt cluster maps.

Both Figures 1 and 2 show inclusion and overlapping among the clusters. In general, tighter and denser clusters are included within the looser, less dense, and usually larger clusters, which are shared among the two or more of the larger clusters. Complete inclusion and almost complete overlapping do not diminish the statistically unique quality of the tighter cluster itself as identified by the algorithm. The computer results from which the six clusters were drawn included many less definite and less significant clusters, but only these six were chosen, since the larger clusters were so vague as to cast doubt on their distinct identity.

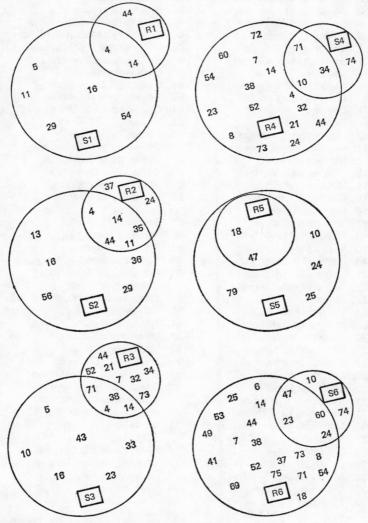

Figure 3 Supply—receipt cluster maps

Figure 4 List of 79 schools of business

1. University of Alabama
2. University of Arizona
3. University of Arkansas
4. Boston College
5. Boston University
6. University of Buffalo
7. University of California (Berkeley)
8. University of California (Los Angeles)
9. Carnegie Institute of Technology
10. University of Chicago
11. City College of New York
12. University of Colorado
13. Columbia University
14. University of Connecticut
15. Cornell University
16. Dartmouth College
17. University of Denver
18. DePaul (Illinois)
19. University of Detroit
20. Emory University
21. University of Florida
22. University of Georgia
23. Harvard University
24. University of Illinois
25. Indiana University
26. State University of Iowa
27. University of Kansas
28. University of Kentucky
29. Lehigh University
30. Louisiana State
31. Marquette University
32. University of Maryland
33. University of Massachusetts
34. Massachusetts Institute of Technology
35. University of Miami (Florida)
36. Miami University (Ohio)
37. University of Michigan
38. Michigan State
39. University of Mississippi
40. Mississippi State
41. University of Missouri
42. Montana State
43. University of Nebraska
44. New York University
45. University of North Carolina
46. University of North Dakota
47. Northwestern University
48. Ohio University
49. Ohio State University
50. University of Oklahoma
51. Oklahoma State University
52. University of Oregon
53. Pennsylvania State
54. University of Pennsylvania
55. University of Pittsburgh
56. Rutgers University
57. St Louis University
58. University of Southern California
59. Southern Methodist
60. Stanford University
61. Syracuse University
62. Temple University
63. University of Tennessee
64. University of Texas
65. Texas Technical College
66. University of Toledo
67. Tulane University
68. University of Tulsa
69. University of Utah
70. University of Virginia
71. University of Washington
72. Oregon State College
73. University of Minnesota
74. Washington State
75. Washington University (St Louis)
76. West Virginia University
77. Western Reserve University
78. University of Wisconsin
79. University of Wyoming

Analysis of the clusters

Each receipt and supply cluster was considered in terms of the set of global and analytical variables discussed earlier in the paper. To facilitate the sketch of the profiles, each cluster of schools was examined relative to all the other schools taken as a unit by the student's t test; that is, each receipt and each supply cluster was compared with all the other schools in the sample on each of the variables shown in Table 1. Only those t values that reached the significance level of 0·05 or better, were used in the analysis.

A table comparing each receipt cluster with its corresponding supply cluster on the entire array of analytical and global variables is not included because only four of the many t values were statistically significant. The comparisons in the descriptions that follow are with respect to the other schools in the population studied.

Cluster-pair 1. The three members of cluster *R1* differed from the other schools in having curricula with less emphasis on management science, special techniques, and case studies; that is, the cluster's main academic emphasis was in the social sciences and general techniques. The members also differed in having an imbalance toward senior faculty and in being located almost exclusively in the New England area.

Cluster *S1* shared with *R1* the lack of an emphasis on management science, but not the lack of an emphasis on special techniques and case studies; that is, schools in cluster *R1* were recruiting their faculty from schools more oriented to special techniques and case studies than they themselves were. Cluster *S1* was not overweighted with senior faculty, had significantly more state support, was concentrated in New England, and was less likely to have members in the Western and Southern regions. The principal difference was that the members of cluster *S1* were more likely to have state support than members of *R1*. Although this appeared to be significant when comparing cluster *S1* with the rest of the 79 schools, a t test of the supply cluster *S1* versus cluster *R1* showed no significant differences, indicating that the supply and receipt schools are very similar to each other.

Cluster-pair 2. The 7 schools of cluster *R2* were located principally in New England and were much more likely to be located there than cluster *R1*. The faculties of this cluster are significantly

Table 1. Some factors distinguishing receipt and supply clusters from remainder of the population of schools of business

Variables	Clusters											
	R1	S1	R2	S2	R3	S3	R4	S4	R5	S5	R6	S6
Analytical												
Faculty size			·05 +				·001 +					·05 +
Faculty growth rate							·001 +					
Student-faculty ratio							·05 +					
Number Ph.D.s awarded, 1960												
Global												
Age of school					·05 +		·001 +		·001 +			·01 +
Prestige rating of school												
Degree of top-heaviness in faculty rank structure												
Shape of faculty rank structure												
1. Top-heavy	·001 −							·001 −	·001 −			·001 −
2. Symmetrical								·001 +				
3. Bottom-heavy								·001 −				
Support of university												
1. Public		·05 +										
2. Private		·05 −										

Type of curricular philosophy

1. Social science	·01−		·001−		·001−	·001−	·001−·001−·05+
2. Management science					·01−	·01−	·001−·01−
3. General techniques	·001−	·001−			·001−	·001−	
4. Special techniques	·001−	·001−					
5. Case studies							·05+

Geographic location

1. New England	·05+	·05+ ·01−			·001−	·001+	·001−·05+·01−
2. Mid-Atlantic	·001−				·01−	·01−	·01−
3. Midwest		·05−	·05−		·001+	·001+	·05−
4. Southeast	·05−	·05−	·05−			·05−	·05−
5. Deep South	·05−		·05−			·05−	
6. Southwest and Mountain States	·001−	·001−	·001−				
7. Far West		·001−	·001−	·01−		·01−	·05−·01−

+ means greater than the sample mean on a given variable.
− means smaller than the sample mean on a given variable.

larger, and the curricula emphasized neither special techniques nor case studies.

The 10 schools of supply cluster, *S2*, were also located predominantly in New England and tended not to emphasize special techniques in its curricula. As in cluster-pair 1, the schools in cluster *R2* received their faculty from a population of schools similar to themselves. No significant differences appeared in the intercluster *t* tests of the clusters *R2* and *S2*.

Cluster-pair 3. The 11 members of cluster *R3* had higher prestige, were less inbred than the average school, and tended not to be located in the Midwestern or Mountain States.

Supply cluster, *S3*, did not differ from the rest of the population except that it supplied more faculty to cluster *R3*; and as in the case of cluster-pairs 1 and 2, the supply and receipt clusters were very similar in all respects.

Cluster-pair 4. The second largest receipt cluster, *R4*, with 18 members, had a significantly higher mean prestige score, graduated far more Ph.Ds, and had a larger and more rapidly growing faculty than that of the other schools. Furthermore, its members supplied and received many more faculty and interacted with more schools. None of the schools in this cluster was in the Deep South.

Supply cluster, *S4*, with only four members, had high prestige, significantly fewer members in the Southeast, the Deep South, or the Mountain States, significantly less emphasis on general techniques curricula, and neither top-heavy nor bottom-heavy faculty rank structures.

Cluster *R4* was more like other schools in having a less symmetrical faculty structure, whereas *S4* was more symmetrical in its faculty structure, suggesting that its members recruited about an even number of people of various age categories. This does not reflect a school with a high growth rate, in which more younger faculty are recruited than middle-aged or older faculty, in contrast to *R4*, which, as Table 1 shows, has a higher rate of growth.

Cluster-pair 5. The two members of cluster *R5*, the smallest cluster, were both located in the Midwest, were significantly older schools, stressing two curriculum types: special techniques and case studies. It tended to be significantly less symmetrical in faculty rank structure than the other schools.

Supply cluster *S5*, with six members, while not as old as the members of *R5*, did complement their curriculum type, having significantly fewer general techniques curricula. Cluster *S5* also supplied many more faculty members and was strongly represented in the Midwest. While both clusters *R5* and *S5* were well defined, they have too few members to justify generalizations on averages of various variables.

Cluster-pair 6. Cluster *R6*, with 22 members, the largest cluster in this study, differed significantly in receiving a higher proportion of its faculty from outside the population of schools and in having almost all its members located in the Midwest.

Cluster *S6*, with only six members, differed from the population of schools in more ways than any other cluster. The *S6* schools had much higher prestige, much larger faculty, more of its own graduates on its faculty, fewer curricula in general techniques and special techniques, and more in case studies. They were less likely to have very few faculty members in the associate professor rank, had more supply and receipt transactions, and interacted with more different schools. Cluster *S6* seemed to have great geographical dispersion, as inferred from the lack of significant positive *t* values for any region, with members in New England, the mid-Atlantic states and the Southeastern states. Cluster *S6*, like cluster *S4*, appeared to be a high prestige group and had a larger faculty than most other schools. This probably explains in part why so small a cluster is such a significant factor in supplying members to a large and rather average group of institutions such as cluster *R6*. These six schools did not emphasize general techniques and special techniques. They emphasized well-defined academic disciplines rather than general professional training. Thus, one can infer that the social sciences, management sciences, and specific case studies receive considerable emphasis in the *S6* schools. Cluster *S6* differs from *R6* in recruiting a higher proportion of their faculty from schools outside the population, and in fewer curricula emphasizing general techniques. This comparison between the supply cluster and the receipt cluster differs from the previous comparisons in that there seems to be a strong difference in the curricular philosophy between this pair of clusters.

If the concept of structural complementarity would serve any useful function in explaining faculty interchange, it would be with respect to curricula, so that it is surprising to find that schools tend to recruit faculty from schools similar to themselves. One possible explanation is that the role-set relationships of faculty members outside a given school are probably affected largely by associations one develops in the course of graduate school training and participation in professional societies. If faculty members tend to associate with colleagues at schools that are similar to their own, they in turn tend to influence the recruitment process by hiring faculty members or graduate students from those schools. This results in an interchange of personnel among fairly similar schools with respect to curricular philosophy and other structural respects. This type of recruitment inadvertently leads to more homogeneity than may in fact be functional for the schools involved. If a faculty diverse in expertise and orientation to teaching and research is a desirable prerequisite for the growth of a professional school, a pattern of recruitment from schools similar to one's own is not likely to promote such diversity and heterogeneity among faculty members. Hence, if the premise is correct that diversity and heterogeneity among faculty members are desiderata for the vitality of a professional school (Simon, 1967), the absence of structural complementarity in the data may well point to a significant failing in the faculty recruitment practices of many schools of business.

Correlates of measures of faculty interchange

In the foregoing discussion, the unit of analysis has been the school cluster. Receipt clusters have been distinguished from supply clusters and each from the rest of the population of schools. A shift from an analysis of a cluster of schools to an analysis of individual schools will be made in an effort to throw additional light on the factors that affect the flow of personnel among these schools. In this analysis, all of the schools in the aggregate shall be considered, that is all 79 schools, for the purpose of ascertaining which independent variables are correlated with the five measures of faculty interchange: (1) inbreeding, a measure of negative interaction among schools; (2) number of faculty supplied, S, a measure of a one-sided tendency to interact with other schools; (3) total number of faculty supplied and received,

$S+R$, a measure of the tendency of a school to interact with other schools; (4) number of schools *qua* schools interacted with, which is a measure of the size of a school's organization-set; and (5) the number of schools with reciprocal faculty interchanges. Table 2 shows some of the correlates of these five measures of faculty interchange.

The inbreeding index was positively correlated with the degree of top-heaviness in faculty structure and a curriculum emphasizing special techniques. Although these correlations are rather small and account for a small amount of variance, they are nevertheless suggestive. A top-heavy faculty may have a high proportion of people who have not explored new theories and new methodologies in their research or in their teaching. Consequently, the Ph.D.s graduating from such schools are not likely to find their way into the outstanding schools of business. Likewise, a curriculum emphasizing special techniques is likely to be highly traditional and lacking in any underlying theoretical character. In short, faculty inbreeding tends to weaken a school's capacity either to attract students or to produce faculty members for other schools.

The index of supply, that is, the tendency to supply faculty to other schools, is positively correlated with the number of Ph.D.s produced, the degree of prestige, faculty size, faculty growth rate, student-faculty ratio, and age of the school. Schools that are old, large in faculty, high in student-faculty ratio, fast growing, prestigious, and prolific in producing Ph.D.s are more likely to supply faculty to other schools than those lacking these characteristics.

The interchange measure, $S+R$, that is, the total number of faculty supplied and received, has a similar set of correlates as in the case of the supply measure, with a high positive correlation between $S + R$ and the number of Ph.D.s produced, degree of prestige, growth of faculty, student-faculty ratio, and age of the school. Among the additions to this list of correlates of $S+R$ is the tendency for schools to be located in the Middle West and a negative correlation with curricula emphasizing special techniques.

A similar roster of positive correlations turns up in connection with the measure of the number of schools interacted with: older

Table 2. Correlates of measures of faculty interchange[a]

Correlates	Per cent of inbreeding	Number of faculty supplied	Number of faculty supplied and received	Number of schools interacted with	Number of schools with reciprocal faculty interchanges
Prestige rating of school		·5135	·5054	·4463	·4291
Age of school		·1819	·1555	·1666	
Number of Ph.D.s		·5245	·5191	·5211	·5183
Faculty size		·4793	·6830	·5837	·5904
Faculty growth rate		·2810	·3393	·3337	·3506
Student-faculty ratio		·2332	·1703		
Type of curricular philosophy					
Special techniques	·1869			−·1955	
Shape of faculty rank					
Top-heavy	·1514			·2105	
Bottom-heavy				−·1954	
Geographic location					
Midwest			·1807	·1963	
Southwestern and Mountain States					−·2401

[a] Kendall tau; level of significance (2-tail) = ·05

schools with larger faculties, with a large number of Ph.D.s produced, with high prestige, and a high faculty growth rate were more likely to interact with other schools of business. There was also a correlation with a top-heavy faculty structure. This finding tends to conflict with the earlier one regarding inbreeding. There a positive correlation was observed between inbreeding and top-heaviness, whereas here a positive correlation was found between the number of schools interacted with and the tendency to top-heaviness in faculty structure. One explanation of this finding involves distinguishing between schools with outstandingly productive full professors whose work makes them highly visible in the academic community, and those in which older full professors have not established themselves in the academic community, and hence neither they nor their schools profit from their senior status.

One of the negative correlations with the number of schools interacted with is by now familiar, namely, the type of curriculum emphasizing special techniques. The only new negative correlation is bottom-heavy faculty structure characterized by a few associate professors and a predominance of either instructors and/or assistant professors. It is not clear why schools with a bottom-heavy faculty rank structure should be negatively correlated with the number of schools interacted with. Such a structure may reflect unusual insecurity among assistant professors caught in a rotating junior staff.

The measure of reciprocal relationships with other schools again yields high correlations with faculty size, Ph.D. output, prestige, and faculty growth rate. In addition, there is a negative correlation with location in the Mountain States.

Table 2 suggests that, except for the measure of inbreeding, four of the measures of faculty interchange have a similar pattern of correlations with the variables that might affect the process: faculty size, number of Ph.D.s produced, age of the school, prestige, and faculty growth rate.

Summary and conclusions

Interorganizational relations involve a variety of complex processes, one of which is an exchange of personnel. Organizations import and export members in the course of pursuing their objectives. An analysis of this facet of interorganizational relations was the purpose of this paper. As a case in point, the flow of faculty members among 79 schools of business was studied. With the aid of a cluster analysis computer program, six receipt (R) and six supply (S) clusters were identified.

Of the supply-receipt cluster pairs, the following summary statements may be made:

$R1$ and $S1$ were distinguished primarily by a lack of certain curriculum types and by a strong regional concentration.

$R2$ had unusually large faculties and a fairly regional concentration, whereas $S2$ faculty sizes were average and the regional concentration stronger.

$R3$ was distinguished principally by high prestige, with no regional tendencies to speak of; the members of $S3$, the faculty sources of these high prestige schools, were not significantly distinct from the other schools in the population.

$R4$ was distinguished by high prestige, Ph.D. output, faculty size, interaction with other schools, and faculty growth rate; $S4$ also had high prestige, symmetrical faculty structure, but few of the merits of $R4$.

$R5$ consisted of principally older schools in the Midwest, recruiting faculty from midwestern private schools.

$R6$ was centred in the Midwest, but recruited faculty from schools distinguished by high prestige, large faculty size, but no pronounced regionality. Here, the receipt and supply clusters can be said to be highly complementary. On the whole, however, there is scant evidence for complementary relationships among the clusters; in other words, receipt and supply clusters are not very different from one another.

A correlational analysis of the five measures of faculty interchange showed that inbreeding was positively correlated with top-heaviness in faculty rank structure. The other four interchange measures – the number of faculty members supplied to other schools, the total number of faculty members exchanged, number of reciprocal exchange relationships, number of schools interacted with – were correlated to a high degree with several common variables: faculty size, prestige, Ph.D. output, and growth in faculty size.

Although 11 independent variables were included in the analysis of the data, it is conceivable that some crucial variables were omitted, for example, the number of faculty publications per year, the presence or absence of a graduate school journal, and the tested scholastic ability of the graduate students admitted by a school. The number of faculty publications and a graduate school journal would add to the visibility of a school, and a high level of scholastic ability of graduate students would increase the probability of producing high calibre Ph.D.s and attracting a high calibre faculty.

Two other methodological and substantive questions should be noted. First, there is a need for a longitudinal analysis of all variables. In the present study, one such variable was examined, the growth rate of the faculty. Similarly, the growth rate of the student body, the growth rate of the Ph.D. programme, and changes over time in prestige and other such derivative variables could well be examined. The dynamic growth of many organizations underscores the importance of growth-rate variables.

Second, the flow of personnel as a phenomenon of inter-organizational relations reflects, among other things, a recruitment decision by organizational decision makers. The recruitment decision is guided implicitly or explicitly by one or more reference organizations (Evan, 1966: 179, 183; Riesman, 1956: 11-37, 70-71). If an analysis of the flow of personnel among schools of business indicates that the recruitment policies of the reference organizations of a school of business are significantly different from those perceived, such a school cannot modify its position in the community of schools of business unless it changes its recruitment policies.

The methodology employed in this paper for studying the flow of personnel among organizations may, with modifications, be applied to all classes of organizations. An extension of such research would contribute to the emergence of models for analysing personnel flows – a relatively neglected and complex problem in organizational theory.

References

AMERICAN ASSOCIATION OF COLLEGIATE SCHOOLS OF BUSINESS (1960), *Faculty Personnel*, St Louis, Mo.

G. B. Baty, W. M. Evan and T. W. Rothermel 141

BERTALANFFY, L. (1962), 'General systems theory – a critical review', *General Systems Yearbook*, vol. 8, pp. 1–20.

BLAU, P. M. (1964), *Exchange and Power in Social Life*, New York, John Wiley.

BONNER, R. E. (1964a), 'On some clustering techniques', *IBM Journal of Research and Development*, January, pp. 22–3.

BONNER, R. E. (1964b), 'Clustering program', working paper, IBM Advanced Systems Development Division, New York, May.

EVAN, W. M. (1966), 'The organization-set: toward a theory of inter-organizational relations', in J. D. Thompson (ed.), *Approaches to Organizational Design*, Pittsburgh, University of Pittsburgh Press, pp. 175–91.

EVAN, W. M. (1968), 'A systems model of organizational climate', in Renato Tagiuri and George H. Litwin (eds.), *Organizational Climate*, Boston, Harvard University, Graduate School of Business Administration, pp. 107–24.

EVAN, W. M. (1972), 'An organization-set model of interorganizational relations', in M. F. Tuite, M. Radnor and R. K. Chisholm (eds.), *Interorganizational Decision Making*, Chicago, Aldine-Atherton Publishing Co., pp. 181–200.

EVAN, W. M., and BLACK, G. (1967), 'Innovation in business organizations: some factors associated with success and failure of staff proposals', *Journal of Business*, vol. 40, pp. 519–30.

GORDON, R. A., and HOWELL, J. E. (1959), *Higher Education for Business*, New York, Columbia University Press.

GROSS, N., MASON, W. J.,and McEACHERN, A. W. (1959), *Explorations in Role Analysis*, New York, John Wiley.

HOMANS, G. C. (1952), *Sentiments and Activities*, New York, Free Press.

KATZ, D., and KAHN, R. L. (1966), *The Social Psychology of Organizations*, New York, John Wiley.

LAZARSFELD, P. F., and MENZEL, H. (1961), 'On the relation between individual and collective properties', in Amitai Etzioni (ed.), *Complex Organizations: A Sociological Reader*, New York, Holt, Rinehart & Winston, Inc., pp. 422–40.

McGUIRE, J. W. (1963), *Business and Society*, New York, McGraw-Hill.

MERTON, R. K. (1957), *Social Theory and Social Structure* (rev. ed.), Glencoe, Ill., Free Press.

PETTIT, R. G. (1964), 'Clustering program, continuous variables', working paper, IBM Advanced Systems Development Division, New York, August.

PIERSON, F. C. (1959), *The Education of American Businessmen*, New York, McGraw-Hill.

RIESMAN, D. (1956), *Constraint and Variety in American Education*, Lincoln, University of Nebraska Press.

SIMON, H. A. (1967), 'The business school: a problem in organizational design', *Journal of Management Studies*, vol. 4, pp. 1–16.

10 P. M. Hirsch

An Organization-Set Analysis of Cultural Industry Systems

P. M. Hirsch, 'Processing fads and fashions: an organization-set analysis of cultural industry systems', *American Journal of Sociology*, vol. 77, January 1972, pp. 639–59.

In modern, industrial societies, the production and distribution of both fine art and popular culture entail relationships among a complex network of organizations which both facilitate and regulate the innovation process. Each object must be 'discovered', sponsored, and brought to public attention by entrepreneurial organizations or nonprofit agencies before the originating artist or writer can be linked successfully to the intended audience. Decisions taken in organizations whose actions can block or facilitate communication, therefore, may wield great influence over the access of artist and audience to one another. The content of a nation's popular culture is especially subject to economic constraints due to the larger scale of capital investment required in this area to link creators and consumers effectively.

This paper will outline the structure and operation of entrepreneurial organizations engaged in the production and mass distribution of three types of 'cultural' items: books, recordings, and motion pictures. Entrepreneurial organizations in cultural industries confront a set of problems especially interesting to students of interorganizational relations, mainly: goal dissensus, boundary-spanning role occupants with nonorganizational norms, legal and value constraints against vertical integration, and, hence, dependence on autonomous agencies (especially mass-media gatekeepers) for linking the organization to its customers. In response to environmental uncertainties, mainly a high-risk element and changing patterns of distribution, they have evolved a rich assortment of adaptive 'coping' strategies and, thus, offer a promising arena in which to develop and apply tentative propositions derived from studies of other types of organizations and advanced in the field of organization studies. Our focal organizations (Evan, 1965) are the commercial publishing house, the movie studio, and the record company. My description of their operation is based on information and impressions gathered from (1) an extensive sampling of trade papers directed at members of these industries, primarily: *Publishers' Weekly*, *Billboard*, and *Variety*; (2) 53 open-ended interviews with individuals at all levels of the publishing, recording, and broadcasting industries; and (3) a thorough review of available secondary sources.

Definitions and conceptual framework

Cultural products may be defined tentatively as 'nonmaterial' goods directed at a public of consumers, for whom they generally serve an aesthetic or expressive, rather than a clearly utilitarian function. In so far as one of its goals is to create and satisfy consumer demand for new fads and fashions, every consumer industry is engaged to some extent in the production of cultural goods, and any consumer good can thus be placed along the implied continuum between cultural and utilitarian products. The two poles, however, should be intuitively distinct. Movies, plays, books, art prints, phonograph records, and pro football games are predominantly cultural products; each is nonmaterial in the sense that it embodies a live, one-of-a-kind performance and/or contains a unique set of ideas. Foods and detergents, on the other hand, serve more obvious utilitarian needs. The term 'cultural organization' refers here only to *profit-seeking firms producing cultural products for national distribution*. Noncommercial or strictly local organizations, such as university presses and athletic teams, respectively, are thus excluded from consideration. A fundamental difference between entrepreneurial organizations and nonprofit agencies is summarized by Toffler (1965, pp. 181–2):

In the non-profit sector the end-product is most frequently a live performance – a concert, a recital, a play. If for purposes of economic analysis we consider a live performance to be a commodity, we are immediately struck by the fact that, unlike most commodities offered for sale in our society, this commodity is not standardized. It is not machine made. It is a handcrafted item. . . . Contrast the output of the non-profit performing arts with that of the record manufacturer. He, too, sells what appears to be a performance. But it is not. It is a replica of a performance, a mass-produced embodiment of a performance. . . . The book publisher, in effect, does the same. The original manuscript of the poem or novel represents the author's work of art, the individual, the prototype. The book in which it is subsequently embodied is a [manufactured] replica of the original. Its form of production is fully in keeping with the level of technology in the surrounding society.

Our frame of reference is the cultural industry system, comprised of all organizations engaged in the process of filtering new products and ideas as they flow from 'creative' personnel in the technical subsystem to the managerial, institutional, and societal levels of organization (Parsons, 1960). Each industry system is seen as a single, concrete, and stable network of identifiable and interacting components. The concept of organization levels, proposed initially to analyse transactions within the boundaries of a single, large-scale organization, is easily applied to the analysis of interorganizational systems. Artist and mass audience are linked by an ordered sequence of events: before it can elicit any audience response, an art object first must succeed in (a) competition against others for selection and promotion by an entrepreneurial organization, and then in (b) receiving mass-media coverage in such forms as book reviews, radio-station air play, and film criticism. It must be ordered by retail outlets for display or exhibition to consumers and, ideally, its author or performer will appear on television talk shows and be written up as an interesting news story. Drawing on a functionalist model of organizational control and facilitation of innovations proposed by Boskoff (1964), we view the mass media in their gatekeeping role as a primary 'institutional regulator of innovation'.

A number of concepts and assumptions implicit in this paper are taken from the developing field of interorganizational relations and elaborated on more fully by Thompson (1967). Studies in this emerging tradition typically view all phenomena from the standpoint of the organization under analysis. It seldom inquires into the functions performed by the organization for the social system but asks rather, as a temporary partisan, how the goals of the organization may be constrained by society. The organization is assumed to act under norms of rationality, and the subject of analysis becomes its forms of adaptation to constraints imposed by its technology and 'task environment'. The term 'organization-set' has been proposed by Evan (1965) as analogous to the role-set concept developed by Merton (1957) for analysing role relationships:

Instead of taking a particular status as the unit of analysis, as Merton does in his role-set analysis, I take . . . an organization, or a class of organizations, and trace its interactions with the network of organizations in its environment, i.e., with elements of its organization-set. As a partial social system, a focal organization depends on input organizations for various types of resources: personnel, matériel, capital, legality, and legitimacy. . . . The focal organization in turn produces a product or a service for a market, an audience, a client system, etc. (Evan, 1965, pp. 177–9).

After examining transactions between the focal organization and elements of its task environment,[1] we will describe three adaptive strategies developed by cultural organizations to minimize uncertainty. Finally, variations within each industry will be reviewed.

Input and output organization-sets

The publishing house, movie studio, and record company each invests entrepreneurial capital in the creations and services of affiliated organizations and individuals at its input (product selection) and output (marketing) boundaries. Each effects volume sales by linking individual creators and producer organizations with receptive consumers and mass-media gatekeepers. New material is sought constantly because of the rapid turnover of books, films, and recordings.

Cultural organizations constitute the managerial subsystems of the industry systems in which they must operate. From a universe of innovations proposed by 'artists' in the 'creative' (technical) subsystem, they select ('discover') a sample of cultural products for organizational sponsorship and promotion. A distinctive feature of cultural industry systems at the present time is the organizational segregation of functional units and subsystems. In the production sector, the technical and managerial levels of organization are linked by boundary-spanning talent scouts – for

1. A focal organization's task environment consists of other organizations located on its input and output boundaries.

example, acquisitions editors, record 'producers', and film directors – located on the input boundary of the focal organization.

To this point, cultural industries resemble the construction industry and other organization systems characterized by what Stinchcombe (1959) calls 'craft administration of production'. The location of professionals in the technical subsystem, and administrators in the managerial one, indicates that production may be organized along craft rather than bureaucratic lines (Stinchcombe, 1959). In the cultural industry system, lower-level personnel (artists and talent scouts) are accorded professional status and seldom are associated with any one focal organization for long time periods. Although company executives may tamper with the final product of their collaborations, contracted artists and talent scouts are *delegated* the responsibility of producing marketable creations, with little or no interference from the front office beyond the setting of budgetary limits (Peterson and Berger, 1971). Due to widespread uncertainty over the precise ingredients of a best-seller formula, administrators are forced to trust the professional judgement of their employees. Close supervision in the production sector is impeded by ignorance of relations between cause and effect.[2] A highly placed spokesman for the recording industry (Brief, 1964, pp. 4–5) has stated the problem as follows:

We have made records that appeared to have all the necessary ingredients – artist, song, arrangements, promotion, etc. – to guarantee they wind up as best sellers. . . . Yet they fell flat on their faces. On the other hand we have produced records for which only a modest success was anticipated that became runaway best sellers. . . . There are a large number of companies in our industry employing a large number of talented performers and creative producers who combine their talents, their ingenuity and their creativity to produce a record that each is sure will captivate the American public. The fact that only a small proportion of the output achieves hit status is not only true of our industry. . . . There are no formulas for producing a hit record . . . just as there are

2. 'Production' here refers to the performances or manuscripts created by artists and talent scouts for later replication in the form of books, film-negative prints, and phonograph records. The physical manufacture of these goods is sufficiently amenable to control as to be nearly irrelevant to our discussion.

no pat answers for producing hit plays, or sell-out movies or best-selling books.

Stinchcombe's (1959, 1968) association of craft administration with a minimization of fixed overhead costs is supported in the case of cultural organizations. Here, we find, for example, artists (i.e., authors, singers, actors) contracted on a *royalty* basis and offered no tenure beyond the expiration of the contract. Remuneration (less advance payment on royalties) is contingent on the number of books, records, or theatre tickets sold *after* the artist's product is released into the marketplace. In addition, movie-production companies minimize overhead by hiring on a per-picture basis and renting sets and costumes as needed (Stinchcombe, 1968), and publishers and record companies frequently subcontract out standardized printing and record-pressing jobs.

The organization of cultural industries' technical subsystems along craft lines is a function of (a) demand uncertainty and (b) a 'cheap' technology. Demand uncertainty is caused by: shifts in consumer taste preferences and patronage (Gans, 1964; Meyersohn and Katz, 1957); legal and normative constraints on vertical integration (Conant, 1960; Brockway, 1967); and widespread variability in the criteria employed by mass-media gatekeepers in selecting cultural items to be awarded coverage (Hirsch, 1969). A cheap technology enables numerous cultural organizations to compete in producing a surplus of books, records, and low-budget films on relatively small capital investments. The cost of producing and manufacturing a new long-play record or hard-cover book for the general public is usually less than $25,000 (Brief, 1964; Frase, 1968). Once sales pass the break-even point (about 7,000 copies for books and 12,000 for records, *very roughly*), the new product begins to show a profit. On reaching sales of 20,000 a new book is eligible for best-seller status; 'hit records' frequently sell over several hundred thousand copies each. Mass media exposure and volume sales of a single item generally cover earlier losses and yield additional returns. Sponsoring organizations tend to judge the success of each new book or record on the basis of its performance in the marketplace during the first six weeks of its release. Movies require a far more substantial investment but follow a similar pattern.

These sources of variance best account for the craft administration of production at the input boundary of the cultural organization. It is interesting to note that in an earlier, more stable environment, that is, less heterogeneous markets and fewer constraints on vertical integration, the production of both films and popular records was administered more bureaucratically: lower-level personnel were delegated less responsibility, overhead costs were less often minimized, and the status of artists resembled more closely the salaried employee's than the free-lance professional's.

At their output boundaries, cultural organizations confront high levels of uncertainty concerning the commercial prospects of goods shipped out to national networks of promoters and distributors. Stratification within each industry is based partly on each firm's ability to control the distribution of marginally differentiated products. Competitive advantage lies with firms best able to link available input to reliable and established distribution channels. In the book industry, distribution 'for the great majority of titles is limited, ineffective, and costly. In part this weakness in distribution is a direct consequence of the strength of the industry in issuing materials. . . . If it were harder to get a book published, it would be easier to get it distributed' (Lacy, 1963, pp. 53–4).

The mass distribution of cultural items requires more *bureaucratic* organizational arrangements than the administration of production, for example, a higher proportion of salaried clerks to process information, greater continuity of personnel and ease of supervision, less delegation of responsibility, and higher fixed overhead (Stinchcombe, 1959). Whereas the building contractor produces custom goods to meet the specifications of a clearly defined client-set, cultural organizations release a wide variety of items which must be publicized and made attractive to thousands of consumers in order to succeed. Larger organizations generally maintain their own sales forces, which may contract with smaller firms to distribute their output as well as the parent company's.

The more highly bureaucratized distribution sector of cultural industries is characterized by more economic concentration than the craft-administered production sector, where lower costs pose fewer barriers to entry. Although heavy expenditures required for product promotion and marketing may be reduced by contracting with independent sales organizations on a commission basis, this practice is engaged in primarily by smaller, weaker, and poorly capitalized firms. Contracting with autonomous sales organizations places the entrepreneurial firm in a position of dependence on outsiders, with the attendant risk of having cultural products regarded highly by the sponsoring organization assigned a low priority by its distributor. In the absence of media coverage and/ or advertising by the sponsoring organization, retail outlets generally fail to stock new books or records.

A functional equivalent of direct advertising for cultural organizations is provided by the selective coverage afforded new styles and titles in books, recordings, and movies by the mass media. Cultural products provide 'copy' and 'programming' for newspapers, magazines, radio stations, and television programmes; in exchange, they receive 'free' publicity. The presence or absence of coverage, rather than its favourable or unfavourable interpretation, is the important variable here. Public awareness of the existence and availability of a new cultural product often is contingent on feature stories in newspapers and national magazines, review columns, and broadcast talk shows, and, for recordings, radio-station air play. While the total number of products to be awarded media coverage may be predicted in the aggregate, the estimation of *which ones* will be selected from the potential universe is problematic.

The organizational segregation of the producers of cultural items from their disseminators places definite restrictions on the forms of power which cultural organizations may exercise over mass-media gatekeepers to effect the selection of particular items for coverage. Widely shared social norms mandate the independence of book-review editors, radio-station personnel, film critics, and other arbiters of coverage from the special needs and commercial interests of cultural organizations. Thus, autonomous gatekeepers present the producer organization with the 'control' problem of favourably influencing the probability that a given new release will be selected for exposure to consumers.

For publishing houses and record firms, especially, it would be uneconomical to engage in direct, large-scale advertising campaigns to bring more than a few releases to public attention. For them and, to a lesser extent, for movie studios, the crucial target audience for promotional campaigns consists of autonomous gatekeepers, or 'surrogate consumers' such as disc jockeys, film critics, and book reviewers, employed by mass-media organizations to serve as fashion experts and opinion leaders for their respective constituencies.

The mass media constitute the institutional subsystem of the cultural industry system. *The diffusion of particular fads and fashions is either blocked or facilitated at this strategic checkpoint.* Cultural innovations are seen as originating in the technical subsystem. A sample selected for sponsorship by cultural organizations in the managerial subsystem is introduced into the marketplace. This output is filtered by mass-media gatekeepers serving as 'institutional regulators of innovation' (Boskoff, 1964). Organizations in the managerial subsystem are highly responsive to feedback from institutional regulators: styles afforded coverage are imitated and reproduced on a large scale until the fad has 'run its course' (Boskoff, 1964; Meyersohn and Katz, 1957).[3]

We see the consumer's role in this process as essentially one of rank ordering cultural styles and items 'preselected' for consideration by role occupants in the managerial and institutional subsystems. Feedback from consumers, in the form of sales figures and box-office receipts, cues producers and disseminators of cultural innovations as to which experiments may be imitated profitably and which should probably be dropped. This process is analogous to the preselection of electoral candidates by political parties, followed by voter feedback at the ballot box. The orderly sequence of events and the possibility of only two outcomes at each checkpoint resemble a Markov process.

This model assumes a surplus of available 'raw material' at the outset (e.g., writers, singers, politicians) and pinpoints a number of strategic checkpoints at which the oversupply is filtered out. It is 'value added' in the sense that no product can enter the societal

3. Boskoff (1964, p. 224) sees the sources of innovations within any social system as the 'technical and/or managerial levels of organization, or external sources. . . . By its very nature, the institutional level is uncongenial to innovative roles for itself.' Changes occur at an increasing rate when 'the institutional level is ineffective in controlling the cumulation of variations. . . . This may be called change by institutional default.' Changes in pop-culture content consistently follow this pattern.

subsystem (e.g., retail outlets) until it has been processed favourably through each of the preceding levels of organization, respectively.[4]

Organizational response to task-environment uncertainties

Our analysis suggests that organizations at the managerial level of cultural industry systems are confronted by (1) constraints on output distribution imposed by mass-media gatekeepers, and (2) contingencies in recruiting creative 'raw materials' for organizational sponsorship. To minimize dependence on these elements of their task environments, publishing houses, record companies, and movie studios have developed three proactive strategies: (1) the allocation of numerous personnel to boundary-spanning roles; (2) overproduction and differential promotion of new items; and (3) cooptation of mass-media gatekeepers.

Proliferation of contact men

Entrepreneurial organizations in cultural industries require competent intelligence agents and representatives to actively monitor developments at their input and output boundaries. Inability to locate and successfully market new cultural items leads to organizational failure: new manuscripts must be located, new singers recorded, and new movies produced. Boundary-spanning units have therefore been established, and a large proportion of personnel allocated to serve as 'contact men' (Wilensky, 1956), with titles such as talent scout, promoter, press coordinator, and vice-president in charge of public relations. The centrality of information on boundary developments to managers and executives in cultural organizations is suggested in these industries' trade papers: coverage of artist relations and selections by mass-media gatekeepers far exceeds that of matters managed more easily in a standardized manner, such as inflation in warehousing, shipping, and physical production costs.

Contact men linking the cultural organization to the artist community contract for creative raw material on behalf of the

4. For a more detailed discussion of the *role-set* engaged in the processing of fads and fashions, with particular application to 'hit' records, see Hirsch (1969).

organization and supervise its production. Much of their work is performed in the field.

Professional agents on the input boundary must be allowed a great deal of discretion in their activities on behalf of the cultural organization. Successful editors, record 'producers', and film directors and producers thus pose control problems for the focal organization. In fields characterized by uncertainty over cause/effect relations, their talent has been 'validated' by the successful marketplace performance of 'their discoveries' – providing high visibility and opportunities for mobility outside a single firm. Their value to the cultural organization as recruiters and intelligence agents is indicated by high salaries, commissions, and prestige within the industry system.

Cultural organizations deploy additional contact men at their output boundaries, linking the organization to (1) retail outlets and (2) surrogate consumers in mass-media organizations. The tasks of promoting and distributing new cultural items are analytically distinct, although boundary units combining both functions may be established. Transactions between retailers and boundary personnel at the wholesale level are easily programmed and supervised. In terms of Thompson's (1962) typology of output transactions, the retailer's 'degree of nonmember discretion' is limited to a small number of fixed options concerning such matters as discount schedules and return privileges.[5] In contrast, where organizations are dependent on 'surrogate consumers' for coverage of new products, the latter enjoy a high degree of discretion: tactics employed by contact men at this boundary entail more 'personal influence'; close supervision by the organization is more difficult and may be politically inexpedient. Further development of Thompson's typology would facilitate tracing the flow of innovations through organization systems by extending the analysis of transactions 'at the end of the line' – that is,

5. Sponsoring organizations without access to established channels of distribution, however, experience great difficulty in obtaining orders for their products from retail outlets and consumers. Thompson's (1962) typology of interaction between organization members and nonmembers consists of two dimensions: Degree of nonmember discretion, and specificity of organizational control over members in output roles. Output roles are defined as those which arrange for the distribution of an organization's ultimate product (or service) to other agents in society.

between salesmen and consumers or bureaucrats and clients – to encompass boundary transactions at all levels of organization through which new products are processed.

A high ratio of promotional personnel to surrogate consumers appears to be a structural feature of any industry system in which: (a) goods are marginally differentiated; (b) producers' access to consumer markets is regulated by independent gatekeepers; and (c) large-scale, *direct* advertising campaigns are uneconomical or prohibited by law. Cultural products are advertised *indirectly* to independent gatekeepers within the industry system in order to reduce demand uncertainty over which products will be selected for exposure to consumers. Where independent gatekeepers neither filter information nor mediate between producer and consumer, the importance of contact men at the organization's output boundary is correspondingly diminished. In industry systems where products are advertised more directly to consumers, the contact man is superseded by full-page advertisements and sponsored commercials, purchased outright by the producer organization and directed at the lay consumer.

Overproduction and differential promotion of cultural items

Differential promotion of new items, in conjunction with overproduction, is a second proactive strategy employed by cultural organizations to overcome dependence on mass-media gatekeepers. Overproduction is a rational organizational response in an environment of low capital investments and demand uncertainty. 'Fortunately, from a cultural point of view if not from the publisher's, the market is full of uncertainties. . . . A wise publisher will hedge his bets' (Bailey, 1970, pp. 144, 170).

Under these conditions it apparently is more efficient to produce many 'failures' for each success than to sponsor fewer items and pretest each on a massive scale to increase media coverage and consumer sales. The number of books, records, and low-budget films released annually far exceeds coverage capacity and consumer demand for these products. The publisher's 'books cannibalize one another. And even if he hasn't deliberately lowered his editorial standards (and he almost certainly has) he is still publishing more books than he can possibly do justice to' (Knopf, 1964, p. 18). While over 15,000 new titles are issued annually, the probability of any one appearing in a given bookstore is only 10 per cent (Lacy, 1963). Similarly, fewer than 20 per cent of over 6,000 (45 rpm) 'singles' appear in retail record outlets (Shemel and Krasilovsky, 1964). Movie theatres exhibit a larger proportion of approximately 400 feature films released annually, fewer than half of which, however, are believed to recoup the initial investment. The production of a surplus is facilitated further by contracts negotiated with artists on a royalty basis and other cost-minimizing features of the craft administration of production.

Cultural organizations ideally maximize profits by mobilizing promotional resources in support of volume sales for a small number of items. These resources are not divided equally among each firm's new releases. Only a small proportion of all new books and records 'sponsored' by cultural organizations is selected by company policy makers for large-scale promotion within the industry system. Most cultural items are allocated minimal amounts for promotion and are 'expected' to fail. Such long shots constitute a pool of 'understudies', from which substitutes may be drawn in the event that either mass-media gatekeepers or consumers reject more heavily plugged items. We see the strategy of differential promotion as an attempt by cultural organizations to 'buffer' their technical core from demand uncertainties by smoothing out output transactions (Thompson, 1967).

Cooptation of 'institutional regulators'

Mass-media gatekeepers report a wide variety of mechanisms developed by cultural organizations to influence and manipulate their coverage decisions. These range from 'indications' by the sponsoring organization of high expectations for particular new 'discoveries' (e.g., full-page advertisements in the trade press, parties arranged to introduce the artist to recognized opinion leaders) to personal requests and continuous barrages of indirect advertising, encouraging and cajoling the gatekeeper to 'cover', endorse, and otherwise contribute toward the fulfilment of the organization's prophecy of great success for its new product.

The goals of cultural and mass-media organizations come into conflict over two issues. First, public opinion, professional ethics, and, to a lesser extent, job security, all require that institutional gatekeepers maintain independent standards of judgement and quality rather than endorse only those items which cultural organizations elect to promote. Second, the primary goal of commercial mass-media organizations is to maximize revenue by 'delivering' audiences for sponsored messages rather than to serve as promotional vehicles for particular cultural items. Goal conflict and value dissensus are reflected in frequent disputes among cultural organizations, mass-media gatekeepers, and public representatives concerning the legitimacy (or legality) of promoters' attempts to acquire power over the decision autonomy of surrogate consumers.

Cultural organizations strive to control gatekeepers' decision autonomy to the extent that coverage for new items is (a) crucial for building consumer demand, and (b) problematic. Promotional campaigns aimed at coopting institutional gatekeepers are most likely to require proportionately large budgets and illegitimate tactics when consumers' awareness of the product hinges almost exclusively on coverage by these personnel. As noted earlier, cultural organizations are less likely to deploy boundary agents or sanction high-pressure tactics for items whose sale is less contingent on gatekeepers' actions.

Variability within cultural industries

Up to this point, we have tended to minimize variability among cultural organizations, cultural products, and the markets at which they are directed. Our generalizations apply mainly to the most *speculative* and entrepreneurial segments of the publishing, recording, and motion picture industries, that is, adult trade books, popular records, and low-budget movies. Within each of these categories, organizations subscribe, in varying degrees, to normative as well as to the more economic goals we have assumed thus far. Certain publishing houses, record companies, and movie producers command high prestige within each industry system for financing cultural products of high quality but of doubtful commercial value. To the extent they do *not* conform to economic norms of rationality, these organizations should be considered separately from the more dominant pattern of operations described above.

Whether our generalizations might also characterize less-uncertain industry segments, such as educational textbook and children's-book publishing divisions, or classical record production is also subject to question. In each of these instances, cost factors and/or degree of demand uncertainty may be quite different, which, in turn, would affect the structure and operation of the producer organizations. Textbook publishers, for example, face a more predictable market than do publishers (or divisions) specializing in trade books: more capital investment is required, and larger sales forces must be utilized for school-to-school canvassing (Brammer, 1967). In the case of children's books, some differences might be expected in that libraries rather than retail stores account for 80 per cent of sales (Lacy, 1968).

Within the adult-trade-book category, coverage in book-review columns is more crucial to the success of literary novels than to detective stories or science-fiction books (Blum, 1959). Review coverage is also problematic: 'Even *The New York Times*, which reviews many more books than any other journal addressed to the general public, covers only about 20 per cent of the annual output. Many books of major importance in specialized fields go entirely unnoticed in such general media, and it is by no means unknown for even National Book Award winners to go unreviewed in the major national journals' (Lacy, 1963, p. 55). We would therefore expect publishers' agents to push novels selected for national promotion more heavily than either detective stories or science-fiction works. Serious novels should be promoted more differentially than others.

Similarly, coverage in the form of radio-station air play is far more crucial in building consumer demand for recordings of popular music than for classical selections. Control over the selection of new 'pop' released by radio-station programmers and disc jockeys is highly problematic. Record companies are dependent on radio air play as the *only* effective vehicle of exposure for new pop records. In this setting – where access to consumers hinges almost exclusively on coverage decisions by autonomous gatekeepers – institutionalized side payments ('payola') emerged as a central tactic in the overall strategy of cooptation employed by producer organizations to assure desired coverage.

Radio air play for classical records is less crucial for building consumer demand; the probability of obtaining coverage for classical releases is also easier to estimate. Whereas producers and consumers of pop records are often unsure about a song's likely sales appeal or musical worth, criteria of both musical merit and consumer demand are comparatively clear in the classical field. Record companies, therefore, allocate proportionately fewer promotional resources to assure coverage of classical releases by mass-media gatekeepers, and record-company agents promoting classical releases employ more legitimate tactics to influence coverage decisions than promoters of pop records employ to coopt the decision autonomy of institutional regulators.

Thompson (1967, p. 36) has proposed that 'when support capacity is concentrated but demand dispersed, the weaker organization will attempt to handle its dependence through coopting'. In our analysis, cultural organizations represent a class of weaker organizations, dependent on support capacity concentrated in mass-media organizations; demand is dispersed among retail outlets and consumers. While all cultural organizations attempt to coopt autonomous consumer surrogates, the intensity of the tactics employed tends to vary with degree of dependence. Thus, cultural organizations most dependent on mass-media gatekeepers (i.e., companies producing pop records) resorted to the most costly and illegitimate tactics; the institution of payola may be seen as an indication of their weaker power position.

Conclusion

This paper has outlined the structure of entrepreneurial organizations engaged in the production and distribution of cultural items and has examined three adaptive strategies employed to minimize dependence on elements of their task environments: the deployment of contact men to organizational boundaries, overproduction and differential promotion of new items, and the cooptation of mass-media gatekeepers. It is suggested that in order for new products or ideas to reach a public of consumers, they first must be processed favourably through a system of organizations whose units filter out large numbers of candidates before they arrive at the consumption stage. The concept of an industry system is proposed as a useful frame of reference in which to (1) trace the flow of new products and ideas as they are filtered at each level or organization, and (2) examine relations among organizations.

References

BAILEY, H. S. (1970), *The Art and Science of Book Publishing*, New York, Harper & Row.

BARNETT, J. H. (1959), 'The sociology of art', in R. K. Merton, L. Broom, and L. S. Cottrell, Jr (eds.), *Sociology Today*, New York, Basic Books.

BLUM, E. (1959), Paperback book publishing: a survey of content', *Journalism Quarterly*, vol. 36, Fall, pp. 447–54.

BOSKOFF, A. (1964), 'Functional analysis as a source of a theoretical repertory and research tasks in the study of social change', in G. K. Zollschan and W. Hirsch (eds.), *Explorations in Social Change*, Boston, Houghton Mifflin.

BRAMMER, M. (1967), 'Textbook publishing', in C. B. Grannis (ed.), *What Happens in Book Publishing*, 2nd ed., New York, Columbia University Press.

BRIEF, H. (1964), *Radio and Records: A Presentation by the Record Industry Association of America at the 1964 Regional Meetings of the National Association of Broadcasters*, New York, Record Industry Association of America.

BROCKWAY, G. P. (1967), 'Business management and accounting', in C. B. Grannis (ed.), *What Happens in Book Publishing*, 2nd ed., New York, Columbia University Press.

CONANT, M. (1960), *Antitrust in the Motion Picture Industry*, Berkeley, University of California Press.

EPHRON, N. (1969), 'Where bookmen meet to eat', *New York Times Book Review*, June 22, pp. 8–12.

EVAN, W. M. (1965), 'Toward a theory of inter-organizational relations', *Management Science*, vol. 11, B217–30. Reprinted in J. D. Thompson (ed.), *Approaches to Organizational Design*, Pittsburgh, University of Pittsburgh Press, 1966.

FRASE, R. W. (1968), 'The economics of publishing', in K. L. Henderson (ed.), *Trends in American Book Publishing*, Champaign, Graduate School of Library Science, University of Illinois.

GANS, H. J. (1964), 'The rise of the problem film', *Social Problems*, vol. 11, Spring, pp. 327–36.

HIRSCH, P. M. (1969), *The Structure of the Popular Music Industry*, Ann Arbor, Survey Research Center, University of Michigan.

KNOPF, A. A. (1964), 'Publishing then and now, 1912–1964', twenty-first of the R. R. Bowker Memorial Lectures, New York, New York Public Library.

LACY, D. (1963), 'The economics of publishing, or Adam Smith and literature', in S. R. Graubard (ed.), 'The American Reading Public', *Daedalus*, Winter, pp. 42–62.

LACY, D. (1968), 'Major trends in American book publishing', in K. L. Henderson (ed.), *Trends in American Book Publishing*, Champaign, Graduate School of Library Science, University of Illinois.

MERTON, R. K. (1957), *Social Theory and Social Structure*, rev. ed., Glencoe, Ill., Free Press.

MEYERSOHN, R., and KATZ, E. (1957), 'Notes on a natural history of fads', *American Journal of Sociology*, vol. 62, May, pp. 594–601.

PARSONS, T. (1960), *Structure and Process in Modern Societies*, Glencoe, Ill., Free Press.

PETERSON, R., and BERGER, D. (1971), 'Entrepreneurship in organizations: evidence from the popular music industry', *Administrative Science Quarterly*, vol. 16, March, pp. 97–107.

SHEMEL, S., and KRASILOVSKY, M. W. (1964), *This Business of Music*, New York, Billboard.

STINCHCOMBE, A. L. (1959), 'Bureaucratic and craft administration of production: a comparative study', *Administrative Science Quarterly*, vol. 4, September, pp. 168–87.

STINCHCOMBE, A. (1968), *Constructing Social Theories*, New York, Harcourt, Brace & World.

THOMPSON, J. D. (1962), 'Organizations and output transactions', *American Journal of Sociology*, vol. 68, November, pp. 309–24.

THOMPSON, J. D. (1967), *Organizations in Action*, New York, McGraw-Hill.

TOFFLER, A. (1965), *The Culture Consumers*, Baltimore, Penguin.

WILENSKY, H. (1956), *Intellectuals in Labor Unions*, Glencoe, Ill., Free Press.

11 M. Aiken and J. Hage

Organizational Interdependence and Intra-Organizational Structure

M. Aiken and J. Hage, 'Organizational interdependence and intra-organizational structure', *American Sociological Review*, vol. 33, December 1968, pp. 912–30.

The major purpose of this paper is to explore some of the causes and consequences of organizational interdependence among health and welfare organizations. The aspect of organizational interdependence that is examined here is the joint cooperative programme with other organizations. In particular, we are interested in relating this aspect of the organization's relationships with its environment to internal organizational behaviour.

Thus this paper explores one aspect of the general field of interorganizational analysis. The effect of the environment on organizational behaviour as well as the nature of the inter-organizational relationships in an organization's environment are topics that have received increasing attention from scholars in recent years. Few studies, however, have examined the impact of the environment on internal organizational processes.

Most studies of organizational interdependence essentially conceive of the organization as an entity that needs inputs and provides outputs, linking together a number of organizations via the mechanisms of exchanges or transactions. (Cf. Ridgeway, 1957; Elling and Halbsky, 1961; Levine and White, 1961; Dill, 1962; James D. Thompson, 1962.) Some types of organizational exchanges involve the sharing of clients, funds, and staff in order to perform activities for some common objective (Levine *et al.*, 1963). The measure of the degree of organizational interdependence used here is the *number of joint programmes* that a focal organization has with other organizations. The greater the number of joint programmes, the more organizational decision-making is constrained through obligations, commitments, or contracts with other organizations, and the greater the degree of organizational interdependence. (Cf. Guetzkow, 1966.) This type of interdependence among health and welfare organizations has variously been called 'functional cooperation' by Black and Kase (1963), and 'programme coordination' by Reid (1964), and is considered a more binding form of interdependence and therefore a more interesting example of interorganizational cooperation. This does not suggest that the cooperation that is involved in joint programmes is easily achieved. On the contrary, there are a number of barriers to establishing such interdependencies among organizations (cf. Johns and de Marche, 1951), and the probability of conflict is quite high, as Miller (1958) and Barth (1963) point out.

The *joint programme* needs to be carefully distinguished from the *joint organization*. The latter refers to the situation in which two or more organizations create a separate organization for some common purpose. For example, the Community Chest has been created by health and welfare organizations for fund-raising purposes. Similarly, Harrison (1959) has noted that the Baptist Convention was created by the separate Baptist churches for more effective fund raising. Guetzkow (1950) has described inter-agency committees among federal agencies, representing a special case of the joint organization. Business firms have created joint organizations in order to provide service functions. These are clearly different from the joint programme because these joint organizations have separate corporate identities and often their own staff, budget, and objectives.

Some examples of joint programmes in organizations other than those in the health and welfare field are the student exchange programmes in the Big Ten. Harvard, Columbia, Yale, and Cornell Universities are developing a common computerized medical library. Indeed, it is interesting to note how many universities use joint programmes of one kind or another. We do not believe that this is an accident; rather, it flows from the characteristics of these organizations. In our study, which includes rehabilitation centres, we have observed the attempt by one organization to develop a number of joint programmes for the mentally retarded. These efforts are being financed by the Department of Health, Education, and Welfare, and evidently reflect a governmental concern for creating more cooperative relationships among organizations. Even in the business world, where the pursuit of profit would seem to make the joint programme an impossibility, there are examples of this phenomenon. Recently, Ford and Mobil Oil started a joint research project designed to develop a superior gasoline. This pattern is developing even across national boundaries in both the business and nonbusiness sectors.

It is this apparently increasing frequency of joint programmes that makes this form of interdependence not only empirically relevant, but theoretically strategic. In so far as we can determine, organizational interdependence is increasingly more common (Terreberry, 1968), but the question of why remains to be answered.

Theoretical framework

The basic assumptions that are made about organizational behaviour and the hypotheses of this study are shown in Figure 1.

The first three assumptions deal with the basic problem of why organizations, at least health and welfare organizations, become involved in interdependent relationships with other units. The type of interdependency with which we are concerned here is the establishment of joint, cooperative activities with other organizations. If we accept Gouldner's (1959) premise that there is a strain toward organizations maximizing their autonomy, then the establishment of an interdependency with another organization would seem to be an undesirable course of action. It is the view here that organizations are 'pushed' into such interdependencies because of their need for resources – not only money, but also resources such as specialized skills, access to particular kinds of markets, and the like (cf. Levine et al., 1963).

One source of the need for additional resources results from a heightened rate of innovation, which in turn is a function of internal organizational diversity. In several ways internal diversity creates a strain towards innovation and change. The conflict between different occupations and interest groups, or even different theoretical, philosophical, or other perspectives, results in new ways of looking at organizational problems. The likely result of this is a high rate of both proposals for programme innovations as well as successful implementation of them (Hage and Aiken, 1967). But organizational diversity also implies a greater knowledge and awareness of the nature of and changes in the organizational environment, particularly when organizational diversity implies not only a spectrum of occupational roles in the organization, but also involvement in professional societies in the environment by the incumbents of those occupational roles, itself a type of organizational interdependency. Together the internal conflicts and awareness of the nature of the organization's environment create strains towards organizational change.

Figure 1. Assumptions and hypotheses about organizational interdependence

---

Assumptions:

I. Internal organizational diversity stimulates organizational innovation.
II. Organizational innovation increases the need for resources.
III. As the need for resources intensifies, organizations are more likely to develop greater interdependencies with other organizations, joint programmes, in order to gain resources.
IV. Organizations attempt to maximize gains and minimize losses in attempting to obtain resources.
V. Heightened interdependence increases problems of internal control and coordination.
VI. Heightened interdependence increases the internal diversity of the organization.

Hypotheses:

1. A high degree of complexity varies directly with a high number of joint programmes.
2. A high degree of programme innovation varies directly with a number of joint programmes.
3. A high rate of internal communication varies directly with a high number of joint programmes.
4. A high degree of centralization varies inversely with a high number of joint programmes.
5. A high degree of formalization varies inversely with a high number of joint programmes.

But innovation has its price. There is a need for more resources to pay the costs of implementing such innovations – not only money, but staff, space, and time. The greater the magnitude of the change or the number of changes within some specified period of time, the greater the amounts of resource that will be needed and the less likely that the normal sources will be sufficient. Some have called organizations that successfully accomplish this task effective ones (Yuchtman and Seashore, 1967). Thus, the leaders of innovating organizations must search for other possibilities, and the creation of a joint, cooperative project with another organization becomes one solution to this problem.

This mechanism for gaining resources, i.e., the establishment of a joint programme, is best viewed as a type of organizational exchange. The leaders sacrifice a small amount of autonomy for gains in staff, funds, etc. While there are strong organizational imperatives against such exchanges, since they inevitably involve some loss of autonomy, as well as necessitate greater internal coordination, the increased intensification of needs for greater resources makes such an alternative increasingly attractive. Still another factor involved here is that some objectives can only be achieved through cooperation in some joint programme. The goal may be so complicated or the distribution of risk so great that organizations are impelled to enter into some type of joint venture. Of course the creation of interdependencies with other organizations also has its costs. The organization must utilize some of its own resources in order to perform whatever co-ordination is necessary. Hence an organization with no surplus resources available could hardly afford a joint programme. Thus there must be some slack in the resource base in the organization before any innovation or cooperative venture is likely.

This is not to argue for the perfect rationality of organizational leaders. Some decisions about change or the choice of a co-operative activity may be quite irrational, and perhaps non-logical (Wilensky, 1967). Indeed much of our argument about the conditions that lead to organizational innovation, i.e., conflict among different occupations, interest groups, or perspectives, is that this is hardly the most rational way to bring about change. Perhaps it is best to view the process as a series of circumstances that propel such events.

While we feel that this line of reasoning is a valid explanation of why organizations enter into interdependent relationships with other organizations via such mechanisms as the joint pro-gramme, alternative explanations have been offered and must be considered. Lefton and Rosengren (1966) have suggested that the lateral and longitudinal dimensions of organizational commitment to clients are factors, at least in health and welfare organizations. These are probably not the primary factors in other types of organizations, such as economic ones. However, our concern has been to attempt to find the most general argument possible to explain organizational interdependence. At the same time we have left unanswered the question of why organizations become diverse in the first place, and their framework may provide one possible answer. Reid (1964) has indicated that complementary resources are also an important factor in understanding organizational interdependence. Without necessarily agreeing or disagreeing with these points of view, we do believe that the first three assumptions in Figure 1 represent *one* causal chain showing why organizations become involved in more enduring interorganizational relationships.

The next theoretical problem is what kind of organization is likely to be chosen as a partner in an interdependent relationship. Here we assume that organizations attempt to maximize their gains and minimize their losses. This is our fourth premise. That is, they want to lose as little power and autonomy as possible in their exchange for other resources. This suggests that they are most likely to choose organizations with complementary resources, as Reid (1967) has suggested, or partners with different goals, as Guetzkow (1966) has indicated. This reduces some of the problem of decreased autonomy, because the probability of conflict is reduced and cooperation facilitated in such symbiotic arrangements (cf. Hawley, 1951). This assumption also implies that other kinds of strategies might be used by the leaders of the organization once they have chosen the joint programme as a mechanism of obtaining resources. Perhaps it is best to develop interdependent relationships with a number of organizations in order to obtain a given set of resources, thus reducing the degree of dependence on a given source. Again, we do not want to argue that organizational leaders will always choose the rational or logical alternative, but rather that they will simply *attempt* to minimize losses and maximize gains. Under circumstances of imperfect knowledge, some decisions will undoubtedly be irrational.

Our last theoretical problem is consideration of the consequences for the organization of establishing interdependent relationships as a means of gaining additional resources. Such joint activities will necessitate a set of arrangements between the participating organizations to carry out the programme. This will mean commitments to the other organization, resulting in constraints on some aspects of organizational behaviour. This in turn will mean an increase in problems of internal coordination, our fifth assumption. It is often difficult to work with outsiders, i.e., the partner in a joint activity. In this circumstance a number of mutual adaptations in a number of different areas will become necessary. One solution to this problem is the creation of extensive internal communication channels, such as a broad committee structure which meets frequently.

But perhaps a more interesting consequence of the joint programme is that it can in turn contribute to organizational diversity. There is not only the likelihood of the addition of new staff from other organizations, but, more importantly, the creation of new communication links with other units in the organization's environment. New windows will have been opened into the organization, infusing new ideas and feeding the diversity of the organization, which means that the cycle of change, with all of its consequences, is likely to be regenerated.

In this way a never-ending cycle of diversity – innovation – need for resources – establishment of joint programmes – is created. What may start as an interim solution to a problem can become a long-term organizational commitment which has a profound impact on the organization. In the long run, there is the tendency for units in an organizational set to become netted together in a web of interdependencies (cf. Terreberry, 1968).

With these six assumptions, a large number of testable hypotheses can be deduced. Indeed this is one of the advantages of a general theoretical framework. Not only does it provide the rationale for the hypotheses being tested, but it can suggest additional ideas for future research. Since we are mainly concerned with the factors associated with high interdependency, and more particularly the number of joint programmes, all of the hypotheses in Figure 1 are stated in terms of this variable.

Organizational diversity implies many different kinds of variables. We have examined three separate indicators of it:

diversity in the number of occupations or the degree of complexity; diversity in the number of power groups or the degree of centralization; and diversity in the actual work experience or the degree of formalization. If assumptions I–III are correct, then the stimulation of change, and more particularly innovation brought about by each of these kinds of diversity, should be associated with a large number of programmes. But this is not the only way in which these variables can be related; and that observation only emphasizes how the internal structure of the organization affects the extent of the enduring relationships with other organizations. The problems of internal coordination and the increased diversity, assumptions V and VI, are also related. Both mechanisms of coordination – communication and programming – are undoubtedly tried, but communication is probably preferred. This increases the advantages of diversity and also helps to bring about greater decentralization and less formalization. Similarly, the greater awareness of the environment, via the infusion of staff from other organizations, feeds this cycle of cause and effect relationships. Therefore, we have hypothesized that the number of joint programmes varies directly with the degree of complexity (Hypothesis 1) and inversely with the degree of centralization and formalization (Hypotheses 4 and 5).

Since our arguments also involve statements about the stimulation of innovation, which in turn heightens the need for resources, it is clear that we would expect the degree of innovation to co-vary with the number of joint programmes. This is hypothesis 2 of Figure 1. While programme change is only one kind of organizational innovation, it is probably the most important, at least from the standpoint of generating needs for additional resources, and thus it goes to the heart of the argument presented in Figure 1. Programme innovation in turn has consequences for the degree of centralization and formalization in the organization, but here we are mainly concerned about the relationship between the rate of organization innovation as reflected in new programmes and the number of joint programmes, and not about these other mediating influences.

The degree of attempted internal coordination is measured by only one variable, namely the rate of communication, but again we feel that this is an important indication of this idea. Given the desire to minimize the loss of autonomy (assumption IV), organizational members must be particularly circumspect when dealing with staff and other kinds of resources from their organizational partners. This largely reduces the options about programming and encourages the elite to emphasize communication rates. Probably special 'boundary spanning' roles (Thompson, 1962) are created; these men negotiate the transactions with other organizations and in turn keep their organizational members informed. The problems of interpenetration by other organizational members will keep the communication channels open and filled with messages as internal adjustments are made. Thus this is the rationale for the third hypothesis.

Study design and methodology

The data upon which this study is based were gathered in sixteen social welfare and health organizations located in a large midwestern metropolis in 1967. The study is a replication of an earlier study conducted in 1964. Ten organizations were private; six were either public or branches of public agencies. These organizations were all the larger welfare organizations that provide rehabilitation, psychiatric services, and services for the mentally retarded, as defined by the directory of the Community Chest. The organizations vary in size from twenty-four to several hundred. Interviews were conducted with 520 staff members of these sixteen organizations. Respondents within each organization were selected by the following criteria; (a) all executive directors and department heads; (b) in departments of less than ten members, one-half of the staff was selected randomly; (c) in departments of more than ten members, one-third of the staff was selected randomly. Non-supervisory administrative and maintenance personnel were not interviewed.

Aggregation of data. This sampling procedure divides the organization into levels and departments. Job occupants in the upper levels were selected because they are most likely to be key decision-makers and to determine organizational policy, whereas job occupants on the lower levels were selected randomly. The different ratios within departments ensured that smaller departments were adequately represented. Professionals, such as psychiatrists, social workers and rehabilitation counsellors, are included because they are intimately involved in the achievement of organizational goals and are likely to have organizational power. Non-professionals, such as attendants, janitors, and secretaries are excluded because they are less directly involved in the achievement of organizational objectives and have little or no power. The number of interviews varied from eleven in the smallest organization to sixty-two in one of the larger organizations.

It should be stressed that in this study the units of analysis are *organizations*, not individuals in the organizations. Information obtained from respondents was pooled to reflect properties of the sixteen organizations, and these properties were then related to one another. Aggregating individual data in this way presents methodological problems for which there are yet no satisfactory solutions. For example, if all respondents are equally weighted, undue weight is given to respondents lower in the hierarchy. Yet those higher in the chain of command, not the lower-status staff members, are the ones most likely to make the decisions which give an agency in ethos.

We attempted to compensate for this by computing an organizational score from the means of social position within the agency. A social position is defined by the level or stratum in the organization and the department or type of professional activity. For example, if an agency's professional staff consists of psychiatrists and social workers, each divided into two hierarchical levels, the agency has four social positions: supervisory psychiatrists, psychiatrists, supervisory social workers, and social workers. A mean was then computed for each social position in the agency. The organizational score for a given variable was determined by computing the average of all social position means in the agency.

The procedure for computing organizational scores parallels the method utilized in selecting respondents. It attempts to represent organizational life more accurately by not giving disproportionate weight to those social positions that have little power and that are little involved in the achievement of organizational goals.

Computation of means for each social position has the advantage of avoiding the potential problem created by the use of different sampling ratios. In effect, responses are standardized by organizational location – level and department – and then combined into an organizational score. By obtaining measures from all levels and all departments, the total structure is portrayed and reflected in the organizational score.

The measurement of organizational interdependence. The degree of organizational interdependence is measured by the number of joint programmes with other organizations. There are several possible measures of the nature and degree of organizational interdependence among social welfare and health organizations. Among these are:

1. The number of cases, clients or patients referred or exchanged.

2. The number of personnel lent, borrowed, or exchanged.

3. The number, sources, and amounts of financial support.

4. The number of joint programmes.

The first two of these were used in an earlier study of interorganizational relationships (Levine and White, 1961). In our research we found that organizations such as rehabilitation workshops and family agencies simply did not keep records of the number of walk-ins or calls referred by other organizations. Similar problems were encountered with exchanges of personnel. Thus, we found great difficulty in using these measures of interdependence. While the nature and amounts of financial support are interesting and important aspects of interorganizational analysis, they are not included in this study.

We asked the head of each organization to list every joint programme in which his organization had been involved in the past ten years, whether terminated or not. A profile of each programme was obtained, including the name of participating organizations, goals of the programme, number and type of clients or patients involved, and source of financial and other resources for the programme. Only existing programmes and those involving the commitment of resources by all participating organizations – such as personnel, finances, space – were included in our analysis.

Since a number of our sixteen organizations had participated in joint programmes with each other, it was possible to check the reliability of their responses. We did not find any difficulties of recall for this period of time. In part this is probably because most of the joint programmes, once started, tended to continue over time. Some organizations had maintained their organizational relationships for as many as twenty years. Then too, the fact that the joint programme is not a minor incident in the life of an organization also facilitates recall. We did discover that organizational leaders tended to think of the purchase of services as a joint programme. To solve this problem we included in our interview schedule a series of follow-up questions about the amount of staff shared and the amount of funds contributed by each organization involved in the joint programme.

The number of existing joint programmes among these sixteen organizations ranged from none to 33. Rehabilitation centres had the highest average number of joint programmes, although the range was quite extensive among some other kinds of organizations in our study (Table 1). The special education department and the hospitals had an intermediate range of programmes. Social casework agencies and homes for the emotionally disturbed had the least number of joint programmes. In every case, however, there was some variation within each organizational category.

Table 1. Average number of joint programmes by type of organization

Type of organizations	Number of organizations	Average number of joint programmes	Range
Rehabilitation centres	3	20·7	8–33
Special education department public schools	1	15·0	15
Hospitals	3	8·3	6–12
Homes for emotionally disturbed	3	2·3	1–3
Social casework agencies	6	1·2	0–4
All organizations	16	7·3	0–33

Findings

A strict interpretation of data would allow us to discuss only the consequences of interorganizational relationships on the internal structure and performance of an organization. This is true because the period of time during which measurement of the number of joint programmes, our measure of organizational interdependence, was made occurred prior to most of our measures of structure and performance. Yet the reasoning in our theoretical framework suggests that these variables are both causes and effects in an on-going process. Strictly speaking, our data reflect the consequences of increased joint programmes, but we shall still make some inferences about their causes.

1. *Organizations with many joint programmes are more complex organizations, that is, they are more highly professionalized and have more diversified occupational structures.* By complexity we do not mean the same thing as Rushing's (1967) division of labour, a measure of the distribution of people among different occupations, but rather the diversity of activities. There are essentially two aspects of complexity as we have defined it: the degree to which there is a high number of different types of occupational activities in the organization; and the degree to which these diverse occupations are anchored in professional societies. One of the most startling findings in our study is the extremely high correlation between the number of different types of occupations in an organization and the number of joint programmes ($r = 0.87$).

The relationship between the occupational diversity of the organization and the number of joint programmes in 1967 is very high, whether we use the number of occupations in 1959 ($r = 0.79$), the number of occupations in 1964 ($r = 0.83$), or the number of occupations in 1967 ($r = 0.87$). While time sequence is not the same as causation, this does suggest that occupational diversity is not solely a function of new programmes. Rather it suggests that organizations that have a high number of joint programmes are organizations that have been occupationally diverse for a number of years.

The addition of joint programmes evidently makes an organization aware of the need for still more specialties. One rehabilitation centre used social workers in a joint programme involving the mentally retarded with several other agencies. It then decided to add social workers to a number of its other programmes. The

Table 2. Relationships between the number of joint programmes and organizational characteristics

Organizational characteristics	*Pearsonian product–moment correlation coefficients between each organizational character-istic and the number of joint programmes*
1. Degree of complexity	
Index of professional training	·15
Index of professional activity	·60[b]
Number of occupations: 1967	·87[d]
2. Degree of organizational innovation: 1959–66	
Number of new programmes (including new programmes that are joint programmes)	·71[c]
Number of new programmes (excluding new programmes that are joint programmes)	·74[d]
3. Internal communication	
Number of committees	·47[a]
Number of committee meetings per month	·83[d]
4. Degree of centralization	
Index of participation in decision-making	·30
Index of hierarchy of authority	·33
5. Degree of formation	
Index of job codification	·13
Index of rule observation	− ·06
Index of specificity of job	− ·06

[a] $P < ·10$.
[b] $P < ·05$.
[c] $P < ·01$.
[d] $P < ·001$.

addition of new specialties may also be necessary in order to help solve some of the problems of coordination created by the joint programmes.

The dependent variable, number of joint programmes, is quite dispersed with a range from 0 to 33 and a mean of 7·3. It is entirely possible that the unusually high correlations for some variables in Table 2 are simply a function of a highly skewed distribution on this variable. Therefore, we computed two non-parametric measures of correlation, Spearman's rank order correlation coefficient (rho) and Kendall's rank correlation coefficient (tau) for the relationship between number of occupations in 1967 and the number of joint programmes. The relationship between these two variables remains strong even when using the non-parametric statistics.

The objection could be raised that the very strong relationship between the number of occupational specialties and the number of joint programmes may also be a function of the type of organization. In Table 1, it was shown that rehabilitation centres had the most joint programmes, followed by the special education department, hospitals, homes for the emotionally disturbed, and finally social casework agencies. The observation that there is a positive relationship between these two variables is valid within three of the four categories of organizations shown in Table 3. That is, within the categories of rehabilitation centres, mental hospitals, and homes for the emotionally disturbed the organizations having the highest number of occupations have the most joint programmes while those having the fewest occupational specialties have the smallest number of joint programmes. Only among social casework agencies does the relationship not hold. It might be noted that only one social casework organization had more than one interorganizational tie.

The degree to which an organization is professionalized is also strongly related to the number of joint programmes. We measured the degree of professionalism in organizations in two ways: first, the degree to which the organizational members received professional training; and second, the degree to which organizational members are currently active in professional activities, i.e., attending meetings, giving papers, or holding offices. The measure of current professional activity was also quite highly related to our measure of the number of joint programmes (r = 0·60). The degree of professional training had little relationship with the number of joint programmes (r = 0·15).

2. *Organizations with many joint programmes are more innovative organizations.* The degree of organizational innovation is measured by the number of new programmes that were successfully implemented in the organization during the eight-year period from 1959 to 1966. The correlation coefficient between joint programmes and new programmes is 0·71, as shown in Table 2. Of course, there is an element of spuriousness in this relationship, since some of the new programmes are joint programmes. If the correlation coefficient is recomputed, eliminating all new programmes that are also joint programmes, we find the same result (r = 0·74).

Table 3. **Number of occupations in 1976 and number of joint programmes by type of organization**

	Number of occupations 1967	Number of joint programmes
Rehabilitation centres		
Rehabilitation centre A	27	33
Rehabilitation centre B	24	21
Rehabilitation centre C	13	8
Department of special education		
Educational organization D	19	15
Mental hospitals		
Mental hospital E	18	12
Mental hospital F	18	7
Mental hospital G	11	6
Homes for emotionally disturbed		
Home H	11	3
Home I	10	3
Home J	7	1
Social casework agencies		
Casework agency K	7	1
Casework agency L	6	0
Casework agency M	5	1
Casework agency N	5	1
Casework agency O	4	4
Casework agency P	1	0

As in the case of number of occupational specialties in the organization, the finding based on non-parametric measures of association between each of these two measures of organizational innovation and the number of new programmes is little different from the results based on the parametric statistical measure.

It could be that the above relationships between degree of organizational innovation and number of joint programmes may simply be a function of complexity. We have argued that the degree of complexity gives rise not only to joint programmes, but also to new programmes. While there is no relationship between professional training and the number of new programmes ($r = -0.18$), there are relatively strong relationships between this variable and professional activity ($r = 0.74$) as well as occupational diversity ($r = 0.67$). When the relationships between the number of joint programmes and the number of new programmes (excluding new programmes that are joint programmes) is controlled for each of these three indicators separately, the relationship between these two variables remains relatively strong (see Table 4). This illustrates that the number of new programmes is related to the number of joint programmes independently of these various indicators of complexity.

Table 4. **Partial correlation coefficients between number of joint programmes and organizational innovation, controlling for indicators of complexity**

Control variables	Partial correlation between number of joint programmes and number of new programmes 1959–66 (excluding new programmes that are joint programmes), controlling for the variable indicated
Indicators of complexity	
Index of professional training	·77
Index of professional activity	·55
Number of occupations: 1967	·46

The key idea in our interpretation is that it is the rate of organizational innovation that intensifies the need for new resources. The higher this rate, the more likely organizations are to use the joint programme as a mechanism for cost reduction in such activities. The fact that some new programmes are joint programmes only strengthens our argument that the joint programme is a useful solution for the organization seeking to develop new programmes.

This interplay between new programmes and joint programmes can be made clear with several examples from our study. One rehabilitation centre with a high rate of new programmes developed joint programmes with several organizations that were primarily fund-raising organizations, as a solution for funding its growth. But in turn these organizations recognized new needs and asked the organization to develop still more new programmes in areas for their clients. This particular agency is presently exploring the possibility of developing special toys for the mentally retarded because one of its joint programmes is with an organization concerned with this type of client.

We may also re-examine the relationships between indicators of complexity and the number of joint programmes. As shown in Table 5, only the relationship between the number of occupations and the number of joint programmes remains strong when the number of new programmes (excluding new programmes that are joint programmes) is controlled (partial $r = 0.75$).

Table 5. Partial correlation coefficients between number of joint programmes and indicators of complexity, controlling for number of new programmes (excluding new programmes that are joint programmes)

Indicators of complexity	Partial correlation between number of joint programmes and indicators of complexity, controlling for number of new programmes (excluding new programmes that are joint programmes)
Index of professional training	·32
Index of professional activity	·11
Number of occupations: 1967	·75

3. *Organizations with many joint programmes have more active internal communication channels.* We measured the degree of internal communication in two ways. First, the number of committees in the organization and, second, the number of committee meetings per month. An active committee structure in an organization provides the potential for viable communication links in an organization. As shown in Table 2, there was a moderately strong relationship between the number of organizational committees and joint programmes ($r = 0.47$) and a very strong relationship between the number of committee meetings per month and the number of joint programmes ($r = 0.83$).

The relationship between the number of joint programmes and the number of committee meetings per month remains moderately strong when the two non-parametric measures of association are computed.

Actually the system of communication for joint programmes is even more complex than this. For example, one rehabilitation agency with the largest number of joint programmes had a special board with the university with which it had many joint programmes and was in the process of establishing another joint board with a second university. Another rehabilitation agency created a special steering committee to suggest and supervise joint programmes: the members of this committee were representatives from other organizations.

Controlling for the indicators of complexity and programme change reduces the relationship between the number of committees and number of joint programmes almost to zero in every case except that of professional training. Thus, the number of committees is evidently a function of these factors.

4. *Organizations with many joint programmes have slightly more decentralized decision-making structures.* In our study, staff members were asked how often they participated in organizational decisions about the hiring of personnel, the promotion of personnel, the adoption of new organizational policies, and the adoption of new programmes or services. The organizational score was based on the degree of participation in these four areas of decision-making. As shown in Table 2, there is a weak, positive relationship between the degree of participation in agency-wide

M. Aiken and J. Hage 179

decisions and the number of joint programmes (r = 0·30). This appears to be measuring the way resources are controlled. A second kind of decision-making concerns the control of work. We measure the degree of decision-making about work with a scale called the 'hierarchy of authority'.[1] This scale had a relationship with the number of joint programmes in the opposite direction to our expectation (r = 0·33). While highly interdependent organizations have slightly more decentralization of decisions about organizational resources, there is slightly less control over work in such organizations. It is difficult to account for this other than that the organizations with a high degree of programme change during the period 1964–6 had less control over work decisions in 1967 than in 1964. This suggests that the rate of change was so high in such organizations during this period that some more rigid mechanisms of social control were adopted in these organizations. Since the highly innovative organizations were also those with more joint programmes, this helps to explain the reversal.

5. *There is no relationship between formalization and the number of joint programmes.* Rules and regulations are important organizational mechanisms that are often used to insure the predictability of performance. There are several important aspects of rules as mechanisms of social control. One is the number of regulations specifying who is to do what, when, where, and why; this we call job codification. A second is the diligency with which such rules are enforced; this we call rule observation. A third is the degree to which the procedures defining a job are spelled out; this we call the index of specificity of jobs.

1. The empirical indicators of these concepts were derived from two scales developed by Richard Hall (1963), namely, hierarchy of authority and rules. The index of hierarchy of authority was computed by first averaging the replies of individual respondents to each of the following five statements: (1) There can be little action taken here until a supervisor approves a decision. (2) A person who wants to make his own decisions would be quickly discouraged here. (3) Even small matters have to be referred to someone higher up for a final answer. (4) I have to ask my boss before I do almost anything. (5) Any decision I make has to have my boss's approval. Responses could vary from 1 (definitely false) to 4 (definitely true). The individual scores were then combined into an organizational score as described above.

Two of these three indicators of formalization, the degree of rule observation and the degree of specificity of jobs, had very small inverse relationships with the number of joint programmes ($r = -0.06$ in each case), but each of these is hardly different from zero. The index of job codification was directly related to the number of joint programmes ($r = 0.13$), but it too is little different from zero, although it is in the opposite direction to our expectation.

We conclude from these findings that formalization is unrelated to the degree of organizational interdependence, suggesting that either this kind of internal diversity is not very important or that we do not have valid measures of this phenomenon. However, there is some problem of interpretation because there was also some movement of the highly innovative organizations toward greater formalization. For example, there is a negative partial correlation between the number of joint programmes and each of the indicators of formalization, i.e., job codification (partial $r = -0.11$), rule observation (partial $r = -0.37$), and degree of specificity of jobs (partial $r = -0.29$), when the number of new programmes during the period 1959–66 is partialled out.

Controls for size, auspices, age, and technology. When each of the relationships between the number of joint programmes and the indicators of complexity, organizational innovation, internal communication, centralization, and formalization are controlled by each of these four variables separately, the relationships shown in Table 2 are little affected. This means that the factors of organizational size, auspices, age, and technology (as we have measured them) have little or no effect on the findings of this study.

Discussions and conclusions

We now return to the issues raised at the outset of this paper. How are organizational structure and interdependence related? How can the study of an organization and its environment be combined? What kinds of organizations are more cooperative and integrated with other organizations?

We noted that there is a greater degree of complexity, i.e., more occupational diversity and greater professionalism of staff, in those organizations with the most joint programmes. The participation in joint programmes is evidently one mechanism for adding new occupational specialties to the organization at a reduced cost. By combining the resources of the focal organization with one or more others, there is the possibility of adding new occupational specializations to the organizational roster. This is especially true because joint programmes are likely to be of a highly specialized nature, providing services and activities that the focal organization cannot support alone.

The involvement of staff in interorganizational relationships introduces them to new ideas, new perspectives, and new techniques for solving organizational problems. The establishment of collegial relationships with comparable staff members of other organizations provides them with a comparative framework for understanding their own organizations. This is likely to affect their professional activities – attendance at meetings of professional societies – as well as reinforce professional standards of excellence. In these ways the involvement of organizations in joint programmes has the effect of increasing the complexity of these social and health welfare organizations.

The heightened interdependence has other important implications for the internal structure of organizations. The partial or total commitment of organizational resources to other organizations is likely to affect various departments and the business office as well as the central programmes of such an organization. Problems of coordination are likely to become particularly acute under such circumstances. The organization is forced to overcome these problems by heightening the frequency of internal communication. A more diverse committee structure and more committee meetings are mechanisms for handling such problems.

We would have expected that the heightened rates of communication would have resulted in more decentralization than appears to be the case. It is entirely possible that the problems of internal coordination may be reflected in some attempts to tighten the power structure, thus leading to less movement towards decentralization than we had expected. Also, the problems of internal coordination may be reflected in greater programming of the organization, or at least attempts in that direction, and this may be the reason why there is a small relationship between heightened interdependency, as we have measured it, and the degree of centralization.

Diversity in occupations (the degree of complexity) and power groups (the degree of decentralization) are related to the number of joint programmes, but diversity in work, as reflected in the absence of rules, is not related to this measure of interdependence. In part this may be a consequence of the sudden increase in the rate of programme innovation. But it may also be that the degree of formalization is not a good measure of diversity. It is the diversity of occupations, including their perspectives and self-interests, along with the representation of these points of view in a decentralized structure, that allows for diversity with the most critical consequences.

Our assumptions help to explain the steadily increasing frequency of organizational interdependency, especially that involving joint programmes. As education levels increase, the division of labour proceeds (stimulated by research and technology), and organizations become more complex. As they do, they also become more innovative. The search for resources needed to support such innovations requires interdependent relations with other organizations. At first, these interdependencies may be established with organizations with different goals and in areas that are more tangential to the organization. Over time, however, it may be that cooperation among organizations will multiply, involving interdependencies in more critical areas, and involve organizations having more similar goals. It is scarcity of resources that forces organizations to enter into more cooperative activities with other organizations, thus creating greater integration of the organizations in a community structure. The long range consequence of this process will probably be a gradually heightened coordination in communities.

References

BARTH, E. A. T. (1963), 'The causes and consequences of interagency conflict', *Sociological Inquiry*, vol. 33, Winter, pp. 51–7.

BLACK, B. J., and KASE, H. M. (1963), 'Inter-agency cooperation in rehabilitation and mental health', *Social Service Review*, vol. 37, March, pp. 26–32.

DILL, W. R. (1962), 'The impact of environment on organizational development', in S. Mailick and E. H. Van Ness (eds.), *Concepts and Issues in Administrative Behavior*, Englewood Cliffs, N.J., Prentice-Hall, Inc., pp. 94–109.

ELLING, R. H., and HALBSKY, S. (1961), 'Organizational differentiation and support: a conceptual framework', *Administrative Science Quarterly*, vol. 6, September, pp. 185–209.

GOULDNER, A. (1959), 'Reciprocity and autonomy in functional theory', in Llewellyn Gross (ed.), *Symposium on Sociological Theory*, New York, Harper and Row, pp. 241–70.

GUETZKOW, H. (1950), 'Interagency committee usage', *Public Administration Review*, vol. 10, Summer, pp. 190–96.

GUETZKOW, H. (1966), 'Relations among organizations', in R. V. Bowers (ed.), *Studies on Behavior in Organizations*, Athens, Ga., University of Georgia Press, pp. 13–44.

HAGE, J., and AIKEN, M. (1967), 'Program change and organizational properties: a comparative analysis', *American Journal of Sociology*, vol. 72, March, pp. 503–19.

HALL, R. (1963), 'The concept of bureaucracy: an empirical assessment', *American Journal of Sociology*, vol. 69, July, pp. 32–40.

HARRISON, P. M. (1959), *Authority and Power in the Free Church Tradition*, Princeton, N.J., Princeton University Press.

HAWLEY, A. H. (1951), *Human Ecology*, New York, The Ronald Press.

JOHNS, R. E., and DE MARCHE, D. F. (1951), *Community Organization and Agency Responsibility*, New York, Association Press.

LEFTON, M., and ROSENGREN, W. (1966), 'Organizations and clients: lateral and longitudinal dimensions', *American Sociological Review*, vol. 31, December, pp. 802–10.

LEVINE, S., and WHITE, P. E. (1961), 'Exchange as a conceptual framework for the study of interorganizational relationships', *Administrative Science Quarterly*, vol. 5, March, pp. 583–601.

LEVINE, S., WHITE, P. E. and PAUL, B. D. (1963), 'Community interorganizational problems in providing medical care and social services', *American Journal of Public Health*, vol. 53, August, pp. 1183–95.

MILLER, W. B. (1958), 'Inter-institutional conflict as a major impediment to delinquency prevention', *Human Organization*, vol. 17, Fall, pp. 20–23.

REID, W. (1964), 'Interagency coordination in delinquency prevention and control', *Social Service Review*, vol. 38, December, pp. 418–28.

RIDGEWAY, V. F. (1957), 'Administration of manufacturer-dealer systems', *Administrative Science Quarterly*, vol. 1, June, pp. 464–83.

RUSHING, W. A. (1967), 'The effects of industry size and division of labor on administration', *Administrative Science Quarterly*, vol. 12, September, pp. 273–95.

TERREBERRY, S. (1968), 'The evolution of organizational environments', *Administrative Science Review*, vol. 12, March, pp. 590–613.

THOMPSON, J. D. (1962), 'Organizations and output transactions', *American Journal of Sociology*, vol. 68, November, pp. 309–24.

WILENSKY, H. L. (1967), *Organizational Intelligence*, New York, Basic Books, Inc.

YUCHTMAN, E., and SEASHORE, S. E. (1967), 'A system resource approach to organizational effectiveness', *American Sociological Review*, vol. 32, December, pp. 891–903.

12 J. E. Schwarz

Maintaining Coalitions

J. E. Schwarz, 'Maintaining coalitions: an analysis of the EEC with
supporting evidence from the Austrian Grand Coalition and the CDU/
CSU', in Sven Groennings, E. W. Kelley, M. Leiserson (eds.), *The Study
of Coalition Behavior*, Holt, Rinehart & Winston Inc., 1970, pp. 235–49.

The ability of coalitions to endure has been of central importance
to a number of political systems, yet there has been little comparative research done on this subject. The purpose of this essay
is to help fill this void by providing a theoretical framework for
thinking about coalition maintenance and by applying this framework to three enduring coalitions. These coalitions are the
European Economic Community (EEC), the Christian Demo-
cratic/Christian Social Union of Western Germany (CDU/CSU),
and the Austrian grand coalition.

At first glance, it is the differences among the coalitions which
stand out rather than the similarities. The EEC, which comprises
France, Germany, Italy, and the Benelux countries, is a coalition
of states having as its base the Treaty of Rome. The direct purpose of the formation of the EEC was to keep alive the movement of European integration. With this spirit in mind, the
Treaty of Rome binds the coalition members in partnership,
although in practice the withdrawal of one or more partners has
been considered a serious possibility.[1]

The CDU/CSU is a coalition of religious and territorial groups.
It has combined Catholics and Protestants in a major Christian
party for the first time in German history. Its territorial partners
are the Christian Social Union, representing Bavaria, and the
Christian Democratic Union, representing the rest of West

1. The major political institutions of the EEC are the Commission, which
is the Community executive and is responsible for initiating almost all
policy proposals; the Council of Ministers, which directly represents the
governments of the member states and has the function of passing almost all
legislation; and the European Parliament, which is composed of national
parliamentarians to whom the Commission is politically responsible.

Germany. The CDU/CSU has been the largest electoral party in West Germany for twenty years, although the Socialists have presented it with major electoral opposition especially during the early years (1949–54) and since 1963.

The Austrian grand coalition comprised the Socialists and the People's Party. These are the two major political parties of Austria – accounting generally for well over 90 per cent of the legislative seats. The formation of the grand coalition in 1945 had the objective of resurrecting the Austrian state. Neither party was able to win a large majority and, hence, both agreed to work for the purposes of national unity until one was able to make large inroads on the other during an election. It is thus obvious that continually close elections were a necessary condition to the longevity of the coalition. But, as we shall see, continually close elections were not sufficient to explain the coalition's endurance. The coalition finally dissolved in 1966 when the People's Party secured a relatively large majority.

This short description of the three coalitions indicates that they were different from one another in many respects. The EEC partners were legally tied together, although withdrawal of members is still a political possibility. Neither the Austrian grand coalition partners nor the groups within the CDU/CSU faced such legal constraints. A second difference is that the EEC and the Austrian grand coalition included all of the major units within the system, whereas this was not the case for the CDU/CSU. A third difference among the coalitions is that progression toward a condition of much closer political integration was the major aim of the EEC and perhaps also of the CDU/CSU, but this was not a goal of the Austrian grand coalition. Such basic differences as these make the similarities to be brought out among the three coalitions all the more striking.

Basic similarities

The most fundamental similarity among the EEC, CDU/CSU, and Austrian cases is that each represents an example of an 'enduring' coalition. An 'enduring' coalition is a set of partners which has been preserved intact over a particularly long period of time. Moreover, an enduring coalition is characterized by a record of functioning at least moderately effectively in making policy.

By having maintained themselves over long periods of time, the three coalitions meet the first criterion. The six partners of the EEC have remained as a unit for over ten years even though a number of observers felt that the EEC would not survive long after its inception. The CDU/CSU partners have kept intact for a period of almost twenty years even though, once again, some observers were sceptical of the coalition's maintenance potential. Finally, the Austrian grand coalition continued in existence for a period of two decades following World War Two.

The coalitions have also functioned at least moderately effectively in making policy. The EEC made substantial strides in the agricultural, industrial tariff, competition, and some aspects of the taxation sector. As governing coalitions or parts of governing coalitions, the Austrian grand coalition and the CDU/CSU have each been responsible for significant amounts of policy outputs.

The ability of the three coalitions to remain intact and in working order for so long can be explained through a theoretical framework (Figure 1) which describes certain other properties these coalitions had in common and which indicates the relationship among these properties. The framework begins with the idea that each coalition was created and maintained amid 'high cost' situations.[2] It was initially the reaction to perceived costly repercussions if the coalition were to fail that motivated each of the coalitions to look upon maintenance as a major goal or good.

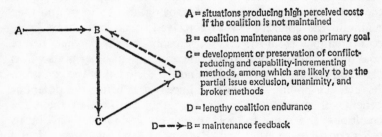

A = situations producing high perceived costs if the coalition is not maintained

B = coalition maintenance as one primary goal

C = development or preservation of conflict-reducing and capability-incrementing methods, among which are likely to be the partial issue exclusion, unanimity, and broker methods

D = lengthy coalition endurance

D-->B = maintenance feedback

Figure 1 Depiction of framework

2. By 'high costs' I mean the existence of highly undesirable consequences which the coalition members perceive may come into being if the coalition were to fail.

The coalition partners did not think in terms of potential coalition alternatives. The coalition was of value in itself.

Looking upon coalition maintenance as a good in itself, the coalition partners developed or preserved methods to decrease internal coalition conflict and increase the coalition's capability to deal with the remaining conflict (Deutsch *et al.*, 1957). A number of methods used by the coalitions were similar. It will be argued that, when maintenance is a major goal, the development of three particular methods is especially encouraged. One of these methods involves the partial exclusion of certain issues from impinging on the coalition's decision-making system; a second method is the establishment of a decision-making system in which either some or all of the members have a veto over important coalition decisions; the third method involves the promotion of a central 'broker' role within the coalition.

The maintenance goal and the development and preservation of conflict-reducing and capability-increasing methods led to the endurance of each coalition over a long period of time. Furthermore, the practice of maintaining the coalition intact and in working order created a feedback which further contributed to the partners' desire to keep the coalition alive in the future and, hence, further increased the likelihood of coalition endurance.

The costs of failure

The background conditions in which the three coalitions were formed and maintained were similar in one important respect: the potential costs involved in not being able to form and then maintain the coalitions were perceived to be very high. These costs stemmed from the relationships among the partners before coalition formation and from competition with other units which for one reason or another could not be included in the coalition. In fact, the potential costs of failure – and hence the potential benefits of success – were so high that partners of the three coalitions tended not to look at their coalition in comparison to other possible alternatives. Rather, the maintenance of the coalition intact and in working order became a value and an end in itself.

Let us first take up the EEC. After World War Two, a number of European statesmen felt that it was imperative to prevent

Franco-German relationships from rupturing once again into armed conflict. Such a goal might be accomplished by tying Germany and France together. This was one of the primary motives which led to the creation of the European Coal and Steel Community and the EEC. In this sense, the potential costs of coalition failure were perceived to be extraordinarily high.

There were also other potential coalition failure costs which accrued from competition with other units in the international system. The importance of the European Communities to each member state in the context of the Cold War added to the potential costs of coalition failure. As time passed, the contribution of the EEC to the capacity of its members to compete economically with the United States has assumed some importance.

The potential costs of failure within the CDU/CSU were anticipated to be the reopening of religious divisions which had, until the coalition's formation, sown great conflict within German politics and, according to some, weakened the resistance of the Weimar Republic to antidemocratic movements. To quote Sigmund Neumann: the coalition was

... a purposeful attempt at an interconfessional Christian party reaching out for the former followers of the Protestant CSVD and DNVP, as well as the Catholic Zentrum. . . . The conscious bridging of the religious schism that had caused havoc throughout German history was foremost in the minds of the founders of the CDU (Neumann, 1956, p. 380).

This potential cost would have been in addition to the cost accruing from immediate Socialist domination of the system had not the CDU/CSU been formed and maintained.

Secher (1958) demonstrates than an extraordinarily high cost situation also faced the Austrian grand coalition partners:

With such a legacy of civil strife, the task confronting the new political leaders in 1945 was formidable indeed. Could the heritage of a generation be disregarded and the once bitterly feuding social and economic groups . . . prevent the revival of political rifts that could only invite totalitarian solutions? . . . To the solution of that problem the whole concept of the coalition is basically oriented.

The point is that the potential costs of failure which faced the partners of each of the coalitions were so great that they have encouraged the partners to view coalition maintenance as a value or an end in itself. The linkage between this goal and coalition preservation has been noted by experts on more than one occasion. That a 'continuing commitment to the undertaking' by the members of the EEC has been of considerable significance to its continued functioning is a theme repeatedly taken up by Lindberg (1963, p. 11). Secher drew attention to the desire of the Austrian partners to maintain their coalition as a significant factor in the actual endurance of the coalition. The importance that Adenauer and a number of Catholic and Protestant leaders in Germany attached to both the creation and maintenance of the CDU/CSU parallels the EEC and the Austrian grand coalition experiences.

The goal of maintenance can lead to the continuation of coalitions in working order by, for example, making each partner more susceptible to compromise. However, the fact that the coalition partners want to keep the enterprise going does not automatically reduce sufficiently those conflicts of interest or even that distrust among the partners which might lead to the dissolution of the coalition. Hence, for a coalition to endure, the maintenance goal must also encourage the development of methods by which the coalition can reduce internal coalition conflict and increase the coalition's capacity to handle the remaining conflict. (Some of these methods may have already developed at the coalition's inception.) Since these methods are of such importance, their nature and their connection to coalition endurance will be examined in greater detail. We shall focus first on the EEC (in the next section) and then undertake to compare the EEC with the other two coalitions (in the section following that).

Methods of maintaining the EEC

Reducing conflict within the coalition

The reduction of conflict within the EEC Council of Ministers has partly taken shape in a conscious effort to insulate the council as much as politically possible from certain stresses and strains. The Council of Ministers, for example, attempts to separate the range of activities covered by the EEC from those activities not within the EEC. By doing this, the partners in the Council of

Ministers have not generally allowed politics from other arenas to interfere with the reaching of agreements in the EEC. Many examples could be given to illustrate the general application and significance of this particular method to the maintenance of the EEC. A recent example was the May 1966 agricultural agreement which was consummated in the midst of the French withdrawal from NATO. A month before the conclusion of these agreements *Le Monde* was prompted to say:

> As far as one can tell, *grande politique* has played practically no role in the development of these negotiations. There was much fear that the French withdrawal from NATO would give Germany a new reason to refuse its part of the Community agricultural policy financing, a bill which will be burdensome for them. But nothing such as that has come about. Everything happens as if the Common Market were much less sensitive to external atmospheric disturbances. There seems to be agreement on the fact that the Community is the place where interests are exchanged with a maximum of synchronization, which is far less exciting for the spirit but permits better resistance to political storms.[3]

One can easily imagine what council negotiations would be like were they generally to turn on matters pertaining to each partner's foreign policy. When on occasion foreign policy matters do intrude upon the EEC, decision making may be seriously disrupted. In fact, the two most serious crises faced by the EEC were both connected to the intrusion of foreign policy into EEC affairs. In the case of the French 1963 veto over British membership in the communities, for example, the Dutch virtually removed themselves from serious EEC work for about two months, and the entire council displayed an unwillingness to proceed further on EEC matters. Thus, the general success the partners have had in separating EEC decisions from other affairs has been of great utility in averting habitual council 'immobilism' and probably eventual dissolution of the EEC as well.

A second way in which the Council of Ministers has attempted to decrease conflict is by reducing the rigidity of policy positions and by insulating itself from certain demands coming from within the Community. The major step along these lines was the council's adoption of the rule to hold its meetings behind closed

3. *Le Monde*, 7 April 1966.

doors. This practice resists the tendency for some commitments to become rigid simply because they were made in public.

Secrecy also enables ministers to make pretensions to their clientele that they have brought an issue before the council. Such pretensions may go some distance in satisfying the clientele. At the same time, the council's business does not become seriously overloaded by divisive issues not of the ministers' making.

A third method used to reduce potential conflict within the EEC, in the form of dissatisfaction, is through insistence on unanimity among all members before a decision of any significance is taken. One characteristic of the EEC is that, according to the treaty, after a relatively short span of time almost all council decisions were to be made by simple or qualified majority. Even before this was to be the general rule, a number of decisions could be made by majority vote. However, the Council of Ministers has rarely availed itself of this opportunity. Between 1958 and 1966, the council had over one hundred opportunities to vote by simple or qualified majority. But it used majority vote on only seven occasions and, of these seven cases, only one dealt with what could remotely be considered to be a major political problem. The recent agreements on taxation illustrate that the council is still very reluctant to allow majority voting. (The council has agreed that majority vote will be possible on relatively minor questions, but unanimity will still be required on questions that are likely to have major consequences.)

What is the importance of the unanimity rule to the maintenance of the EEC? Put simply, the unanimity rule pushes members to make decisions which distribute payoffs on important matters in at least a minimally satisfactory manner for each of the members. Unacceptable payoffs on politically sensitive matters could increase dissatisfaction so that the losing member would be likely to withhold cooperation in administration and future decision making or even to withdraw from the coalition.

But a unanimity rule covering important matters may help to prevent such dissatisfaction. This is not to say that the unanimity rule always decreases dissatisfaction resulting from the aftereffects of sensitive decisions. Where interests are irreconcilable on these matters, as in the dispute among EEC partners over British membership in the Common Market, neither majority rule nor unanimity can reduce conflict. It is where interests can be reconciled that unanimity has its value, through the premium it puts on compromise. The history of the council decision-making process illustrates time and again the significance of the unanimity requirement to obtaining agreements which distributed payoffs more equally and to the greater satisfaction of the losing partner than was initially envisaged. The agreements on agricultural policy in 1961, 1964, and 1966 on competition policy, and on Article 43 of Regulation 15 are among the most notable examples.[4]

The Council of Ministers, then, has acted in three important ways to reduce conflict or dissatisfaction among the partners. The conscious effort to separate EEC affairs from other and more divisive arenas of politics, the policy of holding council meetings behind closed doors, and the policy of requiring unanimity on consequential decisions have undoubtedly been of considerable significance to keeping the EEC alive and intact as a unit.

Increasing coalition capabilities to handle conflict

A number of methods have been developed within the EEC to increase the coalition's capacity to deal with internal conflict. The creation of numerous specialized working committees within the Council of Ministers has greatly increased the council's capacity to deal with technical issues and has substantially increased communication among the partners. The substantive role which the partners had given to the Permanent Representatives, another committee under the council, has also been of significance in increasing communication and understanding among the partners and, thereby, to resolving sensitive issues. Both of these

4. To take the first major Community regulation on competition (Regulation 17) as an example of the encouragement the unanimity principle gives to compromise, see *Agence Europe*, 15 May 1961; 18 September 1961; 22 September 1961; 7 November 1961; 4 December 1961; 11 December 1961; and 19 December 1961. See also Arved Deringer, 'Les règles concernant la concurrence dans le cadre du Marché Commun entrent en vigueur', *Revue du Marché Commun*, vol. 44, 1962, pp. 70–84. With regard to unanimity and the free movement of workers (Article 43 of Regulation 15), see Nederhorst's comments in Assemblée parlementaire européenne, *Débats: Compte Rendu in Extenso des Séances*, no. 48, 1961–2, November 1961, pp. 116–17. For the 1964 agricultural decisions, see *Agence Europe*, 5 November 1963; 7 December 1964; 10 December 1964; and 14 December 1964.

developments have considerably enhanced the ability of the EEC partners to handle conflict in order that agreements can be reached.

Perhaps the most important method, in view of the need to arrive at unanimous agreement on all consequential questions, has been the development and preservation of a political broker to assist the coalition. The broker role has usually been undertaken by the Commission, although the Commission is under no legal compulsion to play this role. Less than a year after the establishment of the EEC, the Commission was already consulting closely with the six partners through the Permanent Representatives, the council work groups, and the national administrations before making specific proposals. By taking national considerations into account and by engaging fuller cooperation of national personnel through the consultative process, the Commission hoped to be able to initiate policy which could bridge national interests in order to obtain unanimity.

The Commission has generally looked upon its broker role as a significant aspect of its work, and the importance of the Commission playing this role to the ability of the partners to reach agreements becomes clear once a comparison of policy making is made. A number of factors were involved in the partners' successful attempts at making policy in the agricultural sector and their relative lack of success in the transport sector. Among the most important of these factors, however, was the positive broker role undertaken by the Commission in the agricultural case and the relative neglect of this role in the transport case. As Scheinmann suggests, the Commission cannot always consummate an agreement by playing the broker role, but 'progress becomes difficult if not sometimes impossible' if this role is not played (Scheinmann, 1966, p. 773).

Maintenance methods in Austria and Germany

Can specific methods to reduce internal conflict and increase capability that we have observed in the EEC be generalized to other coalitions also having maintenance as a goal? At this point we can once again consider the CDU/CSU and the Austrian grand coalition. Almost all of the methods which were developed in the EEC were also operative in one or both of the other two coalitions. These methods include the partial exclusion of certain issues from coalition consideration, the unanimity requirement, the development of a broker role within the coalition, and the proliferation of committees which put the coalition partners in substantially greater contact than they were at the coalition's inception. There is also a final common tendency that leaders of the groups in coalition be allowed to make decisions which bind their respective groups. This tendency was characteristic of the EEC at its inception, but it developed as time went on in the Austrian grand coalition and perhaps in the CDU/CSU as well.

The partial exclusion of certain issues

We have seen that the EEC does not cover most areas of foreign policy and that there has been an effort to keep foreign policy conflict from impinging on the decision-making process of the EEC. A similar situation can be seen operating in the Austrian grand coalition. Here the coalition did not need to face a number of potentially disruptive foreign policy problems because of the neutral position imposed on Austria in 1955. In the case of the CDU/CSU, the general question of the relationship between government and religion was historically a major factor dividing Catholics and Protestants at the national level. The Bonn Republic's fundamental law, however, put the resolution of this question at the *Land* level instead of at the federal level. The effect of this has been to prevent more than partial intrusion of this issue into the decision-making apparatus of the federal CDU/CSU coalition.

The unanimity requirement

The unanimity principle which was so significant in the operation of the EEC was also operative in the Austrian grand coalition. Early in the development of the Austrian grand coalition, according to Secher,

It was agreed to fill every ministerial office with representatives of all parties: a minister from one party and at his side undersecretaries from the other . . . parties. Decisions were to be arrived at jointly, the undersecretaries being required to countersign all orders of the ministers. This improvisation . . . has survived the results of four national and two presidential elections that have provided clear popular majorities for one or the other of the two major parties (Secher, 1958, p. 795).

Unanimity among the two partners thus became a requirement for decisions taken within the Austrian grand coalition.

Merkl has observed the development of the unanimity principle within the CDU/CSU with respect to leadership changes and changes of major policy. He speaks of the CDU/CSU being composed of religious and economic veto groups where, 'A candidate for leadership or a new policy, in order to be accepted, must not arouse the strong opposition of any one group' (Merkl, 1962, p. 638).

We wish to demonstrate as well that the development of dissatisfaction-reducing methods such as the unanimity principle helps coalitions to endure. The utility of the unanimity requirement to the maintenance of the EEC has already been examined. A parallel is suggested by Secher when he contends that the unanimity improvisation and the *Proporz* system which developed along side of it within the Austrian coalition, has resulted in the continuation of cooperation and finding of compromises to keep the coalition 'a going concern', and that this in turn has helped to reduce conflict between the partners 'that was once high enough to break out into civil war' (Secher, 1958, p. 798).

The broker role

As was the case for the partial exclusion of certain issues and the unanimity requirement, a broker role is also evident in each of the three coalitions. We have seen that the Commission of the EEC generally considered the broker function as one of its most important tasks. In the Austrian grand coalition, it was the president of the Austrian republic who actively played the role of a *pouvoir neutre*. Such a role, as Engelmann suggests, was of considerable utility to the continuation of that coalition (1962, pp. 655, 662). Both Merkl and Neumann demonstrate the central importance of Adenauer's activities as a broker to the continued functioning and perhaps to the maintenance intact of the CDU/CSU:

As in our equilibrium model, this system has called for a leader who is basically uncommitted to any one group. While Adenauer could not help being pronounced a Catholic, a man of business associations, and a former local government official of considerable reputation, he has remained far from becoming the herald of any of these groups. He has bent over backwards to win the confidence of Protestants and to get along with organized labor and the states righters. . . . His role as leader has been mainly that of a moderator or mediator among all the groups (Merkl, 1962, p. 638).

A study of CDU/CSU policy making during Erhard's chancellorship would prove useful with respect to an understanding of the significance of a broker to that coalition. Newspaper reports suggest that Kiesinger was chosen to replace Erhard primarily on the grounds that he would fit into a broker role more successfully than Erhard.

Proliferation of committees within the coalition

The proliferation of EEC advisory committees and the growth of council work groups has been a feature of the EEC to which we referred before. A similar development has occurred in the CDU/CSU. But systematic work to relate this kind of development to the maintenance and functioning of coalitions must still be done.

Leadership authority

Each of the enduring coalitions examined in this essay extends considerable authoritative decision-making powers to the leaders of each group within the coalition. This condition has existed since the inception of the EEC. Although responsible to the national parliaments, council negotiators are generally certain that their decisions will be accepted without modification by those parliaments. There has yet to be a case of any national parliament forcing renegotiation of a council decision. The council members can thus negotiate delicate matters and distribute payoffs with the knowledge that these decisions will not be upset by the introduction of new demands at the postdecision stage. The utility of this situation to productive council work is obvious.

The Austrian coalition has exhibited a similar tendency to centralize authoritative decision making into the heads of each of the partners, because little could be accomplished if the leaders negotiated without the knowledge that their respective parties might not carry out the decisions. Engelmann shows, further, that no important decisions were left to the parliamentarians, acting by free vote, to decide.

Finally, Edinger points out that, 'within the CDU/CSU, the focus of actual decision-making power in recent years has been a small group. This inner elite consisted of twenty-three men' (1961, p. 10). But, in order to parallel the other coalitions, it is still necessary to know the extent to which the CDU/CSU leaders specifically represent what Merkl terms the 'veto groups' within the coalition.

Thus all three coalitions partially excluded certain issues, developed the unanimity principle, and provided for a broker role. In addition, both the EEC and the CDU/CSU experienced a proliferation of committees which substantially increased intra-coalition communication, and both the EEC and the Austrian grand coalition gave substantial authority to leaders of the coalition groups to make bargains. We have seen that these methods have been instrumental in helping each of the coalitions to reach its goal of remaining intact and in working order.

Why is it that the coalitions exhibit many of the same methods to reduce internal conflict and to increase capabilities? The following explanation can be suggested in regard to the three methods which all of the coalitions developed. Given the importance of the maintenance goal, which we have observed to be operative in each of the coalitions, the coalition partners will want to be assured that no decision is reached which might eventually cause one of the partners to withdraw. The most direct means to ensure that members find payoffs at least minimally satisfactory to allow them to remain in coalition is by giving each member a veto power on every important coalition decision. But a problem with this strategy is that, in protecting against major dissatisfactions, it may prove difficult to reach decisions at all. Compromise in these situations is induced, of course, if the members desire to keep the coalition alive. A particularly efficient and powerful way to increase even further the coalition's capacity to induce compromise is through the creation and utilization of a *pouvoir neutre*, a broker role. Thus, when coalition members deeply desire to keep their enterprise intact and func-tioning, *both* the unanimity principle and the creation and utilization of a broker are encouraged – as we have seen in the cases of the EEC, the CDU/CSU, and the Austrian grand coalition.

However, there still may be certain issues over which compromise can hardly be induced. Continued intrusion of these issues could overload and break down the coalition regardless of the capabilities at the coalition's disposal. If coalition maintenance is to be achieved, these issues would have to be prevented as much as possible from impinging on the decision-making process. Thus, we have seen that the historically contentious religious issue has been minimized in the CDU/CSU federal coalition and foreign policy issues, which are always potentially difficult to resolve, have been minimized in the EEC and the Austrian grand coalition.

The impact of feedback

Finally, coalition maintenance can be helped along by feedback. This comes about because actual maintenance of the coalition intact and in working order may itself contribute to the partners' desire to keep the coalition alive in the future. The idea that maintenance, once demonstrated, can reinforce the maintenance goal finds a clear example in the EEC. A number of people initially felt that the EEC would soon break apart. In fact, the establishment of the European Free Trade Association (EFTA) by the British was in part based upon the assumption that the EEC partners could be easily divided. That this did not happen and that the EEC actually outperformed the EFTA, however, has undoubtedly contributed to the confidence the EEC partners have in their enterprise and, in this way, to their continued desire to maintain the coalition. In addition, the EEC leaders could use the success of their endeavour in refuting Communist contentions of the impotence of Western European capitalism, again helping to contribute to the members' desire to keep the coalition going.

Maintenance feedback contributed not only to the EEC members' desire to keep the coalition alive, but also to their ability to reach new agreements. The process of trying to secure unanimity among six partners is a long and arduous task, so that there was often a lag of one or two years between the reaching of agreements of major scope in the EEC. Yet, meanwhile, the confidence which the partners increasingly came to put in the

EEC kept a spirit of optimism alive during the lean years that undoubtedly helped the partners to arrive at new agreements. This appears to have been the case at least in the early and mid-1960s.

Successes were relevant to the continued maintenance and effective operation of the EEC essentially because they fed back to reinforce the high costs of failure. Available evidence indicates that by reinforcing the costs of failure feedback also played a useful role in the continued maintenance and effective operation of both the CDU/CSU and the Austrian grand coalition.

Conclusion

Our study suggests that high costs of dissolution and reduction of conflict among the partners play a central role in coalition maintenance. The experiences of the three enduring coalitions we examined conform to this conclusion. We found in each case that the costs of dissolution facing the partners were substantial even at the inception of the coalition, and remained considerable over time partly as a result of each coalition's successes. In addition, conflict management practices were carefully developed or preserved by each coalition to help the coalition avoid as much as possible the deleterious effects of conflict among its partners. By use of these practices, the partners were able to lessen the degree of conflict among themselves and to increase the coalition's capacity to handle the remaining conflict. The most important practices used by each of the coalitions were the partial prevention of certain highly conflictual issues from impinging upon coalition decision-making (i.e., preventing negative spill-over), the requirement of unanimity on all decisions considered vital, and the promotion of a central broker within the coalition.

These factors appear to have contributed greatly to the endurance of the three coalitions considered in this study. To become more certain of the validity of this conclusion, however, the strength of these factors in enduring coalitions must now be compared to their strength in nonenduring coalitions.

References

DEUTSCH, K., *et al.* (1957), *Political Community in the North Atlantic Area*, Princeton, N. J., Princeton University Press.

EDINGER, L. (1961), 'Community and change in the background of German decision-makers', *Western Political Quarterly*, vol. 14, March, pp. 17–36.

ENGELMAN, F. (1962), 'Haggling for the equilibrium: the renegotiation of the Austrian coalition', *American Political Science Review*, vol. 56, September, pp. 651–62.

LINDBERG, L. (1963), *The Political Dynamics of European Economic Integration*, Stanford, California University Press.

LINDBERG, L. (1966), 'Integration as a source of stress on the European Community system', *International Organization*, Spring, pp. 255–6.

MERKL, P. (1962), 'Equilibrium, structure of interests and leadership: Adenauer's survival as Chancellor', *American Political Science Review*, vol. 56, September, pp. 634–50.

NEUMANN, S. (1956), *Modern Political Parties*, Chicago, University of Chicago Press.

SCHEINMANN, L. (1966), 'Some preliminary notes on bureaucratic relationships in the European Economic Community', *International Organization*, pp. 750–74.

SECHER, H. P. (1958), 'Coalition government: the case of the Austrian Second Republic', *American Political Science Review*, vol. 52, September, pp. 791–808.

13 H. Assael

The Political Role of Trade Associations

H. Assael, 'The political role of trade associations in distributive conflict resolution', *Journal of Marketing*, vol. 32, April 1968, pp. 21–8.

Distributive trade associations have often assumed political means to achieve the economic objectives of their membership. Joseph C. Palamountain recognized the deep commitment of trade associations to political action when he wrote in *The Politics of Distribution*:

> The politics of distribution are indissolubly wedded to its economics. . . . Dissatisfied groups try to better their economic lot by invoking governmental aid, while other groups respond with attempts to block or modify the initial proposals (1955, pp. 1–3).

In analysing their pre-World War II activities in the food, drug, and automobile industries, Palamountain found that trade associations effectively initiated or sponsored governmental action. They created lobbies, pushed through Congressional legislation, used Congressional hearings as forums, represented their views at federal trade practices conferences, and influenced governmental agencies.

It is surprising that the political role of trade associations in resolving conflict has received little attention since Palamountain's study. Perhaps in the more economically placid postwar period, distributive conflicts have not been as intense as in the depression. Political action by trade associations to achieve distributive goals may not have been as urgent a part of association programmes. There is some evidence to support this: The Robinson-Patman Act, the Miller-Tydings Act, and the NRA codes were all products of the depression years and were largely engineered by trade associations.

Yet frequent attempts by trade associations to resolve distributive conflicts by political means warrant a re-examination of the politics of distribution. Accordingly, a comprehensive study was undertaken of the political role of retailer, wholesaler, and manufacturer trade associations in nine industries (Assael, 1967). The study relied on an intensive search of trade publications and Congressional hearings from 1947 to 1965 and interviews with key officials of distributive trade associations. The investigation was limited to the role of national associations in resolving distributive issues of national importance, primarily at the federal level.

Two distinct modes of conflict resolution were analysed: political and self-resolution. Political resolution was defined as activities directed to power sources outside the channel system. Although such activities could extend to appeals to private industry or the consuming public for support, association activities are directed primarily to governmental sources in resolving distributive conflicts.

Self-resolution was defined as trade association activities internal to the channel system. Direct negotiations or bargaining between associations in the labour-management sense are rare. Attempts at self-resolution are characterized by appeals to individual channel members or associations for cooperation, joint study groups and committees, cooperative programmes geared to resolving specific issues, and improved channels of communication. Self-resolution could also take non-cooperative forms as when an association successfully exerts pressure on other channel segments for resolution or on its own members for compliance to directives: for instance, a strong retail association effectively boycotting a manufacturer who refuses to fair trade, or the same association inducing wholesalers to boycott a member-retailer engaged in price-cutting.

Judging from the lack of evidence of coercive forms of self-resolution by distributive associations, such practices either have been rare in the postwar period or have taken place at a covert level.

Postwar distributive conflicts

Specific areas of distributive conflict are summarized by industry in Table 1. Ratings of intensity of conflict were derived from a content analysis of the frequency and intensity of conflict as

Table 1. Postwar distributive conflicts in nine industries[a]

	Drug	Auto-mobile	Petrol-eum	Food	Elec-trical products	Tele-vision receivers	Pesti-cides	Liquor[b]	Farm equip-ment[b]
Bypassing wholesaler	vv	*	vv	vv	v	vv	v	v	v
Bypassing retailer	v	vv	v	x	*	v	v	x	vv
Chain vs. independents	vv	*	*	vv	*	*	*	v	*
Discounters vs. traditionalists	vv	v	v	v	vv	vv	*	vv	x
Private vs. national brands	v	*	vv	vv	*	v	*	vv	*
Fair trade	vv	x	v	x	x	vv	x	vv	x
Retail or wholesale inventory levels	x	vv	vv	v	v	vv	v	x	v
Too many dealers	*	vv	v	*	v	v	v	*	v
Price discrimination or discount structure	v	v	vv	vv	v	v	x	v	v
Promotional allowances	x	v	v	v	x	v	v	x	v
Service and warranty	*	vv	*	*	v	vv	v	*	v
Franchise cancellation	*	v	vv	*	x	x	*	*	v
Pressure to accept parts and accessories	*	v	vv	*	x	x	*	*	v
Manufacture involvement in store management	x	vv	vv	v	v	v	x	x	v
Overall intensity of conflict	vv	vv	vv	vv	v	vv	v	vv	v
Intensity of associations' political activities	vv	vv	vv	v	x	v	x	*	x

[a] vv Signifies intense conflict; v signifies moderate conflict; x signifies little or no conflict; * signifies not applicable to industry.

[b] Areas of conflict do not apply to seventeen states where distribution is state-controlled.

documented in government and trade publications. The measure of intensity of political activity was based on reports of activities either initiated or supported by distributive associations.

In several industries experiencing intense conflict, conflict tended to be sharpest in the post-Korean War buyers' market and lessened after 1960.

The study suggests three characteristic causes of most distributive conflicts: First, manufacturers' requirements to maintain production and cover high fixed costs create pressures on dealers to increase sales volume. The result is friction in the areas of price, retail inventory levels, and discount merchandising. Second, absorption by one party of distributive functions previously held by another has resulted in conflict over manufacturers or retailers bypassing wholesalers, sales by factory-owned retail outlets, and control over local promotions. Third, differing interpretations of the role of the wholesaler or retailer stem from differing economic objectives reflecting the trade status and financial resources of the disputants. This has led to conflicts between manufacturers and retailers concerning the franchise, representational policies, and functional discounts. It has also led to conflicts between discount and 'traditional' retailers.

The disparity in many industries between stabilized production rates and unstabilized consumption rates means an inventory buildup at some phase of distribution. The problem is aggravated in times of short demand by the manufacturer's drive to meet high overhead by sustaining production.

Whether a retailer accepts excessive inventory depends on the breadth of his product line and his relative degree of power. In past years, automobile dealers, service station operators, and TV distributors have accepted surplus from the manufacturer under threat of franchise or lease cancellation.

Pesticide and electrical distributors and food retailers are occasionally subjected to pressures to accept inventory. Yet such pressures are ineffective because of the breadth of their product lines. Lack of dependence limits manufacturers' sanctions.

Conflict over retail price policies is another manifestation of differing economic objectives. Food, drug, and liquor manufacturers seek price stability at the retail level to protect their product image. Such action is resented by discount retailers and endorsed by 'traditional' retailers. In some cases, manufacturers' attempts at price control are only half-hearted. The desire to increase production has led some drug, liquor, and television manufacturers to resist fair trade. In the automobile industry, manufacturers' sales organizations have encouraged intense price competition by sanctioning lower prices in factory-owned outlets and by forcing inventory. In their drive for volume, local sales organizations have sometimes operated contrary to central office directives.

The one problem characteristic of all nine industries is absorption of one distributive segment's function by another. The segment losing ground in most cases was the wholesaler. In the food industry, the aggregation of purchasing power by chains and buying cooperatives has permitted the retailer to assume the wholesale function. In the remaining industries, cost savings may warrant the manufacturer's bypassing the wholesaler. Manufacturers in the television and electrical industries have established factory-owned wholesale outlets because they feel the technical services offered by independent distributors are insufficient.

The level of conflict is a function of the traditional role of the wholesaler. In the food and drug industries, wholesalers are losing accounts, and conflict is intense. In the liquor industry, some manufacturers have historically performed the wholesale function. Manufacturers' performance has had less of an impact on the wholesaler and conflict is less intense.

Absorption of distributive functions has also led to conflict between manufacturers and retailers. In the automobile, farm equipment, and petroleum industries, manufacturers have become increasingly involved in the retail sales function through factory-owned and financed outlets. The automobile and drug industries have also seen an increase in direct sales to fleet and institutional accounts. Dealers view these activities as an infringement on traditional functions.

The problems created by differing views of retail management often create a high intensity of conflict because they are rooted in disparate economic objectives.

In most instances, manufacturers seek to exert managerial controls over dealer or distributor outlets. Dealer dependence on the manufacturer in the automobile, petroleum, and farm equipment industries, and distributor dependence in the television receiver industry invest manufacturers with a degree of power which is potentially coercive. Dependence of small canners and distributors on large chains in the food industry has resulted in pressures for lower prices. Reactions of economically weaker segments have been to group together in buyer or seller co-operatives and powerful trade associations. Conflict over distributor management is less intense in the pesticide and electrical industries because of a lower level of dependence on the manufacturer.

Differing viewpoints regarding channel management are evident in the polarization of discount merchandisers and traditional retailers. This polarization has occurred in the drug, liquor, television, and, to a lesser extent, the automobile and petroleum industries. The resulting conflicts have in many cases been more intense than those between manufacturers and their dealers.

The underlying problem in these distributive conflicts is one inherent to channel management: the basic interdependence between organizations that are nominally independent. This interdependence must result in both cooperation and conflict; cooperation for survival, conflict because of different economic goals and ideological motives. Where such interdependence is combined with an imbalance in power – as in the automobile, petroleum, and television industries – the potential for distributive conflict is high. Given the ability of one party to apply pressure successfully, the probability of friction is higher.

A declining economic position of any segment of the channel system will further stimulate conflict. Organizations performing poorly often attribute performance to forces beyond their control rather than to internal management and frequently blame other channel segments. A retailer may regard a manufacturer's policy as coercive in a period of decline, yet the identical policy may be dismissed as a minor irritant during prosperity.

Political resolution of channel conflict

Table 2 lists the most important distributive trade associations in each industry and major political actions initiated or supported by these associations in the postwar period. Primary emphasis is placed on legislative activities.

Table 2. Selective examples of trade association legislative activities from 1947 to 1965[a]

DRUG INDUSTRY

National Association of Retail Druggists
[b]1. Supported McGuire Amendment to FTC Act. Legalizes non-signers clause in interstate commerce. Passed, 1952.
2. Requested national fair trade legislation since 1950.
3. Sponsored Equality of Opportunity Bill: Would limit use of Good Faith defence in Robinson-Patman Act. Introduced periodically since 1956.
4. Sponsored Medical Restraint of Trade Act, 1965: Would prohibit physicians from making profits on products they prescribe.
5. Opposed Kefauver-Harris Amendment requiring generic labelling. Yet bill passed, 1962.
6. Appealed to FTC to investigate direct manufacturers' sales to institutions.

National Wholesale Druggists Association
Supports strengthening of Robinson-Patman and more specific interpretation of Act's intent to provide recognition of functional discounts.

AUTOMOBILE INDUSTRY

National Automobile Dealers Association
1. Monroney Fair Play Bill, 1956: Would amend the FTC Act making it unfair practice for manufacturer to force cars on dealers, and would require manufacturer to buy back surplus cars and assist in equitable liquidation of cancelled dealership.
[b]2. Good Faith Act (Federal Automobile Franchise Act of 1956): Would enable dealers to bring suit in federal court for double damages on proof of unwarranted franchise cancellation.
3. Frequently sponsored legislation since 1955 to allow manufacturers to insert antibootlegging provisions in franchise.
4. Frequently sponsored legislation since 1955 to legalize territorial security clauses in franchise.
5. Phantom Freight Bill, 1955: Would make it unfair competition to charge a dealer for freight in excess of actual transportation charges. Manufacturers subsequently advised practice is illegal.

6. Asked FTC and Justice Department in 1964 to explore anti-trust implications of direct factory sales. Small Business Administration announced investigations into matter in same year.

PETROLEUM INDUSTRY

National Congress of Petroleum Retailers
1. Broke off from National Oil Jobbers Council in 1947 to support enforcement of Robinson-Patman against refiners.
2. Petitioned FTC since 1947 for fair trade code in marketing of gasoline.
3. Frequent legislation offered since 1955 to limit use of Good Faith defence in cases of price discrimination under Robinson-Patman Act.
4. Supported Harris Fair Trade Bill, 1958: Would establish fair trade on TBA lines.
5. Supported Roosevelt-Magnuson Bill, 1960: Would prohibit Tire-Battery-Accessories override commission.
6. Supported Patman amendment to FTC Act, 1961: Would prohibit sales below cost.
7. Supported Antitrust Vertical Integration Amendment: Would require charging company-owned establishments same price as independents for gasoline.

National Oil Jobbers Council
1. Fought NCPR attempts to strengthen Robinson-Patman. Frequent support of legislation to strengthen Good Faith defence in bill.
2. Sponsored legislation in 1949 to nullify FTC ruling ordering refiners to cease offering discounts to independents.
3. Opposed Harris Fair Trade Bill, 1958.
4. Opposed NCPR attempts to establish fair trade code.

FOOD INDUSTRY

US Wholesale Grocers Association
1. Supported Equality of Opportunity Bill, 1958, limiting Good Faith defence in Robinson-Patman.
2. Supported legislation to facilitate enforcement of Robinson-Patman Act and to increase penalties.
3. Fought legislation in 1959 allowing farm cooperatives to be exempt from Robinson-Patman and antitrust laws.

National Association of Retail Grocers of US
1. Supported Equality of Opportunity Bill, 1958.
2. Proposed curtailment of mergers and elimination of discriminatory practices in 1959 before Congressional Committee studying food distribution.
3. Supported legislation in 1964 to strengthen Robinson-Patman by prohibiting predatory price cutting.
4. Appealed for tighter control of conglomerate mergers before National Commission of Food Marketing in 1965.

National Association of Food Chains
[c]Principally attempts at self-resolution of conflict and defensive political activities.

ELECTRICAL INDUSTRY

National Association of Electrical Distributors
[c]Activities geared solely to self-resolution.

TV RECEIVER INDUSTRY

National Appliance and Radio-TV Dealers Association
1. Support for FTC trade practice rules, 1955.
2. Supported FTC task force to study methods to strengthen Robinson-Patman, 1960.
3. Supported Quality Stabilization Bill, 1964: Would establish fair trade on national basis.

LIQUOR INDUSTRY

National Liquor Stores Association
Has primarily supported state and local retail trade associations in attempts to strengthen state fair trade legislation.

FARM EQUIPMENT INDUSTRY

National Farm and Power Equipment Dealers
[c]Activities oriented to self-resolution.

Farm Equipment Wholesalers Association
Supports strengthening Robinson-Patman and more specific interpretation of Act's intent to provide recognition of functional discounts.

---

[a] The table does not purport to list all legislative activities of distributive trade associations but attempts to list the more important examples.

[b] Of those listed, these were the only two association-supported pieces of legislation to pass.

[c] Examples of self-resolution may be found in Table 3.

National distributive trade associations have actively pursued political action in the drug, automobile, food, petroleum, and television industries. Political resolution has been attempted on a local basis in the liquor industry. The farm equipment, electrical, and pesticide industries have been characterized by a complete absence of political activity. What factors encourage trade associations to rely on political rather than self-resolution?

The more intense the conflict, the more likely the resort to political action. The five industries characterized by political action have experienced intense conflict.

Price discrimination by petroleum refiners may encourage destructive price wars. The intensity of this issue caused petroleum retailers to break away from the National Oil Jobbers Council because of its lack of support of FTC efforts to enforce the Robinson-Patman Act. In 1947, they formed the National Congress of Petroleum Retailers to facilitate support of price stabilization and stricter enforcement of Robinson-Patman.

The ability of large food chains to bypass wholesalers and apply pressure on sellers for functional discounts has caused wholesaler and retailer associations to seek methods to strengthen the Robinson-Patman Act. The National Automobile Dealers Association sought and attained legislation to limit powers of franchise cancellation (the Good Faith Act of 1956) as a reaction to the economic threat of inventory forcing. Drug retailers have fought strong inroads from discount operators by seeking a national fair trade law.

In instances where their membership feels a direct economic threat from a stronger channel segment, national associations have sought remedial political action.

When issues within an industry are common to all members, it is likely that a national trade association will become involved and resort to political action. For example, fair trade was an issue affecting all retail druggists. Most druggists took a uniform position on the issue, providing the National Association of Retail Druggists with a common base of support. This permitted the association to exert sufficient pressure on Congress to pass the McGuire Amendment to the FTC Act. Similarly, the scope of manufacturer forcing in the automobile industry prompted the NADA to seek and attain the Good Faith Act.

The local nature of conflict in the liquor industry limits the need and effectiveness of national action. The lack of any dominant problems common to all electrical and pesticide distributors has led the National Association of Electrical Distributors and the National Agricultural Chemicals Association to take a hands-off attitude regarding the resolution of distributive conflicts.

Associations whose membership represents a significant majority of the trade have been more successful in obtaining governmental support. Only two retail associations have been able to attain significant legislation in the postwar period: the National Association of Retail Druggists and the National Automobile Dealers Association. NARD accounts for 92 per cent of the independent druggists. NADA represents 70 per cent of the franchised dealers. Conversely, the National Appliance and Radio-TV Dealers Association, which favours fair trade but has been ineffective in its support, represents only 20 per cent of the eligible dealers and 10 per cent of the eligible distributors.

The most politically active association, the National Association of Retail Druggists, has been able to form a strong cohesive organization because of similarities among its members in economic status, objectives and background. The National Agricultural Chemicals Association can do little to support particular parties to a distributive conflict, since it represents both manufacturers and distributors. The National Appliance and Radio-TV Dealers Association includes both TV distributors and dealers and must also divide its interests among other product categories. *Without homogeneity, these associations have difficulty adopting commonly accepted policies on controversial issues.* With no concise plan of action, there is little chance of applying political pressure.

The most politically active trade associations are formed by the economically weakest segments in the channel structure. The individual druggist, food grocer, automobile dealer, or service station operator is economically insignificant compared to the manufacturer or large retail chain. Retail trade associations in these industries have been politically active. In the food and farm equipment industries, wholesaler associations have been more active than retailer associations because of a progressively deteriorating economic position. The capacity for group action provided by these associations has given small retailers and wholesalers a degree of countervailing power and a means of asserting common economic objectives.

Group action may also be reflected on a more general level, as when one retail association gains the support of another on an issue of national importance. For instance, the National Association of Retail Druggists has been the main advocate of an Equality of Opportunity Bill which would restrict the Good Faith defence in the Robinson-Patman Act. In its drive for passage, NARD has enlisted the strong support of the United States Wholesale Grocers Association, the National Association of Retail Grocers, and the National Congress of Petroleum Retailers. In this instance, group action has surpassed the individual channel system and reflects the interests of a large segment of small retailers on the national level.

Required differences in the structure of distribution between states have led liquor dealers to rely on local and state associations in seeking price controls. Even here, group action could be undertaken in concert as demonstrated by the unified action of members of the Metropolitan Package Stores Association in fighting repeal of the New York State Alcohol Beverage Law's resale price maintenance provisions.

The balance of power maintained between electrical equipment and pesticide manufacturers and their distributors has resulted in complete reliance on self-resolution of distributive conflicts. The ineffectiveness of direct pressure has caused the parties to seek resolution through joint exploration of grievances on either an individual or a group basis.

A ready forum for the expression of grievances provides an inducement to trade associations to seek political resolution. Federal agencies, Congress, and state legislatures are small-business oriented. This attitude gives associations representative of small retailers an advantage in seeking governmental assistance.

In contrast, associations representing manufacturers and chain stores have found that their political efforts often result in government investigations and the threat of regulation. A reading of Congressional hearings in the automobile, petroleum, and food industries demonstrates that political activities of manufacturer and retail chain associations have been defensive. Their spokesmen have consistently opposed rather than initiated legislation. This explains the acquiescent posture of petroleum refiners, food chains, and automobile and drug manufacturers regarding the application of political power.

Despite Congress' sympathy to small business, it has been extremely reluctant to pass restrictive legislation in distribution. *It is the threat of an appeal to government rather than actual legislation that stimulates stronger channel segments to re-examine distributive policies and seek self-resolution.* Congressional hearings in the automobile and petroleum industries and examination of food distribution by the National Food Commission have evoked such a reaction.

A more effective mode – self-resolution

Despite frequent political activity by certain trade associations, the study demonstrates that *most associations have tended to rely on political action as a last resort.* The National Retail Druggists Association sought to limit physician ownership of pharmacies only after a series of unsuccessful meetings with the American Medical Association over a three-year period. The National Automobile Dealers Association sought to limit franchise cancellations, inventory forcing, and direct factory sales by first directing appeals to the Automobile Manufacturers Association and the individual manufacturers. After these appeals failed, it pursued political action.

Most important is the *overall lack of success in achieving specific legislative gains on the national level since World War II.* The only significant legislative results of trade association activities in the postwar period have been the McGuire Amendment and the Good Faith Bill. And both of these acts have had limited effect in achieving their economic objectives. This is scant tribute to political power. Table 2 is full of failures of trade associations in gaining legislation. The strongest trade association, the National Association of Retail Druggists, has in fact met with a series of legislative defeats since passage of the McGuire Act. It has been unsuccessful in its attempts to obtain a national fair trade law and a law prohibiting physician ownership of pharmacies; it also failed to block the Kefauver-Harris amendment.

In addition, most postwar legislative activities represent attempts to strengthen existing statutes – primarily Robinson-Patman and fair trade – rather than to develop new initiatives.

The most effective impact of the application of political power has been elimination of the need for further political activity. The success of political activity by trade associations is not measured by the passage of legislation but by the influence of such activity in furthering self-resolution. This has been the case in the automobile, petroleum, and food industries. In addition, certain associations rely on self-resolution as matters of policy; for instance, the National Association of Electrical Distributors and the National Oil Jobbers Council.

Table 3 cites instances of attempts at self-resolution of distributive conflict initiated or supported by trade associations. A comparison of Tables 2 and 3 suggests that – with the exception of drugs and petroleum – *distributive trade associations have looked primarily inward to resolve conflicts in the postwar period.* And in the industries characterized by frequent political action, there is current evidence of greater reliance on self-resolution.

Table 3. Selective examples of attempts at self-resolution from 1947 to 1965

DRUG INDUSTRY
1. NARD and Pharmaceutical Manufacturers' Association cooperating to help resolve generic labelling dispute.
2. NARD unsuccessfully sought to resolve question of physician ownership of pharmacies through meetings with American Medical Association.

AUTOMOBILE INDUSTRY
1. NADA unsuccessfully attempted to establish lines of communications with manufacturers to discuss declining dealer profits, inventory forcing and franchise cancellation in mid-1950s. NADA then appealed to Congress.
2. NADA appealed to manufacturers in 1958 to assist it in eliminating bootlegging and crosshauling.
3. The Association appealed to manufacturers in 1958 to reinstate territorial security clauses in the franchise.
4. Successfully sought manufacturers' support in 1958 for uniform delivered and posted prices.
5. NADA met with representatives of the Big Three in 1959 to enlist their aid in combating price cutting and misleading advertising. Manufacturers expressed the intention of backing up NADA's programme.
6. Unsuccessful in 1958 in requesting manufacturers to ensure that dealers receive proper number of vehicles to satisfy sales potential of area.
7. NADA formed Task Force Committee in 1961 to seek joint solution of problems. Committee met with manufacturers and recommendations

in areas of profit opportunity and dealer management were jointly approved. Committee is also studying problems in inventory, representation, and service.

8. Since 1962 the Association, through its industrial Relations Committee, has appealed to manufacturers to review policies concerning factory-owned and financed dealerships and direct sales.

PETROLEUM INDUSTRY

1. NCPR and NOJC have formed liaison committee to programme joint activities on dealer management. Sponsor sessions with refiners to voice complaints.
2. American Petroleum Institute, with NCPR support, has asked its member refiners to inform dealers concerning station management, cost accounting, promotional procedures, and TBA rights.
3. NCPR and API's Service Station Advisory Committee developed a model lease for review in 1961.
4. NCPR established Economic Freedom Council in 1961. Council appealed to refiners to make TBA and leasing arrangements public.

FOOD INDUSTRY

1. Manufacturers have sought to alleviate inventory problems through closer integration of merchandising programmes with customers.
2. Manufacturers have sponsored industry-wide studies concerning problems of pricing, private labelling, and shelf-space allotments.
3. Chains and independents have undertaken joint studies of pricing practices and cost structure.
4. Chains and independents have acted jointly on local basis in appeals to manufacturers to change mark-up and promotional practices. In certain areas, price schedules of manufacturers have been standardized and co-operative advertising allowances liberalized as a result.

ELECTRICAL INDUSTRY

Manufacturers cooperate with NAED in publishing distribution policies concerning mutual obligations, discount structure, pricing policies, inventory requirements, advertising, service, and representational policies. NAED maintains a file of current policies. In this way, communication is insured and misunderstanding avoided. Conflicts can be solved within the framework of stated policy. When the conflict area is not covered, the manufacturer's representative generally has authority to negotiate a compromise solution on an individual basis.

TELEVISION RECEIVER INDUSTRY

1. NARDA has sponsored discussions to encourage more selective franchising by manufacturers. Several manufacturers have cut back on their dealer lists.
2. The Association entered into communications with certain manufacturers in 1961 regarding bypassing of dealers and sales through super-

markets. Sales through supermarkets were withdrawn in 1962 after the manufacturer found the plan to be uneconomical. Yet association activity was most likely a factor.

3. NARDA has worked with manufacturers to develop warranty policies of mutual benefit to both dealers and manufacturers.

4. In response to General Electric's stated intention in 1959 to expand direct manufacturer's service, NARDA increased educational activities regarding servicing through its Service Division. GE's current policy is to permit dealers to do their own servicing when of acceptable calibre.

5. To improve communications with manufacturers, NARDA has invited them to become members and attend meetings and conventions. Twelve major manufacturers are now members.

PESTICIDES INDUSTRY
1. NACA serves as informal mediator between member manufacturers and distributors.
2. NACA's Finance Committee successfully mediated problem of inventory forcing by inducing manufacturers to offer distributors early season discounts in advance of peak demand season.

LIQUOR INDUSTRY
Self-resolution of conflict occurs on a limited basis on the state level only. On the national level, the Distilled Spirits Institute and the National Liquor Stores Association have jointly backed an end to state control of distribution and advertising, and a reduction in the excise tax on liquor.

FARM EQUIPMENT INDUSTRY
1. Communications between dealers and manufacturers have been established through Dealer Councils with the support of the National Farm and Power Equipment Dealers Association. These Councils have been instrumental in resolving problems of inventory control and service and warranty claims.
2. The Farm Equipment Institute has established a dealer Contact Committee in response to requests from NFPEDA.

It is unlikely that the political power of the more active trade associations has decreased since Palamountain's investigation. The threat of invoking political action is still important. Yet in terms of actual solutions, *joint industry action was significantly more successful than political action.* Government itself would seem to prefer self-resolution of distributive conflicts as reflected in the urgings of some federal agencies for more industry efforts at self-regulation.

It is possible that reliance on self-resolution in the postwar years is due to prosperity and a lower intensity of distributive conflict. Yet it is also possible that both manufacturers and their middlemen realize the potentially destructive effects of third-party resolution of distributive conflicts. Distributive trade associations would probably be the first to recognize that *one cannot legislate permanent resolution.* Distributive efficiency must necessarily rely on the establishment of mutually acceptable economic objectives and an acceptance of the legitimacy of divergent functional roles and economic goals. In many industries, mutuality of distributive relations has been attained by distribution management guided by a concept of responsible self-regulation.

Political power should become a viable alternative to self-regulation only when the survival of a functionally significant portion of the channel structure is threatened. Fortunately, this point is rarely reached.

References

ASSAEL, H. (1967), *The Politics of Distributive Trade Associations: A Study in Conflict Resolution*, Hempstead, Long Island, Hofstra University Press.

PALAMOUNTAIN, J. C. (1955), *The Politics of Distribution*, Cambridge, Mass., Harvard University Press.

14 L. M. Dewey

Union Mergers

L. M. Dewey, 'Union merger pace quickens', *Monthly Labor Review*, vol. 94, June 1971, pp. 63–70.

The historic merger of the American Federation of Labor and the Congress of Industrial Organizations in December 1955 was expected to set a precedent for affiliated unions with common jurisdictional interests. In the words of the new constitution, it was to encourage 'the elimination of conflicting and duplicating organizations and jurisdictions though the process of voluntary merger in consultation with the appropriate officials of the Federation. . . .'

Ten years later, George Meany noted that relatively few unions had responded. The AFL–CIO president declared: 'I [do not] suggest that we deviate in any way from the principle that such [merger] action must be entirely voluntary. I do, however, strongly suggest that the responsible officers of many unions, who by all logic and common sense should merge, might well take a broader view of the union as an instrument of progress for working people rather than an institution devoted to its own perpetuation for the sake of sentiment and tradition' (Proceedings . . ., 1965, p. 21).

Despite these calls for altruism, overlapping jurisdictions continued to exist in early 1971 – for example, in the textile, shoe, paper, furniture, and retail trade industries. Only when faced with declining memberships in declining industries did some unions reluctantly decide to merge; the number of mergers involving overlapping jurisdictions had fallen far short of its potential. However, there had been a noticeable acceleration of other mergers, as well as of discussions and cooperative actions that in the past had led to the unification of unions.

Table 1. Chronology of labour union merger activity 1956–71

Year	Merging unions	Membership[a]	Affiliation before AFL–CIO merger
1956	International Association of Cleaning and Dye House Workers (AFL–CIO)	20,000	AFL
	Laundry Workers' International Union (AFL–CIO)	73,200	AFL
	(formed the Laundry, Cleaning and Dye House Workers International Union)		
	Barbers and Beauty Culturists Union of America (AFL–CIO)	5,000	CIO
	Journeymen Barbers, Hairdressers, Cosmetologists and Proprietors International Union of America (AFL–CIO)	85,000	AFL
	International Metal Engravers and Marking Device Workers Union (AFL–CIO)	500	AFL
	International Association of Machinists and Aerospace Workers (AFL–CIO)	864,100	AFL
1957	United Paperworkers of America (AFL–CIO)	50,000	CIO
	International Brotherhood of Paper Makers (AFL–CIO)	72,700	AFL
	(formed the United Papermakers and Paperworkers)		
	Allied Independent Unions (Ind.)	1,000	Ind.
	International Brotherhood of Teamsters, Chauffeurs, Warehousemen and Helpers of America (Ind.)	1,231,000	AFL
1958	United Wallpaper Craftsmen and Workers of North America (AFL–CIO)	1,500	AFL
	International Brotherhood of Pulp, Sulphite and Paper Mill Workers (AFL–CIO)	165,000	AFL

Year	Union	Membership	Affiliation
1959	Insurance Agents International Union (AFL–CIO)	11,000	AFL
	Insurance Workers of America (AFL–CIO)	13,000	CIO
	(formed the Insurance Workers International Union, AFL–CIO)		
	American Wire Weavers Protective Association (AFL–CIO)	400	AFL
	United Papermakers and Paperworkers (AFL–CIO)	130,000	AFL
	International Brotherhood of Longshoremen (AFL–CIO)	30,000	AFL
	International Longshoremen's Association (Ind.)	52,000	AFL
1960	Screen Directors Guild of America, Inc. (Ind.)	200	Ind.
	Radio and TV Directors Guild (AFL–CIO)	800	AFL
	Airline Communications Employees Association (Ind.)	1,800	Ind.
	Communications Workers of America (AFL–CIO)	255,400	CIO
	Friendly Society of Engravers and Sketchmakers (Ind.)	500	Ind.
	Machine Printers Beneficial Association of the United States (Ind.)	1,000	Ind.
	National Agricultural Workers Union (AFL–CIO)	4,500	AFL
	Amalgamated Meat Cutters and Butcher Workmen of North America (AFL–CIO)	325,300	AFL
1961	United National Association of Port Office Craftsmen (Ind.)	38,500	Ind.
	National Federation of Post Office Clerks (AFL–CIO)	100,000	AFL
	(formed the United Federation of Post Office Clerks) (AFL–CIO)		

Year	Merging unions	Membership[a]	Affiliation before AFL–CIO merger
	National Postal Transport Association (AFL–CIO)	25,500	AFL
	United Federation of Post Office Clerks (AFL–CIO)	138,500	AFL
	(formed the United Federation of Postal Clerks) (AFL–CIO)		
	International Glove Workers' Union of America (AFL–CIO)	2,200	CIO
	Amalgamated Clothing Workers of America (AFL–CIO)	377,000	CIO
1962	Laundry, Cleaning and Dye House Workers International Union (Ind.)	65,700	AFL
	International Brotherhood of Teamsters, Chauffeurs, Warehousemen, and Helpers of America (Ind.)	1,484,400	AFL
	International Union of Petroleum Workers Inc. (Ind.)	3,500	Ind.
	Seafarers' International Union of North America (AFL–CIO)	75,000	AFL
	Association of Railway Trainmen and Locomotive Firemen (Ind.)	300	Ind.
	International Association of Railway Employees (Ind.)	500	Ind.
	(formed the Federated Council of the International Association of Railway Employees and Association of Railway Trainmen and Locomotive Firemen (Ind.)		
1964	International Photo-Engravers' Union of North America (AFL–CIO)	17,000	AFL
	Amalgamated Lithographers of America (Ind.)	39,000	CIO
	(formed the Lithographers and Photoengravers International Union (AFL–CIO).		

Year	Union	Number	Affiliation
1965	American Federation of Hosiery Workers (AFL–CIO)[b]	5,000	AFL
	Textile Workers Union of America (AFL–CIO)	183,000	CIO
1966	American Communications Association (Ind.)	7,500	Ind.
	International Brotherhood of Teamsters, Chauffeurs, Warehousemen and Helpers of America (Ind.)	1,651,200	AFL
1967	International Union of Mine, and Smelter Workers (Ind.)	75,000	Ind.
	United Steelworkers of America (AFL–CIO)	1,068,000	CIO
1968	Journeymen Stone Cutters Association of North America (AFL–CIO)	1,900	AFL
	Laborers' International Union of North America (AFL–CIO)	474,500	AFL
	National Association of Post Office Mail Handlers, Watchmen, Messengers and Group Leaders (AFL–CIO)	32,800	AFL
	Laborers' International Union of North America (AFL–CIO)	474,500	AFL
	United Packinghouse, Food and Allied Workers (AFL–CIO)	135,000	CIO
	Amalgamated Meat Cutters and Butcher Workmen of North America (AFL–CIO)	353,100	AFL
1969	Federal Tobacco Inspectors Mutual Association (Ind.)	400	Ind.
	National Federation of Federal Employees (Ind.)	95,000	Ind.
	Switchmen's Union of North America (AFL–CIO)	11,300	AFL
	Order of Railway Conductors and Brakemen (Ind.)	18,800	Ind.
	Brotherhood of Locomotive Firemen and Enginemen (AFL–CIO)	39,600	Ind.
	Brotherhood of Railroad Trainmen (AFL–CIO) (formed the United Transportation Union, AFL–CIO)	185,000	Ind.

Year	Merging unions	Membership[a]	Affiliation before AFL–CIO merger
	Railway Patrolmen's International Union (AFL–CIO)	2,500	AFL
	Brotherhood of Railway, Airline and Steamship Clerks, Freight Handlers, Express and Station Employees (AFL–CIO)	270,000	AFL
	Transportation – Communication Employees Union (AFL–CIO)	44,600	AFL
	Brotherhood of Railway, Airline and Steamship Clerks, Freight Handlers, Express and Station Employees (AFL–CIO)	270,000	AFL
	United Weldors International Union (Ind.)	1,900	Ind.
	International Union of Operating Engineers (AFL–CIO)	330,000	AFL
	Railroad Yardmasters of North America (Ind.)	1,900	Ind.
	Railroad Yardmasters of America (AFL–CIO)	4,000	AFL
	Bakery and Confectionery Workers International Union of America (Ind.)[e]	61,000	AFL
	American Bakery and Confectionery Workers' International Union (AFL–CIO)	83,000	([d])
1970	Federated Council of the International Association of Railway Employees and Association of Railway Trainmen and Locomotive Firemen (Ind.)	375	Ind.
	United Transportation Union (AFL–CIO)	262,600	Ind.
1971	United Stone and Allied Products Workers of America (AFL–CIO)	11,100	CIO
	United Steelworkers of America (AFL–CIO)	1,120,000	CIO

United Federation of Postal Clerks (AFL–CIO)	166,000	AFL
National Postal Union (Ind.)	80,000	[e]
National Association of Post Office and General Services Maintenance Employees (AFL–CIO)	13,175	Ind.
National Federation of Post Office Motor Vehicle Employees (AFL–CIO)	8,000	Ind.
The National Association of Special Delivery Messengers (AFL–CIO) (formed the American Postal Workers Union, AFL–CIO)	2,605	AFL

[a] Membership as reported prior to merger.
[b] Formerly part of the Textile Workers.
[c] Merger between Bakery and Confectionery Workers International Union of America (Ind.) and the Teamsters has not been included because of short duration of the alliance.

[d] Formed in 1957.
[e] Formed in 1959.

Anatomy of amalgamation

From the time of the AFL–CIO consolidation until February 1971, 36 mergers involving 77 unions (including those unions involved in two or more mergers) had been recorded (see Tables 1 and 2). Of the total, 20 involved amalgamations between unions affiliated with either the former AFL or the CIO. Thirteen involving 31 unions had occurred since 1967, when the subject was last examined in the *Monthly Labor Review*. Thus, more than one-third of all mergers were consummated in the last three years. Since 1956, there had been seven mergers between AFL and the

Table 2. Affiliation of unions merging prior to and after AFL–CIO merger

Affiliation	Prior affiliation	
	Total of mergers (1956–71[a])	Mergers since 1967
AFL and AFL	12	4
AFL and CIO	7	1
AFL and Independent	8	3
CIO and CIO	1	1
CIO and Independent	2	–
Independent and Independent	4	2
Other[b]	2	2
Total	36	13
	Subsequent affiliation[c]	
AFL–CIO and AFL–CIO	17	6
AFL–CIO and Independent	13	6
Independent and Independent	6	1
Total	36	13

[a] Through 31 March 1971.

[b] The Bakery and Confectionery Workers' International Union of America had been an AFL affiliate, and the American Bakery and Confectionary Workers' International Union was not established until 1957. The National Postal Union (Ind.), one of the five postal unions involved in formation of the American Postal Workers' Union, was organized in 1959 by dissident members of the Postal Clerks.

[c] Affiliation at the time the international Unions merged. As a result of changes in affiliation subsequent to 1956, affiliation totals differ from those shown above.

CIO unions, but only one since 1967. Mergers between former AFL unions had accounted for one-third of all mergers since 1956 and 31 per cent since 1967. Alliances between former AFL and independent unions had accounted for one-fifth of all mergers since 1956, and slightly less than one-fourth of the total since 1967.

Of the 77 unions participating in mergers, 52 were affiliated with the AFL–CIO; the remaining 25 were independent. These ranged in size from several with less than 1,000 members to the largest union, the Teamsters, with 1·8 million members (see Table 3).

Table 3. **Distribution of national and international unions by number of members at the time of merger**

Number of members reported at time of merger	All unions[a]	
	Number	Per cent
All unions	69	100·0
Under 1,000	9	13·0
1,000 and under 5,000	13	18·8
5,000 and under 10,000	4	5·8
10,000 and under 25,000	8	11·7
25,000 and under 50,000	7	10·1
50,000 and under 100,000	12	17·4
100,000 and under 200,000	6	8·8
200,000 and under 300,000	3	4·3
300,000 and under 400,000	3	4·3
400,000 and under 500,000	1	1·4
500,000 and under 1,000,000	1	1·4
1,000,000 and over	2	3·0

[a] Unions participating in more than one merger have been included only once.

A delicate process

The merging of organizations, regardless of their function, requires lengthy and delicate negotiations. Labour unions are no exception, and where efforts to merge were successful they frequently required individual sacrifices for the good of the organization. Many merger efforts failed, and some mergers that appeared inevitable had not been seriously attempted. In some instances, intense rivalry over the years ruled out any attempt to reach an accord. Because negotiations of this nature are not conducted in a public forum, it is difficult to isolate the roadblocks to success.

It is, however, generally agreed that the strong personality required of a successful union president is often a major deterrent. Aside from the personal attributes of the leadership, differences in union structures, including the degree of local or district autonomy, methods of electing officers, and constitutional procedures often require considerable accommodation. In addition, membership pride and loyalty to the union, as well as fear that craft specialization would not be adequately represented, are thought to thwart some consolidations.

While the roadblocks that were responsible for the relatively low rate of amalgamation in the decade after 1955 continued, participants in recent merger discussions cited factors that work toward amalgamation and apparently are becoming increasingly important. Many are directly related to the economics of our time. These include the increasing cost of maintaining a union headquarters and staff. This burden is particularly acute for small, and even medium-sized, unions that are expected to provide the same extensive array of services as larger unions – organizing, negotiation guidance and arbitration assistance, research and education programmes, strike benefits, and lobbying efforts.

Unions in a declining industry are expected to provide all or most of these services, though faced with losses in revenue because of reduced membership. In such cases, the union may have to choose between a cutback in services or an increase in dues, a difficult choice indeed. For unions in industries that have turned to automated techniques, for example, the printing industry, the problems of drastically changed job content threaten traditional craft skills and boundary lines. In other instances, unions are confronted with the need to respond to extensive corporate reorganizations or restructuring in the form of mergers or acquisitions by 'conglomerates'.

To accommodate to these changes, unions may choose a number of alternatives. As a stop-gap measure to deal with declining revenue, unions have increased their dues, although often over their memberships' initial opposition. In recent years, unions have joined forces to lobby on legislative issues of mutual concern and coordinated collective bargaining techniques. In some instances, these cooperative programmes are viewed as substitute measures for organic merger, while in other instances participation in these joint efforts develops a mutual trust, thus paving the way for unity.

The railroad industry

The economic plight of the railroad industry and its impact on employment and union membership have been discussed extensively in the public press and technical journals. In summary, employment, and with it union membership, has been declining over the years as a result of changes in railroad operations and the increasing use of other modes of transportation by travellers and freight shippers. Following the pattern of mergers among major railroad carriers, railroad unions have taken the same route in an effort to trim operating expenses. Since 1967, eight unions with membership predominantly or exclusively in the railroad industry have merged while only two had merged between 1955 and 1967. The 19 railroad unions existing in 1956 had dwindled to 11 by early 1971.

In a historical move, four railway operating unions, representing 221,000 workers and 42,000 retirees, formed the United Transportation Union on 1 January 1969. The four were the Brotherhood of Locomotive Firemen and Enginemen, the Brotherhood of Railroad Trainmen, the Switchmen's Union of North America, and the Order of Railway Conductors and Brakemen (Ind.). Leaders of the unions attributed the merger to the financial drain and staff time required to settle jurisdictional conflicts, the economic savings resulting from fewer offices and a consolidated staff, and the benefits derived from integrated committees, boards and locals. In recognition of the union's importance within the Federation, Charles Luna, president of the new organization and former president of the largest of the four unions, was elected to the expanded Executive Council of the AFL–CIO in 1969. Officials indicated the new organization would attempt to expand through further mergers with other unions in transportation, including those with members in bus and airline operations. On 1 September 1970, the predominantly black 375-member Federated Council of the International Association of Railway Employees and Association of Railway Trainmen and Locomotive Firemen (Ind.), a product of a 1962 unification, became the new union's first merger partner.

For reasons that prompted the formation of the Transportation Union, two railroad unions joined the Brotherhood of Railway, Airline and Steamship Clerks, Freight Handlers, Express and Station Employees, raising the Clerks' membership to almost one-third of a million. On 1 January 1969, the 2,500-member Railway Patrolmen's International Union became an autonomous section in the Brotherhood's Allied Service Division, with a guarantee that its craft would be continued by separate agreements and that distinct seniority and promotional rights for its members would be maintained. With this arrangement, the Patrolmen's organization was to maintain its identity and, in addition, gain the advantages that flow from being part of a large organization.

On 20 February 1969, the 45,000-member Transportation-Communication Employees Union, formerly the Railroad Telegraphers Union, became a division of the Brotherhood. The Transportation union's drive to find a merger partner dates from 1967 when its officers were directed by convention delegates to seek consolidation with other transportation unions. In assessing the merger, the participants noted the added strength that would be gained at the bargaining table.

Unification of the Railroad Yardmasters of North America (Ind.) and its counterpart, the Railroad Yardmasters of America (AFL–CIO), on 1 July 1969 climaxed a long process of negotiations. With identical jurisdiction, the two unions sought to provide a strengthened organization and improved representation. The surviving union, still limited to a single occupation, represents all of the Nation's 5,000 yardmasters.

The recent merger trend in the railroad industry recalls the efforts of Eugene V. Debs, who in 1880 formed the American Railway Union with the objective of uniting all railroad workers regardless of craft. Although hope of achieving this goal was aborted by the Pullman strike, almost a century later the railroad unions appear to be moving towards a modified industrywide organization.

Food processing

Two mergers in the food industry – in meatpacking and in bakery and confectionery products – culminated efforts to eliminate intense rivalries and strengthen bargaining and organizing activities.

In meatpacking, the United Packinghouse, Food and Allied Workers (AFL–CIO) merged with the Amalgamated Meat Cutters and Butcher Workmen of North America (AFL–CIO) in July 1968, after intermittent periods of competition and cooperation dating back to the Packinghouse union's formation in 1937 as an organizing committee.

Sharp changes in the composition of the industry and its operations influenced the decision to join forces. An increasing share of the market had been captured by relatively new, small nonunion producers; major meatpacking companies decided to decrease the size of their production units and to decentralize operations into rural areas; several had become merger targets of conglomerates.

While the membership of the Packinghouse Workers had declined from 150,000 in 1956 to 135,000 at the time of the merger in 1968, the Meat Cutters, because of their foothold in food stores, had grown from 310,000 to 353,000 during the same period. Despite the growth of the latter, there was speculation that food chains would centralize meatcutting operations, thereby threatening jobs of butchers in retail stores.

In February 1971, officials of the Meat Cutters and the 500,000-member Retail Clerks International Association appointed committees to pursue merger discussions on a formal basis. Both unions negotiate for employees of retail stores.

After the 160,000-member Bakery and Confectionery Workers International Union was expelled by the AFL–CIO in 1957 for failing to correct corrupt practices, the Federation established a rival bakery union. The American Bakery and Confectionery Workers' International Union (AFL–CIO) soon surpassed the ousted union's membership, primarily because locals of the independent transferred to the new union. Merger talks had been conducted over a period of years and appeared close to consummation when the independent bakery union, in a surprise move, entered into an alliance with the International Brotherhood of Teamsters (Ind.) in April 1968. Some observers saw this as a tactic to liberalize the merger terms offered by the ABCW. By mutual agreement, ties with the Teamsters were terminated in late 1969, thereby enabling the bakery unions to merge in December. Membership of both totaled 150,000 or 10,000 less than at the times of expulsion and reflected, in part, the dissipation of worker loyalty resulting from rivalry.

Postal system

During 1970, Congress reorganized the postal system as a quasi-government organization. Under the Postal Reform Act, postal unions bargain directly with the new organization rather than attempt to obtain higher wages and improved benefits through Federal legislation. Seven postal unions were cooperating in collective bargaining negotiations through the Council of American Postal Employees and had agreed to be represented by one spokesman.

Delegates to 1970 postal conventions discussed the concept of 'One Big Union', although reservations were expressed concerning craft identity. In February 1971, the presidents of one independent and four AFL–CIO postal unions agreed to merge their organizations into a single unit. The five unions, with a combined membership of close to 300,000, were the United Federation of Postal Clerks, National Association of Post Office and General Services Maintenance Employees, National Federation of Post Office Motor Vehicle Employees, National Association of Special Delivery Messengers, and the National Postal Union (Ind.), the largest unaffiliated postal union.

The new organization, the American Postal Workers Union (AFL–CIO), would be organized as an industrial union with craft departments specializing in the problems of the former organizations. Under the merger terms, none of the five union presidents would be required to relinquish his title, and the head of the new union would be called a 'general president'. Other terms include a uniform *per capita* tax for local unions, election of officers by a membership referendum, and convention voting based on the membership strength of each local. The merger agreement would serve as the constitution of the new union. Its first convention would be in August 1972, with each craft department holding a one-day convention immediately prior to the general session.

Leaders of the five unions were also conducting merger talks with the 210,000-member National Association of Letter Carriers, the largest union in the postal system. The Letter Carriers were also reported to be considering alignment with the Teamsters.

Professional groups affiliate

In addition to mergers at the national level, a number of independent professional associations joined with national unions to gain added strength. Several professional groups outside the maritime industry recently joined the Marine Engineers Beneficial Association. Among these were the 7,000-member Professional Air Traffic Controllers Organization, the California Association of Professional Employees representing 3,700 workers of the city and county of Los Angeles, the 1,700-member Employees' Association of the Seattle-First National Bank, the Engineers and Scientists of California, with 1,140 members, and other smaller groups of engineers and scientists.

Similarly, the National Maritime Union expanded outside its historical representation of seamen. Early in 1970, the American Association of Securities Representatives, with some 5,000 members in brokerage firms throughout the United States, joined the Maritime Union. The decline of the stock market, coupled with brokers' back office problems, resulted in commission cuts and consolidations and was cited as the reason for merging. In March 1971, the 30,000-member Los Angeles Employees Association, an independent organization for 60 years, affiliated with the Service Employees International Union, whose 400,000 members include a sizeable number of State and local government employees.

Prospective mergers

At the turn of the century, the International Typographical Union represented all organized workers in the printing industry. However, as members of a single organization, the crafts felt their interests were not properly represented and formed separate unions. Then, as a result of the industry's changing technology, the unions re-evaluated their positions and concluded that representation for separate crafts may be obsolete.

As a result, the International Stereotypers' and the Electrotypers' Union of North America and the International Typographical Union voted at their 1969 and 1970 conventions, respectively, to merge with the International Printing Pressmen. The merger, if ratified by the membership, would result in a 260,000-member union, representing over 60 per cent of all union members in the printing and publications industry.

The International Brotherhood of Bookbinders were holding merger talks with the Lithographers and Photoengravers International Union, itself a product of 1964 merger, that would result in a union representing 120,000 members. The merger was expected to be completed by Labour Day 1972. A 71-year-old union of bank note and securities engravers, the International Association of Siderographers, with its membership down to 25, indicated it may join the Machine Printers, Die Stampers and Engravers, a union of 425 members.

In March 1971, the International Longshoremen's Association and the International Organization of Masters, Mates, and Pilots met and agreed in principle to merge, citing reduced employment resulting from technological changes. Under the agreement, the 11,000-member Masters Union would become a division of the 50,000-member Longshoremen's Association.

The Air Line Dispatchers Association, with 940 members, was seeking affiliation with a larger AFL–CIO union. Contributing factors included pressure from members who sought to disaffiliate, airline resistance to bargaining efforts in the face of declining profits, and the Federal Aviation Administration's proposal to reduce qualifications and training requirements. Delegates polled in early 1971 on possible merger partners voted for the International Association of Machinists and Aerospace Workers over five other unions. The decision was subject to ratification by the membership.

At the September 1970 convention of the 160,000-member Bricklayers, Masons and Plasterers' International Union of America, delegates endorsed a resolution instructing their leaders to explore merger talks with the Operative Plasterers and Cement

Masons International Association of the United States and Canada, representing 68,000 members. The reasons given for such a merger included overlapping jurisdictional lines, possible lower membership dues, and improved services to the membership by hiring full-time business agents. A month later, delegates to the convention of the United Brotherhood of Carpenters and Joiners of America passed a resolution urging the General Executive Board to negotiate a merger agreement with the Wood, Wire and Metal Lathers International Union, representing members in a similar jurisdiction. The Carpenters, the largest construction union, representing 800,000 workers, and the Lathers, with 16,000 members, had drawn their craft demarcation lines between wood and metal; however, the narrowly defined boundaries often resulted in work allocation disputes.

Any merger agreement reached would provide that all Lathers would assume full rights and benefits equal to length of membership. The alliance would represent a breakthrough in construction trades, where traditional craft lines have been closely guarded, although recent evidence suggests an increasing willingness to lower jurisdictional barriers.

Reference

Proceedings of the Sixth Constitutional Convention of the AFL–CIO,
  9 December 1965.

Part Three
Research on Interorganizational Relations: Types of Networks

In the three research reports comprising Part Three, I would like to draw the reader's attention to different types of interorganizational networks arising from diverse linkages among organizations. In Turk's study we observe the operation of different types of serial or chain-like interorganizational networks. The most complex networks involve several federal agencies, coordinated by the US Office of Economic Opportunity, contracting for anti-poverty programmes with a Community Action Agency – a federation of local community organizations – which, in turn, sponsors the activities of Neighbourhood Youth Corps. In the report by Wiatr we observe a triangular or a quadrilateral network of political parties, interest groups, and the Polish government. And in the last report by Perrucci and Pilisuk we see an approximation to an all-channel network linking interorganizational leaders in a resource network.

Is there a relationship between formal properties of interorganizational networks and types of interorganizational interactions? An analysis of empirical studies of interorganizational relations may well reveal a relationship between formal network properties and types of interorganizational linkages (Evan, 1972, pp. 185–8).

Reference

EVAN, W. M. (1972), 'An organization-set model of interorganizational relations', in M. F. Tuite, M. Radnor and R. K. Chisholm (eds.), *Interorganizational Decision Making*, Chicago, Aldine-Atherton Publishing Co., pp. 181–200.

15 H. Turk

Interorganizational Networks in Urban Society

H. Turk, 'Interorganizational networks in urban society: initial
perspectives and comparative research', *American Sociological Review*,
vol. 35, February 1970, pp. 1–19.

The following report describes a controlled, longitudinal study
at the interorganizational level of analysis, which emphasizes
prediction on the basis of broad assumptions about interorganizational phenomena. The pre-existing organizational characteristics
of the 130 largest American cities were employed to predict
relative levels of interorganizational *activity* in the Federal War
on Poverty and *complexity* within the interorganizational networks that served it.

Recently, sociologists (Levine and White, 1961; Litwak and
Hylton, 1962; Levine *et al.*, 1963; Warren, 1967; Turk, 1969)
have used such familiar concepts as consensus, conflict, exchange,
differentiation, and integration to refer to interorganizational
relations within broad settings. These same concepts may be used
to describe the setting itself in interorganizational terms.

Integration and the specific frame of reference

The present study defines social integration in organizational
terms and provides a test of its ability to predict new interorganizational activities and the complexity of certain networks
within which these activities took place.

Interorganizational consequences of integration. The greater
the integration of a social setting, the greater is its capacity *either*
to support *or* to resist new interorganizational activities and
arrangements. This proposition has been suggested by a discussion of the effects of 'richness' within a social setting in either
providing facilities conducive to the establishment of organizations or constituting means of resisting their encroachment
(Stinchcombe, 1965). Solidarity among organizations and interorganizational networks within the setting could provide the

resources, predictability, and imperative control for new inter-organizational networks. But such solidarity could just as readily provide the basis of a united front against interorganizational emergence or colonization. Thus the direction of the causal connection between prior organizational integration and new networks of organizations will be considered an empirical question until conditions may be specified under which integration leads to either support or resistance.

Local and extralocal integration. A polarity between community and large-scale (mass) society has been suggested by Warren (1956), Vidich and Bensman (1958), Stein (1960), Mott (1965; pp. 165–84), Walton (1968), and others. Gains in the integration of the community are at the expense of integration in mass society and vice versa. This is consonant with the more general idea of an inverse relationship between the solidarity of a social system and that of its subsystems (Riecken and Homans, 1954; Gouldner, 1959; Turk and Lefcowitz, 1962; Starbuck, 1965). From this standpoint one would expect the interorganizational patterns which indicate *local integration* within a regional entity to be negative correlates of the external organizational linkages that determine the level of its *extralocal integration.* However, much of the evidence has been anecdotal and phrased in terms of modalities among individual actors. At the interorganizational level one could also consider the reverse; namely, either mode of integration might provide organizational *facilities* which are required by the other mode, the result being a positive correlation between the two integrative levels.

Comparative urban studies have not always drawn the local-extralocal distinction, largely for want of appropriate data. Those which have concerned themselves with nationwide phenomena such as urban renewal (for example, Hawley, 1963, and T. Clark, 1968) restricted themselves mainly to the role of local integration in pursuing goals whose origin is extralocal in part. It may also be observed that some statistical data may indicate either or both types of integration; for example, export activities may refer to a city's solidarity through the division of labour or to its self-sufficiency and adaptive ability *vis-à-vis* the environment (Duncan and Riess, 1950; Nelson, 1955). They can just as easily refer, however, to its fragmentation and loss of self-determination, since enterprises that operate at the national level may have little or no reason to establish many relations with one another at the local level or with local organizations.

Since the direction of association between local and extralocal integration is not clear at the interorganizational level of analysis, the effects of each form of integration upon new interorganizational phenomena will be described independently.

The demand for new interorganizational phenomena. Although emphasis has been placed upon the effects of organizational integration upon activity levels and complexity within new interorganizational networks, another independent variable merits consideration. Whether expressed directly in some form of mass appeal or – as the present frame of reference would have it – through certain organizational channels, the question of the *demand* for new interorganizational phenomena cannot be avoided. Without at least some demand for them, there will be *no* interorganizational networks either to be facilitated or to be resisted by different levels of local and extralocal integration. Thus the effects of organizational integration will first be described independently of the effects of demand.

Research objectives and hypotheses

The level of a local unit's *extralocal* integration was defined as (1) the number of organizational linkages with the broader society. The level of its *local* integration was defined as (2) the occurrence of community-wide, nongovernmental organizations with coordinative potential and (3) the amount of control exercised by its governmental organization. These variables were used to predict (1) the *activity level* of a new kind of relational network composed of local organizations as well as nonlocally based organizations of a broader society and (2) complexity within a portion of this network. The nature of this network required that *demand* be assessed in terms of the availability of potential clients. The following hypotheses were tested with cities as the local units and federal agencies as the organizational units of the broader society.

(1) *The activity level* of a new interorganizational network having both local elements and externally based societal components is

a function of (a) the pre-existing number of organizational linkages between the local unit and the broader society, (b) prior occurrence of nongovernmental organizations which can coordinate the local unit, and (c) the amount of control exercised by local government.

(2) The establishment of a *complex* interorganizational network having both local elements and externally based societal components is a function of (a) the pre-existing number of organizational linkages between the local unit and the broader society, (b) prior occurrence of nongovernmental organizations which can coordinate the local unit, and (c) the amount of control exercised by local government.

The *directions* of these hypothesized relationships eluded prediction for reasons already given under the specific frame of reference. Although not formulated as an hypothesis, the direction of whatever effect *demand* might have had was assumed to be positive.

Research design

Investigation centred upon the local and extralocal linkages of the 130 incorporated cities in the United States which had 1960 populations of more than 100,000 inhabitants. Each city constituted a separate unit of analysis.

Extralocal integration. The national headquarters of voluntary associations provided a 1960 measure of extralocal integration. Using 21 categories, which ranged from business and health associations through religious and patriotic, the *Encyclopedia of Associations* (1961) listed the number of such headquarters in each of the study cities. Face validity may be claimed, for the number of networks which converge upon one place is just another way of referring to its societal integration – i.e., the external connections of that place. It should also be observed that most of the listed associations represented the interests of a large number of specific organizations or of major role-categories within them. Thus, such an association often reflected what is nationally held in common along certain specialized lines, and the presence of its headquarters within a given city should also signify the *institutional* integration of that city into the broader sociocultural setting.

The older and larger cities were expected to be the ones most intimately and elaborately interwoven with the broader society; and the expectation is borne out by correlations of ·71 and ·69 between the number of national headquarters and size and age respectively. That banking activity may be taken as another indicator of extralocal linkages (i.e., of the city's economic dominance) is borne out by its correlation of ·53 with number of headquarters.

Cities were also ranked according to the number of establishments within each business category which might have an export emphasis – i.e., serve nonresident persons and nonlocal organizations. These data were used to construct an index of the diversity of export ties, which varied directly as the degree of similarity among a city's rankings. That export diversity was associated with the mean of all ranks ($r = $ ·44) implies that the more diversified a city, the larger the *absolute number* of export establishments, whatever their type.

As expected, the number of national headquarters proved to be correlated with the diversity of export establishments ($r = $ ·49). By way of control and also as expected, a similarly constructed index of diversity among maintenance (i.e., nonexport) establishments proved to be weakly correlated ($r = $ ·18) with the headquarters measure. Finally, industrialization, a variable which might confound various organizational measures, was virtually unrelated to this extralocal headquarters index ($r = $ ·12).

The high correlations of the national headquarters measure with size, age of city, banking activity, centrality ratings, and export diversity were virtually unaltered when they were computed separately for each of the five geographic regions. Thus, both the nature of the national headquarters index as well as its uniform correlations with the criterion variables attest to its validity as a measure of extralocal integration.

Local integration. Two organizational indices were used to assess local integration: (1) community-wide voluntary associations were taken to signify the presence of mechanisms for concerted action as well as the absence of highly organized cleavages within the city as of early 1961; (2) 1960 municipal revenue was taken as a measure of integration in terms of control exercised by the city's government over the community's affairs.

Interorganizational activity level. The Economic Opportunity Act (1964) and its amendments inauguarated the interorganizational relations described in the following discussion. It authorized several federal agencies coordinated by the US Office of Economic Opportunity to encourage, negotiate and enter into contractual relations with, and fund the anti-poverty efforts of local organizations or local federations. At least until the cut-off date of 1 April 1966, the *per capita number of poverty dollars* which flowed into a city constituted an excellent index of the activity level of a new network of federal and local organizations within each city.

The generalizability of this index – at least as far as other federal programmes are concerned – is suggested by moderate correlation between *per capita* poverty funding and two programmes of the Department of Housing and Urban Development. The 1959 urban renewal status of cities of this study had been classified as inactive, project planning, contract executed, and project completed (US Housing and Home Finance Agency, 1960). Correlation between this four-point ordinal scale based on 1959 data and *per capita* poverty funding in 1966 is ·30. Another variable, whether or not the city was one of 42 in this study that were part of the first wave of announced Model Cities (*Los Angeles Times*, 17 November 1967), yielded a correlation of ·40 with *per capita* poverty funding.

Interorganizational complexity. That part of the poverty programme called the Neighborhood Youth Corps (NYC) permitted *controlled* inquiry into the occurrence of certain kinds of complex anti-poverty networks. Local organizations or local federations funded to sponsor such projects undertook to provide training, work experience, counselling and placement for disadvantaged youth and young adults. In certain cases this meant that the local sponsor had to seek other organizations as loci of work or training. The American values of self-help, education, and the rights of youth, which these projects symbolized, probably made this component of the War on Poverty even less vulnerable to open public resistance than the rest of the programme.

More important, however, was the occurrence of simple and

complex variants among the interorganizational networks of NYC sponsors and their granting agencies. In one such kind of system, the projects involved the national headquarters and regional offices of both the US Department of Labor, which funded all NYC projects, and the US Office of Economic Opportunity, which funded newly established community organizations called Community Action Agencies. A Community Action Agency was itself an interorganizational system, a federation, since its board consisted of major functionaries from various organized sectors of the community (for example, the mayor or his representative, the school superintendent or a member of his staff, labour union officials, officials of the Catholic Archdiocese, and representatives of various civic groups and associations of businessmen). Sponsorship by a Community Action Agency of one or more of the NYC projects within a given city meant a *complex* interorganizational network. By way of contrast, the *elementary* alternative was sponsorship of NYC projects by one or more autonomous or semi-autonomous organizations having far less broadly-based structures than those of the federative Community Action Agency. Requiring funding by only one federal agency (the Department of Labor), and most often already in existence before the War on Poverty, this less complex form of sponsorship included such organizations as nonprofit welfare agencies, school systems, church groups, labour unions, and municipal departments.

The 130 cities could thus be classified into those served by *complex interorganizational networks* on 6 June 1966 (29 with at least one NYC project sponsored by a Community Action Agency), those served by *elementary interorganizational networks* (43 with NYC projects, none of which were sponsored by a Community Action Agency), and those *without any interorganizational network* of the kind in question (58 with no Neighborhood Youth Corps projects). This scheme yielded two dichotomous (dummy) measures: (1) whether or not the city was served by a complex network and (2) whether or not it was served by an elementary network. The first of these was used as a major dependent variable, the second only for purposes of providing a control condition which was virtually identical in content but different along the key dimension of network complexity.

Demand for the interorganizational network. Demand for these anti-poverty networks was measured by the number of potential clients (rate of *deprivation*) because that number was likely to have effects upon (1) rates of simple petition by the needy, (2) the invocation of War on Poverty norms within the community or by the Federal Government, (3) attempts to avoid depletion of local welfare resources, (4) perception of a ready clientele by initiators of new programmes. Poverty rates, proportion of nonwhite, and proportion of youth out of school were used as indicators of demand.

Results and discussion

Interorganizational activity. All 28 of the independent and control measures were used in a stepwise analysis that permitted any one of them to enter and remain in the regression equation, provided that its partial correlation with interorganizational activity was significant at the ·20 level; the ·20 criterion made it unlikely that an eventually important variable would be overlooked. However, only those standardized partial regression coefficients (*betas*) which reached the ·10 significance level are reported. Spuriousness was minimized by establishing a second regression equation with *all 29 indices*, in order to make certain that all variables making an appreciable contribution in the shorter equation continued to do so in the longer one. The first two columns of Table 1 describe the outcome of these analyses.

Two of the three organizational indicators of integration supported the first hypothesis. The city's extralocal linkages, measured by the number of national headquarters within it, proved to be positively and independently associated with the dollar measure of interorganizational activity in the federal poverty programme; so was the integrative potential of city government, measured by municipal revenue. Contribution by the 1960 Democratic vote probably signified ideological commitment to the War on Poverty, which became manifest in the level of interorganizational activity. Whether the negative effect of socioeconomic status rested upon ideological grounds or whether it signified the absence of organizational channels to the poor cannot be resolved with the data at hand; it should be noted, however, that low education, *not deprivation*, predicted activity level within the anti-poverty network.

Occurrence of complex networks. Two regression analyses tested the second major hypothesis. Techniques and criteria were identical to those just described, except that the prediction measures included level of interorganizational activity in the overall poverty programme and therefore numbered 29. The third and fourth columns of Table 1 show the effects of these measures upon the presence or absence of a complex inter-organizational network which included two federal departments and federation sponsorship of an NYC project. That a complex network rather than programme content had been predicted was assessed by using these same 29 measures to predict the presence or absence of a more elementary NYC network (see the fifth and sixth columns of Table 1) consisting of one federal department and individual organizations. Thus the second hypothesis should be assessed by comparing the two middle columns on Table 1 with the two on the right.

Only one of the integration measures proved to predict complex networks. Mention of community-wide integrative organizations by knowledgeable informants during early 1961 was positively associated with the presence of a complex network in 1966. Indeed, slightly over three-quarters of the complex networks were established within the 76 communities identified as having these associations. The positive effect of funding upon the occurrence of complex networks, as well as their controls, is to be expected and requires no discussion. That educational activity affected the presence of a complex network may either bespeak the community's experience with related programmes or its ideological receptivity to them; but since school systems constituted *alternative* means to sponsorship by the community action agency, the possibility of any regular competition for programmes on their part must be denied. *Only one of the deprivation measures,* the most visible one of race, affected the establishment of a complex network.

Voter turnout, but not partisanship, also helped to predict the complex network. This may suggest turnout as an index of 'moral integration' within the local field, to use Angell's term (1947).

Table 1. Prediction of interorganizational activity in poverty dollars, complex interorganizational networks with CAA sponsorship of NYC projects, and elementary interorganizational networks with other sponsorship of NYC projects on the basis of integration and control measures

Predictor	Prediction of per capita poverty funding (explained variance = 32%)		Prediction of NYC sponsorship by CAA (explained variance = 67%)		Prediction of other NYC sponsorship (explained variance = 24%)	
	r*	beta**	r	beta	r	beta
National headquarters	·31	·18	·40[b]	—	·10[f]	—
Municipal revenue	·48	·28	·44[c]	—	−·02[g]	—
Democratic vote	·38	·21	·38[e]	—	−·06[h]	—
Education	−·34	−·18	−·59[d]	—	−·10[g]	—
Community-wide associations	·07[a]	—	·42	·36[b]	−·18	−·27[l]
Education expenditures	·38	—	·47	·21[e]	−·16	−·33[g]
Nonwhite	·13	—	·36	·40[e]	−·07[h]	—
Vote turnout	·27	—	·31	·46[e]	−·02[g]	—
P.C. poverty funding	—	—	·61	·35[c]	·15	·25[h]

* Zero order product-moment coefficient based upon ordinal data. All correlation coefficients are based on 130 cases. Their unadjusted two-tailed values at the ·05 and ·01 levels are ·18 and ·22, respectively.

** Standardized partial regression coefficient, which has not been tabulated where it failed to achieve p < ·10. Unless noted otherwise, the *beta* is significant at least at the ·05 level.

[a] *Beta* and r were computed as proportions of their ·85 maxima.

[b] *Beta* and r were computed as proportions of their ·45 maxima.

[c] *Beta* and r were computed as proportions of their ·72 maxima. The multiple correlation coefficient, upon whose square the estimate of explained variance in the CAA sponsored network is based, was also adjusted by this value.

[d] *Beta* and r were computed as proportions of their −·72 minima.

[e] p < ·10. *Beta* and r were computed as proportions of their ·72 maxima.

[f] *Beta* and r were computed as proportions of their ·59 maxima.

[g] *Beta* and r were computed as proportions of their −·81 minima.

[h] *Beta* and r were computed as proportions of their ·81 maxima. The multiple correlation coefficient, upon whose square the estimate of explained in the non-CAA sponsored network is based, was also adjusted by this value.

[1] p < ·10. *Beta* and r were computed as proportions of their −·76 minima.

Activity level aside, these forecasters of complex networks are seen to be negative or missing in the case of elementary networks; these appear to have been little more than correlates of funding level – i.e., of inputs to the city. Undue emphasis must not be placed upon the negative signs attached to several of the coefficients, for the complex and elementary dichotomies were constructed so that one is partly the negative of the other. This method allowed the effect of integration upon the creation of complex networks to be measured independently of the network's content or its activity level. Its execution led to unambiguous results. Complex networks proved to be functions of community-wide associations, voter turnout, educational expenditures, and proportion nonwhite. Elementary networks were not. Both kinds of network depended upon poverty funds.

Extralocal and local aspects of the network. Half of the predicted relationships were confirmed. In none of these cases did integration have a negative influence upon the nature of the interorganizational network; thus any inhibitory effect which integration might have had was not in evidence.

The distribution of the observed effects was such, however, to encourage farther examination of the three organizational measures of integration. Multiple regression analysis did not disturb the patterns of association reported earlier between the national headquarters measure of extralocal integration and the criteria used to validate it.

Multiple regression also supported the validity of community-wide associations as a measure of local integration by upholding its previously reported positive association with reform government and provided additional evidence by sharpening the *negative* contribution made by proportion of foreign stock in the population. The latter rate has been taken as a measure of community cleavages (Alford and Scoble, 1965; Alford and Lee, 1968). Assuming the city's age to be an indicator of structural stability permits the positive contribution made by that variable to be taken as further support for the validity of the community association measure. Such support was augmented by the positive effect of a city's location in the West, which may be presumed to indicate a low level of socioeconomic cleavage. Further, *local integration proved to be inversely associated with extralocal integration.* Once the influences of other sources of variation were removed, the number of national headquarters was shown to have a *negative* effect upon the mention of community-wide associations (adjusted *beta* = − ·34, p < ·05). Rather than denying the validity of either index, this event lent strong support to the prevalent theories of mass society we have mentioned.

Prediction of municipal revenue by regression techniques did, however, force a re-evaluation of the meaning of that measure. Two classes of significant and meaningful prediction were observed: (1) *differentiation and interdependence,* attested to by the positive effects of proportion foreign stock, proportion non-white, industrialization, and population density, as well as negative effect (the presumably fragmenting influence) of export diversity, and (2) *extralocal orientation,* witnessed by banking activity, municipal revenue from intergovernmental sources, the city's age, and migration rates that were independent of population growth (which also permitted a contribution to be made by the national headquarters index once their effects were removed).

What appears to be clear and unambiguous, once these additional analyses are considered in the light of Table 1, is that interorganizational activity levels – i.e., inputs to the city from without – depended upon prior extralocal integration (measured by national headquarters), while the existence of complex networks depended upon the city's local integration (measured by community-wide associations). Litwak and Hylton (1962) and Burton Clark (1965) have suggested that interorganizational systems tend to be loosely organized entities. Possibly the rare, closely coordinated version can only exist in a homogeneous *and* highly organized field.

It is equally clear that the municipal revenue measure did not fulfil its intended purpose. Shown to be more than simply an index of government control, its extralocal components might serve to explain the contribution which it made to the prediction of interorganizational activity level. Indeed, it has been suggested that large municipal governments tend to surpass smaller ones in the facilities they have for seeking outside funding (Advisory Commission on Intergovernmental Relations, 1967, pp. 150–53). That it might also signify both cleavages and interdependence among local elements could account for its lack of direct association – either positive or negative – with the occurrence of complex interorganizational networks.

Summary and conclusions

Using the number of national headquarters as its measure, a city's organizational integration into the broader society – its *extralocal integration* – proved capable of predicting the activity level of a new interorganizational network having both local and nonlocal elements. Composed of two federal anti-poverty agencies plus a federation of local organizations at the very least, a complex portion of such a network tended to occur where a high organizational level of *local integration* had been indicated by the pre-existence of community-wide associations. *Demand* – i.e., the practical or normative pressures posed by deprivation rates within the population – was important to these interorganizational outcomes only where organizational integration had been high.

One can only speculate as to the detailed processes involved, but it appears very likely that both the interorganizational links that tie the city to its sociocultural environment, as well as those which connect its internal elements, provide latent or active structures which may be used or modified for new purposes, provide points of articulation, or at the very least serve as models for new interorganizational systems. Prior linkages with the broader society can convey the materials and messages necessary for interorganizational activity, while local integration under common organizations can provide the means or models for the central coordination of elaborate networks. Not only the several other forms which can be taken by these two varieties of negative entropy, but also the conditions under which they enable *resistance* to new linkages or flows, demand future study.

The major conclusion to be drawn is this: *Definition of the urban setting in terms of multi- and interorganizational variables has proven fruitful. These variables were capable of predicting one another's values over time, it appears, without the intervention of nonorganizational sources of variation.* Transactions involving the federal government but different federal agencies were predictable, one from the other; but it is even more impressive that the two most unambiguous predictors of interorganizational transactions involving the federal government were themselves two major categories of nongovernmental organizations. Equally noteworthy in support of the main conclusion is the relative paucity of prediction in terms of population characteristics. Finally, the immediate inverse association which has been claimed between environmental adaptation and local integration – two functional problems of all social systems (Parsons and Smelser, 1956) – could clearly be observed in terms of the kinds of organizations that prevail. The evidence is sufficient to ask whether the organization is not the proper unit in the analysis of modern, large-scale social systems, whether these systems are not interorganizational systems in the main. It is not at all unlikely in macrosociology that such concepts as differentiation and integration refer more readily to relations among organizations than to relations among statuses and roles.

References

ADVISORY COMMISSION ON INTERGOVERNMENTAL RELATIONS (1967), *Fiscal Balance in the American Federal System*, vol. 1, Washington, D. C., US Government Printing Office.

ALFORD, R. R., and LEE, E. C. (1968), 'Voting turnout in American cities', *American Political Science Review*, vol. 47, September, pp. 796–813.

ALFORD, R. R., and SCOBLE, H. (1965), 'Political and socio-economic characteristics of American cities', in the *Municipal Yearbook 1965*, Chicago, International City Managers Association, pp. 82–9.

ANGELL, R. C. (1947), 'The social integration of American cities of more than 100,000 population', *American Sociological Review*, vol. 12, June, pp. 335–40.

CLARK, B. R. (1965), 'Interorganizational patterns in education', *Administrative Science Quarterly*, vol. 10, September, pp. 224–37.

CLARK, T. N. (1968), 'Community structure, decision-making, budget expenditures, and urban renewal in 51 American communities', *American Sociological Review*, vol. 33, August, pp. 576–93.

DUNCAN, O. D., and REISS, JR, A. J. (1950), *Social Characteristics of Urban and Rural Communities*, New York, Wiley.

Economic Opportunity Act of 1964, Public Law, pp. 88–452. (1964), *United States Statutes at Large*, Washington, US Government Printing Office, vol. 78.

Encyclopedia of Associations (1961), Geographic and Executive Index, Detroit, Gale, vol. 2.

GOULDNER, A. W. (1959), 'Reciprocity and autonomy in functional theory', in Llewellyn Gross (ed.), *Symposium on Sociological Theory*, New York, Harper & Row, pp. 241–70.

HAWLEY, A. H. (1963), 'Community power and urban renewal success', *American Journal of Sociology*, vol. 68, January, pp. 422–31.

LEVINE, S., and WHITE, P. E. (1961), 'Exchange as a conceptual framework for the study of interorganizational relationships', *Administrative Science Quarterly*, vol. 5, March, pp. 583–601.

LEVINE, S., WHITE, P. E., and PAUL, B. D. (1963), 'Community interorganizational problems in providing medical care and social services', *American Journal of Public Health*, vol. 53, August, pp. 1183–1195.

LITWAK, E., and HYLTON, L. F. (1962), 'Interorganizational analysis: a hypothesis on coordinating agencies', *Administrative Science Quarterly*, vol. 6, March, pp. 397–420.

MOTT, P. E. (1965), *The Organization of Society*, New York, Prentice-Hall.

NELSON, H. J. (1955), 'A service classification of American cities', *Economic Geography*, vol. 31, July, pp. 189–210.

PARSONS, T., and SMELSER, N. J. (1956), *Economy and Society: A Study in the Integration of Economic and Social Theory*, Glencoe, Ill., The Free Press.

RIECKEN, H. W., and HOMANS, G. C. (1954), 'Psychological aspects of social structure', in G. Lindzey (ed.), *Handbook of Social Psychology*, Cambridge, Mass., Addison-Wesley, vol. 2, pp. 786–832.

STARBUCK, W. H. (1965), 'Organizational growth and development', in J. G. March (ed.), *Handbook of Organizations*, Chicago, Rand McNally, pp. 451–533.

STEIN, M. R. (1960), *The Eclipse of Community*, New York, Harper and Row.

STINCHCOMBE, A. L. (1965), 'Social structure and organizations', in J. G. March (ed.), *Handbook of Organizations*, Chicago, Rand McNally, pp. 142–93.

TURK, H. (1969), 'Comparative urban studies in interorganizational relations', *Sociological Inquiry*, vol. 38, Winter, pp. 108–10.

TURK, H., and LEFCOWITZ, M. J. (1962), 'Toward a theory of representation between groups', *Social Forces*, vol. 40, May, pp. 337–341.

US HOUSING AND HOME FINANCE AGENCY (1960), Fourteenth Annual Report, Washington, US Government Printing Office.

US OFFICE OF ECONOMIC OPPORTUNITY (1966), Washington, US Office of Economic Opportunity.

VIDICH, A. J., and BENSMAN, J. (1958), *Small Town in Mass Society*, New York, Doubleday & Co.

WALTON, J. (1968), 'Differential patterns of community power structure', in T. N. Clark (ed.), *Community Structure and Decision-Making: Comparative Analyses*, San Francisco, Chandler, pp. 441–59.

WARREN, R. L. (1956), 'Toward a reformulation of community theory', *Human Organization*, vol. 15, Summer, pp. 8–11.

WARREN, R. L. (1967), 'The interorganizational field as a focus for investigation', *Administrative Science Quarterly*, vol. 12, December, pp. 396–419.

16 J. J. Wiatr

Political Parties and Interest Representation in Poland

J. J. Wiatr, 'Political parties, interest representation and economic development in Poland', *American Political Science Review*, vol. 64, December 1970, pp. 1239–45.

Discussing the character of the Polish party system elsewhere, I have suggested a label of 'hegemonic party system' for it, as well as for some other party systems based on similar principles (Wiatr, 1964, 1967). The hegemonic party systems stand midway between the mono-party systems and the dominant party systems as defined by Maurice Duverger (1960). In an earlier paper written jointly with Rajni Kothari (1966) we have suggested the following typology of party systems:

1. Alternative party systems, where two or more political parties compete for political power with realistic chances of success;

2. Consensus party systems, where multi-partism does exist but one political party commands in a lasting way the loyalties of a predominant majority of the citizens and permanently runs the government;

3. Hegemonic party systems, where all the existing parties form a lasting coalition within which one of them is accepted as the leading force of the coalition;

4. Mono-party systems;

5. Suspended party systems, where political parties exist but are prevented from regulating political life by other forces (for instance, by the military);

6. Non-party systems, where the government is ideologically hostile toward the political parties as such and does not permit them to function.

Quite obviously, this typology does not exclude mixed types of party systems. On the contrary, the very fact that in political life nothing is absolutely permanent leads to the emergence of transitory types of party systems. However, I am satisfied that the above-mentioned typology better reflects the differences and similarities of the party systems which exist nowadays than the traditional numerical typology of multi-, two-, and one-party systems.

Every party system is a product of history. It is also functionally interrelated with the social, economic and political characteristics of the society in which it operates. The present paper is an attempt to interpret the Polish hegemonic party system from the point of view of its historical roots, its role in the process of interest representation and the interrelation between the economic development of the country and its party system.

History: the emergence and evolution of the party system

The hegemonic party system in Poland is based on the lasting alliance between the three political parties and nonparty political and social organizations. These three are:

1. The Polish United Workers' Party. Founded in December 1948 through the unification of the Polish Workers' Party and the Polish Socialist Party, the membership of the PUWP reached 2 million in the last two years. The party controls the most important positions in the government and has a clear majority of about 51 per cent in all parliaments elected in the last twenty years. In our terminology it is the hegemonic party of the system.

2. The United Peasant Party, founded in November 1949 through the union of the two political parties of the peasantry which had existed previously. With a total membership of about 450,000 and about 25 per cent of seats in the Diet it is the second strongest party in Poland.

3. The Democratic Party, founded nominally in 1939 and more strongly expanded after 1945; its total membership amounts to about 75,000 and it holds about 8·5 per cent of the seats in the Diet.

The three-party alliance is a permanent coalition based on

common participation in the left-wing underground during the Nazi occupation of the country. In January 1942 the various Communist and radical political organizations merged in the new 'Polish Workers' Party', which, after having failed to persuade the anti-Communist underground that the time was ripe for the comprehensive policy of national unity in the struggle against Hitler's Germany, launched a political offensive for a front of national unity led by itself. On New Year's night of 1944 the National Council of Homeland was established as a provisional parliament of the nation. It was composed of the representatives of the Polish Workers' Party, left-wing socialists, left-wing activists of the peasant movement (the so-called 'People's Will' group) and the radical democrats, as well as by the representatives of the left-wing underground armed forces. In July 1944, when the first part of the Polish territory had been liberated by the Soviet Army, the Council created the Polish Committee of National Liberation, which at the end of the year transformed itself into the Provisional Government of the Polish Republic. After the end of the war and on the basis of the Yalta and Moscow agreements between the United States, the Soviet Union and Britain, the new, enlarged government was formed and received diplomatic recognition from the Western powers (the provisional government had been recognized by the Soviet Union previously).

The liberation of the whole country (January 1945), the expansion of leftist political parties and, finally, the legalization of two centrist parties, which joined the coalition after the Yalta and Moscow conferences, resulted in the emergence of six political parties. Four of them (the Polish Workers' Party, Polish Socialist Party, Peasant Party and Democratic Party) were the continuation of political forces which had created the National Council of Homeland during the war. They considered themselves permanent allies and in 1946 founded the Bloc of Democratic Parties for contesting jointly the forthcoming parliamentary election (January 1947). The centrists who joined the provisional government in June 1945 organized themselves in two political parties: the Polish Peasant Party and the Labour Party. The first became a strong political force, while the latter (based on former membership of the pre-war Christian Democracy) never managed to achieve any prominence.

To be sure, the six parties did not represent the whole spectrum of politics. The right-wing parties of the emigration as well as some traditional centre parties (including the right-wing socialist party) refused to recognize the new political situation of the country and launched an armed attack against the new government through the network of their underground organizations. In 1945–7 a state of semi-civil war prevailed in most of the country with casualties of tens of thousands on each side. During the electoral campaign the right-wing underground forces supported the Polish Peasant Party against the Bloc of Democratic Parties. As the result of this the election itself became a part of the civil war and led to a direct show of force.

After the Democratic Bloc's victory in the election the two centrist parties tried to play the role of parliamentary opposition during most of 1947. By the end of the year, however, splits in their ranks, defection to the West of some of their leaders and the pacification of the country by the victory of the government forces over the underground resulted in *de facto* defeat and liquidation of the anti-Communist opposition in all its forms. The two peasant parties merged in 1949, and the Labour Party dissolved itself in 1950, some of its members joining the Democratic Party. Therefore, the end of the 'struggle for power' stage of the Polish post-war history was marked by the consolidation of all legally existing political parties within the permanent coalition and by the consolidation of political power in the hands of this coalition. The war and post-war history of the country explains the roots and characteristics of the party system in the sense that:

1. It allowed us to trace back the origins of the cooperation between the Workers' (Communist) party and the two other leftist parties to the years of the struggle against Nazis during the war;

2. It explains how the logic of revolutionary seizure of power eliminated anti-Communist forces from the political life of the country;

3. It explains the hegemonic role of the Workers' party in the system in terms of the role it played during the critical years when the future of the nation was being decided.

The realization of the new political order resulted in the transformation of the war-time and revolutionary-time coalition into a permanent 'National Front' alliance which, under the leadership of the PUWP, runs the country at the beginning of the second quarter-century period of its post-war history. Within this alliance the hegemonic role of the PUWP is manifest in its five main functions:

1. The party represents and expresses the socialist ideology underlying the entire political system. It determines the fundamental aims and values which constitute the basis for the functioning of the political and socio-political institutions of the country.

2. Through the activity of its members on the institutions of state and social organizations, the party harmonizes the functioning of these institutions with the basic goals of the system.

3. The party determines the general directives of policy-making by the state institutions.

4. The party mobilizes a number of citizens to participate in political decision-making at various levels of government.

5. The party recruits and educates cadres of political leaders operating within the party as well as in the institutions of the state.

The two other parties of the alliance play a different role within the system. Their main functions can be best described as follows:

1. They participate in political decision-making at various levels of government and in the practical execution of these decisions.

2. They constitute additional, although not the only, political representation of the social strata within which they operate (peasants in one case, white-collar workers and craftsmen on the other). It has to be kept in mind, however, that the Workers' party operates among these social strata as well; the peasant membership of the PUWP is about equal to that of the UPP.

3. They constitute forms of political participation not based on clear ideological commitment to Marxism-Leninism 'They are

not,' to quote Wladyslaw Gomulka, 'Marxist parties, but they are independent parties of socialist democracy and of actualization of the current tasks of the joint policy of their members and sympathizers' (1968, p. 437).

In decision-making and decision-executing, in interest representation and in enlarging the possibilities of political participation, the non-Communist parties play an important role. They are no longer considered 'transmission belts' of the Workers' party,[1] but its valuable and independent allies within the whole structure of the political system.

Interest representation and political parties

Since no modern society is absolutely free from differences of interests, the way in which interests are represented within a system of government constitutes a very important characteristic of any system. But let us first address ourselves to the question, what interests do exist within the Polish society?

We can distinguish between two meanings given to the term 'interest' in the current literature. In the first, interest is the policy objective which is favourable to a group of citizens and either less favourable or unfavourable to other groups. In this sense, we say that the increase of prices paid for agricultural products is in the interest of farmers; and – as far as this interest is concerned – we may treat farmers as an interest group. In the second sense, 'interest' is a policy objective which is being pursued by a more or less clearly defined sub-group of citizens. The abolition of capital punishment may be a declared policy-objective of an 'interest group'. However, using this term does not mean that the members of the group *campaign* for something more favourable to them than to the others; obviously it is not the case in our example.

Interest representation includes representation of interests in both these senses of the term. In politics it can, moreover, count less what interest is being represented than how it is represented and to what extent the interest representation is a part of the

1. The application of this term to the non-Communist parties in the early nineteen-fifties reflected a tendency to reduce their role within the system. The trend was, however, reversed after October 1956.

functioning of the policy. In this respect one has to take into account an important precondition of the socialist state: the declared willingness to exclude from the political process the interest of those social classes whose very existence is incompatible with the long-term policy objectives of the socialist transformation of the society. This restricts the interest representation to those interests which are considered to be in harmony with the principles of the system.

Within these restrictions we may enumerate the following types of interest groups:

1. Economic interest groups, such as trade unions, peasant associations (in Poland, Peasant Self-Aid Union, farmers' circles), associations of private (small) business;

2. Professional interest groups, such as the writers' union, General Technical Organization, etc.;

3. Interest groups representing various segments of society such as the Socialist Youth Union, Rural Youth Union, Women's League, and the veterans' organization – Union of Fighters for Freedom and Democracy;

4. Religious organizations, particularly religious socio-political associations of Roman Catholics (Pax, Znak, etc.); the Catholic Church, albeit not an association, may itself be considered a powerful interest group of a special status and structure;

5. National organizations, such as Ukrainian, Byelorussian, Lithuanian, German and Jewish socio-cultural societies;

6. Regional associations, such as an association for the development of Nowy Sacz county, in which prominent people born or educated in this county work in the interests of their mother-region.

The interest representation takes, therefore, two forms. First, within the political parties sectional interests are represented – on the basis, however, of the accepted principle that no party should serve a narrow interest only, but that all parties should seek means of reconciling the various interests with the all-national interest of the country. In this respect, there is a difference between the

Polish United Workers' Party and two other parties. The PUWP is committed to the policy of combining all-national interests (interpreted also as the prospective, historical destiny of the working class) with the current interests of the manual workers, peasants, white-collar workers and professionals, all of them being strongly represented among the party membership and in its leading organs. The UPP and the DP, on the other hand, are committed to combining all-national interests with the special interests of the peasants and craftsmen, respectively. Dyzma Galaj, a prominent theoretician of the UPP and well-known sociologist, defines the peasant character of the UPP by pointing to the following functions of this party: (1) it accepts responsibility for the correct development of economic and 'socio-cultural relations in the countryside'; (2) in the process of socialist education of the citizens it 'takes into account first of all agricultural, mostly peasant population'; (3) it defends peasant interests in direct contacts with agricultural institutions, which show certain 'bureaucratic characteristics'; and (4) it 'looks for those forces among the peasants which can accelerate and deepen the processes of socialist education of the society.' The representation of group interests is, therefore, considered to be a two-fold process. It includes influencing the represented segment of the society in the direction favourable to the general policy of the ruling alliance, as well as defending the interests of this segment in direct contacts with the state authorities.

As far as interest groups in their relations to the political parties are concerned, two characteristics of the system are of special relevance:

1. The political parties, and particularly the PUWP, influence most of the interest groups through the activity of party members within those groups. Except the religious groups (and to some extent also some of the national groups) party members tend to play an important role in the leadership of the interest groups.

2. The political parties (again particularly the PUWP) determine the general line of the activities of the state apparatus and, through delegating their members to the government service, see to it that the administration puts into practice the general line as it has been defined by the political parties.

From these two traits of the system a kind of triangular relationship among the government, political parties and interest group emerges:

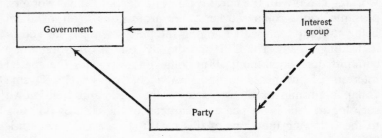

If we take as an example the trade unions, we can say that within the limits of the general objectives of the economic policy they are concerned with: (a) mobilizing the workers to achieve the goals of that policy, and (b) representing their interests in the consultations leading to the definition of policy objectives and economic strategy, as well as during the actualization of this policy. The state apparatus is charged with the task of policy execution; therefore between it and the trade-unions differences of views (or emphasis) can and do emerge. On the factory level workers' self-management is an instrument of reconciling differences of this type.

The above model could be extended and made more complicated in the case of some other types of interest groups. If we take the peasantry, we have the relationships of the following type:

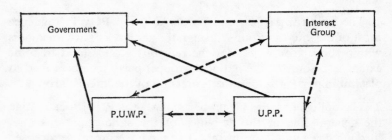

However, a general characteristic of interest representation *vis-à-vis* the state is that the process is in most cases indirect (religious groups being the only exception), the political parties playing the role of moderator among the various interests which have to be represented.

What I want to emphasize is the crucial role of the party system in interest representation and the fact that although the function of interest representation has a universal importance for modern societies, the political forms of this representation differ considerably.

Conclusion

The empirical studies of political parties in Poland are still in their early stage. The analyses I have referred to in the preceding section do not exhaust all the types of problems under study in this field. For instance, the personality characteristics and motivations of the party members are being studied extensively with an emphasis on the influence of political activeness on value orientations and professional performance of party members.

The character of party systems and of political parties themselves in the socialist countries of Eastern Europe is different from that which prevails in the West. It needs to be studied not as a departure from the 'natural' state of things, as seems to be an approach adopted in some area studies, but as a socio-political reality of different character and determined by different types of social conditions. Empirical research on this subject, still in its early stage, does not yet allow us to undertake broader comparative analyses. It might, perhaps, be regarded as a step in this direction.

References

DUVERGER, M. (1960), 'Sociologie des partis politiques', in Georges Gurvitch (ed.), *Traité de sociologie*, vol. 2, Paris.

GOMULKA, W. (1968), *O Neszej Partii* (On Our Party), Warszawa.

KOTHARI, R., and WIATR J. J. (1966), 'Party systems and political pluralism: comparisons between India and Poland', paper presented at the Sixth World Congress of Sociology, Evian, France.

WIATR, J. J. (1964), 'One party system: The concept and issue for comparative studies', in E. Allardt and Y. Littunen (eds.), *Cleavages, Ideologies and Party Systems*, Helsinki, Transactions of the Westermarck Society.

WIATR, J. J. (1967), 'The hegemonic party system in Poland', in J. J. Wiatr (ed.), *Studies in Political Sociology*, Wroclaw, Ossolineum.

17 R. Perrucci and M. Pilisuk

The Interorganizational Bases of Community Power

R. Perrucci and M. Pilisuk, 'Leaders and ruling elites: the interorganizational bases of community power', *American Sociological Review*, vol. 35, December 1970, pp. 1040–57.

The study of community power has developed along two apparently distinct lines, generally referred to as (1) the elitist and (2) pluralist approaches. The elitist tradition has maintained the position that community life is dominated by a relatively small group of men with economic and political power who initiate, direct, and resolve that level of decision-making which has major bearing upon the body politic. Citizen participation in community affairs is either nonexistent or limited to efforts exercised through a few relatively powerless voluntary associations (Hunter, 1953; Miller, 1958; Form and D'Antonio, 1959). The pluralist view, in its most frequently found form, sees power as distributed among a number of organized community groups with domination shifting according to the issues rather than repeated domination by a single power faction across all community issues (Dahl, 1961; Wolfinger, 1960; Polsby, 1963). The role of citizen participation in the pluralist theory is not entirely clear, although great stress is placed upon the ultimate power of the electorate in influencing political leaders, and the opportunity for participation of individuals within various community organizations is sometimes stressed.

Networks of power

Most community power research is guided by a conception of power that is based upon or similar to the views of Max Weber. According to Weber, power is the probability that a person or group can realize their will against opposition (Gerth and Mills, 1946). Despite the reference to 'probability', this conception of power is a heavy burden for the elitist, for it requires leaders to be omnipotent before they can be elites. In order for the probability condition to be operative, power research would have to contain an adequate sampling of decision situations.

The Weberian conception of power is also partly responsible for a research emphasis upon the individual as the unit of analysis. It is striking that both elitist research and pluralist research state that power is contained within institutional systems, and that it is differentially available to individuals and groups according to their place in the larger social subsystems of which they are a part. Yet the use of research procedures which measure the frequency with which persons are reputed to be powerful, or the repeated involvement of the same persons in influencing community decisions, assumes that some aspect of the individual, his passion for involvement or his primary institutional affiliation (e.g., banker, lawyer, industrialist), is sufficient to explain the extent of a person's actual or reputed power in community affairs.

An alternative conception of power, and how to measure it, need not dispute all of Weber's general definition. Our attempt here is to define power, and the occasions for its use, in a way that is particularly relevant for community power research. First, we must assume that the study of community power is most relevant in situations where there is concern over the distribution of scarce values. If they were not scarce, there would be no need to compete for them, and if they were not values, there would be little interest in the competition. Of course, both the elitists and pluralists accept this view. Elitists assume that once you identify persons with reputations for power, or persons with important positions in the community, you are automatically dealing with the most salient community issues. Pluralists are also accepting this view, for it becomes their guiding theoretical justification for seeking out the most controversial community issues. Thus, an acceptance of the view that power is concerned with the distribution of scarce values leads elitists to look for *individuals* most identified with the values (e.g., prestige, wealth, position), and pluralists to look for *issues* that will 'smoke out' those who seek to influence the distribution process.

Both deductions seem to miss an essential point. If power is concerned with the distribution of scarce values in situations that affect large, heterogeneous segments of the community, then it would seem that no one person, through his personal qualities or the resources of his position, can be sufficiently instrumental in initiating or shaping the final outcome on any one or several issues. In other words, no one person commands all the resources sufficient for influencing or intimidating others to see things his way. Persons who influence decision-making, and are thus called powerful (whether in one issue or across many issues), must therefore draw upon the resources of others as well as their own in order to exercise their power. This may all seem quite obvious, for the elitists would point to the fact that when they identify economically dominant leaders in a community they are demonstrating that power does not reside in individuals but in institutional contexts; and the pluralists would point out that the fact that the resources necessary to shape a decision reside in many persons who do not reappear across issues only provides support for their theoretical position. We may then formulate a theoretical statement about a locus of enduring power to which both elitists and pluralists may subscribe; i.e., the resources relevant to the existence of power are dispersed and reside in the interorganizational connections that may be mobilized in specific situations, particularly dealing with allocations of scarce values.

Measurement of power concentration, however, has not been geared to finding such networks of organizational interconnections. Rather, measuring power concentration through the coincidence of individual names requires the elitists to invoke the dubious claims of 'objective interests' (e.g., when all the reputationals are drawn from economic institutions). Finding a coincidence of persons from economic organizations who have a reputation for power does not demonstrate the existence of a *resource network* that is activated on particular issues. Conversely, not finding a coincidence of names among various decision protagonists does not necessarily indicate the absence of a resource network. To date, failure to demonstrate a resource network has only meant that individuals, whether identified by economic position, by reputation for influence, or by activity in one or more community controversies have been the sole measure of power concentration. A network of power could not be found without first defining it and specifying the nature of its measurement.

We start with the proposition, stated earlier, that the resources of a number of persons are required to shape a policy decision and combine it with the view that issues are differentially salient. It is then possible that we will find (1) persons with quite dissimilar 'objective' interests siding together on an issue and giving the appearance of dispersed power, or (2) the emergence of a different set of persons across issues, again giving the appearance of dispersed power, or (3) the coexistence of the same names or same institutional areas or reputational lists, giving the appearance of centralized power. What is clearly needed is the identification of a network of resources that can be drawn upon to shape community decisions, a measurement of the extent of involvement of those networks in decision-making, and a test of the identifiability of persons involved in the network as reputational leaders.

The focus on *overlapping* executive positions has received limited attention in community power research. Freeman *et al.* (1963), in a study comparing several approaches to locating community leaders, develop a measure of 'organizational participation' in which they sought to determine whether a leader's reputation for leadership is a function of the organization in which he holds his formal position. Organizations were classified according to the degree of involvement of its employees in other community organizations. Their data indicate that the top reputed leaders head the organizations whose personnel are most active in community affairs. While this is not the direct measure of overlapping positions that we are suggesting, it clearly indicates the importance of multiple organizational ties to community leadership.

By way of summary, it is our view that community organizations control such resources as money, media, and jobs (see Clark, 1968). Given the assumption that several organizations must combine resources to shape community decisions, power resources must also reside in the interconnections among organizations. An organization leader in a decision-making position automatically has some power within his organization. To the extent that the decisions of his organization affect the larger community, he has more extensive power, and when he is in a position to constrain the decisions of other organizations in the community by overlapping membership, he has still more power.

And when he is part of a chain that interconnects organizations of the community, then we have defined the organizational resources that he is able to call upon to block or promote, or to implement a matter of concern to the community. Thus the community banker who also sits on the executive boards of three other community organizations will occupy a more powerful situation than the banker who does not hold other executive positions. It is not the potency of the individual but the shape of the web (in which he is a node) which depicts the structure of enduring community power.

With this conception of how the resources of power are distributed, and how they are mobilized and brought to bear on community decision-making, the following propositions are offered for consideration.

1. There exists in communities a relatively small and clearly identifiable group of *interorganizational leaders*, or persons who hold high executive (policy decision-making) positions in 'many' organizations.

2. *Organizational leaders*, or persons who hold equally high positions in 'few' organizations, will be less often identified on an *actual* community issue than will their counterpart interorganizational leaders. The two groups will also differ on hypothetical community issues but less so than on real issues.

3. Interorganizational leaders will show greater value homophyly (Lazarsfeld and Merton, 1954) and primary or social ties among themselves than will organizational leaders.

4. Those interorganizational leaders who are part of the same resource network will be judged more powerful by their peers and will show the greatest value homophyly and most frequent social ties.

Design and procedure

The setting for the study is a Midwestern community of 50,000 population, with a diversified economy and a large state university. The general design includes four distinctive tasks: (1) to identify those people in decision-making positions in multiple community organizations and those with a decision-making position in only one or in few such organizations; (2) to assess a sample of persons from both these groups to determine (a) reputations for power in the community, (b) actual participation as influentials in community conflict, (c) value similarity, and (d) personal acquaintances among the interlocking and noninterlocking leaders; (3) to determine from the pattern of interlocking relationships whether any complete and closed networks of interrelationships can be found, thereby creating a resource network sample within the high interlock sample; and (4) given success of the third task, to examine whether members of the network(s) are even more value congruent, better known socially to one another, more often cited as reputational leaders and as key influentials in true community conflict.

The procedure is broken down into several phases to implement the above tasks. The first phase of the project was devoted to developing a list of all organizations in the community with ten or more employees or members. Using such available sources as Chamber of Commerce reports, annual reviews of business and commerce in local newspapers, the city directory, library listings of voluntary associations, and telephone directory, a list of 434 organizations was developed. The only departure from our criteria for inclusion is for lawyers. All law firms were included in the organization list regardless of the number of employees; it was our feeling that lawyers might constitute an important link between organizations and we therefore did not wish to exclude them.

Grouping the organizations by institutional area indicated 44 per cent in business (e.g., banks, manufacturing, commerce); 9 per cent government; 12 per cent business associations and professions (e.g., law firms, medical and bar associations); 8 per cent health and welfare; 14 per cent religion; 3 per cent labour; 2 per cent communications; 3 per cent education; and 8 per cent voluntary associations (e.g., Elks, Moose, Masons, etc.).

For each organization, a list of persons in upper executive and decision-making positions was determined. In most organizations, high position was defined as president or vice-president (or their counterpart in school superintendent, head minister, owner of a business establishment), as well as governing boards such as trustees and directors of banks, manufacturing and commercial firms, and deacons or elders of religious organizations. In law firms, each lawyer was considered to be a holder of a high position. In most cases, the names of organizational executives (president, vice-president, board of directors) were obtained from the same sources used for the organizational list. These were supplemented by such professional indices as: *Who's Who in Commerce and Industry, Martindale & Hubbell Law Directory*, etc. A combination of mail questionnaires and phone calls is used to obtain the names of governing bodies of religious organizations (e.g., elders, deacons, etc.), or the names of the officers of voluntary associations. A total of 1,677 organizational leaders was obtained.

Each organization and organization leader was given a unique number, and a computer program was developed which would generate a matrix of interorganizational connections. Of the 1,677 leaders, 1,368 (82 per cent) held only one upper executive (decision-making level) position; 208 leaders (12 per cent) held high positions in two organizations; 75 leaders (4 per cent) held high positions in three organizations; and 26 leaders (2 per cent) held high positions in four or more organizations. These 26 were designated as interorganizational leaders (IOL). In order to examine the importance of interorganizational ties for community power, it was decided to 'match' each of the 26 IOLs with a person from the leader list who held high positions in only one to three organizations; they were designated as organizational leaders (OL). Matching was on the basis of primary vocational identification. Thus, for each bank president, lawyer, realtor, or doctor that had four or more high organizational positions, we obtained a bank president, lawyer, realtor, and doctor who had at least one but not more than three high organizational positions. The 'matching' was usually done by randomly selecting from a stratum of eligible leaders with the same primary vocation and organization size as the counterpart IOL.

Thus, we obtained a list of 52 leaders, half interorganizational and half organizational, for interviewing. Each of the 52 received a letter describing the project, requesting his cooperation, and indicating that he would be contacted by phone by a member of the project in order to make an appointment for interview. All interviews were conducted by graduate students in sociology, social psychology, and administrative science. Of the 52, 42 co-operated and were interviewed: 20 IOLs and 22 OLs. Each interview lasted about one hour, and consisted of three main sections. The first section was devoted to general demographic characteristics of the leaders, their residence patterns in the community and state, and their level of general social participation in community affairs.

The second section was devoted to measuring power: issue-specific power, both actual (in response to a real issue) and impugned (in response to hypothetical issues); generalized power, in terms of freely generated names and in response to a pre-determined list of names. The measures of power were obtained in two ways: (1) *Issue-specific power*. Respondents were presented with a recent community issue that had produced great public controversy and had involved many individuals and groups in the community. The issue met the criterion of dealing with scarce resource allocation. Respondents were asked to describe the nature of their involvement in the issue, those most instrumental in bringing the issue to the community's attention, and those who held the decisive power in determining how the matter was finally resolved. This reflected our attempt to measure actual power by reconstructing the perceptions of the issue held by our respondents. We also attempted to measure the reputation for issue-specific power by presenting respondents with two hypothetical issues that might face the community in the near future and asking them to give the same information requested for the actual past issue. The hypothetical issues involved the establishment of a town-gown commission to look into the matter of discrimination in off-campus housing and whether a 'black list' of home owners who discriminate should be published; it also involved the decision as to whether or not to establish a Federal Job Corps Center in the community. (2) *Reputational power*. Respondents were first asked to provide the names of ten persons 'most influential in initiating, supporting, and shaping policy decisions which have the most effect on the community as a whole'. This was used to see whether a *freely generated list* of names would be consistent with the names generated by the organizational procedures. The other measure of reputational power was obtained by giving the respondents a list of the 52

R. Perrucci and M. Pilisuk 273

leaders generated as described earlier (which included the name of each respondent) and asking them to rank the ten most influential and powerful persons on the list. They were also asked to indicate the basis of their familiarity with each of the 52 persons, including business dealings, personal friendships, knowledge by reputation only, and no knowledge.

The third section was devoted to the respondents' attitudes on matters of local and national policy including taxes, military expenditures, civil rights legislation, federal intervention in community life, and censorship. Subjects responded here by indicating agreement with items on a six-point Likert-type scale.

In the fourth and final section respondents were presented with a list of names of the 34 community organizations having the greatest number of overlapping members (this is the organizational counterpart to our procedure for measuring IOLs) and were asked to rate each organization on a seven-point scale of 'influence in initiating, supporting or shaping actions which have the most effect in the community'.

The procedures described so far indicate how matched groups of OLs and IOLs (men with multiple executive affiliations) were identified and compared on reputed power, actual decision involvement, attitudes, and social affiliations. The method calls for still further selection from among the IOLs, those with greatest power in accord with findings from the interview data. This latter group is then examined to see whether it meets criteria specified for a closed resource network of organizational interconnections, of social interconnections and a high compatibility of values. The criteria for determining such resource networks will be described in the findings.

The basic analyses in this paper consist of a comparison of interorganizational and organizational leaders on the measure of power, value homophyly, and primary ties. A similar comparison will be conducted for those interorganizational leaders implicated in a common resource network, and those interorganizational leaders who are not involved in a clear network of interconnecting organizations.

Analysis

The original sample of 26 IOLs and 26 matched OLs included

men whose primary occupations are as follows: lawyers, 14; bankers, 12; industrialists, 10; city officials, 4; realtors, 4; school officials, 4; physicians, 2; media owners, 2; making a total of 52 leaders (26 each of OLs and IOLs).

In their general descriptive characteristics, little difference is seen between the IOLs and the OLs. About one-third of each group were born in the community studied, with almost another one-half born in the same state but outside the community. Long-time residence in the community is also a shared characteristic, median years of residence is about 21·0, with only two of the IOLs and three OLs residing in the community fewer than ten years. Over three-fourths of each group completed college, with a sizeable number having completed postgraduate work. The IOLs appear to be slightly younger than the OLs, with the former having a median age of 47·3 and the latter 52·5. Thus the two groups of leaders are at least similar on their occupations, age, education, area of birth, and length of residence in the community.

Let us now turn to the hypotheses. The first hypothesis is the essential starting point in the theory. It states that an examination of organizations and their leaders will reveal a clearly identifiable group of IOLs who hold high executive positions in a number of organizations. From our basic lists of 434 organizations and 1,677 organizational leaders, we found only 26 persons who held high executive positions in four or more organizations. This represents fewer than 2 per cent of all the leaders and suggests that such overlapping organizational ties are sufficiently rare as to be easily identified. The central question now is whether these interorganizational ties are related to the power structure of the community.

Organizational ties and community power

The second hypothesis predicted that IOLs would be more likely to be identified as influential in both a general reputational and actual issue sense than would be OLs. The same difference between the IOLs and OLs should appear, but not as strongly, in being chosen as influential in hypothetical community issues. The procedures used to determine who is influential, and the order in which these procedures are used, are critical for understanding the findings. The first condition presented to the respondents deals with their recollection of those persons who actually exerted the major influence during an important prior issue in the community and, thus, is expected to come closest to measuring actual power. The second and third conditions presented the respondents with two hypothetical issues and asked them to indicate who would be involved in a decisive way. The fourth requested the respondents to provide names of persons who had a general reputation for influence and power. In each of the four conditions the respondents are generating names without any knowledge of an established list of IOLs and OLs that is used later in the interview. Thus, we are in effect determining whether research methodologies that request freely generated names of persons with reputations for power will reproduce the names obtained by our procedures of interorganizational connections. In addition, we will know whether actual power, hypothetical issue power, or a general reputation for power most closely approximates the procedures used in the present paper to determine individuals with multiple organizational ties.

Table 1 shows the basic information provided by IOLs and OLs when they were asked to provide the names of persons involved in a past issue, persons who might be involved in two hypothetical issues, and persons who had a general reputation for power. The names that were produced in the interviews are classified according to whether the person named is an IOL or OL or some other person in the community. Thus, we can determine several things from these data: Are IOLs more likely to be named as community influentials than OLs? When our two groups of leaders are given an opportunity to generate freely the names of community influentials, do they restrict their choices to persons who are IOLs (and OLs), or do they choose outside of these categories?

For each power condition in Table 1, the data provided include the total number of names offered by respondents, the total number of different persons named by the respondents, and the ratio of choices to persons. This ratio gives some idea of the dispersion or concentration of choices for the same persons. It can be seen, in Table 1, first of all, that IOLs are more likely to be identified as influentials than OLs across all four power conditions. The differences are especially pronounced for the actual issue condition and for the general reputation for power. The differences between OLs and IOLs are significant beyond the ·001 level (chi square) for actual issue (Item 1) and for general reputation (Item 4), beyond the ·005 level for the first hypothetical issue (Item 2), are not statistically significant for Item 3. The IOL respondents tend to produce more names from within their own category than do the OL respondents. If we take the number of names generated as some rough index of familiarity with the issues and with the total pool of community influentials, then we would suggest that the IOLs seem more knowledgeable on such matters than do the OLs.

Table 1. Interorganizational leaders (IOL) and organizational leaders (OL). Choices of influentials on actual issues, hypothetical issues and general reputation for power

Issue condit. & selected influen-tial persons	IOL ($N = 20$)			OL ($N = 22$)		
	Total choices	Total persons	C/P[a]	Total choices	Total persons	C/P[a]
Actual issue						
IOL	39	9	4·3	15	6	2·5
OL	4	3	1·3	3	3	1·0
Others	77	36	2·1	55	30	1·8
Hypothet. issue (Town-gown comm.)						
IOL	18	7	2·5	9	5	1·8
OL	5	3	1·7	3	3	1·0
Others	69	42	1·6	60	35	1·7
Hypothet. issue (Job Corps Ctr.)						
IOL	8	5	1·6	6	3	2·0
OL	3	3	1·0	5	5	1·0
Others	70	39	1·8	59	41	1·7
Gen. reputation for power						
IOL	57	13	4·3	42	10	4·2
OL	2	1	2·0	6	4	1·5
Others	67	51	1·3	83	48	1·7

[a] Ratio of choices to persons.

R. Perrucci and M. Pilisuk 277

It is also clear from Table 1 that both groups of respondents are quite likely to select as influential persons other than those from the two leader groups. This might seem to be contrary to our view that the IOLs are most likely to be named as influentials, since our respondents, when given an opportunity to generate names freely, are inclined to name many other than IOLs as influentials. Yet, when we consider that our categories of IOLs and OLs have a very restricted limit to the persons that can be named (26 in each group), and the 'other' category is only restricted by the limits of the total community population, the difference between the choices given to IOLs and to 'others' is not as great as it might appear. Moreover, when we look at the ratio of choices to persons, it is clear that when IOLs are named as influential the choices tend to be concentrated on a few unique persons, whereas when 'others' are named, the choices are clearly less concentrated on the same persons. For example, in the case of the actual past issue, IOLs mentioned 39 names of other IOLs as involved in the issue, with these 39 names representing only nine different persons, whereas the 77 names mentioned by IOLs who were 'others' involved in the issue represented 36 different persons.

Another way of looking at the proclivity of our respondents to listing the IOLs among their choices of powerful persons is to examine the probability of any single individual within the categories: IOL, OL, or 'other' on our respondents' lists. Looking under General Reputation for Power (Table 1), which generated the largest number of names in every category, our 42 respondents listed the names of the 26 IOLs 99 times. An individual IOL, therefore, had 3·8 chances of being named. An OL had only ·3 chance of being named or less than one tenth the likelihood of an IOL. The 'other' category is theoretically open to the entire population of the community. Even if we restrict this to the more realistic figure of 1,677 decision level personnel found in our original list of organizational leaders, the likelihood of choice for an 'other' was less than ·09. And if we were to restrict this analysis to data from the 20 IOL respondents rather than to the entire group interviewed, the likelihood of naming any given individual in the OL or 'other' categories as powerful becomes truly negligible.

The data presented in Table 1, therefore, do provide support for the second hypothesis which predicted that IOLs would be more often identified as influential than OLs, and that differences between the two groups of leaders would be smaller for the hypothetical issues than for the actual issue or the general reputation for power.

Organizational ties and value homophyly

The third hypothesis is concerned with the extent to which the two groups of leaders share similar 'world views' and the extent to which they constitute a group in the sense of social ties. The prediction is that IOLs will reveal greater value homophyly, as indicated by their responses to selected attitude items, and will have more social ties among themselves than will OLs. The main theoretical implication of this hypothesis is that if persons who are involved in overlapping organizational ties have similar value perspectives and shared social ties, it is more plausible to see specific individuals as interchangeable with respect to whether the same 'interests' are being represented on a particular community issue. To move beyond the identification of leaders to the identification of their common views and common ties is essential if we are to obtain a more critical test of the pluralist and elitist views of power and greater clarity in our understanding of the distinction between leaders and ruling elites (Danzger, 1964, p. 711).

IOLs and OLs indicated their degree of agreement with 11 opinion items and one pair of statements describing the way decisions are made in the community. The opinion items were designed to cover issues that have some bearing on matters that might be directly or indirectly related to the community. The roles of the federal government in health and welfare, taxation, segregation, and the university are opinion areas that are not very far removed from matters on which our leaders may have to make decisions, both private and public. The respondents answered the 11 opinion items on a six-point Likert-type scale, ranging from 'agree completely' to 'disagree completely'. The statements describing how decisions are made in the community consist of an elitist and pluralist description.[1]

1. The elitist and pluralist descriptions of the community were taken from Form and Miller (1960).

We set an arbitrary proportion of at least two-thirds of the IOLs or OLs showing agreement (or disagreement) with an opinion item as our index of homophyly. Four items reveal no difference between the IOLs and OLs and no homophyly on the opinion; and one item shows no difference between the leaders but homophyly for both of them. Five of the opinion items show greater value homophyly for the IOLs, and one other falls just short of criterion with 65 per cent agreement among IOLs. Only one item shows greater homophyly for the OLs. Finally, on the statement describing how decisions are made in the community, the IOLs are more likely to agree with the elitist description, but neither group shows over two-thirds agreement on the description (although the OLs came close to two-thirds agreement on the pluralist description). These data indicate that there is some support for the third hypothesis.

Although the differences between IOLs and OLs on value homophyly are not as sharp as they could be, there does tend to be more value agreement among the IOLs. It is interesting to note also that where differences between OLs and IOLs do exist, the pattern is for the IOLs to be the less conservative group. This may be seen in items dealing with integration, tax expenditures and social responsibility toward the disadvantaged. Thus, the people who have more interorganizational ties and are judged more powerful, now appear to resemble the image of a Rockefeller more than a Taft in their attitudes.

The question of the extent of social ties among IOLs and OLs is another aspect of the third hypothesis. Each respondent was presented with a list containing the 52 names of the IOLs and the matching OLs and were asked to (1) rank order the ten persons most influential and powerful in shaping community decisions and (2) indicate the nature of their own social and business ties with each of the 52 persons on the list. Table 2 contains the data on the social and business ties within and between the IOLs and OLs. The ties are shown for all the leaders irrespective of whether they were ranked as powerful, and for ranked leaders only. Differences between IOLs and OLs on the nature of their ties with all leaders are virtually nonexistent (comparison of Columns 1 and 3). Respondents from both groups claimed to have more social ties and more business ties with persons from the IOL list.

However, when indicating the nature of their ties with persons whom they ranked as powerful, it is clear that IOLs have substantially more social ties with persons they ranked as powerful (whether IOLs or OLs) than did the OLs (comparison of Columns 2 and 4). Fifty-four per cent of the IOLs had social ties with other IOLs who were ranked as powerful, as compared to 41 per cent of the OLs who had social ties with IOLs. Similarly, 50 per cent of the IOLs had social ties with OLs who were ranked as powerful, as compared to 36 per cent of the OLs who had social ties with other OLs.

Table 2. **Social and business ties among IOL and OL**

	IOL (N = 20)		*OL (N = 22)*	
	All	*Ranked*	*All*	*Ranked*
IOL Ties:				
Social, social and business	38·4%	54·0%	33·1%	41·1%
Business only	35·6	37·3	37·0	46·2
Reputation only	16·3	8·7	12·9	11·4
Do not know	9·7	—	17·1	1·3
Total	(362)	(150)	(387)	(158)
OL Ties				
Social, social and business	26·9%	50·0%	25·6%	36·1%
Business only	30·4	27·1	30·2	41·7
Reputation only	15·2	18·8	13·8	16·7
Do not know	27·5	4·2	30·2	5·6
Total	(480)	(48)	(441)	(36)

To summarize these data, we might say that an IOL is more likely to be claimed as a social friend and as a business acquaintance by IOL and OL alike. The IOL is more likely than the OL to have numbered among his acquaintances other IOLs and particularly those leaders whom he regards as powerful in the community.

We would conclude, therefore, that there is general support for the third hypothesis in that IOLs are more likely to be socially connected and more inclined to share similar opinions on selected social issues than the OLs. It is also quite clear from the data, however, that the 26 IOLs do not in any sense constitute a single social group sharing common ideas and having common social ties; typically, IOLs have social ties with only about one-half of the other IOLs.

What must also be noted is the quite impressive degree of social and business ties among the interorganizational leaders. The fact that over 90 per cent of the IOLs had social or business ties with other IOLs might be interpreted as an artefact of the methodology since they are selected on the basis of overlapping organizational ties. Yet this methodology does not mean that both social and business ties occur or that these ties must necessarily take place among the IOLs. Moreover, the fact that some 87 per cent of the OLs have social or business ties with IOLs cannot be an artefact of the classification system since OLs are not persons with extensive interorganizational connections. The rather extensive connections of IOLs with other IOLs and OLs are much greater than expected. Whether these connections indicate that there exists a small interconnected group of community leaders with common interests and values – in short, a ruling elite – is the subject of the next section.

Interorganizational ties, resource networks and ruling elites

So far the data have demonstrated that multiple interorganizational ties are somewhat related to coincidence of values, and to concentration of acquaintances from within that broader class of persons with at least one executive level position somewhere in the community. Most important, interorganizational ties are related to community power as measured either by reputation or by participation as an influential in an actual decision. All this is consistent with the hypothesis that a relatively small and homogeneous elite control the effective power in dealing with major policy issues for this community. Yet, these data by themselves would not rule out a limited pluralism in which the most powerful interorganizational figures were aligned in several distinguishable subgroupings of friendship, values and/or organizational affiliations. In this section, therefore, we shall be dealing mainly with the IOLs, attempting to determine whether those IOLs identified as most powerful are also in the same resource networks (i.e., holding high executive positions in the *same* organizations) and reveal considerable homophyly and social ties. The fourth hypothesis predicted that IOLs in the same resource network would show the greatest homophyly and the greatest frequency in interlocking social ties. Thus, if IOLs in the same resource network are identified as having actual or reputational power, and if they have similar opinions and close social ties, then the data would suggest the existence of a ruling elite in the community.

It was found earlier (Table 1) that IOLs were much more likely to have been involved in an actual (past) community issue and to be identified as having a general reputation for power than were OLs. These data were obtained as freely generated names rather than in response to specific lists of names. However, the same pattern is found even when respondents are given a list of names to classify concerning community power. Each of the IOLs and OLs interviewed was shown a list containing 52 names of IOLs and OLs (including the respondent) and was asked to rank the ten persons most influential and powerful in shaping community decisions. The persons ranked as powerful were mainly IOLs. When IOLs did the ranking, 75·5 per cent of their choices were other IOLs, and when OLs did the ranking, 76·5 per cent of their choices were IOLs. Listed below are the names of the ten persons receiving the most choices along with the number of choices received and their average rank order. (All are IOLs.)

Name	Choices	x̄ rank	Position
Selton	19	2·3	Bank President
Moore	18	2·8	Bank President
Patton	17	5·1	Elected City Official
Bessel	16	4·7	President – Industrial Firm
Nance	16	6·0	School System Official
Belton	12	4·1	President – Industrial Firm
Delk	8	6·5	Bank Vice-President
Webb	7	7·3	Lawyer
Perth	7	5·7	Treasurer – Industrial Firm
Cater	7	7·4	Vice-President – Industrial Firm

Thus, of the possible 19 choices that an IOL could receive (each IOL was asked to exclude himself from the ranking), Selton, for example, received 19, with a mean rank of a little over two. In general, the first five names are similar on the number of choices received, but quite different on the general power ranking associated with those choices. Throughout the remainder of the paper we will refer to these ten persons ranked by their peers as the most powerful men in this community, as interorganizational reputational leaders (IORL).

Given the fact that a group of 26 persons with multiple organizational ties (IOLs) were found and that respondents were asked to rank the names of community figures, some ten most reputedly powerful interorganizational leaders were likely to be discovered. But critical to our conception of what elitist theory requires is the detection of a unified network of organizational ties which constitute a power resource to be utilized whenever a major policy decision arises. To do so we must describe criteria for determining the existence of the network itself; only then can we independently list the individuals who provide the interconnecting nodes and check to see the degree of overlap with the list of powerful IORLs already identified.

Our criteria for a network follow from the theory of power presented earlier. It was suggested that the power to shape significant community decisions resides in a number of organizations, each containing *some* of the resources required to initiate influence or constrain decisions; when the resources of these organizations are combined, they can be instrumental and most likely decisive in shaping decisions. It was also suggested that these resource networks could be identified through the overlapping executive positions held by the same person in two or more organizations. The person in the overlapping position is the link between organizations, and the mobilizer of the resources of those organizations. Operationally, a tie exists between organizations if they share even a single person as executive in both organizations. If the connecting individual is an IOL, this may be called a *resource tie*. The network emanates outward with *ties* from some arbitrarily selected organization which has multiple (at least three) IOLs among its decision-making level, the organizational affiliations of these IOLs providing the first remove from the centre. The starting organization is linked to other organizations through further *ties* among the IOLs of the neighbouring organizations. The system is closed in that no organization is related to the network by ties with only one other organization; rather, each organization serves, through its IOL *resource ties*, as a step between two or more other organizations in the system. To specify further, the closed or inbred nature of the hypothesized network is that every organization represented within it should be tied to every other organization in the network. The ties are either first order, i.e., the two organizations share an IOL; or second order, i.e., both organizations are linked through IOLs to a common third organization. No further removes are permitted within the hypothetical resource network. In operational terms, a resource network exists when (1) three or more IOLs share executive positions on the same organization, and (2) these are also linked to each other by one or more other organizational ties, and (3) in such a fashion that the network is 'closed' in the sense that all persons are directly linked to each other by first- or second-order connections.

Plotting a resource network begins with a matrix with the IOLs on one axis and the organizations in which they hold overlapping executive positions on the other axis. From the matrix we can determine which organizations have persons in overlapping executive positions. Following our operational criteria for a network, there are ten organizations which have three or more IOLs holding overlapping positions.[2] The direct and indirect links of the persons involved in each of the ten potential resource networks have been graphically plotted to see whether those criteria in our operational definition of a resource network are present.

Diagramming the interorganizational links revealed that eight of the ten organizations did not produce a complete resource network. The two organizations that did produce a complete resource network are shown in Figure 1. The circles contain the names of the IOLs, and a line between circles shows an overlapping executive position in the organization associated with each letter (see Footnote 2, for the specific organizations represented by the letters).

2. The ten organizations with identifying letters are: D-advisory commission to city government; E, M, P-bank; G, J-welfare organization; L-voluntary association; F, Q-hospital board; S-educational board; T-voluntary association; U-educational board; N, V-industrial firm.

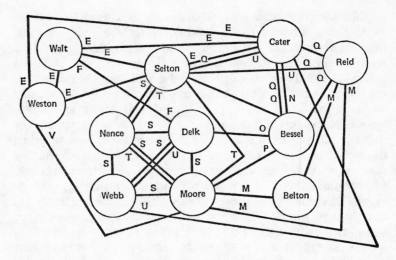

Figure 1 Complete resource network generated from overlaps in organization 'S'

Figure 1 shows the plot of the complete resource network generated from Organization S. This network does not contain the overlaps of Organizations D, G, J, and L. It does contain the overlaps of Organizations E, M, Q, T, and U. It should be noted that the same resource network could also be generated by starting from Organization Q, but *not* from Organizations E, M, T, or U. Thus, to be contained in a resource network as an independent organizational overlap of at least three persons does not mean that the same resource network could be generated. It is not clear what this means for our theoretical view of power. It could mean that the executive overlaps of Organization S and Q are equivalent power centres in that they can activate the same resource network through the persons holding overlapping positions.

It can be seen from Figure 1 that the overlapping executive positions of Nance, Delk, Webb and Moore produce secondary overlapping executive positions that are in turn interrelated and 'feed back' into a self-contained network of overlapping ties rather than continuing to expand outward and resist 'closure'. The three criteria of the operational definition of a resource network are clearly met. It should be remembered that this obtained resource network of eleven persons bound together by ties emanating from their holding executive positions in six organizations is the result of a procedure that started with 1,677 persons holding high executive positions in 434 organizations in the community.

We can now return to the interorganizational reputation leaders (IORL) isolated earlier, and to an examination of the fourth hypothesis concerning the existence of a ruling elite. The questions we are concerned with are whether reputational leaders are drawn from the same resource network and whether they reveal the greatest homophyly and social ties.

Eight of the top ten IORLs isolated earlier are found as members of the resource network described in Figure 1. The primary occupational roles of these eight IORLs in the same resource network include: three bank executives, three industrialists, one educator, and one lawyer. The three persons in the resource network who are not IORLs (Walt, Weston, and Reid) are a bank executive, an insurance agent and the president of an industrial firm. Within the framework of our theory, then, we have (1) identified an existing resource network in the community that can be mobilized to shape decisions in the community, and (2) found that there is a high degree of correspondence between persons involved in the resource network and persons identified as IORLs. The final concern now is to see whether these IORLs in the same resource network think differently about community-related questions and whether they do form a distinct social group.

IORLs in the same resource network were compared with IOLs who are not in a common network on the same twelve opinion items described earlier. What we have done in effect is to take the 20 IOLs and divide them into one group of eight IORLs in a common resource network and the remaining twelve IOLs in another group. Although the numbers are quite small, it is clear that the IORLs in the same resource network show even greater opinion homophyly than the IOLs. IORLs in the same resource network had opinion homophyly on ten of the twelve items, as compared to five items for the IOLs (data not shown). When we contrast these differences between IORLs and IOLs, with those obtained earlier when contrasting IOLs and OLs, it appears that opinion homophyly increases as one moves from OL to IOL, to IORL in a common resource network.

Finally we can look at the nature of the social ties among IORLs in a common resource network. As previously noted in Table 2, about one-half of the IOLs had social ties with the other IOLs whom they ranked as powerful in the community. When we examine the IORLs we find that virtually every person sees every other person socially (data not shown). An eight by eight matrix of IORLs in a common resource network contains 56 possible chooser-chosen patterns concerning social ties (this excludes the diagonal cells). Fifty-three of these cells are filled with a social tie, indicating that virtually every one of the eight IORLs is connected with every other IORL in a single social grouping.

These findings on opinion homophyly and social ties among IORLs in a common resource network support Hypothesis Four and provide additional evidence in connection with our theory of power. As far as their individual and group values and allegiances are concerned, members of common resource networks may in fact be viewed as 'interchangeable' in the parts they play in shaping community decisions. The evidence demonstrates that the question of elitist or pluralist power structure can only be answered in terms of the involvement of resource networks, and not individuals, in specific decision-making situations.

Summary and conclusions

An examination of elitist and pluralist research and theory indicates that neither is completely adequate in its theoretical views on power, and that both are heavily dependent upon measuring power through individuals rather than groups. The present paper has attempted to look at power in terms of inter-organizational ties which result in the creation of resource networks which can be mobilized and brought to bear upon particular community issues. These resource networks can be identified through the overlapping executive positions held by persons in different organizations.

Persons holding executive positions in many organizations (i.e., interorganizational leaders) are more likely than a 'matched' set of persons with few overlapping positions (i.e., organizational leaders) to (1) be identified as involved in past community issues of major proportions; (2) be identified as having a general reputation for power; (3) be similar in their views on community issues; (4) see each other socially; and (5) be identified as powerful from sociometric power choices.

The isolation of a resource network among community organizations indicates that this network quite closely coincides with the interorganizational leaders with greatest reputed power (IORL). These persons are, in turn, found to show the most marked opinion homophyly and to constitute a distinct social group.

The procedures used in this study allow us to test for the existence of a *ruling elite* in community power structure which, we maintain, could not be determined within the framework of existing elitist and pluralist theory. This study of a relatively small Midwestern community (50,000 population) reveals the existence of a small ruling elite who have actual power, common interests, and definite social ties. It is further hypothesized that although this power elite is not necessarily interested or involved in every community decision, when its common values or interests are at stake, it has at its disposal a power resource in the form of ties to the decision-makers of community organizations. In a genuine conflict over major policy, this elite alone is party to this reserve of organized activity and resources necessary to assure an outcome favourable to its interests.

References

CLARK, T. N. (1968), *Community Structure and Decision-Making: Comparative Analysis*, San Francisco, Chandler.

DAHL, R. (1961), *Who Governs?*, New Haven, Yale University.

DANZGER, M. H. (1964), 'Community power structure: problems and continuities', *American Sociological Review*, vol. 29, October, pp. 707–17.

FORM, W. H., and D'ANTONIO, W. V. (1959), 'Integration and cleavage among community influentials in two border cities', *American Sociological Review*, vol. 24, December, pp. 804–14.

FORM, W. H., and MILLER, D. C. (1960), *Industry, Labor and Community*, New York, Harper and Brothers.

FREEMAN, L. C., FARARO, T. J., BLOOMBERG, W., JR, and SUNSHINE, M. (1963), 'Locating leaders in local communities: a comparison of some alternative approaches', *American Sociological Review*, vol. 28, October, pp. 791–8.

GERTH, H. H., and MILLS, C. W. (trans.) (1946), *From Max Weber: Essays on Sociology*, New York, Oxford University Press.

HUNTER, F. (1953), *Community Power Structure*, Chapel Hill, University of North Carolina Press.

LAZARSFELD, P., and MERTON, R. K. (1954), 'Friendship as social process; a substantive and methodological analysis', in M. Berger, T. Abel and C. H. Page (eds.), *Freedom and Control in Modern Society: Papers in Honor of R. M. McIver*, New York, D. Van Nostrand & Co., pp. 21–54.

MILLER, D. C. (1958), 'Industry and community power structure', *American Sociological Review*, vol. 23, February, pp. 9–15.

POLSBY, N. (1963), *Community Power and Political Theory*, New Haven, Yale University Press.

WOLFINGER, R. E. (1960), 'Reputation and reality in the study of community power', *American Sociological Review*, vol. 25, October, pp. 636–44.

Part Four
Strategies for Research on Interorganizational Relations

The problems of conducting research on interorganizational relations are substantially more complex than those encountered in research on intraorganizational relations. For one thing, the difficulties of obtaining access to organizations for observational or survey research are multiplied when a large number of interacting organizations are involved. In addition, the most common research strategies employed by organizational researchers may be either irrelevant or inefficient, posing the need for methodological innovations.

In principle, the most directly applicable strategy for studying organizational interdependence of an economic nature is Leontief's input-output analysis (1966). Although usually applied at the aggregate level of the economy and less often at the regional level, it has rarely been systematically applied at the level of the firm. Stone's essay is a reflection of a growing interest in the potential analytical value of input-output analysis at the organizational level.

Where interorganizational interactions do not entail economic exchanges but rather social exchanges of various sorts, there is a need for devising other methods of mapping organizational networks. Mitchell's analysis of social networks, though principally oriented to personal networks, has implications for the mapping of organizational networks. His distinction between 'morphological' and 'interactional' properties of networks is important; and particularly suggestive is his discussion of such graph-theoretic concepts as connectivity, reachability, and density. Anderson's sociometric analysis is an example of one way of proceeding with the task of interorganizational cartography, so to speak.[1]

1. For another approach, see J. H. Levine, 'The sphere of influence', *American Sociological Review*, vol. 37, February 1972, pp. 14–27.

The data-gathering obstacles to a study of large organizational networks suggest the possible usefulness of computer simulation as a research strategy. However, the effective use of computer simulation models presupposes the development of organizational models sufficiently precise and detailed to guide the simulation. Some models, such as Williamson's differential equations model of interfirm behaviour, may lend themselves to computer simulation and business gaming rather than alternative methods conventionally employed by organizational researchers. The discussion by Cohen and Cyert of computer simulation of various types of decisions of the firm and of oligopolistic markets is suggestive from this standpoint.

Given an interorganizational model that yields significant predictions of a relatively specific and quantitative nature, it is worth considering the usefulness of designing a laboratory or a field experiment. Evan's discussion of the 'organizational experiment' is concerned with the relative advantages of testing organizational hypotheses with the aid of a laboratory or a field experiment. Although laboratory experiments on interorganizational relations have rarely been conducted (Evan and Mac-Dougall, 1967), there is no reason, in principle, why problems of interorganizational interactions cannot be the subject of experimental methodology, as some economists have already discovered (Friedman, 1969). To date, among the very few organizational field experiments thus far conducted, none, to my knowledge, deals with interorganizational relations (Evan, 1971). This research gap will no doubt be filled in the near future.

References

EVAN, W. M. (ed.) (1971), *Organizational Experiments*, New York, Harper & Row.

EVAN, W. M., and MACDOUGALL, J. A. (1967), 'Interorganizational conflict: a labor-management bargaining experiment', *Journal of Conflict Resolution*, vol. 11, December, pp. 398–413.

FRIEDMAN, J. W. (1969), 'On experimental research in oligopoly', *Review of Economic Studies*, vol. 36, October, pp. 399–415.

LEONTIEF, W. (1966), *Input-Output Economics*, New York, Oxford University Press.

18 J. C. Mitchell

The Concept and Use of Social Networks

J. C. Mitchell, 'The concept and use of social networks', in J. C. Mitchell (ed.), *Social Networks in Urban Situations*, Manchester University Press, 1969, pp. 1–29.

The image of 'network of social relations' to represent a complex set of interrelationships in a social system has had a long history. This use of 'network', however, is purely metaphorical and is very different from the notion of a social network as a specific set of linkages among a defined set of persons, with the additional property that the characteristics of these linkages as a whole may be used to interpret the social behaviour of the persons involved. When Radcliffe-Brown, for example, defined social structure as 'a network of actually existing social relationships' (1952, p. 190), he was using 'network' in a metaphorical and not an analytical sense. His use of the word evoked an image of the interconnections of social relationships but he did not go on to specify the properties of these interconnections which could be used to interpret social actions except at the abstract level of 'structure'. Perhaps more often than not the word 'network' when used in sociological contexts is used in this metaphorical way.

One of the ways in which a metaphor may be transformed into an analytical concept is to identify the characteristics on which its heuristic usefulness rests, and then to define these characteristics in terms of general theory. In so far as the idea of social networks is concerned it has been used in sociological writings in a variety of different ways ranging from the purely metaphorical, as we have already seen, to the precise and restricted way required in mathematical graph theory.

In graph theory a finite set of points linked, or partly linked, by a set of lines (called arcs) is called a *net*, there being no restriction on the number of lines linking any pair of points or on the direction of those lines. A *relation* is a restricted sort of net in which there can only be one line linking one point to another in the same direction, i.e., there are no parallel arcs. A *digraph* is a relation in which there are no loops, that is there are no lines which link a point back to itself directly without passing through some other point. A *network* in graph theory is a relation in which the lines connecting the points have values ascribed to them, which may or may not be numerical.

In sociological writings the word 'network' may be applied indiscriminately to any of these somewhat different structures distinguished in graph theory.

The notion of the social network that Barnes (1954) introduced in his study of a Norwegian island parish approximated to that of a digraph in that the connections between the persons were thought of in terms of single links (i.e., there were no parallel arcs) and loops were plainly inapplicable but there was no limit to the number of persons involved. Mathematical graph theory is not restricted to finite nets but in sociology, as we shall argue later, it is usually necessary for pragmatic reasons to work with an identifiable set of persons and the relationships that exist among them. The notion of network used by Bott (1957), Phillip Mayer (1961), Epstein (1961), Pauw (1963) and Adrian Mayer (1966) is closer to the idea of a digraph since they restrict the persons in a given network to a finite number and they do not take particular account of the multiplexity of links of the persons in the network.

The interest in these studies focuses not on the attributes of the people in the network but rather on the characteristics of the linkages in their relationship to one another, as a means of explaining the behaviour of the people involved in them. This concept of a social network is similar to that of a sociogram as used by Moreno and his followers. Studies of sociograms developed mainly by social psychologists took such phenomena as clique formation, leadership, or task performance as their main problems (Festinger, Schachter and Back, 1950; Cartwright and Zander, 1960). In these analyses they related the structure of friendship choices in a group to leadership or the performance of tasks. Out of these studies developed the identification of particular patterns of linkages – for example, the star, the wheel, the chain, the isolate, which could be used in the explanation of how test subjects performed the tasks they were set.

Another aspect of network studies developed by the social

psychologists has been that of communication. Here the interest has been in the way in which rumours, ideas or information in general diffuse among a set of people. The chains of linkage along which the information can flow here have central importance. An example of the application of these techniques to a field problem is the study by Coleman, Katz and Menzel (1957) of the diffusion of knowledge of new drugs among a set of physicians in an American city.

The use of groups of subjects in experimental settings together with questionnaire methods to obtain data has led to the quest for methods of rigorous mathematical analysis of the characteristics of the linkages among the subjects. These concerns, particularly in respect of the flow of communication among a set of people who may know each other, have influenced the way in which sociological graph theory has developed. Witness, for example, the concern in digraph theory with directedness, connectedness, reachability, transmitters, relayers and receivers, strengthening, neutral and weakening points (Harary, Norman and Cartwright, 1965).

Barnes (1954), however, introduced the idea of a social network to describe an order of social relationships which he felt was important in understanding the social behaviour of the parishioners in Bremnes and which was not subsumed by structural concepts such as groups based on territorial location or on occupational activities. He later used the concept to draw the distinction between the type of social network which would characterize a community like that of Bremnes and the type which would be characteristic of a classical tribal society. The interest here is in the morphological features of the network itself and their implications for social behaviour rather than in the flow of communications through the network, though communication-flow is not excluded by Barnes's approach. This step whereby the relationship of the linkages in a network to one another is taken to be a salient factor in interpreting social action is one of the steps whereby the metaphor of a social network is expanded into an analogy and made analytically useful.

This was demonstrated particularly in Bott's study of conjugal roles in London families (1955, 1956, 1957). In this study she correlated the morphological characteristics of the networks of the families she was studying with the allocation of conjugal roles within the family. The attractive feature of Bott's study was that her dependent variable (conjugal roles) was not patently connected with her independent variable ('closed' or 'open' networks of the couples). The elucidation of this unexpected relationship led to a set of illuminating hypotheses about conjugal role behaviour which have stimulated several subsequent inquiries (Udry and Hall, 1965; Nelson 1966; Aldous and Straus, 1966; Turner, 1967).

Epstein (1961) on the basis of an examination of the social contacts of one of his African research assistants over a few days, suggested that Bott's division of social networks into 'closed' and 'open' types could be applied to different parts of a single personal network, the relatively 'closed' parts forming an effective network and the relatively 'open' part an extended network. He used this idea to explain how the norms and values of the local elites in a town percolated into the ranks of the non-elites with whom the elites themselves had no direct contact. He supplemented his earlier paper by showing how gossip which flowed along a chain in the network of a typical member of the social elite of Ndola was transmitted against a background of the norms and values of the social status of the people in that chain.

From the work that has already been done on social networks, however, there appear to be several morphological and several interactional characteristics which are likely to be apposite in any attempt to describe social behaviour adequately. The morphological characteristics of a network refer to the relationship or patterning of the links in the network in respect to one another. They are *anchorage*, *density*, *reachability* and *range*. The interactional criteria on the other hand refer to the nature of the links themselves and are the *content*, *directedness*, *durability*, *intensity* and *frequency* of the interaction in the links. We may now consider each characteristic in turn.

a. Morphological criteria

1. Anchorage[1]

When Barnes originally wrote about social networks he had in mind the general ever-ramifying, ever-reticulating set of linkages that stretches within and beyond the confines of any community or organization. His notion about the 'mesh' of the network refers to the network as a whole and is not related to any specific reference point in the network. This idea is sometimes denoted by the phrase 'the total network'. But the idea of the total network must be a broad generalization. When Barnes, for example, makes the distinction between the total network of small-scale and large-scale societies by referring to the number of separate links that would be necessary to get from any one person and back to him, he is making a generalization about the characteristics of the totality of all links in that society. If this proposition were to be tested it would be necessary to trace the shortest paths of a large number of people in the community from themselves through others and back to themselves and to express the generalization as an average or median number of links. In practice, however, many difficulties would present themselves to a fieldworker who tried to designate the characteristics of 'mesh' of a total network as, for example, the difficulty that in all societies the path from an individual back to himself via his parents would represent a universally minimum path of three steps. The idea of the total network is essentially a general heuristic concept: as with similar general concepts such as Gemeinschaft and Gesellschaft, when it comes to actual fieldwork it is always necessary to specify the context. In so far as social networks are concerned this involves isolating part of the total network and considering the characteristics of that part only.

The criteria to be used in partitioning the total network for detailed examination present a problem. The sociometrists normally work with a distinct group of subjects – the boys in a

---

1. Graph theorists refer to the point source of a 'tree' as the 'root' of the graph (Ore, 1962, p. 59; Busacker and Saaty, 1965, p. 29). As I understand it a 'root' cannot have a positive indegree (i.e., cannot have links coming in to it), a restriction which would make the notion inapplicable to most social networks. In the absence of a better term I suggest the term 'anchorage' to refer to the point of orientation of a social network.

scout troop or the children in a classroom. But the problem for the sociologist is more difficult since he is concerned with the behaviour of individuals in a social situation which may be affected by circumstances beyond the immediate context. The person to whom the actor is orienting his behaviour may not be physically present though he would almost certainly be in the individual's personal network. The behaviour of a child towards another in a classroom, for example, will probably be conditioned by its knowledge that its mother knows the mother of the other. The network links in this case would need to extend beyond the classroom to the parents of the children. How far the links of a network need be traced depends entirely upon the fieldworker's judgement of what links are significant in explaining the behaviour of the people with whom he is concerned. This implies that normally a network must be traced from some initial starting point: it must be anchored on a reference point.

The point of anchorage of a network is usually taken to be some specified individual whose behaviour the observer wishes to interpret. Taking a group as the point of anchorage of a segment of a network, however, involves difficulties arising out of the fact that a group is itself an abstraction derived from a consideration of selected aspects of the total social behaviour of the people considered to be members of the group. A link connecting one group to another can only mean that the groups as wholes are in some sort of relationship to each other. A network anchored on groups in this way could be constructed but care would have to be taken to ensure that the links connecting the groups all represent the same level of abstraction. A more cogent objection to the use of groups as points of anchorage for networks turns on the importance of the idea of multiplexity of social relationships among people in a social network. The relationships that link the people who form a group are by definition single-stranded relationships; those in a network may be multiplex – a fact which might be important in explaining the social action involved. It seems probable that most of the propositions concerning the relationships among groups could be restated at a somewhat lower level of abstraction in terms of the links among the various individuals concerned. If this is so there is much to be said for the presentation of analyses of network relationships as being anchored on an individual chosen particularly because of the part he plays in the events being analysed.

2. Reachability

The degree to which a person's behaviour is influenced by his relationships with others often turns on the extent to which he can use those relationships to contact people who are important to him, or alternatively the extent to which people who are important to him can contact him through these relationships. This is the general idea of reachability in a segment of a network (Harary, Norman and Cartwright, 1965, p. 32). This concept should be differentiated, however, from that of density or 'completeness' which refers rather to the extent to which everyone in a set of ego's contacts knows everyone else. Reachability merely implies that every specified person can be contacted within a stated number of steps from any given starting point. If a large proportion of the people in a network can be contacted within a relatively small number of steps then the network is compact in comparison with one in which a smaller proportion may be reached in the same number of steps. The point may be illustrated by the following three hypothetical networks (Figure 1).

The reachability in each network may be summarized by distance matrices, that is, in matrices where the number of steps taken to reach specified individuals appear in the intersection of the rows and columns for specified individuals, e.g., in distance matrix (c) A can get to E in two steps but to B in three steps. In matrix (a) A can reach all four points in one step: B, 3; C, 2; D, 1; and E can reach no point directly.

There are thus two distinct dimensions in the compactness of a network: (a) the proportion of people who can ever be contacted by each person in the network and (b) the number of intermediaries that must be used to contact others or, in other words, the number of links that must be traversed to reach the people concerned. I am aware of no measure which expresses the compactness of a graph by taking these dimensions into account. A somewhat crude measure may be computed by taking into account the proportion of points reached per person per step. For example in diagram (a) A reaches 4 points in 1 step, 3 in 2, 2 in 3 and 1 in 4 steps, an aggregate of 10 over all possible steps. B reaches 3 in 1 step, 2 in 2 and 1 in 3; C reaches 2 in 1 and 1 in 2; D reaches 1 in 1 step and E reaches none at all. Hence over the 5 × 4 possible steps an aggregate of 20 points are reached, an average of 1·0 points per step out of the possible maximum of 4 or a proportion of 0·25 points per step.

By similar reasoning in diagram (b) A reaches 4 points in 1 step, but no other point in subsequent steps. None of the others in the network reach any point in the 4 possible steps they may take. Thus the aggregate of points reached over all possible steps is 4, an average of 0·20 or proportion of 0·05 points per step. In diagram (c) A reaches 1 point in each of 1, 2, 3 and 4 steps; B reaches 1 point in 1 step; C reaches 1 point in 1, 2, and 3 steps; D reaches none and E reaches 1 point in 1 and 2 steps, an aggregate of 10 points over 20 possible steps or an average of 0·5 or a proportion of 0·125 points per step. Thus network (a) with an index of 0·25 is more compact than network (c) with an index of 0·125, and both are more compact than network (b) with an index of 0·05.

	A	B	C	D	E	
A	0	1	1	1	1	4
B	∞	0	1	1	1	3
C	∞	∞	0	1	1	2
D	∞	∞	∞	0	1	1
E	∞	∞	∞	∞	0	0
	0	1	2	3	4	10

(a)

	A	B	C	D	E	
A	0	1	1	1	1	4
B	∞	0	∞	∞	∞	0
C	∞	∞	0	∞	∞	0
D	∞	∞	∞	0	∞	0
E	∞	∞	∞	∞	0	0
	0	1	1	1	1	4

(b)

	A	B	C	D	E	
A	0	3	1	4	2	10
B	∞	0	∞	1	∞	1
C	∞	2	0	3	1	6
D	∞	∞	∞	0	∞	0
E	∞	1	∞	2	0	3
	0	6	1	10	3	20

(c)

The symbol ∞ indicates that the point at the head of the column cannot be reached from the point at the head of the row no matter how many steps are traversed.

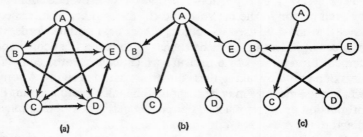

(a)   (b)   (c)

Figure 1

The sociological significance of the notion of reachability lies in the way in which the links in a person's networks may be channels for the transmission of information including judgements and opinions, especially when these serve to reinforce norms and bring pressure to bear in some specified person. This is particularly important where links of this kind lead back to ego.

3. Density

One should not confuse reachability, however, with density. Where the relationships among a set of persons are dense, that is, where a large proportion know one another, then the network as a whole is relatively compact and relatively few links between the persons need to be used to reach the majority.

Density, as Barnes calls it, it used in the sense in which completeness is used in graph theory, i.e., the extent to which links which could possibly exist among persons do in fact exist. In Figure 1(a) we may say that ten links are possible among the five persons involved if we count a link either from A to B or B to A as one link. In fact all these links exist and the network is complete or has maximum density. Barnes proposed a measure of density as

$$200a/n(n-1)$$

where a refers to the actual number of links and n to the total number of persons involved including Ego.

The fact that density and reachability are not directly related one to the other is illustrated by the density and degree of reachability in Figures 1(b) and 1(c). The density of each network would be $800/20 = 40$ per cent. The reachability in the two figures is different, however, 1(b) being somewhat less compact with an average of 0.8 points reached per step than 1(c) with an average of 1.5 points.

In sociological analysis our interest is primarily in reachability since norm enforcement may occur through transmissions of opinions and attitudes along the links of a network. A dense network may imply that this enforcement is more likely to take place than a sparse one but this cannot be taken for granted. The 'pattern' of the network must also be taken into consideration.

4. Range

Some people have many direct contacts while others have few. The first-order range or number of persons in direct contact with the person on whom the network is anchored is likely to be a significant feature of a personal network. A person in contact with thirty others of widely differing social backgrounds would have a wider range network than a person in contact with thirty people of the same general social background.

In general it appears that there is probably a limit to the number of people with whom an individual might be in direct and regular contact, but as yet there does not seem to be enough empirical evidence available to provide an estimate of what it might be.

b. Interactional criteria

As the adjective suggests, the morphological characteristics of personal networks – anchorage, density, reachability and range – refer to the 'shape of the individual's network'. They may be equated with the structural aspects of social behaviour. At the same time the behaviour of individuals *vis-à-vis* one another may be perceived in terms of the characteristics of the interactional process itself: content, directedness, durability, intensity and frequency of interaction. Some of these interactional aspects may be crucial in understanding the social behaviour of the persons concerned.

5. Content

From a sociological point of view the most important interactional aspect of the links in a person's network is that which concerns the meanings which the persons in the network attribute to their relationships. The links between an individual and the people with whom he interacts come into being for some purpose or because of some interest which either or both of the parties consciously recognize. We may speak thus of the content of the links in a person's network. This content may be, among other possibilities, economic assistance, kinship obligation, religious cooperation or it may be simply friendship.

The content of a link in a social network therefore is not directly observable but must be inferred by the observer in the normal course of study. The observer's abstracting the content of network links contrasts with the sociometric approach of using questionnaire methods which deliberately specify the content of the links between the respondents in the study. The use of observation to collect data on networks has consequently led to the recognition of the importance of the concurrence of several contents in one network link. Network links which contain only one focus of interaction are called 'uniplex', or more simply, 'single-stranded' relationships. Those which contain more than one content on the other hand, following Gluckman, are called multiplex, or more simply, multi-stranded or many-stranded relationships (Gluckman, 1955, p. 19; 1962, p. 27).

A multi-stranded relationship is analogous to a multi-channel communication route in so far as effect on social behaviour is concerned, since people in a multi-stranded relationship interact with one another in many different contexts and are therefore less likely to be able to withdraw completely from contact with one another as people in a single-stranded relationship are able to do.

In terms of graph theory, a multiplex relationship may be represented structurally as a set of parallel arcs linking two points, but in terms of the contents of these arcs, sociologically speaking, the separate component arcs might fruitfully be considered to be links in different graphs, as for example a graph of kinship links or a graph of links of economic assistance. This has considerable relevance when the relationship of the content of network links to sociological abstraction in terms of institutions is considered. The importance of looking at the *structural* as well as the *interactional* aspects of network links is that the influence through several links of dissimilar content may be traced. For example, from the point of view of the social behaviour of the people in a personal network, the fact that A is linked to B in terms of kinship and B to C in terms of occupational ties, may or may not affect the extent to which A can enlist C's services for some purpose or other.

6. Directedness

Thus far we have been discussing networks without specifying whether the relationship between the people in the network should be considered either as oriented from one to the other or reciprocal. The problem is particularly germane in sociometric studies where frequently the topic of investigation is friendship choice.

A person may choose another as his friend without having his choice reciprocated, so that the link between the two is essentially a directed one. In some of the problems which could be examined by means of social networks the directionality of the relationships would not be important, but frequently there is a lack of reciprocity in a relationship which lends itself to a more accurate description in terms of a directed network link.

In graph theory, relationships which are not reciprocal may be represented simply by asymmetric adjacency matrices, in which zeros are entered when a relationship is not reciprocated. If the absence of reciprocity is to be distinguished say from indifference, signed graphs could be used in which negative entries could represent the lack of reciprocity and zeros simply the absence of relationships. Where multiplex relationships are involved, however, additional difficulties arise since the direction of flow of interaction in terms of one of the strands of a relationship may be the opposite to the flow in terms of another. Financial aid, for example, may be reciprocated by political support. The reciprocity in terms of different types of goods and service is clearly of considerable importance in understanding social action in many spheres of life. In these circumstances a compound adjacency matrix consisting of the union of several separate matrices which reflect links in terms of specific interactional contents could be used for analytical purposes.

7. Durability

A network exists in the recognition by people of sets of obligations and rights in respect of certain other identified people. At times these recognized relationships may be utilized for a specific purpose – to achieve some object, to acquire or pass on some information, to influence some other person in a desired direction. The recognized rights and obligations are thus potential links in an action-set or communication-set which may come into being for a specific object and disappear again when that object is attained or frustrated. But the underlying consciously appreciated expectations which people have concerning other identified people obviously persist over a longer period than an action- or communication-set, and may last, as in the case of kinship, for a person's lifetime.

8. Intensity

The intensity of a link in a personal network refers to the degree to which individuals are prepared to honour obligations, or feel free to exercise the rights implied in their link to some other person. The intensity of a person's relationship with a close kinsman is likely to be greater than that with a neighbour, for example. Reader, who recognizes this component of the personal network, uses an almost identical definition as 'the "strength" of the ties which bind person to person; the willingness with which the parties are prepared to forgo other considerations in carrying out the obligations associated with these ties' (1964, p. 22).

Measures of intensity are obviously difficult to devise; and for the time being, we must rely on the assessment of the fieldworker for estimates of this important interactional characteristic of personal networks.

9. Frequency

An obvious characteristic of interaction in a network which is amenable to more simple quantification than the other characteristics so far described is the frequency of contact among people in a personal network. A high frequency of contact, however, does not necessarily imply high intensity in social relationships. Contacts with workmates may be both regular and frequent but the influence of these workmates over the behaviour of an individual may be less than that of a close kinsman whom he sees infrequently and irregularly, in the sense that if a man must choose between either meeting the wishes of a close kinsman or those of his workmates, he is less likely to frustrate his kinsman. Although counts of the frequency of contacts have been extensively used by 'interactionist sociologists' in the past, their relevance to network analyses seems to be marginal.

References

ALDOUS, J., and STRAUS, M. A. (1966), 'Social networks and conjugal roles: a test of Bott's hypothesis', *Social Forces*, vol. 44, pp. 576–80.

BARNES, J. A. (1954), 'Class and committees in a Norwegian island parish', *Human Relations*, vol. 7, pp. 39–58.

BOTT, E. (1955), 'Urban families: conjugal roles and social networks', *Human Relations*, vol. 8, pp. 345–85.

BOTT, E. (1956), 'Urban families: the norms of conjugal roles', *Human Relations*, vol. 9, pp. 325–41.

BOTT, E. (1957), *Family and Social Network*, London, Tavistock Publications.

BUSACKER, R. G., and SAATY, T. L. (1965), *Finite Graphs and Networks: an Introduction with Applications*, New York, McGraw-Hill.

CARTWRIGHT, D., and ZANDER, A. (eds.) (1960), *Group Dynamics: Research and Theory* (2nd ed.), Evanston, Ill., Row Peterson.

COLEMAN, J. S., KATZ, E., and MENZEL, H. (1957), 'The diffusion of an innovation among physicians', *Sociometry*, vol. 20, pp. 253–70.

EPSTEIN, A. L. (1961), 'The network and urban social organization', *Rhodes-Livingstone Journal*, vol. 29, pp. 29–62.

FESTINGER, L., SCHACHTER, S., and BACK, K. (1950), *Social Pressures in Informal Groups*, New York, Harper.

GLUCKMAN, M. (1955), *The Judicial Process Among the Barotse of Northern Rhodesia*, Manchester University Press.

GLUCKMAN, M. (1962), 'Les rites de passage', in Gluckman, M. (ed.), *Essays in the Ritual of Social Relations*, Manchester University Press.

HARARY, F., NORMAN, R. Z., and CARTWRIGHT, D. (1965), *Stuctural Models: An Introduction to the Theory of Directed Graphs*, New York, John Wiley & Sons.

MAYER, A. L. (1966), 'The significance of quasi-groups in the study of complex societies', in Banton, M. (ed.), *The Social Anthropology of Complex Societies*, *A.S.A. Monographs* 4, London, Tavistock Publications, pp. 97–122.

MAYER, P. (1961), *Tribesmen or Townsmen: Conservatism and the Process of Urbanization in a South African City*, Cape Town, Oxford University Press.

NELSON, J. I. (1966), 'Clique contacts and family orientations', *American Sociological Review*, vol. 31, pp. 663–72.

ORE, O. (1962), *Theory of Graphs*, Providence, American Mathematical Society, Colloquium Publications, p. 38.

PAUW, B. A. (1963), *The Second Generation*, Cape Town, Oxford University Press.

RADCLIFFE-BROWN, A. R. (1952), *Structure and Function in Primitive Society: Essays and Addresses*, London, Cohen & West.

READER, D. H. (1964), 'Models in social change with special reference to Southern Africa', *African Studies*, vol. 23, pp. 11–33.

TURNER, C. (1967), 'Conjugal roles and social networks', *Human Relations*, vol. 20, pp. 121–30.

UDRY, J. R., and HALL, M. (1965), 'Marital role segregation and social networks in middle-class, middle-aged couples', *Journal of Marriage and Family Living*, vol. 27, pp. 392–5.

19 R. C. Anderson

A Sociometric Approach to the Analysis of Interorganizational Relationships

R. C. Anderson, 'A sociometric approach to the analysis of interorganizational relationships', paper presented at the American Sociological Association in San Francisco, August 1967.

Despite our recognition of the interdependence of organizations, it is rare to find sociological research that deeply penetrates inter-organizational phenomena (Etzioni, 1964; Evan, 1966). Recognizing this deficiency, a group of social scientists at Michigan State University have attempted to explore this unchartered field (Anderson, 1963; Anderson, Damson and Mulvihill, 1965; Damson, 1965; Anderson, Mulvihill and Schwartz, 1966). Our primary objective was to develop a methodological approach for use in the study of the interorganizational relationships of a society. The specific concern was an examination of these relationships as they bear on the process of area development.

Our work, in this particular context, is based in large part on the following postulates:

- Social power is structured.

- The social structure of a region is made up of constellations of interdependent heterogeneous interacting organizations. These represent basic resource holding, allocating, and receiving units.

- The organizations within a region have a fabric of roles that constitute the social organization of that region. Within this structure, individual organizations act and contribute in accordance with role prescriptions of expectations. They perform and coordinate their activities with one another in accordance with the relationship of their own roles to other roles in the structure.

- Organizations are the basic units of power.

- Organizations represent the basic social units responsible for development. Societal development is carried out by some combination of large, small, simple, complex, public or private organizations.

- Organizations are in themselves basic resources of development activity, as are air, water, iron, trees, etc.

- Organizations are control mechanisms by means of which power for development is generated and through which it flows.

- Organizations cannot exist in isolation; every organization is related to a cluster of interdependent organizations.

- Organizations form constellations in order to achieve development goals. As specific issues arise, overlapping constellations of special-interest organizations are formed. A specific organization sometimes cooperates, at other times competes, and at still other times is not involved with other organizations in issue resolution.

- A given organization's involvement and influence in issue resolution and/or in development depend upon the place it occupies in the legitimate order of the organized constellation of organizations affected by the issue and/or the developmental activity. For any given issue, some organizations are more powerful than others. An organization's 'power rank' will generally vary with the issue to be resolved.

With the development of sociometric techniques, it was almost inevitable that these procedures would be used in the study of power and influence in society. However, sociometric techniques generally have not been used to analyse interorganizational relationships. In effect, ours is an exploratory attempt to transpose what traditionally has been a small group, interpersonal approach to a large-scale, interorganizational setting.

Two specific methodologies heavily influenced the design of this sociometric approach. The first was Hunter's nomination-reputational method of social analysis (Hunter, 1953, 1959; D'Antonio and Erickson, 1962). Using a modified version of this technique, we produced an organizational inventory profile of the perceived organized structure of Michigan's Upper Peninsula. The universe of organizations to be included in the sociometric analysis was drawn from this inventory. Secondly, Weiss and Jacobson's set of structured concepts and methodology demonstrated the feasibility of using sociometric analysis in the study of complex structures (1955). While Weiss and Jacobson have done more than anyone else to develop and promote the use of the sociometric approach in the analysis of complex organizations, they do not extend such use beyond intraorganizational activity. The success of sociometric techniques in small group research and Weiss and Jacobson's imaginative use of them in analysing the structure of complex organizations led us to believe that sociometric techniques would provide a useful means of gaining information at the interorganizational level.

In our transposition of traditional sociometric techniques (Lindzey and Byrne, 1968), we obtained sociometric measures indicating dependency ties among an identified universe of organizations, as perceived and recorded by responsible organization members empowered to speak for their respective organizations. The sociometric choices were made in terms of particular criteria and the data obtained provided 'degree-of-dependency' information relating to three interorganizational variables: (1) interaction structures, (2) influence patterns, and (3) status arrangements.

Application of the sociometric technique to economic development of a region

A case study is presented here to illustrate the methodological aspects of our approach. The specific goal of the case study was to identify organizations responsible for economic development in Michigan's fifteen-county Upper Peninsula region, and to discover the dependence relationships existing among them. Organizations included were those that could significantly affect economic development activity in the region by taking one of three alternative courses of action:

1. By actively becoming involved and committing resources to a given development project.

2. By maintaining a neutral position in regard to a given development project, but in so doing acting as a potential influence in either support or opposition to the project.

3. By actively becoming involved and committing resources in opposition to a given development project.

On the basis of a review of existing economic reports and records on the Upper Peninsula, eleven major economic-interest sectors were identified and selected for study. They were Forestry, Mining, Tourism, Agriculture, Business, Manufacturing, Fishing, Utilities, Transportation, Communications and Government Service. It was our belief that each organization identified would be involved in continuing relations with certain others, and that the networks of interdependence would tend to enclose distinct clusters of heterogeneous organizations. We assume that (1) the resources for development in a region are mobilized and controlled mainly by organizations; (2) the actions of one organization have a strong impact on others in a related cluster and a lesser impact outside of the cluster; and (3) decisions affecting the development of the region are not made alone by the inner councils of management in each organization, but by a process that admits the influence of other organizations. Knowledge of the dependency patterns among organizations is thus viewed as an important aspect of the economic planning and development of a region.

Universe of organizations

An interview schedule was designed allowing for open-ended nominations of organizations having a legitimate special interest in one or more of the eleven interest-sector categories. Nominations were made by key informants – persons holding formal and operational positions in specific organizations comprising each of the selected interest sectors. The data were collected on a county basis, that is, informants were asked to nominate organizations that significantly affected development in specified counties of the Upper Peninsula. Data obtained from the interviews were considered to be additive. Thus, as new organizations were nominated, they were added to the inventory list of nominated organizations. This treatment of the data tends to correct for the bias introduced by the selective sampling procedure used. The result obtained is a comprehensive, Warren-type, horizontal and vertical, two-dimensional inventory of organizations (Warren, 1972). These organizations were considered by the informants to be the significant units controlling the economic development activities in eleven economic-interest sectors of Michigan's Upper Peninsula.

In order to obtain a manageable universe of organizations for the sociometric analysis phase of the study, only those organizations receiving multiple nominations were included. Universe reduction using the multiple-nominations meant that only organizations receiving two or more nominations (1) within and/ or between counties, and (2) within and/or between interest sectors were to be included in the study.

Sociometric instrument

The test criterion used to measure interorganizational interaction was the answer to the question: 'What organization does your organization deal with in carrying out its business?'

Organizational officials, representing each organization included in the analysis, were asked to place a check in the appropriate cell in order to rate the relationship of their organization with every other organization in the study. Each rating referred to a point on a multiple-point scale reflecting frequency or intensity of interaction.

To map the dependency patterns among the organizations, we submitted the response choices to a computer matrix rotation process.[1] Each row in the matrix indicated the choices made or given by one respondent for his organization; each column identified the choices received by one organization from all other organizations in the study. Comparing choices given with choices received, we eliminated all nonreciprocated choices from consideration at this point in the analysis.

With the execution of a Boolean matrix, we began by detecting blocks of reciprocally related organizations. The program took each pair of reciprocal choices and searched the matrix for a third organization which was the reciprocal choice of each of the first

1. Francis X. Mulvihill developed the following computer programs for the matrix solutions used:

RLBLTY	representing sociometric scores given and received.
BLOCKS	representing the first ordering of the Matrix of Values.
REORDR	representing the refined permanent recording of Matrix Constellation formations.

No.	Organizations
1.	Iron Mountain News
2.	The Mining Journal
3.	Escanaba Daily Press
4.	City Chambers of Commerce
5.	U. P. Power Company
6.	Lake Shore Engineering Inc.
7.	Clairmont Transfer Company
8.	Wisc.-Mich. Power Company
9.	Inland Steel Company
10.	City & Village Government
11.	Mich. Economic Expansion Comm.
12.	USDA Forest Service
13.	Cliffs-Dow Chemical Company
14.	Soo Line RR
15.	Lake Superior & Ishpeming RR
16.	Abbott Fox Lumber Company
17.	Cleveland Cliffs Iron Company
18.	Michigan Legislature
19.	County Superintendent of Schools
20.	University of Michigan
21.	Michigan State University
22.	U. P. Tourist Association
23.	Area Redevelopment Administration
24.	Cooperative Extension Service (MSU)
25.	FORUM
26.	Keweenaw Land Association Ltd.
27.	Longyear Reality Company
28.	North Range Mining Company
29.	Kimberly Clark of Michigan
30.	Ahonen Land & Lumber Company
31.	Superior Studs, Inc.
32.	Pettibone Michigan Corp.
33.	Mich. & Wisc. Timber Products Assn.
34.	L. H. Shay Veneer
35.	White Pine Copper Corp.
36.	Milwaukee Road RR Company
37.	USDA Soil Conservation Service
38.	County Road Commission
39.	County Sheriff
40.	County Democratic Party
41.	Celotex Corp.
42.	General Telephone
43.	Cloverland REA
44.	Barrett Lumber Company
45.	WLUC-TV Marquette
46.	M. A. Hanna Company
47.	Mead Corp.
48.	Pickands-Mather Mining Company
49.	County Planning Comm.
50.	City & Village Planning Comm.
51.	Sawyer-Stoll
52.	Goodman & Mohawk Lumber Company
53.	County Republican Party
54.	Conner Lumber & Land Company
55.	Michigan Education Association
56.	Drummond Dolomite Inc.
57.	WSOO-Radio
58.	WMUP-TV
59.	Ontonagon Valley REA Power Co.
60.	U. P. Law Enforcement Association
61.	Teamsters' Union

Organization No.   1 2 3 4 5 6 7 8 9 10 11 12 13 14 15 16 17 18 19 20 21 22 23 24

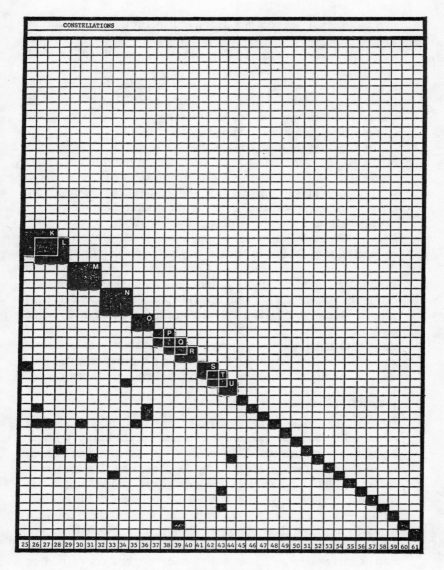

Figure 1 Matrix representation of constellations based on reciprocal choices of 61 selected organizations in response to the question, 'What organization does your organization deal with in carrying out its business?'

two. The search was continued for a fourth, fifth, n^{th} organization. The resulting blocks were put on a temporary list until all blocks based on the original pairs of organizations were listed, at which point these blocks were transferred to a permanent list. In this list, any block which was completely included in some other block was eliminated. This produced a list of organizations in which no block was a subset of any other, although members of any one block might be included in other blocks.

The blocks were then arranged on the diagonal with members of the largest block being listed first. The organizations in each succeeding block which were not included in previous blocks were placed in successive rows and columns. This produced matrices of reciprocal choices along the matrix diagonal.

These clusters along the diagonal are referred to as *constellations*. Constellations are a particular configuration of the original blocks chosen in such a way as to display most lucidly the structure of interaction. Constellations, thus, represent specified groupings of organizations, all of which are reciprocally chosen by one another. These are shown in Figure 1 as darkened squares along the diagonal and are labelled A through U. Some reciprocal choices also appear off the diagonal, the number of these depending upon the complexity of organizational relationships. We believe that of all the possible permutations, this produces a minimum number of off-diagonal configurations.

Interaction structures

In order to illustrate the interactions of each organization in relationship to the constellations thus formed, the idea of constellation sets is introduced. A *constellation set* is a group of organizations, some of which are reciprocally chosen by all members of the constellation – *primary members*; and others which are reciprocally chosen by some, but not all, members of the constellation – *secondary members*. Organizations that interact with members of more than one constellation set are called *liaisons*. *Primary liaisons* are primary members of two or more constellation sets; *secondary liaisons* are secondary members of one or more sets and they may be primary members of one (but not more than one) set. Liaisons might be regarded as actual or potential links between constellation sets.

The constellation sets and the membership (primary or secondary) of the heterogeneous organizations in the sets are illustrated in Figure 2. These constellation sets are based on reciprocal high frequency interaction linkages among organizations.

A few illustrations of the nature of the information provided by this technique are given below.

1. Constellation sets. The sixty-one heterogeneous Upper Peninsula organizations included in this study group themselves into twenty-one identified constellation sets, A through U. The largest set, A, has 47 members and the smallest set, Q, has only seven (See Figure 2). The 'Constellation Frequency' row at the bottom on Figure 2 indicates the number of organizations holding primary and secondary memberships in each constellation set. For example, set A has six primary members (organizations 1, 2, 3, 4, 5 and 6) and 41 secondary members (organizations 7–26, 28, 29, 32, 35, 37–41, 43, 45–50, 53, 55, 56, 59 and 61), for a total membership of 47 organizations. The heterogeneous nature of this constellation set's members can be illustrated by the fact that they represent all eleven economic-interest sectors included in the study.

2. Constellation memberships. We see that The Mining Journal (organization 2) is a primary member of constellation sets A and E; and a secondary member of sets B, C, D, F, G, H, I, J, K, P and R. Some organizations hold memberships in only two constellation sets: for example, the Michigan Education Association and WSOO Radio (organizations 55 and 57 respectively); while others are members of over 12 of the 21 identified sets: The Mining Journal, U.P. Power Company, Lake Shore Engineering, Inc., USDA Forest Service, Cliffs-Dow Chemical Company, and the Soo Line RR (organizations 2, 5, 6, 12, 13 and 14 respectively). The 'Membership Frequency' columns in Figure 2 indicate the number of constellation sets in which each organization holds primary and secondary memberships.

3. Linkages between constellation sets. The data in Figure 2 indicate that all 21 constellation sets are linked by liaison organizations. Every organization in the study occupies a liaison position. For example, the Upper Peninsula Power Company (organization

NO.	Organizations	A	B	C	D	E	F	G	H	I	J	K	L	M	N	O	P	Q	R	S	T	U	P	S	Tot.
1.	Iron Mountain News	P	S	S	S					S			S					S					1	7	8
2.	The Mining Journal	P	S	S	S		S	S	S	S	S					S		S					2	11	13
3.	Escanaba Daily Press			S	P	S			S	S	S												7	4	11
4.	City Chambers of Commerce	P			S	S		S		S	S												3	5	8
5.	U. P. Power Co.				S	S	S	S		S	S	S			S	S			S				3	11	14
6.	Lake Shore Engineering Inc.	P				S	P			S		S		S	S				S	S	S		6	7	13
7.	Clairmont Transfer Co.	S						S	S					S	S	S							2	5	7
8.	Wisc.-Mich. Power Co.	S	S	P			S	S	S			S								S			2	6	8
9.	Inland Steel Co.	S	S			S	S	S	S			S		S									1	7	8
10.	City & Village Government	S	S	S				S	S														1	6	7
11.	Mich. Economic Expansion Comm.	S	S	S	P	S			S														1	5	6
12.	USDA Forest Service	S	S			S	S	S		S	S	S	S			E					S		2	11	13
13.	Cliffs-Dow Chemical Co.	S	S	S	S	P	S	S		S			S					S		S		S	2	10	12
14.	Soo Line RR	S	S	S		S	P	S			S	S	S		S				S		S		3	10	13
15.	Lake Superior & Ishpeming RR	S	S	S		S		P			S		S		S								3	6	9
16.	Abbott Fox Lumber Co.	S	S	S	S	S	S							S	S								2	8	10
17.	Cleveland Cliffs Iron Co.	S	S	S			S	S			S	S	S				S						1	8	9
18.	Michigan Legislature	S	S	S	S				P	S					S	S	S						1	8	9
19.	County Supt. of Schools.	S	S						P	S					S			S	S	S			1	6	7
20.	University of Michigan	S	S		S					S													2	3	5
21.	Michigan State University	S	S	S	S					S					S								1	6	7
22.	U. P. Tourist Assn.	S	S	S						S													1	5	6
23.	Area Redevelopment Administration		S	S						S													1	4	5
24.	Cooperative Extension Service (MSU)	S	S	S				S		P					S								1	5	6
25.	FORUM		S	S	S	S	S			S			P						S				1	8	9
26.	Keweenaw Land Assn. Ltd.	S	S	S	S	S								P									2	5	7
27.	Longyear Reality Co.			S	S									P									2	2	4
28.	North Range Mining Co.	S	S	S			S	S	S			S		P									1	7	8
29.	Kimberly Clark of Michigan	S		S	S	S	S	S						P									1	6	7
30.	Ahonen Land & Lumber Co.				S	S	S	S						P									1	4	5
31.	Superior Studs, Inc.						S	S						P									1	2	3
32.	Pettibone Mich. Corp.	S	S	S			S	S						P									1	5	6
33.	Mich. & Wisc. Timber Products Assn.						S	S						P									1	2	3
34.	L. H. Shay Veneer																			S	S	P	1	2	3
35.	White Pine Copper Corp.	S	S	S			S	S							P								1	5	6
36.	Milwaukee Road RR Co.			S		S	S	S	S						P								1	5	6
37.	USDA Soil Conservation Service	S	S		S	S			S	S						P	S						1	7	8
38.	County Road Commission	S	S	S					S							P		S					2	5	7
39.	County Sheriff	S	S						S								S	P		S			2	3	5
40.	County Democratic Party	S	S	S					S								S	P					1	4	5
41.	Celotex Corp.	S	S	S		S	S	S	S		S			S						S			1	9	10
42.	General Telephone		S						S									P		S	S		2	3	5
43.	Cloverland REA	S	S	S										S				P			S		2	5	7
44.	Barrett Lumber Co.				S	P	S													S			2	3	5
45.	WLUC-TV Marquette	S	S	S	S				S	S														6	6
46.	M. A. Hanna Co.	S	S	S						S	S				S									6	6
47.	Mead Corp.	S	S	S		S	S							S										6	6
48.	Pickands-Mather Mining Co.	S	S	S						S	S	S		S										7	7
49.	County Planning Commission	S	S	S					S	S														5	5
50.	City & Village Planning Comm.	S	S	S	S																			4	4
51.	Sawyer-Stoll					S	S	S				S												4	4
52.	Goodman & Mohawk Lumber Co.					S	S						S											3	3
53.	County Republican Party	S	S						S															3	3
54.	Conner Lumber & Land Co.				S	S	S	S					S											5	5
55.	Michigan Education Association	S							S															2	2
56.	Drummond Dolomite Inc.	S	S	S																S	S			5	5
57.	WSOO-Radio		S					S																2	2
58.	WMUP-TV		S																	S	S			3	3
59.	Ontonagon Valley REA Power Co.	S	S	S																				3	3
60.	U. P. Law Enforcement Assn.			S													S	S						3	3
61.	Teamsters' Union	S	S	S																				3	3
	Constellation Frequency — F	6	5	6	4	4	4	4	4	5	3	4	3	2	3	3	3	3	2	2					77
	— S	41	39	33	24	20	21	21	25	15	15	10	11	5	6	11	8	4	5	7	8	8			320
	— Tot.	47	44	39	28	24	25	18	19	20	13	14	9	9	13	11	7	8	10	10	10	10			403

Primary Membership = ▓
Secondary Membership = S

Figure 2 Constellation sets formed by 61 selected organizations on the basis of response to the question, 'What organization does your organization deal with in carrying out its business?'

5) serves as a primary liaison among three sets (A, B and C) and a secondary liaison among 11 sets (D, E, F, G, H, J, K, L, O, P and S). Note how constellation set A is linked to set M through the secondary liaison of Kimberly Clark of Michigan (organization 29), a primary member of set M and a secondary member of set A.

Figures 1 and 2 make it easy to trace many combinations of potential constellation linkages through primary or secondary liaison relationships of members of individual constellation sets. The data illustrate the extensive interrelatedness of organizations as well as of constellation sets. The interaction structure variable is thus clearly identified and represented by the data presented in these figures.

Many explanations could be offered to account for the grouping of organizations in Figure 1 and 2. For example, the first three primary members of coalition set A are daily newspapers owned by a common publisher. The other three primary members, as well as the majority of the secondary members, are organizations whose operations are in large part dependent upon information dissemination, advertising, and promotion.

Three of the primary members of coalition set M represent the manufacturing-interest sector. The three organizations are based in different locations in the Upper Peninsula and are tied together by the common ownership of one of the organizations by the other two.

The interdependence of the primary members of coalition sets B, C, and D is not based on either common ownership or common functions. These organizations are reputational leaders among organizations comprising communications, tourism, utilities, manufacturing, transportation, mining, forestry, and government services, composing eight of the eleven economic-interest sectors studied (as indicated by the original nominations). This interdependent grouping of influential organizations from different interest sectors can be theoretically accounted for, but without the aid of sociometric measurement it probably could not have been easily identified. The sociometric technique then, provides a convenient mechanism for ordering and mapping the relationships of formally unstructured interaction patterns among heterogeneous organizations.

Influence patterns

Our analysis of the 'influence patterns' variable was made in terms of values assigned for reciprocal relationships and are shown in Figure 3. This analysis rests on the assumption that high frequency business ratings serve as indicators of high levels of influence. In the procedures used, a value of 1 is given for each reciprocal bond an organization has with each primary member of each constellation set. For example, Iron Mountain News (organization 1) has reciprocal bonds with all five primary member organizations of set A; therefore, it is assigned a membership value of five in cell A of the matrix in Figure 3. The News has four reciprocal bonds with primary member organizations of set B, so the value assigned in matrix cell B is four, as is the case with set C. Since Iron Mountain News has reciprocal bonds with only one primary member of constellation sets D, M and R, values of one are assigned in the corresponding matrix cells. A value of two is assigned for its bonds with set J. Because no bonds are established for sets E, F, G, H, I, K, L, N, O, P, Q, S, T and U, no values are assigned in these cells.

The constellation membership values (Figure 3) of Iron Mountain News indicate that the organization is a highly influential member of sets A, B, and C, and a less influential member of sets D, J, M and R. The Teamsters' Union (organization 61) on the other hand, with values of 1, 2 and 1 for sets A, B and C, respectively, and no values assigned for sets D through U, is not a highly influential member of any of the 21 constellation sets in the study.

Status arrangements

In our 'status arrangement' analysis, we are attempting to indicate the selective position of an organization in relation to all organizations included in the study. We assume that an organization holding membership in a number of constellation sets has higher status than an organization with membership in only one. In addition, we assume that a constellation set in which most of the organizations in the study hold membership has higher status than does a constellation set with only a few organizational members, because a large membership constellation, taking a stand on

No.	SELECTED ORGANIZATIONS / Organizations	A	B	C	D	E	F	G	H	I	J	K	L	M	N	O	P	Q	R	S	T	U	Membership Scores	Rank Order
1.	Iron Mountain News	5	4	4	1				2				1						1				2.51	15
2.	The Mining Journal	5	4	3	2	2	2	1	2	1	4	1					1	1		1			4.02	3
3.	Escanaba Daily Press	5	5	4	3	1			3	4	1						2	2	2				4.32	1
4.	City Chambers of Commerce	5		5	1	1	1		1	1													2.65	8
5.	U. P. Power Company	5	5	5	2	1	2	1	1		1	2	1		1	1	1		1				4.04	4
6.	Lake Shore Engineering Inc.	4	5	5		1	3	3		1		1	1	1							1	1	4.18	2
7.	Clairmont Transfer Company	4	5					1	2						1	1							2.51	12
8.	Wisc.-Michigan Power Company	4	4	5				1	1			1							2	1			2.65	10
9.	Inland Steel Company	3	4	5			1	1	2			1	1										2.51	13
10.	City & Village Government	5	3	2	3	1			2	2													2.51	14
11.	Mich. Economic Expansion Comm.	2	2	1	3	1					4												1.81	20
12.	USDA Forest Service	2	1		5	1	1		1		1	2	2	2			1					1	2.79	7
13.	Cliffs-Dow Chemical Company	4	3	3	1	2	5	2	1				1				1			1		1	3.20	5
14.	Soo Line RR	2	2	2		1	3	2			1	3	1	1						1		1	3.06	6
15.	Lake Superior & Ishpeming RR	2	1	2		1	4	3			1		1		1								2.23	17
16.	Abbott Fox Lumber Company	1	2	3	1	2	3							1	1								2.65	9
17.	Cleveland Cliffs Iron Company	3	3	4		1	2	5		1	1		1						2				2.65	11
18.	Michigan Legislature	2	2	1	1				4	1							1	1	1				1.81	21
19.	County Superintendent of Schools	1	1						3	1							1			1	1		1.25	34
20.	University of Michigan	2	1	1					3	4													1.53	28
21.	Michigan State University	3	2	1	1				1	4							1						1.81	22
22.	U. P. Tourist Association	5	3	2	2				1	4													2.37	16
23.	Area Redevelopment Administration	1		2	1				1	4													1.25	35
24.	Cooperative Extension Service (MSU)	2	1	1					1	4													1.39	30
25.	FORUM	3	2			1	1		1		5	2							1				1.95	19
26.	Keweenaw Land Association Ltd.	1	1	1	1	1					5	2											1.39	31
27.	Longyear Realty Company			1	1						5	2											.97	44
28.	North Range Mining Company	1	1	2			2	2			2	3											2.09	18
29.	Kimberly Clark of Michigan		1		1	1	1	1				3											1.25	36
30.	Ahonen Land & Lumber Company				1	1	1	1				3											.97	45
31.	Superior Studs, Inc.					1	1					3											.70	49
32.	Pettibone Michigan Corp.	1	2	2		1	1					3											1.25	37
33.	Mich. & Wisc. Timber Products Assn.						1	1				3											.56	53
34.	L. H. Shay Veneer											2	3								1	1	.56	54
35.	White Pine Copper Corp.	2	3	3		1	1						4										1.53	26
36.	Milwaukee Road RR Company		1		1	2	2	2					3										1.25	38
37.	USDA Soil Conservation Service	2	1		1	1			1	2				3									1.53	27
38.	County Road Commission	2	2	1					1						2	2	1						1.53	25
39.	County Sheriff	1	1												1	2	1						.97	42
40.	County Democratic Party	3	1						1							2							1.11	40
41.	Celotex Corp.	1	1	2		1	2	1		1							2						1.81	23
42.	General Telephone	2							1								2	2	1			1	.70	48
43.	Cloverland REA	1	1	1									1					2					.97	43
44.	Barrett Lumber Company				1	2	2	1					1						2	1	1		1.11	39
45.	WLUC-TV Marquette	2	2	2	1				1	3										2			1.53	29
46.	N. A. Hanna Company	2	3	4					1	1			1										1.67	24
47.	Mead Corp.	2	3	2		1	1						1										1.39	32
48.	Pickands-Mather Mining Company	1	1	2					2	2	1		1										1.39	33
49.	County Planning Commission	2	2	1					1	2													1.11	41
50.	City & Village Planning Comm.	2	2	1	1																		.84	46
51.	Sawyer-Stoll					2	2	1				1											.84	47
52.	Goodman & Mohawk Lumber Company						1	1														1	.56	55
53.	County Republican Party	3	1						1														.70	50
54.	Conner Lumber & Land Company				1	1	1	1					1										.70	51
55.	Michigan Education Association	1							2														.42	58
56.	Drummond Dolomite Inc.	1	1	1																	1	1	.79	52
57.	WSOO-Radio				1				1														.28	61
58.	WMIP-TV				1																1	1	.42	59
59.	Ontonagon Valley REA Power Co.	1	1	2																			.56	56
60.	U. P. Law Enforcement Association				1														1	1			.42	60
61.	Teamsters' Union	1	2	1																			.56	57
	Constellation Set	A	B	C	D	E	F	G	H	I	J	K	L	M	N	O	P	Q	R	S	T	U		
	Constellation Set Score	16.02	13.51	12.95	5.57	3.90	5.85	5.01	4.46	4.04	6.96	3.20	2.51	1.67	1.81	1.95	1.41	1.53	1.53	1.81	1.39	1.53	100	
	Rank Order	1	2	3	6	10	5	7	8	9	4	12	11	13	17	15	14	18	19	16	21	20		

Figure 3 Constellation set and membership scores of 61 selected organizations in 21 constellations formed in response to the question, 'What organization does your organization deal with in carrying out its business?'

an issue, is likely to carry more clout than a small grouping of organizations.

The status variable is analysed in terms of scored measures. These measures consist of a score for each organization, called a *membership score*, and a score for each constellation set, called a *constellation-set score*. The scores are derived from the constellation-set membership value matrix shown in Figure 3. A total membership value for a given organization is obtained by summing across the row for the organization in question; the organization's membership score is then computed by expressing the organization's total membership value as a percentage of the sum of all total membership values obtained from the sample, multiplied by 100. For Iron Mountain News, the score calculated is 2·51. This procedure is repeated for all organizations in the matrix.

Analogously, constellation-set scores, shown in Figure 3, are obtained by first summing each column for a given constellation set to obtain total constellation-set values, and then converting these total constellation-set values into constellation-set scores by expressing them as percentages of the sum of all total constellation-set values and multiplying by 100. In the case of constellation-set A, the score calculated is 16·02. As a result of this computational process, both the column of membership scores and the row of constellation scores will sum to 100.

The data presented in Figure 3 show that the Escanaba Daily Press (organization 3), Lake Shore Engineering, Inc., (6), Upper Peninsula Power Comapny (5), and The Mining Journal (2), exhibit the greatest amount of high-level reciprocal interaction, with respective membership scores of 4·32, 4·18, 4·04 and 4·02. These data are interpreted to mean that organizations 3, 6, 5 and 2 are highly influential and deeply involved in the interorganizational economic business activities of the Upper Peninsula, and on this basis, they are also identified as high-status Upper Peninsula organizations.

The data in Figure 3 show that constellation sets A, B, and C exhibit the greatest amount of high-level reciprocal interaction among their member organizations, as indicated by respective constellation set scores of 16·02, 13·51 and 12·95. We interpret this as indicating high-level interorganizational interaction in Upper Peninsula affairs among constellation sets as well as among their organization members. Therefore, these three constellation sets are considered to be the most influential, high-status sets affecting economic business activities in Michigan's Upper Peninsula. The status of individual organizations as well as of constellation sets are thus reflected in the rank-order designations ascribed to each organization and constellation set in Figure 3.

Conclusion

Our application of sociometric techniques to the study of organizations was an attempt to answer the question, 'Can sociometry be transposed to the organizational level?' Our answer is, 'Yes!'

In adapting the sociometric technique for use with organizations, we used a computer program to trace the sociometric linkages that emerged. The use of our computer matrix rotation process extended the size of the universe that could be analysed by sociometric techniques. With our program, a matrix of over 200 respondents can be dealt with in a very concise and clear manner; computer capacity rather than man's capacity is the limiting factor to the size of a manageable sociometric universe.

In our application of sociometric methods to organizational interaction, we confronted some problems peculiar to the new subject matter. The first of these was that respondents had to report not on their own personal interaction with other persons, but on the interaction of their organization with 60 other organizations. Primarily because of resource limitations for the Upper Peninsula case study, we decided to use only one respondent from each organization. This no doubt increased the chance for respondent errors. Research is needed on the reliability of informants used in this way. For the present, we have assumed that the informants, being high-ranking officials empowered to speak for their respective organizations, were well informed and could reliably reflect their organization's business relations with other organizations.

Regardless of the problems raised by the use of one informant for each organization, we did obtain information of the same kind by interviewing a number of informants and pooling their answers. The techniques of sociometric analysis would be the same regardless of the kind and number of informants used to represent each organizational unit.

Another methodological problem was determining how many and what kind of questions to ask about relations between organizations. In this chapter we have illustrated how the responses to one question, 'What organization does your organization deal with in carrying out its business?' were analysed. In our larger research project, five questions, each designed to measure different types of interdependence, were used, and slightly different patterns of interaction emerged from each question. In our study we theorized that business relations are of central importance in economic development affairs and that the structure revealed by the responses to the above question would be meaningful. Regardless of the theory and the content of the questions, however, the same procedures of sociometric analysis can be applied.

Using the sociometric technique, we confirmed our hunch that organizations vary and are highly selective in their degree of interdependence with others in the field. The interpretation we gave to the data is that organizations which are primary members of the larger constellation sets and which have reciprocal relations with the largest number of other organizations are the most influential with regard to the economic development of the region.

As expected, a substantial proportion of the organizations can be grouped into a few constellation sets on the basis of reciprocal sociometric choices. The first three sets include 49 of the organizations. The 10 largest sets delineated include all 61 of the organizations, 25 of them as primary members and the remainder as secondary members. These constellation sets are not isolated from one another, but are linked by common members. Every organization was found to be linked to every other organization through its constellation set.

After identifying organizational dependencies, we found that they could be accounted for and explained on the basis of (1) complementary differences, in which influential heterogenous, autonomous organizations from widely different interest sectors and wide geographic bases of operation grouped together; (2) supplementary similarity, in which homogeneous, autonomous organizations from common interest sectors, with or without a common geographic area, group together; (3) common ownership; or (4) a common geographic basis of operation. The significance of this fact is that once the coalition sets are identified, explanations for such formations can be made for each set in the matrix.

Some of the formations which emerge could have been predicted on the basis of existing sociological organizational classification schemes; many, however, would have been missed. For example, identification of organizations comprising inter-action sets B and C would be difficult if not impossible without the aid of sociometric techniques. Yet understanding the dependency patterns of those heterogeneous, geographically dispersed organizations is important for explaining why and how economic development occurs in the Upper Peninsula.

In this chapter we have illustrated what interorganizational structures emerge simply on the basis of matching high frequency reciprocal sociometric choices. Once the sociometric data are obtained, it is possible to carry out a number of other analytic procedures. For example, in addition to the analysis reported here, we computed the total sociometric scores received by each organization and rank-ordered the organizations according to amount of dependency. The data also lend themselves to more traditional organizational analysis; the organizations can be classified by interest sectors, as public or private, profit or nonprofit, or by any other grouping of sociological interest. Interorganizational sociometric data may also be subjected to multi-dimensional analytical techniques such as the Guttman-Lingoes Smallest Space Analysis (1967). The sociometric technique, then, can provide the data for many different kinds of analyses of inter-organizational relationships.

References

ANDERSON, R. C. (1963), 'The perceived organized structure of Michigan's Upper Pensinsula', (mimeo).

ANDERSON, R. C., DAMSON, J. E., and MULVIHILL, F. X. (1965), 'The perceived organized structure of Michigan's Upper Peninsula – a sociometric analysis', (mimeo).

ANDERSON, R. C., MULVIHILL, F. X., and SCHWARTZ, J. (1966), 'An analysis of interorganization interaction patterns', (mimeo).

D'ANTONIO, W. V., and ERICKSON, E. C. (1962), 'The reputational technique as a measure of community power: an evaluation based on comparative and longitudinal studies', *American Sociological Review*, vol. 27, June, pp. 362–76.

DAMSON, J. E. (1965), 'An analysis of the perceived organized structure and sociometric application in a region', Master's Thesis, Michigan State University.

ETZIONI, A. (ed.) (1964), *Complex Organizations: A Sociological Reader*, New York, Holt, Rinehart & Winston.

EVAN, W. M. (1966), 'The organization-set: toward a theory of interorganizational relations', in J. D. Thompson (ed.), *Approaches to Organizational Design*, Pittsburgh, University of Pittsburgh Press, pp. 175–91.

HUNTER, F. (1953), *Community Power Structure*, Chapel Hill, University of North Carolina Press.

HUNTER, F. (1959), *Top Leadership, U.S.A.*, Chapel Hill, University of North Carolina Press.

LINDZEY, G., and BYRNE, D. (1968), 'Measurement of social choice and interpersonal attractiveness', in G. Lindzey and E. Aronson (eds.), *Handbook of Social Psychology*, 2nd ed., vol. 2, Reading, Mass., Addison-Wesley Publishing Company, Inc., pp. 452–525.

LINGOES, J. C., and GUTTMAN, L. (1967), 'Nonmetric factor analysis: a rank reducing alternative to linear factor analysis', *Multivariate Behavioral Research*, vol. 2, pp. 485–505.

WARREN, R. L. (1972), *The Community in America*, 2nd ed., Chicago, Rand McNally.

WEISS, R. S., and JACOBSON, E. (1955), 'A method for the analysis of the structure of complex organizations', *American Sociological Review*, vol. 20, August, pp. 661–8.

20 D. Stone

Input-Output Analysis and the Multi-Product Firm

D. Stone, 'Input-output analysis and the multi-product firm', *Financial Analysts Journal*, vol. 25, July-August 1969, pp. 96–102.

The purpose of this article is to demonstrate that Leontief's input-output model (1936) can be used to help the multi-product, vertically integrated firm make short-run strategy decisions. This application of a macro-economic tool is possible because the multi-product firm, if vertically integrated, can be analysed as if it were a complete microcosm of the economy. The vertically integrated firm producing several products is analogous to an economy with a number of interrelated industries. Just as the economy disposes of its output through intermediate and final use, so the multi-product firm uses some of its output and markets the rest to outside customers. The economy deals with the rest of the world through imports and exports; the firm deals with its environment through purchases and sales.

The input-output model was not designed as a tool to suggest the best policies for the economy to pursue. Rather it was intended as a method of showing the implications of changes in the economy on all the parts of the system. In its application to the individual firm the input-output model is likewise not an optimizing device. What is offered here is a tool for showing the firm the implications of changes in its environment or of new activities of its own choosing. With an input-output model the firm is better equipped to make decisions that conform with its overall objectives. The function of running a multi-product firm is highly complex. At present there are no formal analytical tools to help the corporate decision-makers evaluate the firm's activities and select policies to improve them.

One might ask whether this problem of explaining the behaviour of the firm and showing the nature of the decisions that should be made is not already the subject of microeconomic theory. Microeconomic theory is often referred to as 'The Theory of the Firm', whereas, in fact, it is no such thing. Economists have not been interested in the behaviour of the firm. Their concern has been with the behaviour of markets, and how prices are determined. In explaining market behaviour the firm is used only as a conceptual construct. It is needed for linking causes and effects in the market place. However, one cannot take the economist's analytical construct, and hold it up as a useful explanatory model of the real firm.

In the short run the decisions of the firm are somewhat unpredictable because of the complexity of the environment, the multitude of factors affecting each decision, and uncertainty about the future. The firm, more often than not, does not know whether or not a particular decision is consistent with its objectives, however they are defined. The same problem may produce different decisions if it occurs at different times, even though the setting may not appear to have changed. This type of situation defies theorizing. It is not possible to formulate a theory to explain activities that have a significant component of unpredictability.

The multi-product producer has to make more diversified decisions, on more complex issues, than his one-product counterpart. He cannot rely entirely on business acumen and educated judgement. To make discretionary decisions consistent with its objectives the firm needs to have some comprehensive model or rule of thumb to assist it in confronting its complex environment. The firm must make decisions with the highest possible level of awareness of the relevant characteristics of the firm, and understanding of the implications of changes in the market environment for any of the firm's inputs or outputs.

Assisting in the decision-making of the multi-product firm is exactly the role of the input-output model. It is designed to increase the confidence of the firm that it is making subjective decisions in such a way as to maximize the probability of their being consistent with corporate objectives. At present no such confidence is warranted. Not only are the decisions subjective but so is the method of arriving at them.

The input-output model

If input-output analysis is to provide the multi-product firm with a tool for short-run strategy decisions it must provide a wide range of information and absorb a large amount of corporate data. The model will, in fact, show for a firm with stable internal relationships the level of output of each plant and the allocation of that output internally and externally for a given set of market assumptions. It will show the requirements of each plant from other plants. It will also show each plant's materials purchases, its direct nonmaterial costs and its pretax profit. It will also aggregate all this information for the firm as a whole.

The input-output model will show the implications of different market and internal transfer prices, and different sales strategies. It will show the situation with regard to purchased inputs, competitive and noncompetitive, for different output levels. Finally, it will provide the firm's management with the ability to isolate the parts of the system from the whole and to evaluate them separately. They will also be able to see the impact on each part and on the whole system of any change anywhere in the system. It can be an extremely flexible planning tool and yet it makes no assumptions concerning the firm's objectives. It can, in fact, be argued that, given the usual friction in corporate decision-making, the general lethargy in making major structural changes, and the rigidity of supply and distribution practices for most firms, a single input-output table could serve as a model of a multi-product firm for a number of years.

The input-output tables familiar to most readers are those showing flows in the entire US economy. In this national model the core of the table is a matrix listing all industries down its left-hand side, and the same industries across the top. In the version for a single firm, shown in Table 1, instead of seeing the major industrial groupings in the national economy we have a multi-product, multi-plant firm split into its component plants. To simplify matters, we assume that each plant produces a single product. Figures are in dollar amounts.

The 'Shipments and Receipts' section at the top of the table shows shipments of a plant. These are divided into shipments to the company's other plants, and those to outside purchasers. Reading across each row on the top left-hand corner, one sees

Table 1. Input-output transactions table

Shipments and receipts	Internal shipments				Outside sales					Total ship-ments
	Plant A	Plant B	Plant C	Total internal ship-ments	Retail sales	Whole-sale sales	Foreign sales	Net inven-tory change	Total outside sales	
INTERNAL RECEIPTS										
Plant A	×	15	10	25	20	30	15	10	75	100
Plant B	19	×	75	94	40	56	10	15	121	215
Plant C	6	0	×	6	10	50	39	15	114	120
Total internal receipts	25	15	85	125	Totals 70	136	64	40	310	435

Costs and profit				Totals
OUTSIDE PURCHASES				
Product A	15	10	0	25
Product B	0	30	1	31
Product C	0	2	2	4
Other products	5	21	4	30
Total purchases	20	63	7	90

NON-MATERIAL
COSTS AND PROFIT

Interest	20	40	4	64	x	x	x	x	x	x
Overhead	8	17	2	27	x	x	x	x	x	x
Labour	5	15	1	21	x	x	x	x	x	x
Other product and selling costs	15	50	5	70	x	x	x	x	x	x
Total non-material costs	48	122	12	182	x	x	x	x	x	x
Pretax profits/(loss)	7	15	16	38	x	x	x	x		
Total non-material costs and profit	55	137	28	220	x	x	x	x		
Total non-material costs, profit and purchases	75	200	35	310	x	310	x			
Total inputs	100	215	120	435	x	x	435			
Current capital employed	140	500	400	1040	x	x	x	x	x	x
Return on capital	5	3	4	4	x	x	x	x	x	x

the shipments of a particular plant to each of the plants listed at the top of the column (by reading down each column, one sees the purchases of each plant from all the plants listed on the left). Sales by each plant to customers outside the firm are shown in the upper right-hand portion. The 'Total Shipments' column shows the level of total shipments for each plant, and is the sum of shipments to other company plants and to outside customers.

In the 'Costs and Profit' section of the table, the top portion is composed of materials purchased by each plant, of products they make themselves and other products. The lower portion of the table shows nonmaterial costs and profit, and the bottom section shows invested capital and rates of return.

We now have a comprehensive summary of the firm's operations, providing a dollar breakdown of sales and of costs at a given level of output. To use the input-output model as a planning tool, one can by use of Table 2 estimate the amounts of each input that would be required for any level of total shipments. The coefficients in Table 2 represent the proportion of shipments represented by each input, and one may simply multiply any given level of shipments by these coefficients to determine how much of each material and nonmaterial input would be required. This information is provided separately for each plant.

Starting off with the company's sales forecast, an additional step is required to go from actual dollar sales to dollar shipments by the company's plants. This is because of the internal shipments between company plants, as shown in Table 1, which are not reflected in final sales. Table 3 shows the dollar value of shipments from each plant required for $1 of its sales. This coefficient is shown separately for each of the company's three products.

This small table is called the direct and indirect coefficient table. It is this table which creates the analytical flexibility of input-output analysis. By multiplying each element in each column in this table by the total of outside sales and net inventory change for the plant listed at the top of the column and then adding across each row one will have the appropriate total output of each plant. This means that one can find the total output needed from all the plants for any set of outside sales. In other words, we have a set of simultaneous equations which, when solved, will show the operating levels of the firm's plants for a given set of budgeted sales. With these total shipments levels, we can return to the direct coefficient table and create a new transactions table appropriate to the new shipments levels. Therefore, the firm has the opportunity of seeing the implications of any number of different budgeted sales forecasts on the whole firm's operations. It can see all shipments inside and outside the firm, purchases, labour requirements (wage bill divided by the wage rate), costs by plant, profit or loss made by each plant, and of

Table 2. Direct-coefficient table
(Proportion of output represented by each input)

	Plant A	Plant B	Plant C
Plant A	×	·07	·08
Plant B	·19	×	·63
Plant C	·06	0	×
Total internal receipts	·25	·07	·71
Product A	·15	·05	0
Product B	0	·14	·01
Product C	0	·01	·02
Other products	·05	·10	·03
Total purchases	·20	·30	·06
Interest	·20	·18	·03
Overhead	·08	·08	·02
Labour	·05	·07	·01
Other product and selling expenses	·15	·23	·04
Total nonmaterial costs	·48	·56	·10
Pretax profit	·07	·07	·13
Total nonmaterial costs and profit	·55	·63	·23
Total nonmaterial costs, profit and purchases	·75	·93	·29
Total inputs	1·00	1·00	1·00

Table 3. Value of shipments required per dollar of sales

	Product A	Product B	Product C
Plant A	1·021	0·072	0·127
Plant B	0·233	1·016	0·659
Plant C	0·061	0·004	1·008
Total	1·315	1·092	1·794

course all of this information aggregated for the firm as a whole. It is up to the corporate executives to choose their sales objectives – the model will not choose one – and the model (if accurate) will take over from there.

Limitations

We must briefly consider the assumptions behind the model. In fact, there is only one assumption essential to the model and that is that the direct coefficients are absolutely fixed for the length of the time the table is used unchanged. However, this assumption has five implications for a system made up in dollar terms. These are: (1) that the technological relationships indicating a specific quantity of x needed to produce a given amount of y does not change; (2) that there are constant returns to scale; (3) that there are no changes in the relative prices of inputs and outputs; (4) that the plant's operating efficiency does not change; (5) that no input substitution is possible. The first assumption is reasonable considering we are discussing specific plants. The others appear to pose definite limitations to the usefulness of the model.

The hardest of these assumptions to live with is the assumption of stable relative prices or, more probably, stationary prices. This assumption can be avoided by building the product flow part of the table in physical volume terms and creating the coefficients of Tables 2 and 3 from that volume table. After the production levels have been found one can then multiply through by the correct transfer prices appropriate to the base year table. The assumption of constant returns to scale is not unreasonable for product inputs but definitely breaks down with the direct non-material costs and profit. The way around this is to do the analysis in marginal terms and have different sets of marginal coefficients for different operating ranges. For example, it might be zero nearly all the time for rent. After the run is completed the increments would be added to the base table. For product inputs the average and marginal coefficients would be the same. Generally the assumption of stable efficiency is not unreasonable for only a few years. If, however, the plant is modified or there is a change in production efficiency then the coefficients would have to be adjusted. Finally, the assumption that no substitution is possible can also be gotten around by manually shifting the coefficients between alternative sources running the programme and analysing the effect on the whole system and on the parts.

There are three other problems with the model. These are the difficulty in handling inventory changes where some part of the change is planned and the rest is unforeseen; the problem of determining the coefficients for purchases of outside products; and what to do about the vacuum left by not having explicit capacity constraints. Generally, inventory change is assumed to be planned but it is not a proportion of the plant's total output. For this reason it is included in the forecast area of the table with outside sales. Competitive purchases and capacity constraints are handled together. The purchase of products which are also produced by the firm only causes a problem when they are made not because of special product characteristics or the special location of the requirement, but rather when the purchases are due to a shortage of capacity. In this case the easiest solution is to exclude the availability of the purchase, run the model, examine the excess required, subtract an appropriate amount from outside sales and then rerun the model so as to find out how much raw materials should be absorbed. Then the excess requirement could be put down as a purchase and total outside sales could be restored. This is similar to the method of handling competitive imports in the national input-output model. The solutions to some of these problems may appear to be a little clumsy or troublesome but in fact they work and the nuisance element is a small price to pay for having such a conceptually simple, yet analytically flexible, planning tool.

Conclusion

1. It is not possible to formulate an operational theory to explain the behaviour of the firm in the short run. Although the objective of the firm in the long run may be to maximize net income, in the short run it is not possible to show how the firm's decisions relate to this objective. The reasons for this are as follows:

In the real world the firm is not forced to maximize profits particularly in the short run. The firm can and does allow competing objectives to influence short-run decisions.

D. Stone 333

The short-run environment is highly complex and where the firm must make decisions rapidly it may be unable to relate all the variables that must be considered to its objectives.

The firm has only part of the required information on the environment.

Not all the information the firm has is reliable.

The firm may be uncertain about the future.

The decision-makers of the firm do not think with one mind. There are inevitably differences of interpretation and opinion.

The firm in the short run is subjected to numerous and often conflicting internal and external institutional pressures.

Under these conditions the decision-makers in the firm cannot predetermine a complete quantifiable objective function.

2. It is not reasonable to expect that firms can optimize their operations in the short run. All they can do is attempt to meet minimum targets of various sorts. These might include: growth, short-run profits and earnings stability. Since there is no theory to tell the firm how to achieve its objectives it has to use simple rules of thumb and general business acumen.

3. Simple rules of thumb and educated judgement may suffice for the single-product firm but are more dangerous for its multi-product, vertically integrated, counterpart. The operations of this type of firm are much more complicated to analyse. Not only does the multi-product firm have on a larger scale the same problems as the single-product firm, but it also has problems peculiar to itself, such as:

How can the firm determine the primary and secondary plant and product interdependencies?

Given these interdependencies how should the firm allocate its resources between product lines?

How can the firm relate changes in one part of its production system to the rest of it?

How can the firm test the implications of alternative policies on such a complex system?

How can the firm estimate the effects of changes in any of its input or output markets?

How should the firm select transfer prices for products shipped from one of its plants to another?

How can the firm be sure that all the plant budgets are mutually consistent?

Simple rules of thumb are insufficient for solving complex problems.

4. Input-output analysis, slightly modified from its more familiar economy-wide application, can be used to investigate the behavioural options open to the multi-product firm. It will not show the firm how to optimize its operations, but it will help the firm decide what to do by increasing its awareness of the implications of its actions. The model will do the following things for the firm:

It will provide the firm with a summary of its entire operation. It will show it all the internal flows of product between plants as well as each plant's sales to the firm's markets. It will show each plant's product purchases, its nonmaterial costs and pretax profit. Of course, all this information will be available for the firm as a whole. Furthermore, the framework of an input-output table will ensure that all information will be internally consistent.

The mathematical properties of input-output analysis will enable the firm to see the effects of different sets of sales forecasts for its plants. It will also point out the slacks and bottlenecks which would result with different price and quantity assumptions of final sales. Even though the model will not maximize profits it will show the level of profits for every plant for each set of sales forecasts.

By making certain manual adjustments one can use the model to show the effects of substitution between alternative sources of supply. One may not find the best pattern of distribution but one does have the opportunity of improving on the current one.

With this model the multi-product firm is more likely to make decisions consistent with its objectives. The model increases the firm's understanding of its own operations and allows it to rapidly test the impact of any changes in its environment or in its own policies.

5. This model does not replace any existing one; rather it fills a

void. Since no theory of the firm can be developed for the short run no optimizing model like linear programming can be used to formulate over-all strategy decisions. This is because it is not possible to express a quantified objective function for the firm. Optimizing models can only be used for decentralized decisions where the specific objectives involved can be clearly defined in a quantified form.

6. The contribution of input-output analysis in this microeconomic context is to provide a flexible short-run planning tool for the multi-product firm. It is therefore possible to improve the decisions of such a firm by bringing them closer to its objectives, even though one cannot formulate a theory to explain its behaviour.

Reference

LEONTIEF, W. W. (1936), 'Quantitative input-output relations in the economic system of the United States', *Review of Economics and Statistics*, vol. 18, August, pp. 105–25.

21 K. J. Cohen and R. M. Cyert

Simulation of Organizational Behaviour

K. J. Cohen and R. M. Cyert, 'Simulation of organizational behavior', in J. G. March (ed.), *Handbook of Organizations*, Rand McNally & Co., 1965, pp. 308–33.

This chapter will be devoted to a review of several computer models which have been developed for the simulation of organizational behaviour. In selecting the particular computer models which we shall discuss, we have attempted to give specific examples of each of the major types of simulation studies which are of interest to organization theorists. However, we certainly have made no attempt to mention every worthwhile simulation of organizational behaviour which has been developed. Thus, our review of the literature should be regarded as being illustrative rather than exhaustive. Moreover, we have made no attempt to mention the large number of simulation models which have been formulated in the literature of economics and operations research, even though many of them clearly can be regarded as models of the behaviour of some particular organizations.

Simulation of a department store buyer

Cyert, March, and Moore (Cyert and March, 1963, pp. 128–48) have developed a simulation model which describes in considerable detail the processes used by a department store buyer in deciding the amount of merchandise to order and the price of the various items. They have validated the model by comparing the buyer's actual decisions in a large number of circumstances with the simulated decisions made by the model under the same conditions. The results of these tests strongly suggest that their model is in reality a proper description of this department store buyer's decision processes.

The organization chosen for intensive study is one department in a large retail department store. This store is organized into several merchandising groups, each of which has several departments. The store has a total of over 100 major departments. Cyert, March, and Moore studied, with varying degrees of intensity, the price and output decisions in about a dozen of these departments. From these dozen they chose one for intensive investigation, and the specific simulation model they formulated is literally a model of decision-making by the buyer (i.e., the manager) in that specific department. However, they state that the decision processes observed in that one department could be generalized with trivial changes to other departments in the same merchandising group and could be generalized with relatively modest changes to most other departments outside the immediate group. Because of the great similarity in operation among department stores, the model probably represents most aspects of decision-making by retail department store buyers in general.

Cyert, March, and Moore have found that the department store buyer makes relatively independent price and output decisions. There are loose connexions between these decisions, but for the most part they are made with reference to different goals in response to different stimuli. There are two general goals that the department pursues. (a) A sales objective: The department expects (and is expected by the store) to achieve an annual sales objective. (b) A mark-up objective: The department attempts to realize a specified average mark-up on the goods sold. Organizational decision-making occurs in response to problems (or perceived potential problems) with respect to one or the other of these goals, so that the behaviour of the department is problem-oriented.

The buyer in a department forms sales 'estimates' that are consistent with its sales goal and develops a routine ordering plan for advance orders. These orders are designed to avoid over-commitment, pending feedback on sales. As feedback on sales is provided, results are checked against the sales objective. If the objective is being achieved, reorders are made according to standard rules. This is the usual route of decisions.

Suppose, however, that the sales goal is not being achieved. Under such circumstances a series of steps is taken.

First, the department's buyer attempts to change its environment by negotiating revised agreement with either its suppliers or other parts of its own firm or both. Within the firm, the buyer seeks a change in the promotional budget that will provide greater promotional resources for the goods sold by his department. Outside the firm, he seeks price concessions from manufacturers that will permit a reduction in retail price. If either of these attempts to relax external constraints is successful, reorders are made according to appropriately revised rules.

Second, the buyer considers a routine mark-down to stimulate sales generally and to make room for new items in the inventory. The buyer ordinarily has a pool of stock in his department available for mark-downs, and he expects to have to reduce mark-up in this way on some of the goods sold. He will attempt to stimulate sales by taking some of these anticipated mark-downs. Once again, if the tactic is successful in increasing sales sufficiently, reorders are made according to slightly revised rules.

Third, the buyer searches for new items that can be sold at relatively low prices (but with standard mark-ups). Most commonly, such items are found when domestic suppliers are eliminating lines or are in financial trouble. A second major source is in foreign markets.

In general, the buyer continues to search for solutions to his department's sales problems until he finds them. If the search procedures are successful, all goes well. In the long run, however, a solution may be found in another way. The feedback on sales not only triggers action, it also leads to the re-evaluation of the sales goal. In the face of persistent failure to achieve the sales goal, the goal adjusts downward. With persistent success, it adjusts upward.

The buyer's reaction to the mark-up goal is analogous to, but somewhat different in impact from, his reaction to the sales goal. On the basis of the mark-up goal (and standard industry practice), price lines and planned mark-up are established. Feedback on realized mark-up is received. If it is consistent with the goal, no action is taken, and standard decision rules are maintained.

If the mark-up goal is not being achieved, the buyer searches for ways in which he can raise mark-up. Basically, the search focuses on procedures for altering the product mix of the department in the direction of increasing the proportion of high mark-up items sold. For example, the buyer searches for items that are exclusive, for items that can be obtained from regular suppliers below standard cost, and for items from abroad. Where some of the same search efforts led to price reduction (and maintenance of mark-up), when stimulated by failure on the sales goal, here they lead to maintenance of price and increase in mark-up. At the same time, the buyer directs his department's major promotional efforts towards items on which high mark-ups can be realized. In some instances, the buyer has a reservoir of solutions to mark-up problems (e.g., pressure selling of high mark-up items). Such solutions are generally reserved for problem solving and are not viewed as appropriate long-run solutions. Finally, as in the case of the sales goal, the mark-up goal adjusts to experience gradually.

In order to explore the implications of their analysis of the department store buyer's decision processes, the authors developed a computer model to describe the processes. The model was programmed for an IBM 650 Ramac electronic digital computer. By letting the model run on the computer, it was possible to simulate the decisions of the department store buyer under a wide range of circumstances. In this manner, the properties of the model and the type of behaviour it produces could be explored in as much depth as desired. It was also possible to test the empirical validity of the model by presenting it with the facts about a number of actual decision situations that the real department store buyer faced, and then comparing the simulated decisions of the model with the actual decisions made by the buyer in these circumstances.

Cyert, March, and Moore tried to develop a model of decision-making by a department store buyer that would yield testable predictions. In interpreting the results of the tests, however, two qualifications are necessary. First, they did not attempt to formulate a model that would simulate all possible decisions the buyer made. Thus, for example, employment decisions were not considered at all. Second, even where the authors were successful in developing a model, they were constrained by the availability of data. The value of data for the purpose of testing models has not always been considered by the store in determining their information-storage system. Despite these limits, the authors were able to develop models for the major price and output decisions and to subject all but one of the major components of those models to some empirical test.

The output determination model consists of three segments – sales estimates, advance orders, and reorders. In each of the empirical tests made by Cyert, March, and Moore, the data used were *not* the same data from which the model was developed.

The sales estimation model is composed of the rule for estimating sales for the six-month period and of the rules for the estimation of the sales of individual months. The data available were for a two-year period, so that the test was far from conclusive. However, there is no reason to believe that the model would not be equally valid for a larger sample of data. The first part of the model, the estimation of total sales for a six-month period, predicted the total within 5 per cent in each of the four test instances. With the set of monthly rules, the model predicted about 95 per cent of the monthly sales estimates within 5 per cent. Cyert, March, and Moore stated that the predictive power could be increased still further by additional refinement of the rules, but they did not choose to expend further resources in that direction.

The advance orders segment of the model and the sales estimation segment are related, so that discrepancies between predicted and actual results are difficult to allocate precisely between the two segments. Unfortunately, the department store did not keep its records of advance orders any length of time, so no extensive test of this part of the model was possible. Cyert, March, and Moore were able to accumulate only four instances in which the predictions of the model could be compared with the actual advance orders. The results are given in Table 1.

Table 1

Season	Predicted advance orders	Actual advance orders
1	18,050	16,453
2	26,550	24,278
3	36,200	35,922
4	43,000	35,648

The reorders segment is one that it is most important to test. The fact is, however, that the data on reorders are not kept in any systematic fashion, and it was not possible to make any kind of test.

The situation with regard to adequate data for testing purposes was much better for the pricing models. In each case the model was subjected to a large sample of actual situations and performed adequately.

In order to test the ability of the mark-up model to predict the price decisions that will be made by the buyer on new merchandise, the authors drew an unrestricted random sample of 197 invoices. The cost data and classification of the item were given as inputs to the computer model. The output was a predicted price. Since the sample consisted of items that had already been priced, it was possible to make a comparison of the predicted price with the actual.

The definition of a correct prediction was stringent. Unless the predicted price matched the actual to the exact penny, the prediction was classified as incorrect. The results of the test were encouraging: of the 197 predicted prices, 188 were correct and nine were incorrect. Thus, 95·4 per cent of the predictions were correct. An investigation of the incorrect predictions showed that with minor modifications the model could be made to handle the deviant cases. However, at this point Cyert, March, and Moore felt that the predictive power was good enough so that a further expenditure of resources in this direction was not justified.

In order to test the sales pricing model, a random sample of 58 sales items was selected from the available records. For each item, the appropriate information as determined by the model was used as an input to the computer. The output was a prediction of the price that would be set by the buyer. Again Cyert, March, and Moore used the criterion that to be correct the predicted price must match the actual price to the penny. Out of the 58 predictions made by the model, 56 were correct.

In testing the mark-down part of the model, the basic data were taken from 'mark-down-slips', the primary document of this department store. These slips did not show the information which would enable the items to be categorized properly for use in the model. It was necessary therefore, to use direct methods such as interrogation of the buyer and sales personnel to get the information needed to classify the items so that the model could be tested. All of the data used were from the previous six-month period. It would be possible on a current basis to get the information which would enable the model to make the classifications itself as part of the pricing process.

The test for a correct prediction was the same as before, namely, correspondence to the penny between the predicted and the actual price. A total sample of 159 items was selected and predictions made of the mark-down price for each item. Of the 159 prices predicted, 140 were correct and 19 were wrong. This was only 88 per cent of the predictions correct to the penny, the poorest record of the three models. Although this model did not do as well as the other two, the outcome was clearly statistically significant.

The tests made support the model, even though there is a scarcity of data. It seems quite clear from this work that it is possible to develop a computer model that will simulate accurately all of the decision-making activity of the buyer. The major questions relate to the generalizability of the model across buyers and to the amount of explanation provided by this type of model. We shall discuss the second question later in this chapter. On the former question, the authors argue that the basic model can be generalized to other departments with appropriate changes in the parameters. They have not, however, attempted as yet to apply the model elsewhere.

A general model of price and output behaviour

A general behavioural model of price and output determination in oligopoly firms has been developed by Cohen, Cyert, March, and Soelberg (Cyert and March, 1963, pp. 149–82). This model is not a direct attempt to simulate the behaviour of any specific business firm, but rather an attempt to illustrate in specific quantitative form some general hypotheses about oligopoly behaviour and to derive some of the implications of these hypotheses. The general behavioural model is formulated as a computer model. The same essential model, with possibly different parameter values and initial conditions, is intended to simulate the price and output decisions of each firm in an oligopoly market. When an additional computer model of the market-wide interactions between the several firms is included, these models can then simulate the behaviour of an oligopoly market, as well as that of each component firm, over time.

The set of simulation models for an oligopoly industry contains an extremely large number of initial conditions and parameter values. In order to try to determine which of these are most important, and to understand the roles played by these most important parameters and initial conditions, a multiple regression procedure was used by the investigators. This consisted of generating a large number of random samples of sets of initial conditions and parameter values, simulating the oligopoly model for a long period of time using each set of these values, and then using multiple regression analysis to determine which particular parameters and initial conditions had the greatest effect on a number of selected key model outputs. The results of this exploratory technique are described more fully below, following a description of the oligopoly model itself. The latter is presented in terms of the internal decision processes postulated for any one firm.

In each time period, every firm in the Cohen-Cyert-March-Soelberg model makes three basic decisions. First, it must determine the selling price to be charged for its product. Since this essentially is a differentiated oligopoly market, selling price is a decision variable which may differ from firm to firm. Second, each firm must decide on its rate of production for the period. Finally, a general sales and marketing strategy must be chosen by the firm. This involves a determination of the amount of sales effort it will exert and the dollar expenditures it will make on sales promotion.

Associated with each of these decisions in the Cohen-Cyert-March-Soelberg model is a set of relevant goals. 'Each decision is related (at least in the first instance) with its own set of goals. Decisions within one decision area are made primarily with respect to the immediately relevant set of goals. The major interconnections among goals come through feedback, through expanded search where local goals cannot be achieved, and through certain checks on the feasibility of proposed action' (Cyert and March, 1963, p. 150).

Each firm is assumed to have three sets of goals relating to profits, inventory and production, and sales. The profit goal is an aspiration level for the firm's profits, and it has the most direct impact on the pricing decision. The inventory goal consists of minimum and maximum limits on inventory size relative to sales, while the production goal is a production-smoothing objective in the form of constraints on variations in the output level. Both the inventory and production goals have direct effects on the output decision. The firm's sales goals consist of aspiration levels for market share and for sales. The sales goals primarily affect sales strategy, but through interconnections, they also have an important effect on price.

Because the firm's decision process in the Cohen-Cyert-March-Soelberg model is segmented into three sets of decisions each having its own set of goals, it is convenient to think of each firm as being departmentalized into three subdivisions. 'These subdivisions – pricing, production, sales – are relatively independent of each other. Each makes decisions independently, subject to cross departmental pressures' (Cyert and March, 1963, p. 151).

Each firm makes its decisions on the basis of feedback from past results, adjusting both its goals and its procedures on the basis of such feedback. When problems are perceived to exist, each firm will search for solutions to these problems, but the firm avoids search behaviour when problems are not perceived.

In a steady state of equilibrium, production in one time period would be precisely equal to sales of the preceding time period. However, both in reality and in the model, such a steady state is rather infrequently attained and, when attained, is subject to shocks that usually make it transitory. In a dynamic environment, the firm seeks to establish a production level that is consistent with a set of changing inventory and production-smoothing goals.

With respect to inventory, the two critical values are the excess limit and the runout limit. The excess limit is a size of inventory that leads to complaints from the rest of the firm about the excessive cost of maintaining inventory. The excess limit gradually increases as sales increase. The runout limit is a size of inventory that leads to complaints from the rest of the firm about the loss of sales and sales position due to stockouts. As sales increase, the runout limit also increases.

These excess and runout limits define three possible conditions. So long as current inventory lies between the limits, the proposed inventory level will show a small growth of inventory reflecting the aspirations of the inventory-production division. If current inventory exceeds the excess limit, proposed inventory will be reduced from the overly high level. If current inventory is below the runout limit, proposed inventory will be increased.

Proposed production is determined by proposed inventory and a sales forecast, subject to demands for production smoothing. The sales forecast is an exponentially weighted moving average of past sales data. Proposed production is equal to the forecasted sales plus the difference between proposed inventory and current inventory. The production-smoothing goal consists of an upper and lower production limit. If proposed production is within these limits, it is produced. If proposed production is outside these limits, actual production is set at the limit nearer the proposed level. Normally, the upper production limit is the maximum production attained in the last several periods, the exact number of past periods considered being a parameter of the model. Similarly, the lower production limit is the minimum production in the last several periods. However, if production is actually set at one of these limits, that limit is changed in the direction of the proposed production. As long as proposed production is within the upper and lower limits, these limits tend to contract. When proposed production is outside these limits, the limits tend to expand. A firm which has a history of variable production learns to allow future variability, while a firm which has a history of smooth production will tolerate rather little variability in its future production.

These rules define the output decision in the model. In addition, the inventory-production part of the model exerts some pressures on other parts of the system. First, so long as goals are met, organizational slack (excess operating cost) is increased. Second, when the inventory-production goals are not met, pressure is put on the sales division to adjust sales to inventory-production needs – that is, to smooth sales by reducing them when production is high or inventory low, and by increasing them when production is low or inventory high.

In the model, a firm's selling price is determined by adjusting present price in the face of feedback on goals, costs, and competitors' behaviour. While this adjustment is primarily responsive to a comparison between actual profits achieved and the profit goal, it is also sensitive to pressure from the sales department for price reduction.

The profit goal of a firm changes over time in two ways. First, it tends toward actual achieved profits, since the profit goal is a lagged function of profits. Second, the parameters involved in this function change on the basis of experience. The authors postulate two different functions for changing the profit goal on the basis of experience, one operating when profits achieved exceed the goal, the other when profits are less than the goal. Whenever the profit goal is achieved without extra search effort being exerted, the firm learns to attend more to recently experienced success. When the goal is achieved after initial failure triggers search activity, the firm learns to attend less to recently experienced failure. When the goal is not achieved even after extended search, the firm learns to attend more to recently experienced failure.

In setting its selling price, the firm first checks three environmental characteristics – costs of manufacture, the effects of past price changes, and long-run competitors' price behaviour. First, if exogenous costs have increased, proposed price is increased proportionately to the change in costs. Then, if profit performance has improved after a prior price change (either up or down) that was induced by a prior profit failure, the price-change rule is altered to produce future action more in the direction of the action taken. In contrast, if the prior action has been followed by a poorer performance, the rule is shifted in the other direction. Thus, 'successful' price cuts will stimulate more vigorous price cuts in comparable circumstances; 'unsuccessful' price cuts will stimulate less vigorous cuts and possibly even price raises. Similarly, 'successful' and 'unsuccessful' price raises lead to revision in the rule.

Finally, the firm also checks the long-run price behaviour of competition, specifically of the lowest-priced major competitor. Here an elaborate program checks the relative price of the competition in relation to the relative price position of the firm. A series of steps involving market-share and sales goals has been developed. It is possible, depending on the way competition has moved and the effects on market-share and sales goals, for the firm to match a relative price decrease completely, partially, or not at all, and similarly with a relative price increase. Thus, no simple, strict rules are developed as in such economic models as the 'kinked demand curve'. Rather, all of the actions of a firm in the real world are possible.

After these checks on the environment are made, the firm considers price from the point of view of its profit and sales goals. If profit goals are being met and there is no pressure for price reduction from the sales department, then price remains constant, organizational slack increases, and sales-effectiveness pressure decreases. If profit goals are not being met and there is no pressure from the sales department for price reduction, the firm considers its past experience in this situation and raises, cuts, or maintains price according to what has been 'successful' in the past.

Under certain circumstances, however, there will be pressure from the sales department for price reduction. There are two forms that this pressure might take. The more moderate pressure simply indicates trouble on sales goals. The more extreme pressure (which we might call 'emergency' pressure) indicates not only trouble relative to the sales goal, but also a recent adverse change in short-run competitive price position. The feedback on price competition is faster than other types of feedback. If the firm has achieved its profit goal and the standard pressure for a price reduction is applied, it will cut price somewhat, while if emergency pressure is applied, it will cut price to restore the previous relative price position. If the firm is not achieving its profit goal, the pressure from the sales division for price reduction is potentially in conflict with the profit goal. Consequently, there is more resistance in the firm to price reduction. If the pressure being applied is of the emergency variety, the firm acts to restore the price position; but it also initiates a search program for other alternatives to price cutting. If only standard pressure is being exerted, no price action is taken, but the search program is triggered.

The search program consists of five steps pursued sequentially (one each time period) until the need for search is removed. These steps are the following:

1. Organizational slack is reduced.

2. Inventory excess limit is reduced.

3. Pressure is placed on sales for improved performance.

4. Expenditure for sales promotion is increased.

5. If all of the other procedures fail, the profit goal is reduced.

6. Return to (1) and cycle again.

The order of the search procedures changes in response to experience.

Since the model is concerned with price and output determination, no attempt was made to construct a detailed market strategy decision. There are, however, three different sales goals for a firm. First, the firm compares its actual sales level with a sales-level goal that is a function of its recent experience. Second, the firm compares its market share with a market-share goal that is also a function of its recent experience. Finally, the firm has a competitive-price goal, for it does not want its short-run relative price position (i.e., price change *vis-à-vis* competitors) to change adversely (i.e., to a higher relative price).

In the short run, the competitive price goal represents the objectives of the sales force. When relative price position changes adversely, the sales force complains and requests remedial action, because its own job then becomes harder. Such a feedback is fast, being received each time period in the model. Feedback information on the sales level and the market share is somewhat slower. Cohen, Cyert, March, and Soelberg assume that sales and market share are computed relatively infrequently, the exact frequencies being parameters of their model.

In making its market strategy decisions, the firm first checks its sales goals. If the latest reports on sales and market share indicate that these goals have been achieved, the sales department simply continues its present policies, accompanied by an increase in sales slack (i.e., a decrease in 'sales-effectiveness pressure') and an increase in general organizational slack. If the market-share goal is not being met but the sales goal is, then sales-effectiveness pressure is increased. If the market-share goal is being met but the sales goal is not, there is an increase in the percentage of sales revenue expended on sales promotion.

If neither market-share nor sales goals are achieved, sales-effectiveness pressure is increased, and the sales department puts pressure for remedial price action on the pricing department. If the short-run relative price position has changed adversely, the request is an emergency one, while if the relative price position has not changed adversely, the request is of the standard type.

Both market-share and sales goals change in approximately the same two ways that the profit goal changes. 'Each goal is a weighted average of the previous goal and the immediate past experience. Whenever the goal is achieved the weights attached to recently experienced success are increased, and the weights attached to recently experienced failure are decreased. Whenever a goal is not achieved, the weights attached to recently experienced failure are increased, while the weights attached to recently experienced success are decreased' (Cyert and March, 1963, pp. 157–8).

We have described in some detail the decision-process model of any firm in this oligopoly simulation. The entire oligopoly model is made up of several such firms, together with some additional mechanisms which describe the interactions of these firms in the market place.

There are two major ways in which the several oligopoly firms interact in the market place. First, the collective actions of all the firms determine the total level of market demands. Second, the individual actions of each firm relative to the collective actions of all firms determine the share of demand which will be generated for each firm. In addition, there is also one minor way in which the firms interact, namely, the attention which each firm pays to relative price changes *vis-à-vis* its major competitors.

In each time period, the total level of market demand is a function of the weighted average level of prices set by all firms, the weighted average level of sales-effectiveness pressure for all firms, the weighted average level of sales-promotion expenditures by all firms, and an exogenous factor. Each of the weighted averages in this function uses actual sales level for the previous time period for each firm as the weighting factor.

The share of market captured by any one firm is a somewhat complex function of its relative sales-effectiveness pressure, its relative price level, its relative promotion expenditures, and its previous share of market. All of these relative measures are *vis-à-vis* the total industry levels of these variables.

The computer program for the model was written in an algebraic programming language, 20-GATE, and the model was simulated on a Bendix G-20 electronic computer. The computer model generates a detailed time series of decisions, internal organizational results, goals, etc., for each firm in the industry. The exact nature of this output depends on a rather large number of initial conditions and parameters.

To study the impact of selected internal firm parameters on the model, the authors simplified the industry by treating only the case where there are only two firms in the industry. They further considered only one set of market parameters and a market in which the exogenous factor contributing to total demand is subject only to modest random fluctuations around its mean.

To summarize, we can say that the detailed general model of price and output determination in a modern oligopolistic firm portrays the process of decision-making in terms consistent with a behavioural theory of the firm. The firm has multiple goals whose values change with the firm's experience. The firm solves problems in each of its decision areas more or less independently and uses search procedures which are learned from experience. The firm also adjusts decision rules on the basis of the feedback of experience.

A simulation of market relationships in the West Coast lumber industry

Balderston and Hoggatt have developed a quasi-realistic computer simulation of the West Coast lumber industry (1962). We choose to classify this as an illustrative or intellective simulation study, rather than a descriptive simulation study of real organizations, because Balderston and Hoggatt intended their model to bear only a loose resemblance to the actual industry, and they did not attempt to study in detail the decision processes of several firms in that market.

The Balderston-Hoggatt model is a study of the dynamic behaviour of firms in a two-stage market. In this model, supplier firms sell to wholesale intermediaries, and these wholesalers in turn resell to customer firms. There are flows of information, materials, and money between firms at the different vertical stages of this market, but no horizontal communication within the same stage is allowed in this model.

The model is driven by the wholesalers. They send search messages to suppliers (manufacturers) to discover the quantities the supplier is prepared to sell and the price he is asking. Similarly, the wholesalers send messages to the retailers to determine the quantity demanded and the price. If the transaction is profitable to the wholesaler on the basis of his tests, the transaction is completed. The material is shipped directly to the retailer. The wholesalers carry no inventory, but handle the financing of the transactions.

A market period ends when all the wholesalers have completed their searching, that is, when there is no longer any wholesaler who wishes to send a search message. At the end of the period, two important categories of action take place. First, price and output decisions are made by manufacturers and retailers for the next period. For the retailer, the decision includes not only bid prices and quantities but also the price and quantity for selling in the final market. Second, decisions to enter and leave the industry are made at this time. The decision criterion in each case is quite simple. If a firm has a negative cash position, it leaves the industry, and if average profits for any class of firms are higher than some given level, a new firm enters.

There are two basic parameters in the model which can be changed without affecting the other relations. One of these is the cost of sending a message. There is only one cost for sending a message, regardless of which of the three classes of participants sends it. In developing an experimental design for testing certain hypotheses of the model, four different message costs were used: 0, 12, 48, and 192. The second basic parameter of the model is the method of formulating a criterion by which a firm in one class decides with which firm in another class it will deal. Thus, a manufacturer must have a preference ordering of wholesalers to decide to which one he will sell. Retailers must also have a preference ordering of wholesalers and wholesalers must have preference orderings for both manufacturers and retailers. The authors have used two methods in the model. One preference ordering is based on experience. It is a number which depends on the relation of transactions to orders and the actual quantity shipped. The higher the number, the more preferred is the particular firm. The second method is to determine a preference ordering on the basis of random numbers. The experimental design then consists of a complete run of the model for each cost and each method of preference ordering. This gives a total of eight runs, which form the basic data for analysis. These data are used in the testing of a series of hypotheses the authors have constructed.

The first set of hypotheses ignores the potential interactions among variables and concentrates on the relationship of one variable to another. Accordingly, these are called elementary hypotheses. These hypotheses are concerned with three factors: (a) market stability, (b) the effect of changing message costs, and (c) the effect of the alternate methods of preference ordering.

The hypotheses on market stabilization are generated from classical economic theory for the most part. Thus, the authors examined the three sets of prices in the model – offer prices, bid prices, and retail prices – for evidence of a trend toward equilibrium. In addition, hypotheses concerning the flow of the physical commodity through the system, the number of firms in each class, and the amount of profit were tested. In the case of the other two classes of hypotheses, the attempt was made to determine the effects of parameter changes in message cost and preference-ordering on the same set of variables as above.

In addition to the elementary hypotheses, certain hypotheses related to specific characteristics of the internal structure were tested. In particular, the effects of changing the two parameters – message cost and preference-ordering – on the average firm size were tested. The authors then went further and attempted to isolate the various causal mechanisms in the model. This was done in lieu of analytical reduction of the model which, in the case of most simulation models, is not possible.

Conclusions

An examination of recent work in organization theory underscores the need for using computer simulation methodology in future research. A major defect in much of the research to date has been its inability to utilize our knowledge of the micro components, such as work groups and decision-making units, for deriving implications about the behaviour of the total system, i.e., of the organization in which the micro components are embedded. Current work in organization theory tends to get bogged down in two ways. First, the separate segments of an organization are usually studied independently. Thus, the structure of the work group is analysed, then the problems of supervision are studied, then the processes of management are considered, and so on for other segments of the organization, including its environment. In these studies, however, inadequate attention is often paid to the interactions which occur between these segments when they are part of the same organization. Second, the techniques used for trying to understand each individual segment often involve studying the effects of only one or two variables at a time, even though many different variables may be jointly responsible for the observed behaviour.

Clearly, this type of work is a useful beginning in helping us obtain a better understanding of organizations. However, before we can say that we have a complete understanding of any organization, it is necessary to show that our knowledge of the individual components can be put together in a total system, i.e., an organization can be synthesized, which allows for the interactions of all the relevant variables and of all the structural components. The behaviour of an individual subsystem in isolation may be very different from its behaviour when it interacts with other subsystems. Since the ultimate aim of organization theory is to explain and predict the behaviour of organizations, not of individual components, it is necessary to have a method which allows us to construct and manipulate a total organization. Computer simulation techniques provide one such method.

Computer models and man-machine simulations offer an unparalleled means by which we can:

1. Formulate extremely detailed and highly precise models of organizational behaviour.

2. Test the empirical validity of these models;

3. Experimentally manipulate the models in a way which is usually prohibited in real-world organizations;

4. Predict the future behaviour of existing or redesigned organizations;

5. Train people to behave more effectively in an organizational setting. We are convinced that in the future much fundamental research in organization theory concentrating on the behaviour of entire organizations will be done using simulation models.

References

BALDERSTON, F. E., and HOGGATT, A. C. (1962), *Simulation of Market Process*, Berkeley, University of California, Institute of Business and Economic Research.

CYERT, R. M., and MARCH, J. G. (1963), *A Behavioral Theory of the Firm*, Englewood Cliffs, N.J., Prentice-Hall.

22 W. M. Evan

The Organizational Experiment

W. M. Evan, 'The organizational experiment', in *Organizational Experiments*, Harper & Row Publishers Inc., 1971, pp. 1–5.

Of the various research methods currently used in the field of organization theory several are well established – almost institutionalized – and others are still looked on with some skepticism and even suspicion. Perhaps the most common mode of research is the case study or the field study which typically involves an intensive analysis of one or more organizations or organizational subunits. This method consists of such techniques as participant and nonparticipant observation, interviewing, and the analysis of documentary materials. That this method is admirably suited to studying the complexities of large-scale organizations is evident upon examining such outstanding studies as Selznick's on the TVA (1949), Blau's on two government agencies (1963), Lipset, Trow, and Coleman's on the International Typographical Union (1956), and Gouldner's on a mine and gypsum plant (1954). In these exemplary studies, the authors, guided by Weber's theory of bureaucracy or Michels' theory of the iron law of oligarchy, have abstracted – from their concrete observations – propositions about organizational dynamics.

As a strategy for generating insights and propositions, the case study is invaluable. It is not, however, a method of testing propositions; nor does it provide a basis for generalizing particular findings to a class of organizations or to organizations in general. Moreover, the case study does not lend itself to a systematic investigation of the antecedents and consequences of organizational structures. Although a longitudinal study of organizations can ascertain changes in structure over time, the range of variation or the contrasts observed in a case study may be too limited for analysis.

The various limitations of the case study of a particular

organization, whether it be a government agency, a hospital, a research laboratory, a university, a business organization, or a labour union, have stimulated social scientists to make use of the sample survey. This method enables the researcher to explore the relationships among a large number of variables in the context of a sample of organizations. In recent years there has been a marked growth in the use of the sample survey in studies of organizational problems. Several notable examples of applications of survey methodology are Woodward's study of the relation of technology to organizational structure in a sample of 100 manufacturing firms in England (1965). Gross's study of the relation of goals to the power structure of a sample of 68 universities (1968), and Gross and Herriott's study of the interaction of principals, teachers and students in a sample of 507 schools (1965). Such surveys have made important contributions to the field; nevertheless, they illustrate the two principal problems that beset users of survey methodology: how to overcome the cross-sectional bias so as to study changes over time and how to infer causal relations from correlational data.

The panel technique, one method of overcoming the cross-sectional bias of surveys, involves conducting repeated interviews with the same sample of respondents over time, thus yielding data on processes of change (Lazarsfeld and Fiske, 1938). Although applied with considerable sophistication to the study of voting behaviour, consumer behaviour, and attitude change, the panel type of survey has not yet been extended, with a sizeable sample, to organizational research.

The difficulties of inferring causal relations from correlational data have preoccupied the attention of Lazarsfeld (1959), Simon (1954), Blalock (1964), Duncan (1966), and others. Some of their models have been used effectively in disentangling causal relations from correlational data. A case in point is the analysis by Gross and Herriott of the relationships among the principal's professional score, teacher professional performance score, teacher morale, pupil academic score, and pupil's family income (1965, pp. 48–57). And yet because of the large number of variables typically investigated in a sample survey, the various causal models are likely to leave many problems concerning the interrelationships among the variables unanswered. For this as well as other reasons, the question of whether social scientists are sufficiently exploiting the experimental method, whose strength lies in reducing some of the ambiguities in inferring causality, merits attention.

The use of the experimental method is still relatively infrequent in organizational research. The reluctance to explore the potential utility of experimental designs is not unrelated to the scepticism long expressed about the feasibility of the experimental method in the social sciences. Toward the end of the nineteenth century, Durkheim asserted that

> When ... [phenomena] can be artificially produced at the will of the observer, the method is that of experiment, properly so called. When, on the contrary, the production of facts is not within our control and we can only bring them together in the way that they have been spontaneously produced, the method employed is that of indirect experiment, or the comparative method. ... Since ... social phenomena evidently escape the control of the experimenter, the comparative method is the only one suited in sociology (1950, p. 125).

Over one-half of a century later, C. A. Moser (1965, p. 16), in a similar vein, claimed:

> It is regarded by many as a truism that the social scientist is rarely able to conduct strictly controlled experiments and, consequently, to establish the causative connections which are held to be the essence of scientific progress. There is no denying that strictly controlled experimentation is rarely feasible with human populations and that this does account for the tentativeness of many social research results.

And quite recently, Price, though acknowledging the superiority of experimentation as a method of verifying propositions on organizational phenomena, predicts that its use will not 'expand significantly in the near future' (1968, p. 122).

Notwithstanding these expressions of doubt and pessimism, small-scale efforts have been made to develop an experimental approach to organizational problems, beginning in the late forties with Bavelas's laboratory experiments on communication nets (1950), and with Coch and French's field experiment at the Harwood factory on resistance to changes in production (1948). In this paper a laboratory as well as a field experiment, if concerned with an organizational problem, will be referred to as an *organizational experiment*.

Concept of the organizational experiment

Compared with the case study and the sample survey, the organizational experiment has the virtue of increasing the chances of establishing causal relations among variables of interest to the researcher. But there is yet another attribute which not only defines the nature of an organizational experiment but also identifies its potential contribution to the body of theory on organizations, viz., it investigates variables relating to organizational structure and process.

Paradoxically, there is still little consensus as to the meaning of these basic concepts – witness the recent efforts of Pugh and his colleagues to define and measure structure in terms of five dimensions: specialization, standardization, formalization, centralization, and configuration (1968). As the field of complex organizations develops, these concepts of structure and process will be progressively defined in relation to other fundamental concepts and postulates of special and general theories. For present purposes, *organizational structure* refers to the relatively durable properties of the arrangement of subsystems of an organization, such as the degree of hierarchical differentiation with respect to skill, rewards, and authority (Evan, 1963), and *organizational process* refers to recurrent activities that contribute to the transformation of organizational inputs into outputs and mediate the relations between the organization and its environment (Evan, 1966; 1968). Without going into the rationale for these tentative definitions, which would take us far afield, an *organizational experiment* – whether conducted in the laboratory or in the field of an ongoing organization – tests under controlled conditions propositions relating to variables of organizational structure and process. In studies employing nonexperimental research methods, however, generic problems of structure and process tend to be neglected. Yet, if a general theory of organization is to be developed in the years to come, it will probably be cast in terms which will include concepts of structure and process.

In the case of the organizational laboratory experiment, properties of structure and process are simulated (in the laboratory, not on the computer) by various means. Whether to simulate properties of structure and process, which properties to simulate, and how to simulate them are still moot questions. According to one view, a simulation should be

... both rich in properties and made up mostly of real and iconic properties. ... A [simulation] that is very rich in properties is as difficult to observe, control, and analyze as the world it represents. But a [simulation] that is poor in properties depends, more than a rich one, upon a theory sufficiently developed to translate its results into terms relevant to an understanding of empirical reality. ... In the present state of theory, we require [simulations] close to the upper bound of richness; the upper bound being dictated by the desire to isolate and manipulate theoretically significant variables without undue complication. ... As theory accumulates, [simulations] should become less rich and use more analogue properties (Zelditch and Evan, 1962, pp. 52, 54).

A pervasive problem in designing laboratory simulations, as well as other types of experiments, is fulfilling the demands for both internal and external validity, as cogently formulated by Campbell (1963). Internal validity is concerned with whether the experimental stimulus creates treatment effects which are unconfounded by various extraneous variables that the experimental design sought to control; external validity 'asks the question of generalizability: To what populations, settings, treatment variables, and measurement variables can this effect be generalized?'(1963, p. 214). Simulating many properties of organizational structure and process in the laboratory may increase external validity at the cost of decreasing experimental control and hence of internal validity.

The questions whether and how to simulate organizational structures and processes do not, of course, arise in the case of the organizational field experiment. Any theoretical or practical problem of structure and/or process can be the subject of an organizational field experiment. As in the case of the laboratory experiment, of critical import is whether the experimental design meets the standards of both internal and external validity. In short, the organizational experiment deals with problems of structure and process of organizations, whether in the laboratory or in ongoing organizations.

Functions of the organizational experiment

Although the concept of the organizational experiment was

defined in terms that have consequences for the building of theory in the field of organizations, it does not follow that the only function of experimentation is to *test* theory. 'Theoretical experiments' and 'crucial experiments' are by no means the only types of experiments performed in science (Kaplan, 1964, pp. 147–54); nor are they yet as common in the social sciences as in the natural sciences. Another important function of the organizational experiment, apart from verification, is the exploration of hypotheses, whether well grounded or poorly grounded in theory. Such exploratory experiments are particularly useful in the present stage of development of the theory of organizations.

An additional function of the organizational experiment, of considerable import for theory as well as practice, is the ability of the researcher, particularly in the laboratory, to experiment with organizational innovations. As Bass puts it,

. . . only in simulation can really radical innovations be tried; for no survey or case observation can uncover, nor can any field study be attempted of, an organizational idea which is untried, untested, and seemingly uncertain in outcome (1963, p. 122).

Structural properties of organizations that depart, for example, from prevailing hierarchical principles of authority and inequality of rewards can be simulated in the laboratory (Evan and Simmons, 1969). If the researcher should discover that an organizational innovation – which might readily be dismissed as a mere 'utopian' organizational design – is both 'efficient' and 'effective', in Barnard's usage of these terms (1938, pp. 55–8), he might eventually succeed in persuading the executives of an ongoing organization to test his innovative design in a field experiment. In effect, organizational innovations can be developed and implemented by means of organizational experiments in the laboratory as well as in real-world organizations.

To be sure, ideas for 'utopian' organizational designs need not originate in laboratory experiments. In one study the researchers initiated a field experiment to increase 'industrial democracy' in manufacturing organizations in Norway without first conducting a related experiment in the laboratory (Thorsrud and Emery, 1960). This raises an important question as to the relationship among the several research strategies we have discussed, viz., the case study, the sample survey, the organizational laboratory experiment, and the organizational field experiment.

Methodological integration

Regardless of the research strategy, the organizational researcher is faced with the problem of the grounds for generalizing the findings of his study. In the case of the sample survey, the nature of the sample of organizations provides a relatively clear-cut criterion for generalizing the findings to a particular population of organizations. But what of the case study, the organizational laboratory experiment, and the organizational field experiment? One answer is to rely on a relevant theory to bear the brunt of generalization. If, however, theories of organization are not yet sufficiently developed to guide the researcher in his efforts at generalization, he will, of necessity, look further afield. Campbell, as we have seen, has grappled with this problem in some detail and with great acuity. If in designing an experiment, the researcher avoids the four sources of external invalidity – which are, according to Campbell, interaction effects of testing and the experimental variable, interaction effects between selection bias and the experimental variable, reactive effects of experimental arrangement, and multiple-treatment interference (1963, p. 215) – then he can have some confidence in the representativeness of his findings.

Another basis for generalizing the findings of a given study is for the researcher to relate his results not only to those of studies employing similar methods – especially if he replicates a particular study – but also to results stemming from studies using dissimilar methods. In other words, if, for example, the findings of a case study are confirmed by those of a laboratory experiment and a sample survey, or if the results of a laboratory experiment are confirmed by those of a field experiment and a survey, in either case the researcher would be more confident about the generalizability of his findings than in the absence of confirmations from studies employing dissimilar research methods. Otherwise put, generalizability of findings is enhanced by the coordination or integration of findings from studies using different research methods (Zelditch and Evan, p. 60).

The interrelationships of the research methods discussed above may be represented in various ways. One way of diagramming some of the relationships is by means of the flow chart in Figure 1. Although other feedback loops are possible – e.g., sample survey to case study, laboratory experiment to sample survey, case study to laboratory experiment, field experiment to laboratory experiment, etc. – the rationale for those shown in Figure 1 is probably more readily defensible. A case study or field study of an organization can identify one or more salient variables or relationships

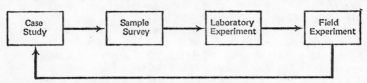

Figure 1 Interrelationships of research methods

which a researcher may then wish to investigate by means of a sample survey. The major relationships uncovered in the survey will probably leave unanswered questions concerning their dynamics. The researcher may then choose to pursue the problem of the relationships among the key variables in the laboratory. If the experiment yields a relationship of general significance to theory and/or practice, the researcher may wish to test its external validity – not to mention its practical import for organizational design or innovation – in a field experiment. The fact that the literature in organization theory does not provide a single instance of a methodologically integrated sequence of studies similar to the one sketched above is not an argument as to its feasibility or utility but rather an indication of a glaring deficiency in the field. An entirely plausible reason for this deficiency is the lack of appreciation displayed by many researchers with respect to laboratory and field experimentation. Given the necessary resources, research programs can be designed with methodological integration in mind, but the omission of any link in the sequence can have serious consequences for the resulting generalizations; and the links which are usually omitted are those involving experimental methodology. This should not be taken as a criticism of alternative research strategies, but rather as an attempt to place experimental techniques in their proper perspective. Notwithstanding the halting progress thus far made in developing and applying the organizational experiment there is no question but that the field of organization theory is now more receptive than heretofore to this relatively new research strategy.

References

BARNARD, C. I. (1938), *The Functions of the Executive*, Cambridge, Mass., Harvard University Press.

BASS, B. (1963), 'Experimenting with simulated manufacturing organizations', in S. B. Sells (ed.), *Stimulus Determinants of Behavior*, New York, Ronald Press, pp. 117–96.

BAVELAS, A. (1950), 'Communication patterns in task-oriented groups', *Journal of the Acoustics Society of America*, vol. 22, pp. 725–30.

BAVELAS, A., and BARRETT, D. (1951), 'An experimental approach to organizational communication', *Personnel*, vol. 27, pp. 366–71.

BLALOCK, H. M. (1964), *Causal Inference in Nonexperimental Research*, Chapel Hill, University of North Carolina Press.

BLAU, P. M. (1963), *The Dynamics of Bureaucracy*, rev. ed,. Chicago, University of Chicago Press.

CAMPBELL, D. T. (1963), 'From description to experimentation: interpreting trends as quasi-experiments', in C. W. Harris (ed.), *Problems in Measuring Change*, Madison, Wis., University of Wisconsin Press, pp. 214–16.

COCH, L., and FRENCH, J. R. P., JR (1948), 'Overcoming resistance to change', *Human Relations*, vol. 1, pp. 512–32.

DUNCAN, O. D. (1966), 'Path analysis: sociological examples', *American Journal of Sociology*, vol. 72, July, pp. 1–16.

DURKHEIM, E. (1950), *The Rules of Sociological Method*, trans. by S. A. Solovay and J. H. Mueller, Glencoe, Ill., Free Press.

EVAN, W. M. (1963), 'Indices of the hierarchical structure of industrial organizations', *Management Science*, vol. 9, April, pp. 468–77.

EVAN, W. M. (1966), 'The organization-set: toward a theory of inter-organizational relations', in J. D. Thompson (ed.), *Approaches to Organizational Design*, Pittsburgh, Pa., University of Pittsburgh Press, pp. 175–90.

EVAN, W. M. (1968), 'A systems model of organizational climate', in R. Tagiuri and G. H. Litwin (eds.), *Organizational Climate*, Harvard University, Graduate School of Business Administration, pp. 107–24.

EVAN, W. M., and SIMMONS, R. G. (1969), 'Organizational effects of inequitable rewards: two experiments in status inconsistency', *Administrative Science Quarterly*, vol. 14, June, pp. 224–37.

GOULDNER, A. W. (1954), *Patterns of Industrial Bureaucracy*, Glencoe, Ill., Free Press.

GROSS, E. (1968), 'Universities as organizations: a research approach', *American Sociological Review*, vol. 33, August, pp. 518–43.

GROSS, N., and HERRIOTT, R. E. (1965), *Staff Leadership in Public Schools: A Sociological Inquiry*, New York, John Wiley.

KAPLAN, A. (1964), *The Conduct of Inquiry*, San Francisco, Chandler.

LAZARSFELD, P. F. (1959), 'Evidence and inference in social research', in D. Lerner (ed.), *Evidence and Inference*, New York, Free Press, pp. 107–38.

LAZARSFELD, P. F., and FISKE, M. (1938), 'The 'panel' as a new tool for measuring opinion', *Public Opinion Quarterly*, vol. 2, pp. 596–612.

LIPSET, S. M., TROW, M. A., and COLEMAN, J. S. (1956), *Union Democracy*, Glencoe, Ill., Free Press.

MOSER, C. A. (1965), *Survey Methods in Social Investigation*, London, Heinemann.

PRICE, J. L. (1968), 'Design of proof in organizational research', *Administrative Science Quarterly*, vol. 13, June, pp. 121–34.

PUGH, D. S., HICKSON, D. J., HININGS, C. R., and TURNER, C. (1968), 'Dimensions of organization structure', *Administrative Science Quarterly*, vol. 13, June, pp. 64–105.

SELZNICK, P. (1949), *TVA and the Grass Roots*, Berkeley and Los Angeles, University of California Press.

SIMON, H. A. (1954), 'Spurious correlation: a causal interpretation', *Journal of the American Statistical Association*, vol. 59, pp. 467–79.

THORSRUD, E., and EMERY, F. E. (1960), 'Industrial conflict and industrial democracy', in J. R. Lawrence (ed.), *Operational Research and the Social Sciences*, London, Tavistock Publications, pp. 439–47.

WOODWARD, J. (1965), *Industrial Organization: Theory and Practice*, London, Oxford University Press.

ZELDITCH, M., JR, and EVAN, W. M. (1962), 'Simulated bureaucracies: a methodological analysis', in H. Guetzkow (ed.), *Simulation in Social Science: Readings*, Englewood Cliffs, N.J., Prentice-Hall, pp. 48–60.

Part Five
Designing and Managing Interorganizational Systems

Given the state of the art in research on interorganizational relations, it may seem both premature and hazardous to concern oneself with normative questions of designing and redesigning interorganizational systems. The application of any model – positive or normative – to a real world problem requires a deep familiarity with the realities in question. This truism holds for organizational as well as interorganizational systems. While going beyond positive research to normative research may seem unwarranted to some organizational researchers, others would contend that it is a critical and indispensable means for advancing knowledge in this field.

Each reading in Part Five suggests a potentially useful approach to redesigning interorganizational systems. Stern focuses on organizational strategies for resolving interorganizational conflicts. He relates different mechanisms for resolving interorganizational conflicts to varying degrees of perceived vertical interdependence among organizations, particularly those that are members of a channel of distribution. At the high end of perceived interdependence, it is possible to institutionalize supraorganizational mechanisms such as the development of superordinate goals and to have recourse to conciliation, mediation and arbitration. At the low end of perceived interdependence, a bargaining model is appropriate for the resolution of interorganizational conflict.

Posner outlines a programme for increasing the effectiveness of the Antitrust Division of the Department of Justice as a regulatory agency. Applying some concepts of classical economic theory combined with cost-benefit analysis, Posner develops various proposals to enhance antitrust enforcement. By formulating an instrumental conception of law enforcement, he argues for selective enforcement that will maximize the efficiency with which the goals of antitrust laws are pursued. To implement his instrumental view of law enforcement, Posner advocates various organizational changes within the Antitrust Division, such as hiring economists in addition to lawyers, providing for more hierarchical control of the staff, especially the trial lawyers, and providing for planning and evaluation to determine priorities in the use of the organization's resources.

The last reading by Stern and Craig addresses itself to the role of technological innovations in effecting interorganizational linkages. The use of computer-based communication systems to link organizations belonging to the same channel of distribution – assuming it can be implemented without violating antitrust law – is but a special case of the potential use of communication systems transcending the boundaries of organizations.

In effect, the authors of the three papers in Part Five advance a mixture of strategies for redesigning interorganizational systems: organizational, economic, legal and technological. Clearly, these strategies are not independent of one another nor do they exhaust the normative approaches to redesigning interorganizational systems. As in the case of other facets of organizational research as well as organizational decisions, an experimental perspective is the better part of wisdom:

All formal organizations are recurrently confronted with dilemmas of organizational design. The researcher in organization theory, as in other scientific disciplines, can create various structures in the laboratory and learn why they have predictable or unpredictable results. He will thereby discover deeper knowledge about the phenomena he is concerned with. Likewise, if executives, regardless of type of organization, adopt what might be called a 'cybernetic conception of decision making', namely, that managerial decisions are neither ineffable nor infallible but rather hypotheses to be tested in order to learn from both successes and failures, they will be more willing to entertain the idea of instituting a program of field experiments as an integral part of the operations of their organization (Evan, 1971, p. 263).

Reference

EVAN, W. M. (1971), 'Editor's postscript', in W. M. Evan (ed.), *Organizational Experiments*, New York, Harper & Row.

23 L. W. Stern

Managing Conflicts in Distribution Channels

L. W. Stern, 'Potential management mechanisms in distribution channels: an interorganizational analysis', in D. N. Thompson (ed.), *Contractual Marketing Systems*, Heath Lexington Books, 1971, pp. 111–45.

Introduction

The purpose of this paper is to suggest potential mechanisms that might be employed to manage, reduce, or resolve conflict in distribution channels. Very little work has to date been done in applying to the field of marketing the findings of sociologists, labour relations experts, or political scientists on resolving conflict. Conflict in distribution may be viewed behaviourally, as a form of opposition which is opponent-centred; based on incompatibility of goals, aims, or values of opposing firms; direct; and personal; in which the opponent or opposing firm controls the goal or object desired by both parties. Such conflict – behaviour which thwarts, injures, or destroys an opponent – is present in all socioeconomic systems, including channels of distribution.

For any given socioeconomic system, some degree of conflict may be highly functional for the long-term viability of the system. At some point, excessive conflict becomes dysfunctional and produces adverse effects on the system. Conflict should not be treated as all good or all bad. Boulding nicely characterizes the view taken here:

We are not 'against' conflict. It is indeed an essential and for the most part useful element in social life. There is, however, a constant tendency for unmanaged conflict to get out of hand and to become bad for all parties concerned (Boulding, 1961, p. 1).

In this paper, the potential conflict management mechanisms suggested are organized into categories which are consistent with the various degrees of perceived vertical interdependence among channel members. Viewing vertical interdependence on a continuum from high to low, the categories and the specific mechanisms discussed under each can be outlined as shown in Figure 1.

	Degree of perceived interdependence High←————————————— —————→Low			
Category	Supra-organizational	Interpenetration	Boundary	Bargaining and negotiation
Specific mechanisms	superordinate goals; conciliation and mediation; arbitration; special-purpose mechanisms: (1) commissions of inquiry (2) observers	membership: exchange-of-persons programmes; ideological: (1) education, (2) propaganda; membership anc ideological: cooptation	diplomacy	bargaining strategy

Figure 1

As is pointed out below, certain mechanisms facilitate the implementation and reinforce the effectiveness of others (for example, establishing superordinate goals facilitates conciliation and mediation). In addition, productive bargaining and negotiation underlie and make possible the enactment of almost all of the mechanisms proposed.

It is important to note at the outset, however, that if dysfunctional conflict within distribution channels is to be managed, reduced, or resolved, it will be essential for the members involved to come to grips with the underlying causes of the conflict issues which arise among them. And the specific mechanism employed will depend not only on the cause of the conflict but also on the structure of the channel itself. The scope of this paper is, nevertheless, limited to suggesting potential conflict management mechanisms irrespective of issues, causes, or channel structure.

Supraorganizational mechanisms

In channels of distribution characterized by a high degree of interdependence and interaction among members, we might expect to come upon fertile ground for the institutionalization of supraorganizational conflict resolution mechanisms. The supraorganizational mechanisms discussed below are: (1) establishing superordinate goals; (2) employing conciliation and mediation;

(3) submitting to arbitration; and (4) establishing special-purpose mechanisms. In order to implement such instruments, channel members would have to view themselves as part of a channel *system* and thereby recognize, overtly, their functional interdependence. Even in these situations, however, members will generally have different sets of active goals (or at least different preference orderings for the same set of goals), and thus the conditions for conflict will continue to exist among them.

Establishing superordinate goals

Superordinate goals are those ends greatly desired by all those caught in dispute or conflict, which cannot be attained by the resources and energies of each of the parties separately, but which require the concerted efforts of all parties involved.

If a superordinate goal or goals could be established within a channel of distribution, this would not only lead directly to a reduction in conflict among members but would provide the motivational basis for adopting other resolution mechanisms. More than any other device, superordinate goals could facilitate functional accommodation. Thus, mediation between groups or organizations in conflict is likely to be most beneficial when effective appeal can be made to a superior value-consensus which transcends group or organizational differences (for example, the preservation of the system itself, common larger interests, shared norms, and so on). Superordinate goals can also provide the foundation for meaningful contacts, communication, and negotiation – as well as interorganizational problem-solving.

Conflict resolution requires an integration of the needs of both sides to the dispute so that they find a common goal without sacrificing their basic economic and ethical principles. The difficult task is, obviously, to articulate a goal or common interest on which all parties can agree.

The establishment of a superordinate goal requires equitable participation and contribution from all parties in interdependent activities.

If the establishment of superordinate goals is going to lead to effective problem-solving among organizations in a channel, mutual identification must be high among the participants. As

Parsons observes: 'The focus of the integrative problem on a trans-organizational level . . . is the problem of the determination of the loyalties of the participants . . .' (1960, p. 47). Clearly, then, the varied loyalties of channel members are limiting factors to the establishment of superordinate goals.

As indicated above, a superordinate goal can be an explicit desire by channel members to resist a threat to the channel's survival or growth from some outside pressure (for example, competitive, legal). In such situations, the channel members set aside their differences for the sake of defence. To some extent, it makes no difference if the threat from the outside is real or is simply perceived; it will tend to increase cohesion within the channel. Not only is it likely to result in the reduction of minor conflicts within the channel, but also it may lead to a heightened sense of identity as an interorganizational system and a greater degree of consensus of opinion and purpose.

It is also likely that the process of meeting a threat external to the system will serve to displace or transfer hostility between and among channel members to the common enemy. Because of the information exchanged and because of the monetary and psychological costs jointly borne by the parties during the time of combating the threat, future relationships between the parties may be significantly different than they were during previous interactions. Channel members may gain empathy by seeing, perhaps for the first time, other channel members' points of view even though these viewpoints are presented in a different context than under normal circumstances. Finally, the original conflict issues – prior to the threat occurrence – may decay over time as energies are directed at the outside threat.

Employing conciliation and mediation

The process of reconciliation presumably leads to the convergence of opposing images held by the conflicting parties. In theory, conciliation is the passive role of attempting to bring harmony and a spirit of cooperation to a negotiation over conflicting issues and primarily involves adjustment of the dispute by the parties themselves. It is likely that, in many distribution channels, independent wholesalers serve as conciliators between their suppliers and their customers and may occasionally serve as mediators. Here, the term intermediary has a double meaning, pertaining to marketing tasks assumed as well as to conciliatory functions performed.

Mediation implies more active intervention by the third party than does conciliation. Mediation is the process whereby the third party attempts to secure settlement of a dispute by persuading the parties either to continue their negotiations or to consider procedural or substantive recommendations that the mediator may make. Thus, conciliation is primarily adjustment of the dispute by the parties themselves, while mediation is guidance by a third party to an acceptable accommodation. In the following discussion, unless otherwise stated, we concentrate on the more intricate process of mediation.

Functional attributes of mediation. Mediation essentially involves operating on the field of the conflicting parties in such a way that opportunities or trading moves are perceived which otherwise might not have been perceived. Solutions might be given an acceptability simply by being suggested by the mediator and hence acquire a degree of saliency which is important in making them mutually acceptable. One party often finds it difficult to accept a proposal suggested by an opposing party, whereas if the same proposal is suggested by a neutral mediator, it can be accepted without difficulty. Effective mediation succeeds in clarifying facts and issues, in keeping parties in contact with each other, in exploring possible bases of agreement, in encouraging parties to agree to specific proposals, and in supervising the implementation of agreements.

The mediator's role. In large part, a mediator of channel conflicts should concern himself with getting the conflicting parties together (perhaps over some noncontroversial procedural problem, such as types of forms used in billing), deflating the conflict situation by providing pertinent facts, raising doubts about positions already assumed, and expanding the area of agreement by suggesting alternative solutions to the problem.

Another function of the mediator is to restructure conflict situations by isolating nonrealistic elements of aggressiveness so that the contenders can deal directly with the divergent claims at issue. Once he has ascertained the real as opposed to the stated positions of contending parties, he can suggest proposals in the area of the real demands or leak information to the various sides about what each side will settle for. Through control of the communications structure, the mediator can reinforce or minimize the intensity of the position of one party as it is transmitted to the other.

To the extent that a mediator exercises independent initiative (as in the case of McKinsey and Company or other consultants), he becomes an entrepreneur of ideas and may, as such, play an extremely important role in structuring the network of interorganizational relationships.

The history of distribution in the United States has shown that, if the disputants allow the conflict to continue long enough, the federal or state government will assume the mediator's role. In the latter case, mediation can rapidly lead to compulsory arbitration or adjudication in the guise of legislation which all parties might find difficult to live with over the long run (for example, the Robinson-Patman Act).

Submitting to arbitration

Arbitration is another supraorganizational conflict management mechanism which can be applied to channel situations. It is felt to be inferior to the mechanism of conciliation and mediation for the resolution of conflict in distribution channels, because imposed resolution often leaves each disputant feeling his position was poorly understood. The 'solution' may be viewed as inequitable, and the dispute may easily surface again in slightly different form.

Arbitration can be compulsory or voluntary. Compulsory arbitration is a process wherein the parties are required by law to submit their dispute to a third party whose decision is final and binding. In a channel context, the government (or the courts) have served to settle disputes, as was the case when the automobile dealers and manufacturers clashed publicly over certain distribution policies and when fair trade pricing was a conflict issue between resellers and manufacturers.

Voluntary arbitration is a process wherein parties voluntarily submit their dispute to a third party whose decision will be considered final and binding.

Conflict resolution through voluntary arbitration requires at least three prior commitments among the disputants:

1. They have to agree that some form of settlement – even one involving the loss of a position – is preferable to continued conflict.

2. They have to agree to resolve the conflict on the basis of legal standards rather than according to political, economic, or social criteria.

3. They have to agree to the jurisdiction of a specific court, commission, or committee.

Thus, in arbitration, a preliminary bargain must be struck, in the sense that the parties have to agree to submit to arbitration. It is hoped that channel members would, in the process of undertaking such a bargain, understand that the whole question of relying on law and law enforcement to truly resolve conflicts among them is suspect, because it is doubtful whether permanently legislated solutions can be equitably applied to future conflicts in different channel contexts. As Assael (1968) has found, internal (intrachannel) conflict resolution has proven, historically, to be more satisfactory, from both a micro and a macro viewpoint, than external or legally imposed resolution.

Establishing special-purpose mechanisms

Two intriguing supraorganizational mechanisms are suggested in the political science literature. Brief mention is made of them here, because they could prove useful in helping to resolve, manage, or reduce conflict in distribution channels.

Commissions of inquiry. Although such commissions are frequently slow in operating, have no effective sanctions, and sometimes serve only as a substitute for action, it is likely that, in situations of considerable friction in the channel, the need for in-depth information, independently gathered, might warrant their establishment. One issue of importance in the drug industry involves the problem of physicians owning pharmacies.

Observers. The dispatch of neutral observers to the scene of hostilities by, say, trade associations comprised of the channel members in dispute might be useful in verifying disputed facts and in acting as a restraining influence. Although such a mechanism is similar to conciliation, the information received about the conflict might be reported to the trade association and published in a factual manner in the trade magazine of the association. With the supposedly fresh insight generated by the information, especially as it relates to the various positions taken on the issue, conciliation may be facilitated.

Interpenetration mechanisms

Organizations with frequent interactions may be more likely to develop patterns of conflict resolution or management in their interrelationships than those whose relationship consists of only occasional events. Interpenetration mechanisms provide means for increasing the number of meaningful interactions among channel members and, concomitantly, for reducing conflict within the channel. In this section, we suggest two primary approaches to interpenetration – membership and ideological.

Membership

According to Lasswell and Kaplan, conflict among groups varies inversely with their mutual permeability. 'The permeability of a group is the ease with which a person can become a participant' (1950, p. 35).

Interaction among the various representatives in trade association-sponsored events is undoubtedly infrequent. What is even more desirable is the creation of a network of primary relations among channel members. The possibility for creating such a network is present within many channels because the relations formed within a channel are functionally important to the members; therefore, as Galtung suggests, their conflict-preventing value may be considerable (1959, p. 74). But even on a relatively infrequent basis, the arranging of interorganizational collaboration on a common task jointly accepted as worthwhile and involving personal association of individuals as functional equals should result in lessened hostility among the organizations.

Perhaps one of the most meaningful interpenetration mechanisms, in this respect, might be an exchange of persons programme among channel members, similar to those implemented in international relations.

Exchange of persons. In distribution channels, exchange of persons could take place on several different levels of an organization or at all levels. Thus, as part of his initial executive training programme, the recruit (perhaps fresh from college) could spend a prescribed period of time working in the organization of suppliers, middlemen, and/or customers. A salesman employed by a manufacturer could, on a periodic basis, spend a specified period of time as an employee of a wholesaling or retailing firm selling the latter's assortment of products of which the original manufacturer's product may be only one of several. In like fashion, traffic and inventory personnel could be exchanged as well as other line and staff personnel. For certain types of employees, such as relatively prominent executives, it might even be possible to work out a sabbatical system similar to that of universities, so that these executives could replenish themselves by taking positions either closer to or farther away from the ultimate market in which the product of the particular channel is sold.

The best type of exchange might involve not merely a transfer of persons but common enterprises, jointly initiated and carried out on a relatively large scale.

Ideological

Basically, ideological penetration refers to informational, propaganda, and educational activities aimed at managing, resolving, or reducing conflict. Some of the aims of such activity may be: (1) simply to enhance knowledge and understanding; (2) to cultivate goodwill among channel members, gain prestige, and perhaps to undermine the goodwill and prestige of a competitor competitive channel; and (3) to shape attitudes among the personnel of another channel member so as to influence its management to follow a certain course of action.

Effective ideological penetration, independent of kind, should lead to a reduction of bifurcation of images and to the definition of common symbols among conflicting parties. What the channel propagandist (or educator) may be seeking is some sort of ideological conversion. For example, the effort by many manufacturers and wholesalers to influence retailers to think in terms of return-on-investment criteria rather than in terms of gross profit margins would, if accomplished, represent an ideological conversion, as well as result in changes in retail operating methods. In order to achieve such a conversion, it would be wise for the channel member performing the educational role to:

1. Avoid actions that would have the effect of humiliating the target organization(s);

2. Attempt to achieve a high degree of empathy with respect to the values of members of the target organization(s);

3. Adopt a consistent attitude of trust toward the target organization, including an open statement of one's own plans and intentions;

4. Make visible concessions for one's cause and maintain a consistent set of positive activities which are an attempt at the explicit realization of the goals of the organizations involved and, hopefully, of the channel as a whole.

Specific mechanisms. We have already mentioned the sales training programmes conducted by manufacturers for their middlemen's sales forces. Another specific mechanism that has often been employed to achieve ideological penetration is the wide dissemination of trade publications and reprints.

Also, the development of professional ethics in an industry, either through interactions among trade associations or the Trade Practice Conferences of the Federal Trade Commission, may often serve as a normative structure through which increased coordination is achieved among channel members. Similarly, channel members can coalesce to achieve public relations ends. Such a phenomenon occurs regularly in those industries where the retailers are small and the manufacturers and distributors are large.

All other things being equal, educational programmes will have maximum effects when information is presented as part of the ordinary action of a group or organization carrying out its usual socioeconomic function. Thus, it would appear that ideological conversion, if that is the aim, would be easier in on-the-job training situations where channel members interact directly with one another in the performance of a common task than through trade publications or other general information programmes. A unique approach, which is somewhat in between the on-the-job and the general information approaches, might be the establishment of either libraries or training schools or both by channel members, either individually or collectively. In the case of collective efforts, this would take the form of a supraorganizational mechanism; individual efforts would be an ideological penetration mechanism.

Perhaps ideological penetration can be best accomplished through the process of uncertainty absorption by one channel member for others in the system. This mechanism has been described elsewhere in a channel context and is, therefore, only briefly discussed here. Uncertainty absorption takes place when inferences are drawn from a body of evidence and the inferences, instead of the evidence itself, are then communicated. All channel members face uncertainty in their respective task environments and, as Cyert and March point out, 'firms will devise and negotiate an environment so as to eliminate the uncertainty. Rather than treat the environment as exogenous and to be predicted, they seek ways to make it controllable' (1963, p. 120). There is, however, little likelihood that such a situation will occur. One can expect a high degree of uncertainty to prevail in almost all commercial situations. The problem is to reduce the uncertainty to the point where meaningful predictions are possible, based on probability distributions, and to achieve at least some degree of consensus on a realistic perception of the environment in which firms operate. Once this realistic perceptual consensus is established, one can expect at least some reduction in conflict that was based on incongruent views.

Combinations of membership and ideological penetration

Perhaps the most effective type of interpenetration in terms of changing the goals, attitudes, or behaviour of the target organization occurs when the penetration involves both membership and ideology. An important mechanism in this respect is cooptation.

Cooptation is the process of absorbing new elements into the leadership or policy-determining structure of an organization as a means of averting threats to its stability or existence (Selznick, 1949, p. 13).

Cooptation may be a response to the pressure of specific centres of power within a channel of distribution.

A channel member, given a position of power and responsibility with regard to the generation of policy decisions throughout the channel, should gain increased awareness and understanding of the problems which the channel as a whole faces. Also, as Thompson and McEwen observe, 'By providing overlapping memberships, cooptation is an important social service for increasing the likelihood that organizations related to one another in complicated ways will in fact find compatible goals.'

By thus reducing the possibilities of antithetical actions by two or more organizations, cooptation aids in the integration of the heterogeneous parts of a complex society. By the same token, cooptation further limits the opportunity for one organization to choose its goals arbitrarily or unilaterally (Thompson and McEwen, 1969, p. 195).

It might also be said that cooptation of channel members encourages their ideological transformation, so that they subsequently tend to carry the ideology of the coopting unit into their other membership groups. Cooptation makes inroads on the process of deciding goals and means. Not only must the final choice be acceptable to the coopted channel member(s), but to the extent that cooptation is effective, it places an outsider in a position to determine the occasion for a goal decision, to participate in analysing the existing situation, to suggest alternatives, and to take part in the deliberation of consequences. When an established organization is coopted, the coopting organization becomes in some measure dependent upon the coopted organization for administration. Using the administrative machinery of the coopted organization requires one to pursue the interest and goodwill of those who control it, the leaders of the coopted organization. And, finally, as Etzioni observes, cooptation may be used to create a semblance of communication from others to those in control without effective communication really existing. Manipulated or fictitious cooptation only conceals the need for real communication and influence (Etzioni, 1958, p. 261). It is perhaps for this latter reason that the term coopted has fallen into such disrepute among students seeking change on college campuses today. The same reaction could easily occur in distribution channels.

It may not, of course, always be feasible or desirable to institute penetration processes similar to those mentioned in this section. If this is the case, channel members may have to rely heavily on activities taking place at the boundaries of their various organizations if conflict is to be reduced or resolved. The following section turns to a discussion of possible boundary mechanisms for resolving conflict or for, at least, coming to grips with conflict situations.

Boundary mechanisms

For the purposes of this section, assume that the relevant boundary of an organization is its legal boundary. Given this assumption, a boundary position can be defined as one for which some role-senders are located in other organizations. The personnel of an organization who are concerned primarily with foreign (external) affairs are called, in this context, boundary persons. Thus, in the role-set of a boundary person are his role-partners in other organizations. Within a channel of distribution, two key classes of boundary personnel are, obviously, salesmen and purchasing agents.

Activities between and among personnel operating at the boundary of organizations within distribution channels may be significant in reducing conflict just as they are significant in creating it. Their boundary roles make these persons continual mediators between organizations, for they should be able to justify the position of either side to the other and thereby should be instrumental in bringing about compromise. In the long run, the roles of these boundary specialists should become routinized through the emergence of opposite numbers, thereby reducing the likelihood of interorganizational conflicts accruing from threats to the status of organizational representatives. What is suggested as a conflict resolution mechanism, then, is the institutionalization of some form of channel diplomacy.

Diplomacy

Using an analogy from international relations, channel diplomacy is the method by which interorganizational relations are conducted, adjusted, and managed by ambassadors, envoys, or other persons operating at the boundaries of member organizations. Channel members must persuade, negotiate with, and exert pressure upon each other if they wish to resolve conflict, because, with the exception of the government, there is generally no superior above them that can impose a settlement. Therefore, they must engage in, cultivate, and rely upon diplomatic procedures. Taken in its widest meaning, the task of diplomacy is fourfold:

1. Diplomacy must determine its objectives in the light of the power actually and potentially available for the pursuit of these objectives.

2. Diplomacy must assess the objectives of other members and the power actually and potentially available for the pursuit of their objectives.

3. Diplomacy must determine to what extent these different objectives are compatible with each other.

4. Diplomacy must employ the means suited to the pursuit of its objectives.

The tasks involved in the implementation of diplomatic procedures and processes are similar to those involved in the implementation of negotiation and bargaining discussed later. The functions of a channel diplomat would, again in the widest interpretation, be to help shape the policies he is to follow, to conduct negotiations with channel members to which he is assigned, to observe and report on everything which may be of interest to the firm employing him, and to provide information concerning his firm to the operatives in counterpart channel organizations.

Strains on boundary personnel

Individuals who operate at the boundaries of organizations are subject to important strains which tend to impede their ability to aid in the resolution of conflict. In a study of such boundary personnel as salesmen, credit expediters, and traffic managers, Kahn, *et al.*, concluded that,

Lacking formal power over role senders outside his work unit, a person at the boundary has a reduced ability to guarantee that the performance of these outsiders will be as he needs and wishes. In compensation for this lack of formal authority, a boundary person relies heavily on the affective bonds of trust, respect, and liking which he can generate among the outsiders. But these bonds are unusually difficult to create and maintain at the boundary. For the outsiders, the failings of a person's unit are all too easily identified as failures of the person, thus weakening their affective bonds with him.

[A consequence of the role senders' inadequate understanding of boundary positions] is the failure of role senders, especially in other departments, to appreciate the urgency or necessity of a boundary person's requests to them. They are likely to present him with self-interested demands and to be intolerant if these demands are not met.

A person in a boundary position is faced, therefore, with a sizable body of role senders whose demands are hard to predict and hard to control. . . . Most difficult of all, the boundary person faced with such demands has at his disposal only limited power resources with which he may attempt to induce their modification (Kahn *et al.*, 1964, pp. 123–4).

Assuming that all boundary personnel face strains similar to those enumerated above, the question remains: Who are the most appropriate individuals within an organization to assume the role of diplomat in resolving channel conflicts? It is essential that the status of the diplomat be high enough so that the power which the diplomat holds is at least relatively obvious to the parties with whom he interacts.

To prepare the channel diplomat for this role, it would seem important that he be given thorough indoctrination in and knowledge of organizational procedures and operations if he is to resolve the uncertainty which his role prescribes. In addition, to prevent occupants of these positions from developing too strong an identification with specific channel members, it might be wise to periodically shift such boundary persons among the different members of the channel.

Bargaining and negotiating

It might be reasonably argued that no matter what conflict management mechanism is adopted by policy-makers within a channel, resolution is always the result of bargaining – the making of commitments, offering of rewards, or threatening of punishments or deprivation – between and among the members. Insights into effective bargaining and negotiation should facilitate the employment of the mechanisms suggested previously. And channel members often can be viewed as interest groups in opposition over scarce resources. If channel members do not (or only vaguely) perceive themselves as part of a distribution system and, instead, take the position of interest groups, then a bargaining model is more appropriate to deal with the conflict which arises among them.

In a channel context, the term bargaining refers to the negotiation of an agreement for the exchange of goods or services between two or more organizations. Negotiation is a process through which the parties interact in developing potential agreements to provide guidance and regulation of their future behaviour. Here, the two terms will be used interchangeably, unless otherwise noted.

Within a channel, the bargaining may at first appear to be a fixed-sum game, that is, whatever solution is arrived at will yield the same total benefit, even though the division of returns will vary. However, solutions frequently yield a greater total benefit to the channel in, say, the form of higher sales or lower costs. Bargaining, under these conditions, takes on the characteristics of a variable-sum game. In addition, there is, within a channel:

... a curious mixture of cooperation and conflict – cooperation in that both parties with a certain range of possible solutions will be better off with a solution, that is, a bargain, than without one and conflict in that, within the range of possible solutions, the distribution of the total benefit between two parties depends on the particular solution adopted (Boulding, 1962, p. 314).

The strategy of bargaining

Two questions appear central in developing a bargaining strategy: (1) How much is it necessary to concede? and (2) How can the other side be induced to accept less favourable terms than it wants? Schelling notes that 'to "win", a party must make his commitment appear irrevocable to the other party'. On the other hand, if one party can demonstrate to the other that the latter is not committed, or that he has miscalculated his commitment, the former may undo or revise the latter's commitment (Schelling, 1960, p. 28). If bargaining is going to be effective in leading to integrative problem-solving, it is essential to prevent the other party from holding a committed position in order to claim a disproportionate share of the joint gain. In other words, it is important to attempt to keep the other party flexible or to help him abandon a committed position once it has been taken, because integrative or cooperative bargaining requires free and open exploration without preconceived ideas or dogmatic positions.

A stable bargaining situation depends on the development and maintenance of trust and mutual respect between bargainers. One obvious reason for trusting another channel member is the awareness that this member has incentives for behaving in a trustworthy fashion and that its leaders recognize these incentives. In some cases, trust or distrust is based on what is known about another member's past behaviour. Trust is likely to develop if the other member has engaged in helpful behaviour (as defined by the furtherance of the goals of the affected member), distrust if it has engaged in harmful behaviour.

If a channel member wants to be trusted, it should demonstrate that its helpful actions are freely taken and that it adopts policies harmful to the interest of other channel members only when compelled to do so by forces beyond its control.

Some suggestions which seem useful for establishing trust in channel relations come from the political science literature. One suggestion is the taking of unilateral steps to reduce tension. Adapting Osgood's theory to a channel context, one could say that for such a unilateral act to be effective in inducing another channel member to reciprocate, it should (1) be clearly disadvantageous to the member making it, yet not cripplingly so; (2) be such as to be clearly perceived by the other member as reducing his external threat; (3) be such that reciprocal action by the other member is available and clearly indicated; (4) be announced in advance and widely publicized to all channel members (its nature, its purpose as part of a consistent policy, and the expected reciprocation); and (5) not demand prior commitment to reciprocation by the other member as a condition of its commission (Osgood, 1959).

Compromise, like trust, is a prerequisite in successful bargaining. Negotiations are possible only if each side is prepared to give up something in order to gain some of its objectives. The difficulty with the compromise outcome is that the basic problem may not be solved and may continue to be a source of tension.

The willingness to negotiate a compromise depends, of course, on correct assessment of the conflict situation. Such assessment and the following accommodation is possible only if each party is aware of the relative strength of the others. If implicit assessment is difficult, mediation may help, for one of the key functions of the mediator is to make such indices readily available to the parties. The conflicting parties will be able to negotiate to the extent they share a common system of symbols allowing them to arrive at a common assessment.

With regard to the loss of face problem, the logic of bargaining and compromise is not appropriate for the settlement of ideological differences. The negotiators cannot bargain over an ideological principle, as might be represented by the small business ethic versus the desire for efficiency on the part of large businesses, without compromising their moral position. There is an all-or-none quality to moral principles. Thus, in order to prevent the two types of differences from getting confused, it may be best to send to the channel bargaining table pragmatic, task-oriented men (rather than ideologues, as some top corporate executives must be) with at least some system perspective and intimate understanding of the nature of the channel structure, so that the members can avoid bargaining over ideological issues.

Several major problems face the negotiator, however, even if he is vested with appropriate authority. Thus, negotiators face the dual problems of (1) securing consensus among the operating executives within his own firm; and (2) compromising between the demands for flexibility by conflicting channel members and the demands for rigidity by the executives in his own firm. These same problems serve to place constraints and limitations on negotiation as a conflict resolution mechanism in distribution channel relations.

Constraints and limitations

We have already mentioned one major limitation on the scope of the negotiation in channel relations – the difficulty of settling ideological differences through bargaining. In fact, it is likely that establishing superordinate goals is the only means to settling ideological differences. We have also noted that negotiation is governed by, and operates within, bounds acceptable to the firm from which the negotiator comes. In this respect, leaders on each side in the bargaining situation must avoid courses of action which threaten the leadership positions of their counterparts. Where there is genuine interest in maintaining the bargaining relationships, studies indicate that leaders on both sides clearly take into account the limitations that their opposite numbers must contend with and minimize behaviours that produce embarrassment or problem-creating consequences for them.

Clearly, there is no point in negotiating in the absence of some possibility of success. The problem is more complicated, though, if the purpose of one or more of the parties is not agreement but rather the pursuit of a side effect. Such side effects can be positive or negative, for example, to maintain contact (to keep channels of communication open), to gain more knowledge of the other party's true position, to reveal the intentions of the other side, to deceive (to buy time, for example), to permit a forum for propaganda, or to affect a third party (the government, consumers, suppliers, middlemen outside the negotiation, and so on).

Lastly, although this list is not exhaustive, public debate among the channel members is likely to hurt the chances of achieving an effective accommodation through negotiation. Taking a public position in advance of negotiation lays the groundwork for competition to enter, even when the firms would be expected to interact in a collaborative manner. Taking a public position intensifies the problems mentioned above, for when a negotiator deviates from a fixed public position, it means that he is openly going against the desires of his firm. As we have already taken pains to point out, compromise is a prerequisite to bargaining, and therefore it may be impossible to negotiate successfully in channel situations if one side takes a specific and adamant public position.

Other mechanisms

We have not discussed the conflict resolution mechanisms of (1) avoidance or withdrawal (sometimes referred to as conflict denial or passive settlement); and (2) the use of force, counter-threats, and deterrence (balance-of-power mechanisms). We have also not explored fully the use of law and law enforcement or the creation of authority in a supersystem. These mechanisms have been placed outside the scope of this paper because they are either (1) obvious and may require no purposive effort on the part of channel members to institute; (2) dependent for their initiation on some manifest coercive power on the part of members; or (3) maintain the conflict in a suspended and oftentimes unstable state. Nevertheless, by omitting an examination of them, we do not mean to imply that they are unimportant.

References

ASSAEL, H. (1968), 'The political role of trade associations in distributive conflict resolution', *Journal of Marketing*, vol. 32, April, pp. 21–8.
BOULDING, K. E. (1961), 'Opening remarks', in E. Boulding (ed.), *Conflict Management in Organizations*, Ann Arbor, Michigan, Foundation for Research on Human Behavior.
BOULDING, K. E. (1962), *Conflict and Defense*, New York, Harper & Brothers.
CYERT, R. M., and MARCH, J. G. (1963), *A Behavioral Theory of the Firm*, Englewood Cliffs, New Jersey, Prentice-Hall, Inc.
ETZIONI, A. (1958), 'Administration and the consumer', *Adminstration Science Quarterly*, vol. 3, September, pp. 251–64.
GALTUNG, J. (1959), 'Pacifism from a sociological point of view', *Journal of Conflict Resolution*, vol. 3, March, pp. 67–84.
KAHN, R. L., WOLFE, D. M., QUINN, R. P., and SNOCK, J. D. (1964), *Organizational Stress: Studies in Role Conflict and Ambiguity*, New York, John Wiley & Sons, Inc.
LASSWELL, H. D., and KAPLAN, A. (1950), *Power and Society*, New Haven, Yale University Press.
OSGOOD, C. E. (1959), 'Suggestion for winning the real war with communism', *Journal of Conflict Resolution*, vol. 3, December, pp. 295–325.
PARSONS, T. (1960), *Structure and Process in Modern Societies*, Glencoe, Ill., The Free Press.

SCHELLING, T. C. (1960), *The Strategy of Conflict*, Cambridge, Mass., Harvard University Press.

SELZNICK, P. (1949), *TVA and the Grass Roots*, Berkeley, California, University of California Press.

THOMPSON, J. D., and MCEWEN, W. J. (1969), 'Organizational goals and environment', in A. Etzioni (ed.), *Complex Organizations: A Sociological Reader*, 2nd ed., New York, Holt, Rinehart & Winston, Inc.

24 R. A. Posner

A Programme for the Antitrust Division

R. A. Posner, 'A program for the Antitrust Division', *University of Chicago Law Review*, vol. 38, Spring 1971, pp. 500–513, 531–6.

In two previous articles, I have criticized a number of facets of current antitrust enforcement policy, ranging from the attitudes of the enforcers toward their role, at one extreme, to specific provisions in merger guidelines issued by the Antitrust Division, at the other, and covering a good many points in between (1969, 1970). The articles are not wholly negative; they suggest both new enforcement mechanisms and new substantive policies. But they do not attempt to present a rounded programme of antitrust enforcement. The present piece, drawing on the earlier suggestions but with a good many additions and some revisions, outlines such a programme. For the sake of brevity, I limit my attention to the Antitrust Division of the Department of Justice, and I take its existing powers and resources as a given. Within these limits I have tried to be practical and specific, as well as reasonably comprehensive, and to consider philosophical as well as practical objections to the suggested programme. Necessarily, many important details of the programme have been omitted.

Presumptuous as such an exercise may seem, it is at least timely. It is fashionable nowadays to exhort institutions to re-examine the priorities under which they operate. Never has the Antitrust Division had greater reason to heed this exhortation. The rapid growth of the economy in recent years has not brought a corresponding increase in the resources of the Division. At the same time, the Supreme Court's virtual abandonment of anti-trust law to the discretion of the enforcement agencies has vastly increased their domain, tempting them to fritter away resources in glamorous and political, but surely marginal, operations: consider the Division's late absorption with conglomerate power and organized crime. With the collapse of the conglomerate bubble the Division may have entered a period of drift and uncertainty.

Toward practical goals for antitrust

Setting forth the goals of antitrust enforcement ought to be a straightforward enough process but is not. Before we can get to the goals themselves we must clear three hurdles. We must consider first whether it is proper to have goals of antitrust enforcement at all, other than the goal of challenging every violation of antitrust law or at least every *per se* violation. If the answer is yes, we must next consider whether it is proper, in fashioning antitrust goals, to exclude considerations other than economic efficiency, such as the merits of favouring small business or altering the distribution of income. If the answer is again yes, we must consider finally how to choose among schools of economic thought that disagree on the consequences for efficiency of various market practices and conditions.

The propriety of regarding law enforcement as a means rather than an end

The programme of antitrust enforcement proposed in this paper – indeed, the very idea of the Antitrust Division's adopting a programmatic approach – rests upon an instrumental conception of law enforcement. According to this view, public agencies should consider the enforcement of the laws committed to their responsibility not as an end in itself but as a means of advancing with maximum efficiency the fundamental goals behind the laws. As a corollary, the agency may properly decline to proceed even against clear-cut violations of law when the resources that would be required in proceeding against them could be utilized more effectively in other phases of the agency's work. Obvious as these propositions may seem, they are rejected (particularly the second) by those in charge of the Antitrust Division where, for example, it has long been proclaimed and to the best of my knowledge actual policy to prosecute any and all violations of the so-called *per se* rules, no matter how trivial.[1]

1. As the Division has many times stated: 'The Courts have time and again held that price-fixing agreements are illegal *per se*. Such practices will continue to be prosecuted whenever and wherever they are found to exist.'

When Congress enacts a regulatory law, such as the Sherman Act or the later antitrust statutes, it normally wants compliance, of course; but that is an intermediate rather than a final end. Behind the law will be found some practical goal that the law is designed to achieve. It has been argued, for example, that Congress in the Sherman Act[2] forbade conspiracies in restraint of trade and other monopolistic practices to the end of increasing output in the industries that would be affected by the Act (Bork, 1966). That was the purpose of the legislation; the specific prohibitions written into it were merely the means of its attainment. When deciding whether to commence a case or investigation, and in other judgements concerning the allocation of its resources, an enforcement agency should always ask which use of the resources in question will 'buy' the largest quantity of the particular 'good' (greater output, or whatever) that the statute is intended to 'produce'. This will sometimes entail not proceeding against clear, but unimportant, violations.

Several objections are made to this approach. It is said that enforcement officials have no authority to forgive violations; that their arrogation of the power to do so injects an unhealthy element of discretion into law enforcement; that the notion of equal justice is offended; and that the moral authority of law is impaired. None of these objections is compelling.

If a legislature appropriated sufficient funds to enable an enforcing agency completely to extirpate an illegal practice, and the agency declined to proceed against all violations, the legislature could rightly complain that its will was being thwarted. But usually the funds appropriated are too limited to permit total enforcement. By so limiting the agency's resources, the legislature makes an implicit judgement, no less authentic than the initial and unqualified declaration of illegality, and perhaps more authoritative since subsequent in time, that there shall be less than total enforcement. Partial enforcement may take the form of responding inadequately to all complaints or not at all to some. If the latter course can in a particular instance be justified as a better

News release quoted in *The Federal Antitrust Laws with Summary of Cases Instituted by the United States* 86 (1952–56 Supp.) (CCH ed. 1957). More important than that they say it is that they mean it.

2. 15 USC § *et seq.* (1964).

approximation to the basic goals of the legislation, the legislature should not complain that its will has been overridden. It can and should insist that the agency justify the enforcement policy selected.

The objection to 'discretionary justice' (Davis, 1969) is based upon the absence of standards – 'discretion' being conceived as the opposite of 'rule' – which opens the door to arbitrary and oppressive enforcement. The approach urged here avoids that objection because it furnishes a standard to guide the exercise of administrative discretion: the standard of efficiency. Of course, to be a meaningful check on improper discretion, a standard must be reasonably precise. An extensive literature expounding the application of cost-benefit or systems analysis – techniques for evaluating the relative efficiency of alternative programmes – in a variety of public-administration contexts (Hitch and McKean, 1965; McKean, 1958; Prest and Turvey, 1965; Schlesinger, 1968) suggests that the standard of efficiency does have content and is operational. But the reader must finish this paper before deciding whether an efficiency standard is, as I believe, reasonably clear and definite. Assuming it is, the objection based on notions of equal justice falls too. Equality in the administration of law requires only that similar cases be treated similarly. A rational and impartial ground for distinguishing otherwise similar cases is consistent with the principle of equality.

The final objection to the instrumental conception of law enforcement is that it undermines the moral authority of the law. To condone violations merely because prosecution is not cost-justified is, one could argue, to deny that there is an unqualified duty to obey the law. Were it necessary, I would argue that, with respect to a wide variety of public regulations, the duty to obey is not an unqualified one. Holmes's 'bad man' conception of law (1920, pp. 167–75), under which the command of the law is conceived to be not that we obey but that we obey or suffer the consequences, seems to me highly persuasive in those situations where the offending conduct is not altogether devoid of social utility.[3]

3. By 'conduct devoid of social utility', I mean conduct whose private benefits to the actor society has decided have a weight of zero in determining the permissibility of the conduct. A person acts wrongfully, I assume, if, weighing the benefits to him from a murder against the punishment and other

The prohibitions of antitrust law are of this type. Had we an adequate system of antitrust penalties, so that the full social cost of an antitrust violation were borne by the violator, there would be no moral objection, I believe, to his committing the violation. Since, no matter how carefully the antitrust laws are administered, we cannot be sure that they will not occasionally forbid conduct having a net social product, the recognition of a 'right' to violate – providing the violator pays the full cost of his violation – is in society's best interests.

If it is correct that the function of legal norms and sanctions, in many settings and specifically that of the antitrust laws, is not to establish categorical prohibitions but to make the violators of legal rules bear the costs that their conduct imposes on society, then enforcement agencies are entitled to decline to enforce the law where enforcement is not cost-justified in the light of alternative uses to which the agency could put its resources. The same conclusion can be reached without accepting any part of Holmes's approach: by distinguishing the duty to obey the law, which may be an unqualified duty, from the duty to enforce it, which cannot be unqualified if only because public agencies lack the necessary resources.

Economic efficiency and other values

Assuming the propriety of an approach to law enforcement that seeks to maximize the efficiency with which the relevant legislative goals are pursued, even at the occasional price of ignoring clear-cut violations, we have yet to consider what, in the present context, those goals are. As mentioned earlier, Professor Bork has argued that the framers of the Sherman Act, the basic antitrust statute, were concerned primarily with precisely the objection that a classical economist would make to monopoly: it reduces the value of output. A profit-maximizing monopolist will sell less of his product, and at a higher price, than would competing firms. Those who bought the product before it was monopolized but consider the new (monopoly) price too high will switch to substitutes that before the price increase they considered less desirable. The reduction in the monopolist's output thus dimin-

---

costs that he will bear, and finding the former to predominate, he commits the murder.

ishes the satisfaction of consumers. It is in this sense that monopoly reduces the overall value of the economy's output. Of course, those consumers who continue to buy the product after it is monopolized, but at a higher price, are dissatisfied too; but their loss is exactly balanced by the gains to the owners of the firm from monopolizing. Professor Bork adds that the concern with output constitutes the 'main tradition' in the judicial interpretation of the Sherman Act (1965).

One may wish to dispute his weighting of the various strands in the legislative judicial history of the Sherman Act but it is surely correct that concern with limitations of output (although usually not expressed in just those terms) has always been one of the important themes of antitrust law. The hard question is what weight the Antitrust Division should assign to other values in formulating its enforcement policy. I suggest none. Two objections to incorporating as antitrust standards such policy considerations as hostility to big business on moral or political grounds, or desire for a more equal distribution of income and wealth or to protect existing enterprises from being destroyed by competition, or commitment to Jeffersonian conceptions of the optimum organization of the economy seem to me decisive. The first is futility. The antitrust laws do not provide effective tools for bringing about an organization of industry that is inefficient in an economic sense, however much it is to be desired on other grounds. If, consistent with Judge Learned Hand's famous articulation of the social policies of the antitrust laws,[4] a monopoly were broken up into units that were smaller than the efficient scale of the industry, the resulting organization of the industry would be unstable. Some firms would expand their output to take advantage of the economics of scale and the least efficient firms would leave the industry. The antitrust laws cannot, in general, do more than temporarily retard the process by which an industry attains an efficient scale of operation.

My second objection applies less to judicial application of antitrust policy than to the enforcement policies of the antitrust agencies, but it is with the latter that I am primarily concerned. There is no analytic procedure for weighing costs in economic

4. United States v. Aluminum Co. of America, 148 F.2d 416, 429 (2d Cir. 1945).

efficiency against benefits in a more equitable distribution of income and wealth or in other social values. That is not to deny that these things are weighed by legislatures and courts, but the judgement involved is political (in a noninvidious sense) rather than technical or professional and the staff of the Antitrust Division is an inappropriate body for making broad political judgements.

My conclusion is that in the formulation of policy, certainly in areas where there are no hard and fast legislative or judicial rules of antitrust, the Antitrust Division had best confine itself to the economic criterion: maximizing the value of output. That is the course, it seems to me, of effectiveness and of professionalism. The rules that the Supreme Court has read into the Sherman Act by interpretation raise, however, an additional question. Suppose the rule that tie-in agreements are illegal *per se* can be justified only by reference to social policies other than concern with limitations of output – and therefore should never, on the foregoing analysis, have been adopted. It has been adopted, however, and its application involves no reference to those policies. None the less, a judicial rule establishing that certain conduct is within a statutory prohibition does not obligate an enforcement agency, morally or otherwise, to bring cases challenging that conduct. The decision to prosecute properly depends on an ordering of priorities to govern allocation of the agency's limited resources and the courts have no authority to displace that judgement. There is no rational principle that can guide the Division in deciding how much money to spend combating practices that reduce economic efficiency, and how much on practices that increase (or have no clear effect upon) it. A judgement to increase resources devoted to uncovering violations of the tie-in rule would have to be political, in the sense of lying outside of the professional competence of the Division's staff; and such judgements, I have argued, are to be avoided.

The search for an economic consensus

If it is desirable and proper that antitrust policy rest on a point of economic theory – prevention of monopolistic restrictions of output – then it is reasonable to turn to the economics profession for guidance in reducing the general goal to a set of usable guidelines. Unfortunately, the profession is deeply divided on the critical issues. Virtually every initiative that the Antitrust Division has taken, or would take, has had or would have its defenders among reputable economists. The Assistant Attorney General in charge of antitrust will rarely be competent to evaluate competing schools of economic thought, and, if he is, he is likely to have his own *parti pris*.

The least unsatisfactory solution that occurs to me is for the antitrust chief (with the help of economist advisers) to identify those questions on which there is a consensus of professional opinion – a very substantial majority position (with mere numbers weighted by experience and distinction) – and to build his policy on that common ground. Not every economist believes that reciprocal buying is a monopolistic practice, although many do, but perhaps there are some practices that all or substantially all economists condemn as monopolistic. As it happens, there is enough common ground among economists on the monopoly question to provide an ample as well as secure base for a programme of antitrust enforcement.

The consensus approach is likely to be challenged on the ground that it gives 51 per cent of the votes in formulating antitrust policy to a minority school of industrial-organization economists, many of whom, as it happens, are or have been professors at the University of Chicago. But such an objection misconceives how professional opinions are formed. Academic economists writing in professional journals are unlikely to decide on nonprofessional grounds what kind of antitrust enforcement they would like to have and then concoct economic evidence to support their preferences. Any who did would quickly lose all standing in the profession and their opinions would rightly be ignored in the search for a consensus of professional economic opinion on a question. When a substantial number of highly distinguished economists agree with their brethren on a number of relevant points of antitrust policy, while disagreeing forcefully on others, the prudent antitrust administrator committed to the economic criterion of antitrust enforcement will channel enforcement resources to the areas of agreement and avoid areas where economic science is highly uncertain.

We can begin to delimit the area of concordance by distinguishing between two kinds of arguably monopolistic practice: the single-firm 'abuse' and the horizontal 'combination'. An abuse, as used here, is a practice by which a single firm, without entering into any express or implied agreement with competitors, seeks to increase its power over price and output. The firm may enlist the aid of noncompeting firms, such as suppliers or customers, as in exclusive-dealing and tying arrangements, but there must be no combination of competitors. In contrast, a combination case, as I use the term, is one where there is a conspiracy, merger, or other concert of action between competitors. This usage differs from that employed in the Sherman Act, whose combinations, conspiracies, and restrictive contracts may be vertical as well as horizontal.

The attempted distinction involves problems of characterization (most acutely with respect to resale price maintenance), but it serves to distinguish the area of consensus from the area of debate. Almost all economists in the relevant fields agree that horizontal combinations can restrict output; many economists, including some very distinguished ones, doubt that abuses can, except in very unusual circumstances. It follows, under the consensus approach here urged, that the Antitrust Division should with few exceptions confine itself to combination cases.

This may seem a breathtaking constriction of the Division's scope of activity. The excluded class includes vertical and conglomerate mergers,[5] arrangements subject to section 3 of the Clayton Act[6] (unless imposed by a conspiracy among competing firms), many single-firm monopolization cases such as the pending suit against IBM,[7] and many resale price maintenance cases. Although the emphasis in the Division's operations has always leaned heavily to the combination, not the abuse, case, a marked change of direction is proposed. But if the reader accepts the

5. With the occasional exception of some market-extension, potential-competition, and substitute-competition mergers, properly classifiable as horizontal.

6. 15 USC § 14 (1964).

7. United States v. International Business Machs. Corp., Civil No. 69 Civ. 200, (US Antitrust Cases Summaries – 1961–70 Transfer Binder) *Trade Reg. Rep.* ¶ 45,069 at 52,707 (Case 2039) (SDNY, filed 17 January 1969).

proposition that the goal of antitrust enforcement should be to increase the value of output in the economy, and that in giving content to this strictly economic goal antitrust enforcers should be guided by the best professional economic opinion, then he should agree that it is foolish to devote substantial resources to extirpating practices about whose effects economists profoundly disagree, when, as we shall see, there is so much to be done about practices that all agree limit output.

The appeal to an economic consensus enables us not only to narrow our attention to horizontal combinations but also to establish priorities for enforcement attention within that broad area. At present, two questions relating to combinations are particularly controversial. The first is whether a limitation of output, similar to what would be brought about by a cartel,[8] is inherent in the very condition of a highly concentrated market, even if there is no collusion among the firms in the market. If the question is answered in the affirmative, as it is by many economists, it seems to follow that the limitation can be removed only by changing the concentrated structure of the market, that is, by dismembering the largest firms. If, on the other hand, as is implicit in the theory of oligopoly proposed by George Stigler (1964), noncompetitive pricing by oligopolists without detectable collusion is nothing more than a special case of cartelization ('tacit collusion'), then one can argue that the criminal and injunctive penalties used to control ordinary cartels can be used against oligopoly pricing as well and there is no need to have recourse to structural remedies.

The consensus approach requires rejection of the interdependence theory of oligopoly and the structural solutions to which it points. Simple prudence dictates the same result, for the empirical foundations of the interdependence theory have lately been badly shaken. This leaves open the question, which turns

8. 'Cartel' as used in this paper means any 'horizontal combination' as earlier defined that can fairly be characterized as a price-fixing agreement or the equivalent. Apart from the case of resale price maintenance, discussed later, there are a number of other ambiguous arrangements which may or may not be cartels depending on the circumstances. Customer and territorial limitations in distribution are examples. My own, not fully examined view is that they are analytically about the same as resale price maintenance, but I do not attempt an adequate treatment here.

largely on issues of judicial competence, how far to push anti-cartel measures; we return to it in a later section.

The second controversy relating to combinations involves the definition and appraisal of 'barriers to entry'. The term is used in two different senses and it is important to distinguish them. It is used in a broad sense to denote any condition that would delay the immediate entry by new competitors into a market in which firms were charging a price above cost, and in a narrower sense to denote a condition that imposes on a new entrant higher long-term costs of operating in the market than are borne by firms already there. Large capital requirements are an example of a barrier to entry in the first sense, a regulatory policy barring new entrants (such as that of the Civil Aeronautics Board with regard to trunk-line carriers) an example of a barrier to entry in the second sense.

The importance of the distinction lies in the fact that barriers in the first sense are transitory while barriers in the second sense need not be, so *prima facie* the latter are far more serious. In a market where established customer contacts are very important or where new products are heavily advertised, it may take a while for a new firm to get established; but there is no presumption that the costs of getting established are any higher than those which the established firms in the market bore, so there is no reason to expect that entry will not occur if a monopoly price is charged in the market. In a market where entry is in the grace of a regulatory agency, grudgingly bestowed, firms in the market may be able to change monopoly prices indefinitely without entry occurring.

I do not mean to imply that a lag in entry may not be an important factor in whether a serious limitation of output is possible. It becomes necessary, however, to compare the probable length of the lag with the probable duration of any enforcement proceeding undertaken to eliminate the condition responsible for the lag. Economists disagree, moreover, on the importance of various entry-retarding conditions. No one doubts that it would take longer to establish a new auto manufacturer than a new supermarket, but the real questions lie elsewhere. Does advertising make it easier or harder for a new entrant to get established? Harder, some say, because the new entrant must overcome the accumulated goodwill that advertising has created for the existing brands; probably easier, say others, because the new entrant can ride the coat-tails of the existing firms, who have helped create public acceptance of the product, and because the higher price that established firms must charge in order to cover their advertising expenses creates attractive opportunities for the new entrant to market his goods as off-brand or private-brand merchandise through retail chains that have their own reservoirs of consumer goodwill. The difficulty of assembling capital for investments is another point of dispute. The way such questions are answered has significant implications for the proper direction of antitrust enforcement. If advertising and capital requirements slow the rate of entry materially, as some believe, then there is a stronger argument for attacking practices that contribute to those conditions, such as a merger that permits more advertising by enabling economies of scale in advertising to be obtained, or vertical integration, which, if carried far enough in an industry, may force a new firm wishing to enter at one level to enter, with a larger investment, at both. Unfortunately, there is no consensus on these matters – which is a major reason why there is also no consensus on the significance of abuses. Many of them, like vertical integration, are plausibly sinister only if one believes that increasing the capital requirements for entry is likely to make a big difference in the speed of entry. In contrast, there is general agreement that barriers to entry in our second, more limited sense are quite serious.

Donald Turner has suggested still a third sense in which the conditions of a market may impose a barrier to entry.[9] Even when the cost of entry is the same for the new entrant as for the established firm, there may be nonrecurring costs of entry, he believes, that will favour the latter. The established firms will already have incurred extensive start-up costs – in advertising, in making arrangements with distributors and suppliers, in developing the product, and in testing the demand for it – that the prospective new entrant has first to incur. Those are sunk costs to the established firms and they can ignore them in pricing. This gives them a built-in price advantage over the new entrant.

The argument is highly speculative. It reverses the common-sense expectation that it is often rougher to be the first firm in an

9. In his forthcoming treatise on antitrust law with Phillip Areeda.

industry than the second because the second can learn from the mistakes of the first. It assumes, rather incredibly, that a firm can 'coast' indefinitely on the initial advertising campaign, the initial product specifications, the initial distributor organization – as if firms did not, in fact, advertise continually, improve their products continually, and renew continually their contacts with suppliers and distributors.

Turner's most plausible example of a nonrecurring cost of entry is the premium that a new entrant must pay in order to borrow money for the risky venture of trying to penetrate a new market. Once the new firm has become established in the market, it can presumably renew the initial loan at a lower rate, while the new entrant will have to pay a higher. It is not so clear that this is in fact a nonrecurring cost. After all, the established firms will have to bring out new products from time to time and investment in them may be quite risky (the Edsel). Large multi-product firms, an important category of new entrants, may be able to make new investments at substantially reduced risk. A major source of entry, in a practical sense, is the expansion of smaller firms already in the industry, and they may not have to pay a substantial premium for expansion capital. But I am willing to grant Turner's assertion that a new entrant will face higher initial capital costs in order to point out an important offsetting factor: the expectation, which ought to justify incurring some risk premium, of abnormally high profits. Firms earning monopoly profits are unlikely to cut their prices to their costs in order to prevent or repel the entry of firms having somewhat higher costs at the start. The theory of the dominant firm (which applies with equal force to cartels, and for which there is some empirical support) teaches that the profit-maximizing strategy in the face of threatened entry is not to fix a price low enough to prevent entry from occurring but to fix a higher price, at which entry occurs. The gradual contraction of monopoly profits under the second response is preferable to their immediate disappearance under the first. If a new entrant has permanently higher costs than the existing firms in the market, there may be a price at which they can forestall entry indefinitely while continuing to enjoy some monopoly return, but since Turner assumes merely a temporarily higher cost for the new entrant, the strategy is unavailable.

A final point, passed earlier, can be resolved by reference to the consensus approach. We said that the economic test of an anti-competitive practice is whether it tends to make the value of output less than what it would be under competition. Some economists believe that monopoly has other important adverse consequences – on innovation, on technical efficiency, and on the quality of service. But there is no consensus on these points; the effect on output is the only well-established objection to monopoly. One can find economists who doubt even that, but our standard is consensus, not unanimity.

Institutional changes

Virtually all of the resources of the Division would be allotted to price fixing, patents, and regulatory proceedings, with the last playing a much larger role in the Division's overall activity than at present. Merger enforcement would absorb few resources because few if any mergers vulnerable under my proposed guidelines have occurred for some time. Price fixing would be handled differently from today, with great emphasis placed on economic considerations and evidence quite foreign to the experience of most antitrust lawyers. The guiding principle of the entire operation would be the goal of maximizing the output of the economy.

I have summarized the substantive aspects of the programme as starkly as possible in order to underscore the importance of institutional change to the success of the programme. Such a programme could not be implemented without significant reforms in three areas: personnel, supervision, and planning.

Personnel

It goes without saying that the role of economists in the Division would be markedly different from the present. With the occasional exception of the special economic assistant to the chief of the Division (another happy innovation of Donald Turner), the Division's economists today are handmaidens to the lawyers, and rather neglected ones at that. The indifference (and sometimes hostility) of lawyers toward economists in the antitrust enforcement agencies is an old story. The lawyers are in firm command and the better economists are not attracted.

Such a situation would be disastrous if the Division sought to adopt the programme proposed here, and not only because the programme presupposes a much higher degree of economic competence and larger economic input to the decision-making process than heretofore. Economists are familiar with maximizing strategies, cost-benefit analysis, and the business or enterprise approach. Lawyers are not. The essence of the approach suggested here is that the Antitrust Division transforms itself into a kind of business, producing an output that consists of reducing monopolistic misallocations of resources and seeking to maximize that output net of input costs. This approach would bewilder or even horrify the average lawyer in the Antitrust Division, who thinks of his job in terms of enforcing the antitrust laws as Congress wrote them and the courts interpret them. The programme can succeed only if economists are well represented among the supervisory personnel of the Division.

The use of economists knowledgeable in industrial organization in key managerial roles in the Division seems to me preferable to the use of businessmen or management specialists. This is an empirical judgement, based on the notable lack of success that programme review officers of the Bureau of the Budget seconded to the Department of Justice have had in introducing efficient planning and management techniques into the various divisions, notably the Antitrust Division. I do not attribute their failure entirely, or even primarily, to the resistance of the lawyers, but more to the Budget officers' unfamiliarity with the highly specialized character of the Division's 'output'.

Supervision

The present organization of the Antitrust Division is highly decentralized. The closest organizational analogy, although a far from perfect one, is to a large litigating law firm. In most periods the Division is dominated by the individual trial lawyers and supervision is minimal. They owe their authority and independence partly to the trial lawyer's distinctive personality and partly to the accumulation of skills and experience that makes them valued by private firms and hard to replace by the Division – but mostly to default. The traditions of supervision and hierarchy are very weak in the Division. For many years section chiefs received no greater compensation than senior trial lawyers and they still conceive of themselves by and large as conduits and office managers rather than as leaders. The total number of officials above the section-chief level in the Division can be counted on one's fingers – this is an organization of several hundred professionals.

Any student of organizations will tell you that a 'flat' hierarchy of this sort is all very well if the desire is to encourage maximum autonomy at the bottom level, but that it is ill suited to a more centralized operation. It would be only a slight exaggeration to say that, in the early 1960s, the only real coordination of antitrust policy took place in the Solicitor General's office, where coherent theories were formulated for the antitrust cases bound for the Supreme Court. The Court has expressed its dismay at the liberties taken by the Solicitor General with the theories urged by the Division in the lower court,[10] but the lack of theoretical coherence in the Division's positions made major surgery unavoidable.

Donald Turner took the first step toward correcting the Division's excessive decentralization by creating an 'Evaluation Section' whose function was to review all proposals for investigation and for complaint and all important documents filed by the Division during trial. This worthwhile innovation has been retained by his successors. The staff of the Evaluation Section consists of good young lawyers who are free from any trial or investigative responsibilities. The function of the section, however, is essentially negative: to check the excesses of the enthusiastic trial lawyer and to assure a modicum of uniformity and consistency of policy. The initiative remains with the trial sections, which usually means, as noted, with the trial lawyers themselves.

The kind of programme proposed in this paper demands a quite different structure. I cannot formulate the details, but a broad outline follows. The Division would be divided into five bureaus – four line bureaus and one staff bureau. The staff bureau would be the Bureau of Planning and Evaluation, discussed in the next subpart. The line bureaus would be the Bureau of Regulated Competition, the Bureau of Investigations, the Bureau of Trials,

10. United States v. Arnold, Schwinn & Co., 388 US 365, 371–2 n.4, 374 n.5 (1967).

and the Bureau of Compliance. The first would be responsible for participation in regulatory proceedings, interagency committees, and other proceedings. It would consist of economists and lawyers. The second bureau, also consisting of economists and lawyers, would be responsible for surveying nonregulated markets and developing evidence of anticompetitive effects, mostly price fixing. The third, consisting of lawyers, would try cases prepared by the second. The Bureau of Investigations would furnish expert economic witnesses for the Bureau of Trials. Quite possibly the neat separation of trials and investigations proposed here is infeasible, judging by the FTC's unfortunate experience with such a separation in the 1950s. But however accomplished, it is important so far as practicable to confine trial lawyers to trials in recognition of the specialized character of the trial lawyer's function. The aptitudes required by a good trial lawyer are quite different from those required in the judicious design of policy, appraisal of economic evidence, and selection of cases, and the failure to recognize this has resulted, I believe, in costly underspecialization. Finally, a compliance bureau seems essential in view of the well-documented deficiencies of the Division in the administration of equitable remedies (Adams, 1951; Elzinga, 1969; Posner, 1970); if it is to have greater success than the existing Judgments Section, such a bureau will have to include economists as well as lawyers.

Each bureau would be headed by a bureau chief, and would be divided into several small sections, each headed by a section head. The bureau chiefs would be supervised by the Director of Operations in administrative and operational matters, and by the Director of the Bureau of Planning and Evaluation in policy matters, including the selection of cases.

The foregoing description is incomplete and simplified, but it conveys the essential purpose of the reorganization: to reduce the dominant role of trial lawyers in the direction of the Division's affairs and to create a more vertical system of hierarchical control.

Planning

A position of Director of Policy Planning was created by then Assistant Attorney General Orrick in 1963 and continued by his successors. Not one of the extremely able men who have filled the post has done any planning worthy of the name. Initially little more than a speech-writing job, it later became a supervisory position. The principal unit supervised was the Evaluation Section. A superficial reason why the Directors of Policy Planning have never done any planning is that they have never been given a staff whose function was planning, rather than riding herd on trial lawyers or something else equally removed. The more basic reason is that the Antitrust Division has never conceived for itself a role in which planning would be something more than homiletics. Planning is meaningful only in the context of a programmatic approach to antitrust enforcement, heretofore lacking.

The first job of the Bureau of Planning and Evaluation would be to design a substantive programme – to determine priorities in the use of the Division's resources – of which the proposals in this paper may be viewed as a very rough cut, and also to co-ordinate the activities of the line units of the Division in carrying out the programme. The second job would be to evaluate the programme, using statistical measures discussed at length elsewhere (Posner, 1970), and to revise it from time to time in accordance with the results of the evaluation. The third job would be to formulate a legislative programme for submission to Congress, specifying any changes in legal authority or the level of appropriations that appeared appropriate in view of the Division's programme. The Bureau would be advised by an advisory board consisting of distinguished private economists.

Conclusion

The programme presented here, entailing as it would a rather drastic overhauling of antitrust enforcement, is not – I predict – about to be adopted by the Antitrust Division and is in that sense an academic exercise. But perhaps not completely. After all, such a programme would be the culmination of perceptible trends in the Division's recent history. Moreover, to return to an earlier point, the trend of antitrust decisions in the Supreme Court has given new importance to the devising of a programme for the Division. The Court's often remarked tendency in the antitrust area to declare principles so sweeping as to be incapable of practical and consistent application had by 1967 reached such a point with regard to mergers that the Division either had to declare its own rules to channel the discretion of its trial staff or permit anti-merger enforcement to become virtually random. The response was the Merger Guidelines.[11] One may fault these guidelines in many places but what is significant for the present discussion is that the Division felt obliged to articulate a set of goals based not upon statutory or judicial language but upon the policy grounds assumed to underlie such language and that it attempted to fashion a set of priorities under which, grudgingly to be sure, the Division indicated that it was prepared to condone some apparent violations of the merger law as it had been interpreted by the Court. What is this but an embryonic form of the programme suggested here?

References

ADAMS, W. (1951), 'Dissolution, divorcement, divestiture: the pyrrhic victories of antitrust', *Indiana Law Journal*, vol. 27, Fall, pp. 1–37.

BORK, R. H. (1965), 'The rule of reason and the per se concept: price fixing and market division', *Yale Law Journal*, vol. 74, April, pp. 775–847.

BORK, R. H. (1966), 'Legislative intent and the policy of the Sherman Act', *Journal of Law and Economics*, vol. 9, pp. 7 ff.

DAVIS, K. C. (1969), *Discretionary Justice – A Preliminary Inquiry*, University of Illinois Press.

ELZINGA, K. G. (1969), 'The antimerger law: pyrrhic victories', *Journal of Law and Economics*, vol. 12, April, pp. 43–78.

HITCH, C., and MCKEAN, R. (1965), *The Economics of Defence in the Nuclear Age*, Cambridge, Harvard University Press.

HOLMES, O. W. (1920), 'The path of the law', *Collected Legal Papers*, New York, Harcourt, Brace & Howe, pp. 167–75.

MCKEAN, R. (1958), *Efficiency in Government Through Systems Analysis, with Emphasis on Water Resources Development*, New York, John Wiley.

POSNER, R. A. (1969), 'Oligopoly and the antitrust laws: a suggested approach', *Stanford Law Review*, vol. 21, pp. 1562–606.

POSNER, R. A. (1970), 'A statistical study of antitrust enforcement', *Journal of Law and Economics*, vol. 13, pp. 365–419.

PREST, A. R., and TURVEY, R. (1965), 'Cost-benefit analysis: a survey', *Economic Journal*, vol. 75, December, pp. 683–735.

SCHLESINGER, J. R. (1968), 'Systems analysis and the political process', *Journal of Law and Economics*, vol. 11, October, pp. 281–98.

STIGLER, G. (1964), 'A theory of oligopoly', *Journal of Political Economy*, vol. 72, February, pp. 44–61.

11. *Department of Justice Merger Guidelines, 1 Trade Reg. Rep.* ¶ 4430, at 6,681 (1968).

25 L. W. Stern and C. S. Craig

Interorganizational Data Systems

L. W. Stern and C. S. Craig, 'Interorganizational data systems: the computer and distribution', *Journal of Retailing*, vol. 47, Summer 1971, pp. 73–91.

The purpose of this chapter is to explore the probable evolution of Interorganizational Data Systems (IDS) in channels of distribution. Operationally defined, an IDS is a computer-based communications system directly linking two or more firms for the purpose of information exchange. The article examines the consequences of such systems in terms of the changes their introduction makes in the communications and power structure within the distribution network. Here, a channel of distribution shall be considered as 'a set of institutions which performs all of the activities (functions) utilized to move a product and its title from production to consumption' (Bucklin, 1966, p. 5). Particular stress is placed on the channels made up of independent wholesalers and retailers.

Just as a firm has a production lead-time, it has an information lead-time. An event occurs in the marketplace – e.g., a stockout in a hard goods store in Des Moines, Iowa. Several alternative actions are possible, depending on how critical this stockout may be: (1) as immediate phone call to the wholesaler, (2) an order sent through the mails and requiring several days, or (3) a wait until the next visit of the wholesaler's salesman. The wholesaler follows a similar procedure, depending on the demand generated from the retailers. If a telephone call (or TWX or TELEX) is placed, the manufacturer has current information to act on, and the needed merchandise can be shipped. If he also faces a stockout, the necessary production orders are made. However, if normal channels of communication were used all along the line, several weeks or more may have elapsed since the initial stockout occurred. This, together with the necessary manufacturing and delivery lead-time, may result in a delay of several months before the retailer again has sufficient stock.

A great deal has been done to reduce production cycles and delivery time, but much remains to be done to lessen the information lead-time. The greatest advances ought to be in information handling, since data can travel at the speed of light while physical products are relegated to slower modes of transportation. The situation is somewhat analogous to the fabled race between the tortoise and the hare; information has the ability to arrive first, but often does not.

The ideal situation would be for the manufacturer to know not only when stockouts occur, but what the inventory levels are at all points in his channels of distribution. This desired state should soon become a reality if interorganizational data systems come to full fruition. Manufacturers would be able to ascertain the demand patterns within each retail establishment carrying their brands. Thus, the time between an action-requiring event at one level of the channel and action at another level could be measured in seconds rather than in days or weeks.

Machine-to-machine interaction

The developments that will eventually lead to direct machine-to-machine interaction within the channel of distribution fall into two basic categories: (1) technology and (2) applications. The first shows what is actually possible, and the second indicates what people are willing to accept. Each aspect will be discussed briefly.

Technology

In the area of computer technology, hardware and software capabilities have expanded rapidly. Early computer systems were limited to batch-processing. As direct-access storage devices were developed and central processing units grew larger, multiprocessing became a reality. Terminals coupled with advanced programming systems have made time-sharing possible. Considerable effort in today's computer industry is spent in producing more sophisticated terminals. In fact, specialized firms have come into being solely to manufacture terminals that interface with major computer manufacturers' main frames.

A number of corporations currently tie remote locations to their central offices through terminal networks. Often the terminals at remote locations are stand-alone computers that can batch-process local requirements when not sending or receiving data. Likewise, many large universities have small computers strategically positioned throughout their campuses that act as input-output devices for a large central computer. At The Ohio State University, for example, the central data facility contains a System 360 Model 75. Throughout the campus, IBM 1130s (a small stand-alone computer) are linked on-line, allowing jobs to be entered at remote locations, compiled and executed by the 75, and printed out on the 1130s printer. (During slack time, turnaround is instantaneous.)

In sum, hardware and software have been sufficiently developed to allow for direct machine-to-machine interaction throughout a distribution channel. Many firms and institutions are employing this on a daily basis. The computer manufacturers are developing and pushing communications-based systems and the 1970s, in addition to seeing the fourth and possibly fifth generation of computers, will also be the 'time of the terminal'.

Applications

Airlines and the military have done some of the pioneering in the use of terminals. SAGE and SABRE have attained almost legendary stature. Faced with large amounts of data, and with a desire for efficient and improved customer service, the airlines were left with no other alternative but to computerize. In essence, the airlines had to have accurate information available immediately. The obvious eventual outgrowth of the airlines' individual reservations systems is a common data bank to speed inter-airline booking.

Most major hotel chains now have computerized reservations systems to assure their guests of rooms in distant cities. Additionally, there are private firms offering instant confirmation of theatre tickets, which can be purchased directly at numerous remote locations. The terminal produces hard-copy output which serves as the actual ticket.

Computer utilities are growing rapidly and serve many different

L. W. Stern and C. S. Craig 411

types of users. General Electric, Service Bureau Corporation (IBM), CDC, Honeywell, and scores of others offer computational time-sharing services with languages such as BASIC, QUIK-TRAN, PL/I, FORTRAN, ALGOL, and COBOL. Firms such as KEYDATA offer specific application packages that handle invoicing, inventory updating, order entry, and credit checking. In addition to the on-line terminal service, reports are prepared periodically on the main system and sent to the user (Parkhill, 1966, p. 80).

Some commercial service bureaus are providing their clients with highspeed terminals for transmission and receipt of data. This eliminates many of the time delays associated with service bureau operations and gives the firm many of the advantages of an in-house computer without some of its drawbacks.

The feasibility and limited use of on-line checkout systems is yet another example of innovative applications. Inventory control is revolutionized by having the cash register tied directly into the firm's data-processing systems, so that when a sale is rung up on the selling floor, all the relevant files are immediately updated. This, coupled with effective means of inventory control (e.g., IBM's IMPACT), allows the retailer to maintain a specific level of customer service while, at the same time, keeping his inventory investment at a minimum.

In manufacturing industries, data terminals are becoming an accepted part of the production floor. Not only are completed work orders recorded, but new ones are transmitted directly from the computer's master file. An in-line IBM 1030 system allows a firm to keep track of its raw material, work-in-process inventory, and finished-goods inventory. At the same time, efficient production scheduling and loading can be achieved. The system provides shop-floor terminals that allow direct man-to-machine interaction.

The use of terminals for order-entry and routine inquiry has increased significantly in the past ten years. To date, most of this usage remains intrafirm, but it is highly feasible to expand it beyond the boundaries of the firm. The technology is available, and some firms are making imaginative use of terminals. In short, there is every reason to believe that interorganizational data systems will soon become a reality.

The potential for IDS within distribution channels

Interdependency is pervasive among firms within any given distribution channel. The form that this interdependency takes is clearly illustrated by the economic input-output analysis pioneered by Leontief (1965). The various sectors of the economy are related to each other in terms of the goods they supply and the goods they demand. In like manner, firms require internal and external information. To date, efforts have been directed toward internal information systems or information-gathering systems. Little effort has been directed at the exchange-of-data function among firms linked together vertically.

The direction and probable evolution of efforts aimed at the exchange-of-data function have been portrayed graphically in Figure 1. The evolutionary stages that interorganizational data systems will follow in response to a need for a more rapid exchange of information are traced. The information flow pictured is bi-directional. Confirmation of information receipt merely reverses the process requiring the same number of intermediaries.

In each of the three stages pictured (precomputer stages are not considered), some actionable event occurs in Firm A – e.g., an order point is reached for some item carried in inventory. In Stage I, the computer system generates a low-stock list at the end of each day. Early the following morning, the list is reviewed and a determination is made regarding the items to reorder. Depending on the urgency of the item, an appropriate vehicle for contacting the supplier (Firm B) is selected. The order may be mailed or, if time is of the essence, telephoned. The process is continued at the other end, with a person receiving the order and performing preliminary checks. After the initial editing stages, the order is sent to data processing where it is entered into the system (keypunched, inscribed directly on tape, or entered directly through an on-line terminal). The computer generates an action notification. Internally, Firm B reacts in two ways: it (1) initiates action to solve the problem, and (2) confirms receipts of the order. The procedure for order confirmation is the converse of the original procedure followed by Firm A.

This type of system is characterized by a large number of intermediaries with two major results: (1) more error points, and (2) delays at each handling point. By eliminating the first, the second

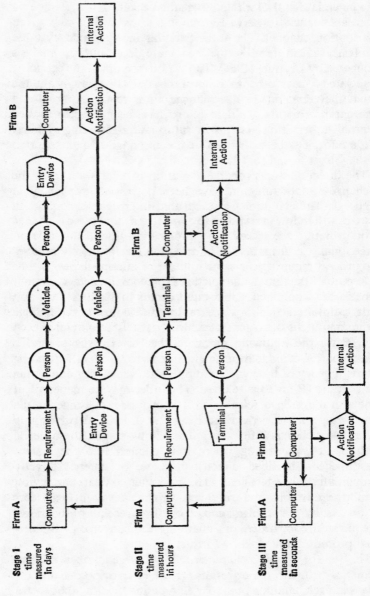

Stage I
time measured
in days

Stage II
time measured
in hours

Stage III
time measured
in seconds

Figure 1

is also reduced. These factors are significantly increased in any distribution channel where there are multiple levels.

Stage II represents an elimination of some of the intervening steps. The figure shows the flow of data from a terminal to a computer. For each order confirmation, the flow moves in the opposite direction. Time between events has diminished, and the information lag time has been reduced.

Stage III depicts the eventual evolution of interorganizational data systems within the distribution channel. All intermediaries have been eliminated. An event in Firm A triggers an immediate response from Firm B. The information lag time is nonexistent. All that remains is production lead-time and the delivery of the merchandise. Thus, Stage III represents the type of data system linking all the members of the channel of distribution envisioned by the authors.

Eventually, every firm will probably have some sort of data-processing device. These may range from simple terminals to extensive computer installations, but the majority will have a small computer. The recent announcement of the IBM System/3 points in this direction, making a computer available at a cost the small firm can well afford. Those firms that cannot justify the purchase or lease of their own computers will probably have pooled access to computers through either suppliers or trade associations. This idea is merely an extension of the computer utility concept. The major difference is that it should become an integral part of the firm's operation instead of an outside service.

Assuming some form of data-processing hardware in each firm, machine-to-machine interaction will undoubtedly become the dominant mode of communication among firms over the long run. What firm is going to rely on the United States mail system when it has at its disposal the quickest and most efficient means of communication available? In the time it takes to address and stamp an envelope, the computer can transmit an entire order to the vendor's computer and receive confirmation.

The larger firms that have computers with direct-access storage devices and multiprocessing capabilities will be able to transmit orders as the need arises. Firms with less sophisticated hardware will have to pool their order requirements and batch-process them periodically. The receiving vendor's computer will, of necessity, have multiprocessing capabilities (or be dedicated to order receipt and processing). As the order is received, the inventory file is checked for availability, and an order confirmation is issued immediately. This confirmation is not mailed but is transmitted directly back to the ordering firm's computer. In some instances, the confirmation will indicate a stockout condition. If this occurs, the ordering computer either cancels the order (if alternative sources of supply exist) or makes allowance for the back-order condition in its own files.

The preceding discussion has been limited to the inventory-order-writing cycle. This has been done to simplify the explanation. This does not suggest, however, that this is the only portion of the firm's operations that could be included in the inter-organizational data system. Virtually every facet of the firm's dealings with other firms will be affected. For example, much has been written about the 'checkless society'. In an 'ultimate' system, the commercial interorganizational data system will, of necessity, interface with the financial community's system.

Behavioural consequences of IDS

A number of behavioural changes will no doubt occur when all firms have computers, or easy access to them, and are using them not only for their internal information systems, but also as the basis for their external relations regarding distribution. We concentrate below on suggesting some of the consequences of IDS on communication and power within distribution channels (Stern, 1969).

Communication

Once IDS has been instituted within a distribution channel, the most immediate and obvious change will be an increase in the speed with which communication takes place. When a stockout occurs, or an order point is reached at the retail level, it will not be days or hours before the appropriate wholesaler knows about it, but seconds. Likewise, the manufacturer of the item will also know of this condition when it happens. This linkage brings each level of the channel temporally closer together. It is not only the retailer who will be able to perceive shifts in ultimate consumer markets as they happen, but all key members of the channel.

The wholesaler's computer will also act to pool the requirements of his customers and send a grouped requirement to the source of supply. This mode of communication will cause a certain amount of routinization within the channel and also serve to limit the alternatives open to each member of the channel. Obviously it will require complex software, including preprogrammed decision rules. Order points, EOQs, sources of supply, and the message content of the order will all have to be determined in advance. The computer cannot assume or derive implicit meanings; therefore, instructions must be specified in advance. (Advances in heuristic programming may help in this area.)

For example, assume that a customer in a department store buys a hand tool. The cash register is connected to the store's computer and, as the sale is rung up, the inventory file is updated. If it is a credit transaction, the consumer's account is first checked, and then his account is debited. If this transaction causes the stock to fall below a given minimum, the store's computer contacts the wholesaler's computer. The latter's computer confirms receipt and transmits the planned delivery date.

The department store's computer does not contact all possible vendors for that particular hand tool. It contacts one and possibly has one or two alternative sources. This restriction is primarily due to the associated transaction cost because, for every vendor added to the system, internal files must be maintained. When one considers all the items carried in the typical retail store, a complete listing of all potential suppliers would become prohibitively expensive. The vendor's computer must also have records established for the retailer, and the vendor cannot afford to maintain these records unless he is assured of a certain minimum volume of business.

Further rigidity is imposed by system requirements. Hardware compatibility should pose no insurmountable obstacle, since software interfaces can be written to anticipate many problems. However, each system will have specific requirements. The vendor's computer requires certain data to complete transactions, and these data must be supplied by the ordering computer. The order confirmation will take a certain form so that the ordering computer can update its on-order file or contact an alternative source of supply. The system will not be economical unless the setup cost to include a firm can be recouped through sufficient sales volume. The necessary volume can be attained only if alternatives are limited and firms are selective in their interactional patterns.

In addition to the great speed with which data will be sent through the channel, greater accuracy will result. Once the retail salesperson has correctly keyed in the purchased item, the same information will pass unaltered to the other levels in the channel.

In the best of all possible worlds, all internal data systems would be compatible and able to communicate freely with one another. However, industry requirements vary from channel to channel. Further, if patterns of systems development continue much as they have in the past (i.e., most systems are tailored to the individual firm's requirements), systems will continue to be unique. Unless trade associations and computer manufacturers exert considerable pressure for a high degree of standardization, members in the same channel will not be able to interact freely and speedily. Firms will not be able to switch to competitive systems without substantial changes. The problem is somewhat analogous to switching computer manufacturers. (Even with emulators and compatibility features, switching from one manufacturer to another represents a major undertaking.)

Most of the foregoing factors will serve to increase the permanence of the information flows. As permanence increases, certain members will become more dependent on other members, have fewer viable alternatives, a greater commitment to a specific channel, and a tangible stake in its operation. These factors are germane to understanding the emergence of a locus of power within any given channel.

Power

In a channel of distribution where the locus of power is firmly established (e.g., vertically integrated systems), there will be little appreciable change in the power structure due to the introduction of IDS. Generally, the established locus will be the driving force behind the evolving IDS.

Where the members are loosely organized, however, a locus of power is expected to emerge. For example, in a channel characterized by a loose coalition of independent retailers and wholesalers, where no middleman is particularly dominant, one of the wholesalers may take the lead in developing IDS, thereby 'tying' a number of the retailers to him. As a consequence, it is likely that the market will sustain a 'shakeout' with a few large wholesalers emerging and displacing the smaller ones. Those wholesalers who do not establish a clientele large enough to support an IDS will probably fail. In a channel situation similar to that posed above, the member(s) best able to establish strong dependency bonds and limit alternatives for those with whom they deal will dominate, and IDS is seen as a means to this end.

Positionally, wholesalers are probably best able to assume leadership in the development of IDS in such channels. It would not be feasible, from an economic perspective, to maintain a great number of parallel flows, since each data link represents a cost. In any channel with more than two retailers and more than two manufacturers, the number of links can be minimized by employing a wholesaler. With a large number of possible links, the saving can be substantial. The emergence of wholesalers as power loci is an example of technological determinism. *Ipso facto* their position in distribution channels bestows power on them in this regard.

Interorganizational data systems portend great promise for wholesalers in another area – computer services. A wholesaler is in an ideal position to help smaller retailers with inventory management, accounts receivable, payroll, and other applications beyond the capabilities of the latter's own equipment. Besides establishing the permanence of the flows between wholesaler and retailer, revenue could be derived from the services performed. Many commercial service bureaus thrive on performing these same services for their clients. A parallel trend is developing in the field of banking, with large banks performing various computer-related tasks for their correspondent banks. Wholesalers could have a price advantage over service bureaus in that retailers' inventories and related functions are subsets of their own and should, therefore, not require extensive additional programming.

Numerically, data links present a problem. A wholesaler within a given channel should be able to minimize the total number. By virtue of his position, the wholesaler will be able to mitigate another problem – compatibility. Compatibility problems are exacerbated by the number of links. Since his problems are similar to those of the retailers with whom he deals, he can do much to standardize this interface. Problems facing manufacturers, however, are much different from those facing retailers and wholesalers. Some manufacturers, in fact, will link directly to major retailers, but in most instances – especially those involving medium and small-size retailers – the effort will not be justified, since wholesalers can perform the same function with greater facility. Moreover, with the wholesaler-retailer links established, the wholesaler can readily build the wholesaler-manufacturer links. With a large exclusive domain of retailers, a wholesaler will be able to exert power over manufacturers. By controlling inventories, maintaining receivables, and helping to prepare the payroll, the wholesaler will further entrench himself in the retailer's operation.

By maintaining retailers' inventory files, the wholesaler can order his own stock more intelligently and can also communicate demand trends to manufacturers, who can then plan production accordingly. By performing these services, the wholesaler is increasing the dependence of both the retailer and the manufacturer on him.

Data systems will also likely cause greater vertical integration in the channel. Data links will direct the flows upward and downward. Very little communication will take place on a horizontal level. If one retailer is out of a certain item, he will not check directly with other retailers, but address his inquiry to the wholesaler who maintains all the inventory records. The vertical nature of the data links will enhance the power of the channel member at the locus, and other members will experience difficulty in forming effective coalitions to offset the power inequality.

One word of warning should be interjected lest wholesalers become enamoured of their projected roles in channels of distribution. Some wholesalers will probably fail because they are unable to generate sufficient sales to support a computer system; others may be replaced by large switching networks. If the wholesaler merely assists in the flow of goods and services and does not take actual possession, he will no longer be necessary. Manufacturers will establish their own pooled-data points. This will give them direct information of retailers' requirements. With this immediate information, together with advances in physical distribution, a wholesaler as a field storage location may no longer be necessary.

Thus, the advent of interorganizational data systems could be either a boon or a bane for wholesalers. The direction depends on their own initiatives. If they succeed in developing the data links with the retailers with whom they deal, the manufacturer will have no alternative but to rely upon them.

Implications for managerial strategy

One of the primary implications of the proposed advent of IDS is that of survival. The firm must embrace the new technology quickly. Once data links have been established, it will be difficult to make competitive inroads, and firms slow to adopt the technology may be doomed to failure. Being an early innovator will allow the firm to grow appreciably in size. The wholesaler who acts quickly to tie up his current customers and those of his competitors will prosper. He will be providing them with faster delivery, lower prices, better inventory control (resulting in smaller inventory investment), and many additional services.

Once the data link is established, it will be relatively easy for a wholesaler to add merchandise carried by other types of wholesalers. Retailers within the wholesaler's market outreach will become more dependent on him as a source of supply for all their needs. Thus, the number of wholesalers will diminish while the size of those remaining will increase substantially. Entry of new firms will be difficult due to the capital necessary to establish a comparable IDS and because of the firmly entrenched positions of the remaining wholesalers.

In addition to increased sales, the wholesaler (or centralizing member) will be able to derive additional revenue from service-bureau-type operations. The wholesaler will be able to provide inventory control, accounts receivable, billing, payroll, and sales-forecasting services for his retailers. The wholesaler will also be able to secure such valuable information as reports on sales by specific area, type of store, and method of display, and then pass it on to relevant manufacturers.

There will also be a change in the composition of personal

selling expense. A wholesaler will no longer need as many salesmen to call on retailers. As soon as an order point is reached, the order will be placed. There will, however, be a need for technical personnel to implement the system. Advisory personnel will be needed to help retailers with merchandising techniques. Thus, the total personnel expense will probably remain relatively constant; the change will be in the character of the personnel.

There will be a reduction in the order-delivery cycle. This results from requirements being generated simultaneously throughout the channel. Manufacturers will be better able to plan their production, since they will know the amount of inventory in the entire channel, not simply in their own warehouse. They will be able to spot changes in demand patterns occurring at the retail level and alter their production accordingly. The reduction in the order cycle will be accompanied by fewer out-of-stock conditions. The delivery side of the cycle will be reduced through the advances that will occur in logistics. Better decision-making will result through more complete and timely information at all levels of the channel.

A final word of warning is required, however. The discussion here has been in terms of existing institutions innovating and changing their present ways of doing business. If existing channel members fail to innovate, new organizations will be formed to capitalize on the opportunities that exist. The new firms will be stronger and will possess the technical expertise to implement interorganizational data systems. These firms will grow and prosper, while the old firms will rapidly lose their place in the market.

References

BUCKLIN, L. P. (1966), *A Theory of Distribution Channel Structure*, Berkeley, California, Institute of Business and Economic Research, University of California.

LEONTIEF, W. W. (1965), 'The structure of the US economy', *Scientific American*, April, pp. 25–35.

PARKHILL, D. F. (1966), *The Challenge of the Computer Utility*, Reading, Mass., Addison-Wesley.

STERN, L. W. (1969), *Distribution Channels: Behavioral Dimensions*, Boston, Mass., Houghton Mifflin.

Further Reading

Models of Interorganizational Relations

F. E. Emery and E. L. Trist, 'The causal texture of organizational environments', *Human Relations*, vol. 18, 1965, pp. 21–32.

W. M. Evan, 'The organization-set: toward a theory of interorganizational relations', in J. D. Thompson (ed.), *Approaches to Organizational Design*, Pittsburgh, University of Pittsburgh Press, 1966, pp. 175–91.

W. M. Evan, 'A systems model of organizational climate', in R. Tagiuri and G. H. Litwin (eds.), *Organizational Climate*, Boston, Division of Research, Harvard Business School, 1968, pp. 107–24.

E. W. Kelley, 'Theory and the study of coalition behavior', in S. Groennings, E. W. Kelley, M. Leiserson (eds.), *The Study of Coalition Behavior*, New York, Holt, Rinehart & Winston, Inc., 1970, pp. 481–89.

S. Levine and P. E. White, 'Exchange as a conceptual framework for the study of interorganizational relationships', *Administrative Science Quarterly*, vol. 5, March 1961, pp. 583–601.

E. Litwak and L. F. Hylton, 'Interorganizational analysis: a hypothesis on coordinating agencies', *Administrative Science Quarterly*, vol. 6, March 1962, pp. 397–420.

E. Litwak with the collaboration of J. Rothman, 'Toward the theory and practice of coordination between formal organizations', in W. R. Rosengren and M. Lefton (eds.), *Organizations and Clients*, Columbus, Ohio, Charles E. Merrill Publishing Co., 1970, pp. 137–86.

J. Marschak, 'Elements for a theory of teams', *Management Science*, vol. 1, January 1955, pp. 127–37.

A. Phillips, *Market Structure, Organization and Performance*, Cambridge, Mass., Harvard University Press, 1962.

J. D. Thompson, *Organizations in Action*, New York, McGraw-Hill, 1967.

J. D. Thompson and W. J. McEwen, 'Organizational goals and environment goal-setting as an interaction process', *American Sociological Review*, vol. 23, February 1958, pp. 23–31.

H. B. Thorelli, 'Organizational theory: an ecological view', *Academy of Management Proceedings*, 27th Annual Meeting, Washington, D.C., 26–9 December, 1967.

M. F. Tuite, M. Radnor and R. K. Chisholm (eds.), *Interorganizational Decision Making*, Chicago, Aldine-Atherton Publishing Co., 1972.

R. L. Warren, 'The interorganizational field as a focus for investigation', *Administrative Science Quarterly*, vol. 12, December 1967, pp. 396–419.

P. E. White and G. J. Vlasak (eds.), *Inter-Organizational Research in Health: Conference Proceedings*, US Department of Health, Education and Welfare, National Center for Health Services Research and Development, 1970.

E. Yuchtman and S. E. Seashore, 'A system resource approach to organizational effectiveness', *American Sociological Review*, vol. 32, December 1967, pp. 891–903.

Research on Interorganizational Relations

B. Aaron, 'Interunion representation disputes and the NLRB', *Texas Law Review*, vol. 36, October 1958, pp. 846–62.

H. Assael, 'Constructive role of interorganizational conflict', *Administrative Science Quarterly*, vol. 14, December 1969, pp. 573–82.

A. I. El-Ansary and L. W. Stern, 'Power measurement in the distribution channel', *Journal of Marketing Research*, vol. 9, February 1972, pp. 47–52.

W. N. Chernish, *Coalition Bargaining*, University of Pennsylvania Press, 1969.

W. M. Evan, 'An organization-set model of interorganizational relations', in M. F. Tuite, M. Radnor and R. K. Chisholm (eds.), *Interorganizational Decision Making*, Chicago, Aldine-Atherton Publishing Co., 1972, pp. 181–200.

W. M. Evan, 'Power bargaining and law: a preliminary analysis of labor arbitration cases', *Social Problems*, vol. 7, Summer 1959, pp. 4–15.

W. M. Evan and J. A. MacDougall, 'Interorganizational conflict: a labor-management bargaining experiment', *Journal of Conflict Resolution*, vol. 11, December 1967, pp. 398–413.

A. L. Gitlow, 'Union rivalries', *Southern Economic Journal*, vol. 18, January 1952, pp. 338–49.

M. Gort and T. F. Hogarty, 'New evidence on mergers', *Journal of Law and Economics*, vol. 13, April 1970, pp. 167–84.

H. Graham, 'Union mergers', *Industrial Relations*, vol. 25, 1970, pp. 552–66.

J. M. Gustafson, 'The United Church of Christ in America: actualizing a church union', in N. Ehrenstrom and W. G. Muelder (eds.), *Institutionalism and Church Unity*, New York, Association Press, 1963, pp. 325–51.

J. Kitching, 'Why do mergers miscarry?' *Harvard Business Review*, vol. 45, November–December 1967, pp. 84–101.

S. Levine, P. E. White and B. D. Paul, 'Community interorganizational problems in providing medical care and social services', *American Journal of Public Health*, vol. 53, August 1963, pp. 1183–95.

S. Macaulay, 'Changing a continuing relationship between a large corporation and those who deal with it: automobile manufacturers, their dealers and the legal systems', *Wisconsin Law Review*, Summer 1965, pp. 483–575, Fall 1965, pp. 740–858.

P. W. Macavoy, *The Economic Effects of Regulation*, Cambridge, Mass., MIT Press, 1965.

J. J. Mol, 'The merger attempts of the Australian churches', *The Ecumenical Review*, vol. 21, January 1969, pp. 23–31.

Note, 'Coordinated-coalition bargaining: theory, legality, practice and economic effects', *Minnesota Law Review*, vol. 55, January 1971, pp. 599–633.

R. A. Posner, 'A statistical study of antitrust enforcement', *Journal of Law and Economics*, vol. 13, October 1970, pp. 365–419.

W. Reid, 'Interagency co-ordination in delinquency prevention and control', *Social Service Review*, vol. 38, December 1964, pp. 418–28.

L. J. Rosenberg and L. W. Stern, 'Conflict measurement in the distribution channel', *Journal of Marketing Research*, vol. 8, November 1971, pp. 437–42.

L. R. Sayles and M. K. Chandler, *Managing large systems: organizations for the future*, New York, Harper & Row, 1971.

L. Scheinman, 'Some preliminary notes on bureaucratic relationships in the European Economic Community', *International Organization*, vol. 20, Autumn 1966, pp. 750–73.

P. Selznick, *TVA and the Grass Roots: A Study in the Sociology of Formal Organizations*, Berkeley, California, University of California Press, 1949.

G. J. Stigler and C. Friedland, 'What can regulators regulate? The case of electricity', *Journal of Law and Economics*, vol. 5, October 1962, pp. 1–16.

W. L. Warner, D. B. Unwalla and J. H. Trimm (eds.), *The Emergent American Society: Large Scale Organizations*, New Haven, Conn., Yale University Press, 1967, pp. 121–57.

H. B. Wells, 'A case study on interinstitutional cooperation', *Educational Record*, vol. 48, Fall 1967, pp. 355–62.

Strategies for Research on Interorganizational Relations

J. A. Barnes, 'Networks and political process', in M. J. Swartz (ed.), *Local-Level Politics*, Chicago, Aldine-Atherton Publishing Co., 1968, pp. 107–30.

J. A. Barnes, 'Graph theory and social networks: a technical comment on connectedness and connectivity', *Sociology*, vol. 3, 1969, pp. 215–32.

B. M. Bass, 'Business gaming for organizational research', *Management Science*, vol. 10, April 1964, pp. 545–56.

W. M. Evan and J. A. MacDougall, 'Interorganizational conflict: a labor-management bargaining experiment', *Journal of Conflict Resolution*, vol. 11, December 1967, pp. 398–413.

J. W. Friedman, 'On experimental research in oligopoly', *Review of Economic Studies*, vol. 36, October 1969, pp. 399–415.

G. K. Garbett, 'The application of optical coincidence cards to the matrices of digraphs of social networks', *Sociology*, vol. 2, September 1968, pp. 313–32.

W. Z. Hirsch, 'Input-output techniques for urban government decisions', *American Economic Review*, vol. 58, May 1968, pp. 162–70.

J. H. Levine, 'The sphere of influence', *American Sociological Review*, vol. 37, February 1972, pp. 14–27.

C. W. Nelson, 'Input-output applications for the multi-activity firm', in W. F. Gossling (ed.), *Input-Output in the United Kingdom: Proceedings of the 1968 Manchester Conference*, London, Frank Cass and Co., Ltd., 1970.

A. Rapoport and W. J. Horvath, 'A study of a large sociogram', *Behavioral Science*, vol. 6, October 1961, pp. 279–91.

T. B. Roby, 'Computer simulation models for organization theory', in V. H. Vroom (ed.), *Methods of Organizational Research*, Pittsburgh, Pa., University of Pittsburgh Press, 1967, pp. 171–211.

H. B. Thorelli, 'Game simulation of administrative systems', in W. Alderson and S. J. Shapiro (eds.), *Marketing and the Computer*, Prentice-Hall, 1963, pp. 334–48.

Designing and Managing Interorganizational Systems

B. J. F. Mott, *Anatomy of a Coordinating Council*, Pittsburgh, Pa., University of Pittsburgh Press, 1968.

R. A. Posner, 'Oligopoly and the antitrust laws: a suggested approach', *Stanford Law Review*, vol. 21, June 1969, pp. 1562–606.

L. W. Stern, 'Antitrust implications of a sociological interpretation of competition, conflict, and cooperation in the marketplace', *The Antitrust Bulletin*, vol. 16, Fall 1971, pp. 509–30.

Acknowledgements

Permission to reproduce the following Readings in this volume is acknowledged to these sources:

1 *The Quarterly Journal of Economics*
2 *The Quarterly Journal of Economics*
3 Rand McNally College Publishing Company
4 John Wiley & Sons Inc.
5 Macmillan Inc.
6 Aldine Publishing Company
7 American Economic Association
8 *Administrative Science Quarterly*
9 *Administrative Science Quarterly*
10 The University of Chicago Press
11 American Sociological Association
12 Holt Rinehart and Winston Inc.
13 American Marketing Association
14 Bureau of Labor Statistics, US Department of Labor
15 American Sociological Association
16 American Political Science Association
17 American Sociological Association
18 Institute for African Studies, University of Zambia
19 Robert C. Anderson
20 The Financial Analysts' Federation
21 Rand McNally College Publishing Company
22 Harper & Row Publishers Inc.
23 D. C. Heath and Company
24 The University of Chicago Press
25 New York University Institute of Retail Management

Author Index

434 Author Index

Subject Index